# REVELATION

Sacra Pagina Series

Volume 16

# Revelation

Wilfrid J. Harrington, O.P.

Daniel J. Harrington, S.J.
Editor

A Michael Glazier Book
THE LITURGICAL PRESS
Collegeville, Minnesota

Cover design by Don Bruno.

A Michael Glazier Book published by The Liturgical Press.

1    2    3    4    5    6    7    8    9

**Library of Congress Cataloging-in-Publication Data**

Harrington, Wilfrid J.
    Revelation / Wilfrid J. Harrington.
        p.    cm. — (Sacra pagina series ; v. 16)
    ''A Michael Glazier book.''
    Includes bibliographical references.
    ISBN 0-8146-5818-0
    1. Bible. N.T. Revelation—Commentaries. I. Bible. N.T.
Revelation. English. Harrington. 1993. II. Title. III. Series:
Sacra pagina series ; 16.
BS2825.3.H335   1993
228'.077—dc20                                                                93-15197
                                                         CIP

FOR
JOAN AND MICHAEL GLAZIER

Níl malairt chuí le fáil ar chara dílis
ní féidir a luach a mheas.
Sláníoc na beatha is ea cara dílis.
                    (Síorach 6:15-16).

# CONTENTS

Editor's Preface      xi

Preface      xiii

Abbreviations      xvii

## *Introduction*

  I. Literary Form      1

 II. Authorship and Date      8

III. Background      9

IV. Purpose      12

 V. Lines of Interpretation      14

VI. An Outline      17

VII. Theological Perspectives      23

General Bibliography      39

## *Translation, Notes, Interpretation*

### I. Prologue, Address, and Inaugural Vision

1. Prologue (1:1-3)      43

2. The Address (1:4-8)      45

3. Vision of One Like a Son of Man (1:9-20)      49

### II. The Messages to the Seven Churches

4. Message to Ephesus (2:1-7)      54

5. Message to Smyrna (2:8-11)      58

6. Message to Pergamum (2:12-17)      60

7. Message to Thyatira (2:18-29)      63

8. Message to Sardis (3:1-6)      67

9. Message to Philadelphia (3:7-13)     69
10. Message to Laodicea (3:14-22)     73

### III. The Scroll Vision

11. The Heavenly Temple (Ch. 4)     78
12. The Lamb and the Scroll (Ch. 5)     83

### IV. The Seven Seals

13. The First Four Seals (6:1-8)     89
14. The Fifth Seal (6:9-11)     92
15. The Sixth Seal (6:12-17)     95
16. The Sealing of the Faithful (7:1-8)     97
17. Song of Victory (7:9-17)     100
18. The Seventh Seal (8:1-5)     103

### V. The Seven Trumpets

19. The First Four Trumpets (8:6-13)     105
20. The Fifth Trumpet (First Woe) (9:1-12)     108
21. The Sixth Trumpet (Second Woe) (9:13-21)     111
22. The Open Scroll (Ch. 10)     114
23. The Temple Measured (11:1-2)     118
24. The Two Witnesses (11:3-14)     120
25. The Seventh Trumpet (11:15-19)     125

### VI. The Woman and the Dragon

26. The Woman and the Dragon (12:1-6)     128
27. Victory in Heaven (12:7-12)     131
28. Dragon and Woman (12:13-18)     135

### VII. The Two Beasts

29. The First Beast (13:1-10)     137
30. The Second Beast (13:11-18)     142

### VIII. Salvation and Judgment

31. The Companions of the Lamb (14:1-5)     146
32. Proclamation of Judgment (14:6-13)     149
33. The Harvest (14:14-16)     153
34. The Vintage (14:17-20)     156

## IX. THE LAST PLAGUES

35. Song of Moses and the Lamb (15:1-4) 158
36. The Angels of the Bowls (15:5–16:1) 160
37. The First Four Bowls (16:2-9) 162
38. The Fifth Bowl (16:10-11) 165
39. The Sixth Bowl (16:12-16) 165
40. The Seventh Bowl (16:17-21) 168

## X. THE HARLOT AND THE BEAST

41. The Harlot and the Beast (Ch. 17) 170

## XI. THE END OF BABYLON

42. The Fall of Babylon (18:1-8) 176
43. Dirges Over Babylon (18:9-19) 179
44. The Judgment of Babylon (18:20-24) 182
45. The Vindication of God's People (19:1-10) 185

## XII. THE END OF EVIL

46. The End of the Beasts (19:11-21) 189
47. The End of Satan (20:1-10) 195
48. The Last Judgment (20:11-15) 202

## XIII. THE NEW JERUSALEM

49. The New Heaven and Earth (21:1-8) 206
50. The New Jerusalem (21:9–22:5) 212

## XIV. EPILOGUE AND CONCLUSION

51. Epilogue and Conclusion (22:6-21) 220

Excursus. Positive Eschaton Only:
Revelation and "Universal Salvation" 229

Complete Translation 237

### Indexes

1. Principal Ancient Parallels 261
2. Subjects 267
3. Authors 269

# EDITOR'S PREFACE

Sacra Pagina is a multi-volume commentary on the books of the New Testament. The expression *Sacra Pagina* ("Sacred Page") originally referred to the text of Scripture. In the Middle Ages it also described the study of Scripture to which the interpreter brought the tools of grammar, rhetoric, dialectic, and philosophy. Thus *Sacra Pagina* encompasses both the text to be studied and the activity of interpretation.

This series presents fresh translations and modern expositions of all the books of the New Testament. Written by an international team of Catholic biblical scholars, it is intended for biblical professionals, graduate students, theologians, clergy, and religious educators. The volumes present basic introductory information and close exposition. They self-consciously adopt specific methodological perspectives, but maintain a focus on the issues raised by the New Testament compositions themselves. The goal of *Sacra Pagina* is to provide sound critical analysis without any loss of sensitivity to religious meaning. This series is therefore catholic in two senses of the word: inclusive in its methods and perspectives, and shaped by the context of the Catholic tradition.

The Second Vatican Council described the study of "the sacred page" as the "very soul of sacred theology" (*Dei Verbum* 24). The volumes in this series illustrate how Catholic scholars contribute to the council's call to provide access to Sacred Scripture for all the Christian faithful. Rather than pretending to say the final word on any text, these volumes seek to open up the riches of the New Testament and to invite as many people as possible to study seriously the "sacred page."

DANIEL J. HARRINGTON, S.J.

# PREFACE

The reader faced for the first time with the Book of Revelation is, understandably, bewildered. This book, more than any other New Testament writing, demands commentary. All the more urgently, indeed, as approach of the magical year 2,000 fuels expectation of the End. Fundamentalist interest in Revelation is bound to heighten during this last decade of our second Christian millennium. M. E. Boring aptly observes: "If responsible interpreters do not make the effort to set forth the message of Revelation in terms that are faithful both to the Scripture and to our own times, this task goes by default to others" (*Revelation*, 59). This commentary is one response to that challenge.

It is a challenge. In the first place, it is not easy to classify Revelation. The work is certainly apocalyptic. Yet, its author is, professedly, a prophet; and he writes a letter. His text is open to more than one line of interpretation. Modern critical scholars agree on the proper approach to the work: they all insist that it must be read in its own historical setting. But they are not agreed as to the nuances of its message.

My own fascination with Revelation is not new. Over twenty years ago, I published a commentary on the book: *Understanding the Apocalypse* (Washington: Corpus, 1969). I believe that the opening words of my Preface there still apply:

> It seems to me that two factors, above all, have led to the preparation of this commentary on the Apocalypse of John. In the first place, I have long known the strange attraction of the book. This I had felt, vaguely, at a first reading; but as I came to understand the literary form of the work and, in some measure, to appreciate the quality and significance of it, its appeal grew stronger. On the other hand, I became aware that, to many people, it is indeed a sealed book. It occurred to me that I might be able to open up the book to such as these, to help them to find in it an abiding Christian message.

I do strive, in the present commentary, to open up Revelation and to convey its Christian message. Today, I can call on a clearer understanding of apocalyptic; much scholarly work has been done in this area during the past two decades. Also, we now have a better grasp of the historical and social setting of the book: a first-century C.E. province of the Roman Empire. Above all, I have come to recognize important aspects ✓ of Revelation that had escaped my notice in the earlier study.

This said, the method of procedure here is that standard in biblical commentary. First, I provide an introduction which, necessarily in the case of Revelation, begins by explaining the apocalyptic genre, goes on to fill in the social and religious background, and indicates John's purpose in writing. Next I provide a new (literal) translation of each section of Revelation, followed by notes which deal with matters of text and content that require clarification. Then I treat the passage as a whole in a manner that takes cognizance of its literary character, its theological significance, and its relevance to our situation. Bibliographies direct the reader to important modern studies which elucidate the views embraced or which, not infrequently, propose alternative interpretations.

It is clear that John knows well the Churches he addresses. He is disturbed by attitudes in the Churches—notably, a willingness to come to terms with the prevailing social environment. He perceives a radical incompatibility between that Roman world and the gospel message. In his dualistic view, the perennial conflict between good and evil is being played out in terms of Rome and Church. Christians may not, in any measure, be followers of the Beast (Rome).

I maintain that John's is a minority position. First-century Christians had, by and large, learned to live with and within the Roman system. John stands as a challenge: a reminder, then and now, that the demands of Caesar may be in conflict with the claims of God. He does propose his view with prophetic singlemindedness and apocalyptic exuberance. Yet, in doing so, he seems to be motivated by a singularly un-Christian vindictiveness—witness the awesome plagues and the ultimate merciless extermination of "the inhabitants of the earth." This is explained by his theological perception of the contemporary situation and by the apocalyptic vehicle of his thought. It is modified, indeed transformed, by two factors. A key figure in his book, the agent and presence of God himself, is the Lamb *who was slain*. I argue that, in John's view, God's victory *has* been won: on the Cross. Hence the paradox that, in Christian terms, the victim is the victor. In the second place, I discern, throughout the book, the theme of "universal salvation." Or, better expressed, that the *eschaton*, God's final word, is positive: it speaks only salvation. The message of Revelation is more than a word of encouragement to those suffering tribulation. It is a promise of wider hope.

There is a tendency to view Revelation as crisis literature. In that case, its appeal would extend only to Christians who find themselves in a situation of active persecution. In fact, its appeal has always been wider. I argue that the communities of John's concern are not victims of relentless persecution. He, rather, prepares his readers for the reaction that must inevitably follow his proposed defiance of Rome. Revelation continues to offer encouragement to all who find themselves in conflict with an ethos that is inimical to the standard of the gospel.

The liturgical character of Revelation must be stressed. It is not only that the book is spangled with heavenly liturgies. Revelation is a letter that carries explicit direction for its reading in a liturgical assembly (Rev 1:3). It was designed to be *heard*. Somewhat as with a radio drama, the listener assimilates its words imaginatively. This is an important feature of our interpretation of the work. I suggest that, before turning to study of the text, one read the whole of Revelation. Or, even better, one might listen to it, well read. With this in mind, I have provided a complete translation of the book.

The focus of my study is on Revelation as a profoundly Christian text, albeit one firmly influenced and colored by John's Jewish heritage. My approach is at once literary, historical, and theological. Apart from a brief sketch of lines of interpretation, I have not ventured a history of Revelation's interpretation. Nor have I followed the path of structuralist analysis. I have not, as a rule, outlined alternative interpretations. This does not indicate lack of appreciation of other approaches. It is an acceptance of what may realistically be achieved within the compass of a single volume.

I have, to my satisfaction at least, discerned what I believe to be John's purpose, and I have sought to present it in a coherent fashion. I am conscious that there is more than one acceptable line of interpretation of a work that is so rich as poetic literature, so exuberant in its imagery, so profound in its theology. At the end of the day, I hope that I present a reading of Revelation that is faithful to John's text. I trust that I may help the reader to find meaning here and guide her and him to listen to John's word to their situation.

In the study of any biblical writing, one typically finds some commentators more congenial than others. There will be many reasons, the most significant being a shared reader response to the text. For my part, I have been most influenced by G. B. Caird, M. E. Boring, J. P. M. Sweet, and, to a lesser extent, G. A. Krodel. This is largely because I share with them a discernment of John's conviction of Christian victory as the victory of the Cross, the victory of the slain Lamb. With them, I discover in Revelation a firmly optimistic perspective. As to an assessment of the historical background, I owe much to the study of L. L. Thompson. It is salutary to acknowledge how much one may learn from great scholars of the past, such as H. B. Swete and R. H. Charles. My indebtedness, of course, spreads far, far wider. A very special word of thanks is due to my friend,

Michael Glazier, whose persuasion encouraged me to take on this task. My warm thanks, too, to Daniel Harrington, S.J., who read my manuscript and made many helpful suggestions—all of which I was happy to adopt.

WILFRID J. HARRINGTON, O. P.

# ABBREVIATIONS

Works referred to with some frequency in *Notes* and *Interpretation*.

Boring     M. Eugene Boring, *Revelation*. Interpretation. (Louisville: John Knox, 1989).

Caird     G. B. Caird, *The Revelation of St John the Divine*. (London: A. & C. Black; New York: Harper & Row, 1966).

Charles     R. H. Charles, *A Critical and Exegetical Commentary on the Revelation of St John*. 2 vols. International Critical Commentary (New York: Scribner's, 1920).

Hemer     C. J. Hemer, *The Letters to the Seven Churches of Asia in their Local Setting*. (Sheffield: JSOT, 1986).

Krodel     G. A. Krodel, *Revelation*. Augsburg Commentary on the New Testament. (Minneapolis: Augsburg, 1989).

Sweet     J. P. M. Sweet, *Revelation*. Pelican Commentaries. (London/Philadelphia: SCM/Westminster, 1979).

Swete     H. B. Swete, *The Apocalypse of St John*. (London: Macmillan, 1922³).

Thompson     L. L. Thompson, *The Book of Revelation. Apocalypse and Empire*. (New York and Oxford: Oxford University Press, 1990).

## *Biblical Books and Apocrypha*

| | | | |
|---|---|---|---|
| Gen | Nah | 1-2-3-4 Kgdms | John |
| Exod | Hab | Add Esth | Acts |
| Lev | Zeph | Bar | Rom |
| Num | Hag | Bel | 1-2 Cor |
| Deut | Zech | 1-2 Esdr | Gal |
| Josh | Mal | 4 Ezra | Eph |
| Judg | Ps (*pl.*: Pss) | Jdt | Phil |
| 1-2 Sam | Job | Ep Jer | Col |
| 1-2 Kgs | Prov | 1-2-3-4 Macc | 1-2 Thess |
| Isa | Ruth | Pr Azar | 1-2 Tim |
| Jer | Cant | Pr Man | Titus |
| Ezek | Eccl (*or* Qoh) | Sir | Phlm |
| Hos | Lam | Sus | Heb |
| Joel | Esth | Tob | Jas |
| Amos | Dan | Wis | 1-2 Pet |
| Obad | Ezra | Matt | 1-2-3 John |
| Jonah | Neh | Mark | Jude |
| Mic | 1-2 Chr | Luke | Rev |

## Periodicals

| | |
|---|---|
| AsSeign | Assemblées du Seigneur |
| AUSS | Andrews University Seminary Studies |
| Bib | Biblica |
| BibLeb | Bibel und Leben |
| BibOr | Biblica et orientalia |
| BJRL | Bulletin of the John Rylands University Library of Manchester |
| BK | Bibel und Kirche |
| BR | Biblical Research |
| BTB | Biblical Theology Bulletin |
| BTS | Bible et terre sainte |
| BVC | Bible et vie chrétienne |
| BZ | Biblische Zeitschrift |
| CBQ | Catholic Biblical Quarterly |
| CP | Classical Philology |
| EspV | Esprit et vie |
| EstBib | Estudios bíblicos |
| ETL | Ephemerides Theologicae Lovanienses |
| EvQ | Evangelical Quarterly |
| EvT | Evangelische Theologie |
| ExpTim | Expository Times |
| Greg | Gregorianum |
| HTR | Harvard Theological Review |
| Int | Interpretation |
| ITQ | Irish Theological Quarterly |
| JBL | Journal of Biblical Literature |
| JETS | Journal of the Evangelical Theological Society |
| JR | Journal of Religion |
| JRS | Journal of Roman Studies |
| JSJ | Journal for the Study of Judaism |
| JSNT | Journal for the Study of the New Testament |
| JTS | Journal of Theological Studies |
| Neot | Neotestamentica |
| NJBC | New Jerome Biblical Commentary |
| NovT | Novum Testamentum |
| NRT | La nouvelle revue théologique |
| NTS | New Testament Studies |
| PIBA | Proceedings of the Irish Biblical Association |
| RB | Revue Biblique |
| RelSRev | Religious Studies Review |
| RevExp | Review and Expositor |
| RevThom | Revue Thomiste |
| RHPR | Revue d'histoire et de philosophie religieuses |
| RivB | Rivista biblica |
| RSR | Recherches de science religieuse |
| SBFLA | Studii Biblici Franciscani Liber Annuus |

| ScrB | Scripture Bulletin |
|------|--------------------|
| SJT | Scottish Journal of Theology |
| ST | Studia theologica |
| TAiK | Teologinen Aikakauskirja Teologisk Tidskrift |
| TGl | Theologie und Glaube |
| TLZ | Theologische Literaturzeitung |
| TQ | Theologische Quartalschaft |
| TynBul | Tyndale Bulletin |
| TZ | Theologische Zeitschrift |
| VD | Verbum domini |
| VetChrist | Vetera Christianorum |
| VoxEv | Vox Evangelica |
| WTJ | Westminster Theological Journal |
| ZNW | Zeitschrift für die neutestamentlichen Wissenschaft |

# INTRODUCTION

## I. *Literary Form*

### Apocalypse

The word *apokalypsis,* "revelation," the first word of the Book of Revelation, came in time to designate a type of Jewish literature which appeared about 200 B.C.E. to 100 C.E. Some scholars characterize and stress the literary form of these writings as the disclosure of heavenly mysteries. Others look to their content and particularly to their eschatology. It would seem, in fact, that both approaches may and should be sustained. Specifically, apocalypse has been helpfully defined as: "A genre of revelatory literature with a narrative framework in which a revelation is mediated by an otherworldly being to a human recipient, disclosing a transcendent reality which is both temporal, insofar as it envisages eschatological salvation, and spatial insofar as it involves another, supernatural world" (J. J. Collins, *The Apocalyptic Imagination,* 4).

It may be conceded that Revelation matches up. It is, indeed, revelatory, and there is a narrative framework. The mediators throughout are otherworldly. John is a human recipient of visions and a human visitor to the heavenly world, for Revelation does take for granted the existence of another, heavenly world beyond this world of ours. This is not a complete explanation, however. While its apocalyptic dimension is hardly in question, it is really not possible to slot Revelation into one, readily definable form. Before considering this aspect, it is well to look at major Jewish apocalypses that have, directly or indirectly, influenced the author of Revelation.

### Major Jewish Apocalypses

The major extant Jewish apocalypses that are earlier than, or contemporary with, Revelation, are 1 Enoch, Daniel 7–12, 4 Ezra, 2 Baruch, and The Apocalypse of Abraham.

1

*1 Enoch.* 1 Enoch (Ethiopic Enoch) is the oldest of three apocalyptic writings attributed to Enoch (Gen 5:18-24). Originally written (mainly) in Aramaic, it is now best represented in an Ethiopic version (in two recensions). It is a compilation of five "Books" or sections of unequal length and of differing dates:

| Chs. | 1–36 | The Book of the Watchers | [third century B.C.E.] |
|------|------|--------------------------|------------------------|
|      | 37–71 | The Similitudes (Parables) | [first century C.E.] |
|      | 72–82 | The Astronomical Book | [before 200 B.C.E.] |
|      | 83–90 | The Book of Dreams | [ca. 165 B.C.E.] |
|      | 91–108 | The Book of the Epistle of Enoch | [200–175 B.C.E.] |
|      |      | [Apocalypse of Weeks (93:1-10 and 91:11-17)] | |

In general, the work reflects the historical events preceding and following the Maccabean Revolt (167–164 B.C.E.). It was to have a notable effect on early Christian tradition. For instance, the legend of fallen angels (an elaboration of the story of the "sons of God" in Gen 6:1-4) comes from the Book of the Watchers. Here we shall look at the Epistle of Enoch (G. W. E. Nickelsburg, *CBQ* 39 [1977] 309-28).

This "Book" of the complex 1 Enoch offers something like a cross-section of the apocalyptic genre with its different literary forms. The tendency had been to view apocalyptic only along the pattern of Revelation and Daniel 7–12. The truth is, as Enoch illustrates, that the apocalyptic message may be conveyed in varied literary forms. We find Woes; for example:

> Woe to you who repay your neighbor with evil;
> for you will be repaid according to your deeds (95:5).

The Woes reflect the author's view of the world, an upside-down world. Sinners, though in rebellion against God, prosper. The faithful righteous are oppressed, with no redress in sight. The second line of each "Woe" couplet promises that the situation will be righted. The Exhortations, addressed to the righteous, come in two types. First, a judgment on sinners:

> Fear not the sinners, O righteous;
> for the Lord will again deliver them into your hands,
> so that you may execute judgment on them as you wish (95:3).

But also a more positive approach:

> Be of good courage,
> for you were formerly worn out through afflictions and tribulations,
> but now you will shine as the luminaries of heaven (104:2).

The reversal announced in Woes and Exhortations is underscored by description, in lurid detail, of future judgment. This is a feature of the

*Apocalypse of Weeks* (93:1-10 and 91:11-17). History, from creation to the end, is divided into ten "weeks." The first seven weeks end with the choosing of the elect. The remaining three offer three judgment scenes: a prelude to the endless series of weeks stretching through eternity. The heart of the message is that, in the coming judgment, God will punish the wicked and save and reward the righteous. Thereupon, creation will become what God had ever intended it to be.

In chapters 102-104 we have an address to the righteous and to the sinful: first to the dead (102:4-103:8) and then to the living (103:9-104:8). Again we find the contrast between the present situation and its reversal at the judgment. Here and now, sinners flout the law of God and persecute the righteous: a state of imbalance and tension. The imbalance will be righted when God will judge sinners and reward the righteous. The author lays claim to the insight of revelation: "I know this mystery: I have read the tablets of heaven and have seen the holy writings" (103:2).

The whole of chapters 92-105 is a "letter" from the author ("Enoch") to his contemporaries (for these are the "latter generations"). "I will speak these things, my children, I, Enoch, and let you know according to that which was revealed to me from the heavenly vision, that which I have learned from the words of the holy angels, and understood from the heavenly tablets" (93:2).

The author speaks of a world of violence and oppression. He claims vision of a heavenly realm—but a realm that is operative in our world, bringing about salvation. Because of this, his message takes on an eschatological quality. Still, the message is firmly addressed to the present. A sure hope of God's imminent intervention and of his reversal of the gross imbalance summons the oppressed community to faith, courage, and even joy in the here and now.

*Daniel 7-12.* While Daniel 7-12 is unquestionably the first full-blown apocalypse in the Hebrew Bible (Dan 1-6 being related stories) it is, most likely, not the earliest Jewish apocalypse. It would have been pre-dated by some of the Enochic material. Otherwise, Daniel 7-12 deserves to stand as the masterpiece of Jewish apocalyptic. It can be dated almost precisely to 165 B.C.E.—shortly before the death of Antiochus Epiphanes (the "villain" of Daniel). Daniel 7-12 consists of three visions (chs. 7; 8; 10-12) and a prophecy (ch. 9), all parts of a composite whole. Along the line, revelation is mediated by an angel. In each unit there is an historical pattern, an eschatological crisis, and the prospect of judgment and ultimate salvation.

In a series of visions, Daniel 7-12 traces the course of history, with stress on the ultimate, inevitable victory of the people of God. Daniel maintains that history is wholly under divine control. That is just the point. He tells the story of the past in such a way that the persecuted

Jews may understand that their sufferings had a place in God's purpose. The book looks always to the final victory, to the time of the end, to the coming of the kingdom. It sees the messianic age about to dawn, beyond the time of tribulation. God's victory over the forces of evil is assured and those who serve him faithfully will have a glorious part in his triumph. Daniel, like apocalypse in general, presupposes the existence of a supernatural world beyond the visible one. The apocalyptic seer has an entree into the heavenly reality.

One feature of apocalyptic is determinism. There are two camps—the righteous and the wicked. And it is presupposed that there is little or no chance that the wicked will change allegiance. One must always keep in mind the cultural setting of apocalypticism. There is the powerless minority, effectively defranchised by the dominant group, who are not going to relinquish their power-base. What can the oppressed do? The temptation to look towards a "soft" solution beyond death is rightly questioned in our day. The Book of Daniel, however, looks only to a divine intervention. And it firmly follows the road to determinism: "Go your way, Daniel, for the words are shut up and sealed until the time of the end. Many shall purify themselves, and make themselves white, and be refined; but the wicked shall do wickedly, and none of the wicked shall understand; but those who are wise shall understand" (12:9-10). This is an aspect of apocalypticism that needs to be faced and challenged. In Revelation, John handles it by appeal to a prophetic insight. (See J. J. Collins, *The Apocalyptic Imagination*, 68–72.)

*4 Ezra.* The apocalypse 4 Ezra (2 Esdras) was written after the fall of Jerusalem (70 C.E.). Now prefaced by a Christian introduction in Greek (chs. 1-2), the Apocalypse of Ezra (chs. 3-14), is a Jewish work of about 90–120 C.E., written in Hebrew. The work is extant in a Latin version. The Apocalypse is structured in seven scenes (dialogues and visions). We note points relevant to the study of Revelation. In the first vision, Ezra confronts a woman who is grieving for the death of her only son. Abruptly, she is transformed into a city with massive foundations. The angel Uriel appears and explains to Ezra that the woman was Zion and that God had shown him the glory of the future, restored Jerusalem.

The second vision (chs. 11-12) opens with the statement: "I saw an eagle coming up out of the sea; it had twelve feathered wings and three heads" (11:1). Here, the eagle is Rome; the heads, most probably, are the emperors Vespasian, Titus, and Domitian. The eagle vision may be understood as a reinterpretation of the fourth beast of Daniel 7. The third vision (ch. 13) introduces "a figure like that of a man" (13:3) who "sent forth from his mouth as it were a stream of fire" (13:10). One is reminded of Revelation 19:15, 21 ("the sword of his mouth").

*2 Baruch and The Apocalypse of Abraham.* The work known as 2 Baruch is closely related to 4 Ezra. The text is preserved in a Syriac version translated from Greek. The Hebrew original was composed about 95 C.E. Like 4 Ezra, it is a response to Rome's conquest of Jerusalem. The Apocalypse of Abraham, extant only in a Slavonic version, was written in Hebrew or Aramaic in the first or second century C.E. It faces the problem of the prominence of evil in the world, especially in the shape of idolatry.

*The Sibylline Oracles.* The genre of sibylline oracles had a long tradition—reaching back to the fifth century B.C.E.—before it was adopted by Jews (and Christians). The Sibylline Oracles are extant in fourteen books (second century B.C.E. to seventh century C.E.). They are not, strictly, apocalyptic, but they do have interest for a study of Revelation. One feature of the Oracles is condemnation of Rome for immorality and arrogance. Of more immediate interest is their use of the Nero legend. There was widespread belief that Nero had not died but had fled to the Parthians and would return, at the head of a Parthian army, to wreak vengeance on a Rome that had rejected him (*Nero redux*). In the Oracles, this legend was given an eschatological slant. Another, later form of the legend had Nero return from the dead (*Nero redivivus*). Here are the principal Nero-related passages:

> A great king will flee from Italy like a runaway slave
> unseen and unheard over the channel of the Euphrates. . . .
> The fugitive from Rome will also come, brandishing a great spear,
> having crossed the Euphrates with many myriads (4:119-120; 138-139).
> For the Persian [Nero] will come onto your soil like hail . . .
> a savage-minded mighty man,
> with a full host numerous as sand,
> bringing destruction on you (5:93-97).
> A man who is a matricide will come from the ends of the earth. . . .
> He will destroy every land and conquer all . . .
> he will destroy many men and great rulers,
> and he will set fire to all men as no one else ever did (5:363-369).
> Celebrate, if you wish, the man of secret birth,
> riding a Trojan chariot from the land of Asia
> with the spirit of fire . . .
> going against everyone, having crossed the sea,
> then dark blood will pursue the great beast (8:153-157).

John had ample precedent for his use of the Nero legend.


## Literary Freedom

The author of Revelation obviously knows the Old Testament thoroughly. He has, demonstrably, been heavily influenced by Daniel and

Ezekiel. While there is no absolutely sure quotation, reminiscences are readily discernible, and John's use of certain biblical passages is beyond question. One can presume that he knew the Book of Wisdom; it would have prompted his liberal transformation of the Egyptian plagues in his own plagues of trumpets and bowls. It can scarcely be doubted that he would have known some of the earlier or contemporary Jewish apocalyptic writings. Our rather frequent quotation (in the Commentary) of texts from works such as 1 Enoch is not meant to assert that John must have known such works; it simply demonstrates that he is part of a recognizable tradition.

It is one thing to acknowledge that John was familiar with the Old Testament and contemporary apocalyptic. It is more significant and more important to recognize his remarkably creative use of earlier and contemporary texts. He displays a dazzling mastery of his Bible. A measure of this mastery is the fact that, though one may catch an Old Testament echo in every verse of the book, never once does he quote verbatim; his grasp of Scripture is free and creative. Not only does John never quote his Old Testament sources, he regularly modifies them. Indeed, he frequently gives them a paradoxical twist, standing them on their head. We not only may, but must, assume a parallel freedom in regard to his nonbiblical sources. John's own text, in its setting in Revelation, is the basis of interpretation—not any source, evident or presumed.

This creative literary freedom of John is a major interpretative key. It may well explain why he never quotes directly. True, he quarries his material in Old Testament and existing apocalyptic writings. Then, like a skilled stone-cutter, he shapes the material to his own liking. He disdains the use of bricks. To put it another way: he delights in vivid imagery because images stimulate his own fertile imagination. Images play about in his mind and emerge in surreal exuberance. One must be prepared to play along with him, ready to be dazzled and delighted—and shocked.

It is well to keep in mind that Revelation was meant to be *heard*, to be listened to: "blessed they who hear" (1:3). It has a dramatic dimension. Heard in the setting of an early Eucharistic liturgy, the scenes would have unfolded with theatrical effect. And the images would have flooded the imagination of the hearers. Carried along by the powerfully evocative language, encouraged and warmed by the firm word of hope, the worshiping community could have cried "Amen! Come, Lord Jesus!"

## Literary Genre

Revelation is an intertextual work—a network of references to other texts. It is a mixed genre. It does not wholly conform to any known ancient literary convention. It is revelatory literature; that much is clear. It has unmistakable apocalyptic characteristics. Yet, John presents himself as a prophet. To complicate the issue, he has cast his work in letter form. We are left with a prophetic-apocalyptic writing, in the form of a letter to specific Christian communities.

The letter form arguably points to a Pauline influence. This is of interest. While there is, certainly, a traditional linkage of Johannine writings (Fourth Gospel, Letters, Revelation) with Asia Minor, Paul's association with Asia is certain. John surely would have known some, at least, of Paul's letters. It must be acknowledged that, on closer examination, a relationship between Revelation and the Fourth Gospel is not as obvious as has been alleged. On the face of it, a largely apocalyptic writing might be expected to have closer affinity with Paul than with the Fourth Gospel (see Fiorenza, "The Quest for the Johannine School" 402–27).

Recognition of apocalyptic *and* prophetic dimensions of Revelation goes a long way towards explaining seemingly contradictory trends in the work. Standard apocalyptic sharply distinguishes the righteous from the wicked, most emphatically in an eschatological denouement when the righteous will be rewarded and the wicked definitively punished. In contrast, the distinction, in prophecy, between righteous and wicked is nuanced. Here, the wicked may repent and change their ways; the righteous stand in need of admonition and of exhortation to faithfulness, and may be threatened with ultimate rejection.

At first sight, Revelation firmly fits the apocalyptic mold. Dichotomy of righteous and wicked seems firm and sustained. On the other hand, there are forceful warnings to Christian readers ("the righteous"), and not only in the prophetic messages to the Churches (chs. 2–3). More remarkable is a discernible thread reflecting a concept of "universal salvation." (See "Excursus," p. 229). If one reads Revelation strictly as an apocalypse, this thread may be missed or ignored. When one acknowledges the prophetic dimension, it may more readily be discerned and traced. The recognition that Revelation is a mixed genre will predispose one to expect inconsistency. The argument in this commentary is that John does indeed strike an optimistic note. It follows from his thoroughly Christian acceptance of the seriousness of God's deed in Christ. While his apocalyptic imagery and language suggest the severity of God's judgment of the wicked, the dominant image of the slain Lamb shows that God's word of judgment was spoken in the Cross. John has recognized that God's activity will ever seem paradoxical to human assessment.

One may suppose that John is ambivalent or unrealistic. He seems to be wholly unworldly. Yet, he looks to the destruction of Rome: an admission that redemption is, somehow, to be achieved within history.

Revelation in no way suggests that God will wave a magic wand and transform our vale of tears into a garden of Eden. The struggle between good and evil is a dirty, bloody affair. Slowly, humankind is beginning to learn that violence is not a formula for peace. After two world wars unleashed in Europe in half a century, the European Community is not only a sign of hope but a marvellously positive achievement. Just war is, arguably, a wholly un-Christian concept. But it does point to a painful dilemma. The Christian ideal is the victory of the Cross. Yet, can it be Christian to condone oppression? The path of violence should, more than any other way that Christian concern might suggest, be subjected to the stern critique of the Cross. While one may confidently claim that non-violent resistance to oppression is always a Christian response, violent resistance to oppression may or may not be an authentically Christian option. One must be prepared to live with one's decision. But one may not invoke Revelation, properly understood, in support of violence.

## II. *Authorship and Date*

### *Authorship*

Four times (1:1, 4, 9; 22:8) the author of Revelation names himself John. Christian tradition has, on the whole, identified him with John, son of Zebedee. The earliest witness is Justin (ca. 150 C.E.) who in his *Dialogue with Trypho* declares: ''A man of our number, by name John, one of the apostles of Christ, prophesied in a revelation vouchsafed to him that those who believe in our Christ will dwell for a thousand years in Jerusalem'' (cf. Rev 20:4-6). About the turn of the century the identification was accepted by Irenaeus, the Muratorian Canon, Clement of Alexandria, Tertullian, and Hippolytus. Origen says explicitly that John the Apostle had written both Revelation and the Fourth Gospel.

Dissident voices were first heard in the third century. The earliest was that of the Roman priest Gaius (Irenaeus, *Adv. Haer.*, 3.28.2). The Montanists were invoking Revelation in support of their doctrines and the reaction of Gaius was radical: he attributed Revelation to the heretic Cerinthus—a veritable cutting of the Gordian knot. Far more important was the view of Denis of Alexandria (d. ca. 265). On the ground of a critical literary and theological analysis of both writings he concluded that Revelation could not have been written by John, author of the Fourth Gospel. The opinion of Denis was recorded by Eusebius (*Hist. eccl.*, 7.25) who seems to have accepted it (3.39.5-6). It was in the Eastern Church, especially, that there was hesitancy about Revelation. Cyril of Jerusalem and Gregory of Nazianzus did not number it among the New Testament writings; John Chrysotom and Theodoret never referred to it. It does not figure in the Syriac versions of the New Testament. The negative witness represents no more than a fraction of the patristic tradition. However, the dissidents had on their side the evidence of conflicting data and the strength of scholarly research.

Today it is widely accepted, or at least seriously argued, that any linkage of Revelation with the Fourth Gospel is, at best, tenuous. Indeed, the letter format and the Asian provenance of John's work would suggest some Pauline association. The best we may claim is that the author of Revelation is an otherwise unknown Christian prophet, likely an itinerant prophet, and, probably, a Palestinian by birth. Not very impressive, it might seem. Yet, it is rather more than can be said of the authors of many other biblical writings.

### Date

The strongest external evidence for the date of Revelation is the testimony of Irenaeus: it was written in the reign of Domitian (81–96 C.E.). The clearest internal evidence is the use of the name "Babylon" for Rome. In Jewish literature this name is associated with Rome precisely as second destroyer of Jerusalem. Its use indicates a date after 70 C.E. We may date Revelation, approximately, 90–95 C.E. (see Collins, *Crisis and Catharsis*, 25–83).

## III. *Background*

Domitian's reign is the most likely political background of Revelation. Domitian has been characterized as megalomaniac and tyrannical. He is said to have fostered the imperial cult and encouraged use, in his regard, of the divine title *dominus et deus*. He might be regarded as another Nero. Such assessment made for an assumption that, in his time, there was widespread oppression and persecution of Christians in Asia. This, in turn, was said to account for the anti-Roman stance of Revelation and for the book's emphasis on "tribulation," understood as active persecution.

The truth is, the dominant portrait of Domitian is a studied caricature. Our standard sources are Pliny the Younger, Tacitus, Dio Chrysostom, and Suetonius who wrote in the reign of Trajan (98–117 C.E.), and Dio Cassius a century later. Trajan marks a transition from the Flavians (Domitian being the last of that line) to the Antonines; his reign was seen to usher in a new era. Contemporary writers, to emphasize the change, employed the device of contrast with Domitian. The blacker the picture of Domitian, the brighter, in contrast, looked that of Trajan.

The standard, unflattering portrait of Domitian is, consequently, highly suspect. Indeed, Roman writers contemporary with him—Quintilian, Statius, Martial, Silvius Italicus—paint a quite different picture. He is not a cruel tyrant but a competent and social-minded ruler. He did not modify the imperial cult by seeking divine honors beyond his predecessors. The title *dominus et deus* is never bestowed on him by his court writers. As for Revelation, the single martyr (Antipas) named in the messages to the Churches scarcely suggests widespread persecution. In short, the reign of Domitian would not, of itself, have been radically inimical to the Christian way of life. (See L. L. Thompson, *The Book of Revelation*, 95–115.)

### The Imperial Cult

In the Roman provinces the imperial cult contributed significantly to the people's understanding of their relationship to the emperor. The cult developed prominently in the province of Asia, being firmly implanted there during Augustus' reign. Of the seven cities listed in Revelation 2–3, all but Thyatira had imperial temples. The Churches of Revelation were located where the imperial cult was most securely in place.

For Christians, emperor-worship was but a facet of a larger problem. It went without saying that they could acknowledge as divine only the one, true God. Furthermore, for them, sacrificing itself was at stake: Jesus was the one supreme and final sacrifice. To the extent, then, that imperial cult was propagated, Christians would be under serious threat. It is not surprising that a fundamental conflict in Revelation is centered on the true worship of God and his Christ versus the false worship of the beast.

### Social Location

Our evidence strongly suggests that Christians, on the whole, lived peacefully in Asia. There is no need to presume that they were an oppressed minority. Not even Revelation itself supports such a view. What does emerge, unmistakably, is John's unequivocally negative attitude to the Roman Empire and to the Asian society that reflected the values of the Empire. Christians in general—witness the writings of Paul, 1 Peter, and the author of the Pastorals—had recognized the Roman order. John would have none of it. In his view, Christians were pitted unyieldingly against the evil empire. The political order of Rome was wholly corrupt; it belonged to the Satanic realm. In a nutshell, the conflict and crisis in

Revelation between Christian commitment and the social order derive from John's perspective on Roman society rather than from significant hostilities in the social environment.

Within the Roman Empire the inhabitants of Asia enjoyed a coherent, ordered structure of life. By and large, Christians fitted into that social situation. John set out, deliberately, to dislocate Christians. He not only cast Rome as demonic, but depicted Roman rule as oppressive and stressed the threat of persecution. Opposition to the dominant social forces in place is expressed in negative and hostile rhetoric. The current situation is described in terms of crisis. John not only urged the rejection of everything Roman: he firmly predicted the end of Rome.

## A Minority View

An apocalyptic group tends to be sectarian, seeing itself as the true remnant. Such an attitude does figure in Revelation. At the same time, if John called for radical separation from Rome, he did not call for a break with existing Christian communities. He was sharply critical of some within those communities—the Nicolaitans, Jezebel—but he did not regard them as outsiders. He certainly called for reform. He tried to polarize the Churches in Asia by claiming that there is only one proper Christian attitude towards the contemporary world. He was clear that it is wrong for a Christian to settle for any form of accommodation to that world, because the Roman world is demonic through and through. Might it not be that John's real target was within the Church: Christians who had settled for a quiet life in the Roman environment? One may easily guess at John's reaction to Christians of the Pastoral communities, if he had ever encountered any.

We may ask: if Revelation addressed only a crisis situation, could it have the wider appeal it has enjoyed? John and his Christians were not in a situation of actual persecution. Rather, located within the Roman society, John radically attacked that social order. He firmly opposed the larger Christian community that had developed a modus vivendi with the contemporary social order. He and his adherents were a "deviant" group that chose to oppose the public order—in this instance wielding a literary weapon. He and they represented alienation, but an alienation of their choosing. John was a realist. He could not fail to see that his rejection of Rome, his opposition to everything Roman, if it prevailed among Christians, would invite a stern reaction from the "demonic" empire. Any Christian community, built along his lines, would necessarily be on a collision course with any authority structure built on power. In his perspective, persecution was an inevitable and imminent prospect. The book will appear attractive to any Christian of any age who feels frustrated by his or her world or Church. If Revelation is not to be linked with actual upheaval and crisis, it may be seen as representing an uncompromising minority view. There is its challenge.

## IV. *Purpose*

The prophet John was a committed Christian and a man profoundly concerned. He had found in Jesus Christ his way to God—indeed, the very image of his God. He rejoiced that there were those in the cities of Asia who shared his discovery and his vision. Yet, these Christian communities were his concern. They were small and helpless, so few even in a single province of the empire. The tide of the Roman world flowed steadily against them. What worried him above all was that there were among them some who felt that they might swim with the tide. This was madness!

John saw, with prophetic conviction, that something was rotten at the heart of Rome. His was a firmly dualistic vision: there is God, and there is evil. And Rome was wholly evil. Not all Christians saw it so. There is no evidence that John had any knowledge of, let alone any association with, the Christian communities to whom the Pastoral Letters were addressed. These Christians had come to terms with the world in which they lived. They were to be model citizens of that world. The author of 1 Timothy could recommend prayers "for kings and all who are in high position, that we may lead a quiet and peaceful life" (2:2). In short, the Pastorals present a Church coming to terms with the world: an eminently sensible Church, concentrating on structure, orthodoxy, and respectability. It is the sort of Church with which we are familiar because, historically, the Christian Church has followed the Pastoral model.

The author of Pastorals looked to an ongoing world and asked that Christians should be good citizens. The question remains: is the label "good citizen" too high a price to pay for passive acceptance of institutions and structures that are, in fact, sinful? If, for John, the answer was categorically clear, it was not equally obvious to others in his communities. Something had to be done. He decided to write. Given the Christian situation as he perceived it, it was not surprising, and well nigh inevitable, that what he wrote was an apocalypse.

John's is a minority voice. He had adopted a radical stance. He wrote to and for the like-minded, and challenged those who would see things differently. Throughout history, Christian movements have been inspired by particular sayings of the Lord. Francis of Assisi, for instance, embraced Lady Poverty in response to the Lucan Jesus: "whoever of you does not renounce *all* that he has . . .'' (Luke 14:33). It is at least arguable that John had taken to heart the admonition: ''it shall not be so among you'' (Mark 10:43)—that total rejection of the Gentile style of rule and authority. John pushed it a step further. He viewed all authority based on power as demonic. As a prophet, he could not settle for half-measures. The civil authority of his day, the Roman imperium, was, without doubt, based on power and bolstered by a sycophantic religious system. The whole set-up, to his eyes, was demonic. Surely history has substantiated that John's assessment of power-structures is not too wide of the mark. He is writing to and for Christian communities. He clearly perceives the threat to Christians that is constituted by a worldly authority pattern. A prophetic perception indeed when one regards the naked ecclesiastical power of Christendom and a more subtle power-play in the contemporary Church.

John faced an uphill battle. Some, likely many, even in the Asian communities of his concern, had come to terms with the Roman world. He had a two-fold reason for his attack on Rome. First, his conviction that imperial Rome was an instrument of Satan. Second, he had to wean his fellow-Christians from their willingness to work within the contemporary social system and, even, from their admiration for features of that world. On both scores his depiction of Rome was negative in the extreme. He could not find a good word to say in favor of the empire. More than that, he strove to stress, in a wholly unambiguous manner, the fatal fragility of the empire despite its appearance of invincibility. It carried within itself the seed of its own destruction. And, sharing as he did a widespread early Christian expectation of an imminent end, he predicted that the fall of the empire would be soon. Surely, then, it was utterly foolish for Christians above all to place their trust in a regime that was sick unto death.

Furthermore, because the fall of Rome would presage the end, it behooved Christians to play their part in the dissolution of the evil empire. If rejection must be total, resistance must be passive. Ironically, victory is won through defeat! The victim is the victor! Resistance, even passive resistance, would inevitably invite the reaction of Rome: a power-based authority can brook no dissension. John was urging his Christians to resistance. In the assurance that he would be heeded, he warned, repeatedly and without apology, of tribulation. After all, Christians are disciples of the slain Lamb—the disciple is not greater than the Master.

John, a prophet, had chosen to write an apocalypse. It was a genre ideally suited to his purpose. It gave him full scope to paint the empire in the most lurid colors. He could depict history as a stark struggle between the forces of evil and the worshipers of God and of the Lamb. He could encourage his hearer-readers, a constant feature of apocalyptic. His encouragement was paradoxical. Victory was won on the cross. Faithful

Christians would surely shed their blood. John could promise, with more assurance than the author of the Book of Wisdom: "In the eyes of the foolish they seem to have died . . . but they are at peace . . . they will govern nations and rule over peoples" (Wis 3:2-3, 8). He would encourage, not by conjuring up false hope of miraculous intervention but by his reinterpretation of the suffering of Christians. The beast could, and would, strike mercilessly and savagely; no doubt of that. The enduring comfort was that the powerless victims would be, and would be seen to be, the ultimate victors. There is comfort rooted in realism.

It was not John's last word. It was the *prophet* John who spoke the limitless graciousness of God. In his manner he voiced the conviction of Paul: "God has consigned all to disobedience, that he may have mercy upon all" (Rom 11:32).

## V. *Lines of Interpretation*

Revelation is largely, if not exclusively, an apocalyptic work. While in the early Greek and Syriac Churches it was treated with some suspicion, and was largely ignored, it was readily accepted in the Latin Church. Commentators on the book, however, seem not to have understood it or, at least, not to have appreciated the literary form and imagery of apocalyptic. And there was a preoccupation with millennialism—an interpretation, often literal, of the thousand-year reign of Revelation 20:1-6. Down the ages, the book has been subjected to varied and contradictory expositions. Yet the picture is not as confusing as it seems; in practice, we may discern four principal lines of interpretation.

### 1. *Non-historical or "idealist" interpretation*

In this view, the book is concerned with ideas and principles—with timeless truths. Its purpose is to depict the perennial struggle of good and evil and the ultimate triumph of the kingdom of God. It is not really concerned with the early Church; not at all with the Church of later times. While this aloofness from historical reference may enable it to have relevance for all periods of the Church's history, it is cavalier in its ignoring of specific historical references to the first-century setting of Revelation. The work is made irrelevant to the situation perceived by John and its first readers. And the fact that Revelation is cast as a letter and thus meant to address, directly, its original recipients, is ignored.

## 2. World-historical (Church-historical) interpretation

In this approach, Revelation is regarded as a detailed prophecy of identifiable historical events—in short, as an inspired forecast of the whole reach of human history. A variant form discerns seven stages in the history of the Church. In either case, the upshot is that the interpreter sees John as predicting the course of history down to the interpreter's own time. Indeed, the alleged historical references have to be so contrived that the time of the interpreter may be regarded as the promised last age. There are obvious flaws. The view presupposes a misunderstanding of biblical prophecy, which is taken to be prediction of future events of world history. Also, there has to be constant, and contradictory, revision of alleged historical references, as the end stubbornly refuses to materialize. And, until recently, the "world-history" envisaged was, in practice, European history only. Most damaging of all, the book, in this perception, could have meant nothing to its first readers.

## 3. End-historical ("futurist") interpretation

In light of this interpretation, Revelation is taken to be exclusively concerned with happenings at the close of the age. Even the seven Churches of chapters 2-3 are not real Churches of first-century Asia but seven periods of Church history. The "dead" Church of Laodicea becomes the apostate Church of the interpreter's own time. The rest of the book looks to the end of the world and the events that will usher in the second coming of Christ. Since chapters 4-22 predict only those events that are to happen in the last years of world history, and since the interpreter stands at the threshold of the end, the whole book is meaningless not only for its first readers but for all subsequent generations up to the last. Boring (49) scathingly observes: "It is this interpretation that has become so pervasive among media 'evangelists' and the purveyors of pop-eschatological literature." Something needs to be said about this most recent version of the interpretation in question.

Premillennial dispensationalism is a brand of fundamentalist eschatology that is notably prevalent in the United States. An indication of its popularity is the best-seller success of a book by Hal Lindsay: *The Late Great Planet Earth* (Grand Rapids: Zondervan, 1970). This is also the position that underlies the teaching of the major contemporary television evangelists. The term "dispensationalism" refers to the theory that God "dispenses" or administers the divine purpose throughout history in seven distinct and successive stages, called "dispensations." The seventh dispensation is that of the millennium (Rev 20:1-6). "Premillennial" distinguishes this view from other beliefs about the return of Christ at the close of history. Premillennialists believe that Christ will return before the millennium. After a brief reign of Antichrist, he will come to destroy decisively the powers of evil in the great battle of Armageddon.

The concept of a millennium—understood literally as a thousand-year reign with Christ on earth—and the final battle of Armageddon shows the influence of Revelation on the dispensationalist stance. History is rapidly moving to a showdown: the final, decisive battle of good and evil will be fought in the valley of Megiddo (Rev 16:16). Even if some dispensationalists interpret Ezekiel 38–39 as envisaging a world-wide nuclear holocaust, the climactic moment will still occur in the valley of Megiddo. A further refinement is the "rapture"; this time the single text 1 Thessalonians 4:16-17 is pressed into service. Using vivid apocalyptic language, Paul had underlined the truth that all the faithful will live with the Lord forever. He spoke of all being "caught up" ("rapt up") to meet the Lord of the parousia—hence the "rapture" of the dispensationalists. True believers will, at the end, be "raptured" from the earth and thus will escape the gruesome destruction of the rest of humankind.

Here we have not only gross misinterpretation of Revelation (and other biblical texts), but something unsavory and even dangerous. The idea of an elect minority being shunted to the safe regions of the upper air while a vengeful Lamb destroys the inhabitants of the earth is scarcely Christian. Politically, it could be maintained that world-wide nuclear war is really part of God's plan for his world. All of this is far removed from the theology of John of Patmos.

## 4. *The contemporary-historical ("preterist") interpretation*

This method presupposes that Revelation is wholly concerned with the circumstances of John's day ("contemporary" meaning John's contemporaries). In its extreme form it maintains that the author was wholly preoccupied with his own time; his book has no reference whatever to later ages. While the view makes the work meaningful to its original readers, it renders it basically meaningless for all subsequent readers. Taken more flexibly, the view implies the application of historical method to the study of Revelation. It assumes that Revelation, no differently from any other New Testament writing, is set in a particular first-century situation. On this understanding, it is the method followed by all modern critical biblical scholars. One may add that present-day scholars do, in practice, adopt some elements of the "idealist" interpretation. Revelation is surely concerned with the struggle between good and evil and with the ultimate triumph of the reign of God. These were concerns of John and of his Asian contemporaries. To understand Revelation properly, one must begin with the communities to which it was written. This approach I have outlined above, and keep constantly in view throughout the commentary.

## VI. *An Outline*

The author of Revelation wrote in idiosyncratic Greek. Some of his un-Greek idiom may be due to the fact that his native tongue was Semitic, most likely Aramaic. But this cannot be the whole story: his peculiar grammar and syntax appear studied and are not due to a poor grasp of Greek. It has been suggested that John wrote as he did in conscious protest against Hellenistic culture—his was "an act of cultural pride of a Jewish Semite" (Yarbo Collins, *Crisis and Catharsis*, 47). The distinctive style pervades the book—a factor in the cumulative argument that speaks for a unified, structured work. This is not to say that it is easy to discern the precise structure intended by John. There are unmistakable features, notably, reference to three scrolls (1:11; 5:1; 10:1); and four septets: messages (chs. 2–3), seals (6:1–8:1), trumpets (8:2–11:9), and bowls (chs. 15–16). There have been many attempts to trace an elaborate sequence throughout. While the book is surely not shapeless, it seems to me that little is to be gained by imposing a logical plan on a work of such imaginative power and such deep religious feeling. It is more helpful to propose a summary of the book, one which may suggest a line of interpretation.

### Summary

*Overture* (Ch. 1). The prologue (1:1-3) introduces Revelation as a letter of the prophet John to be publicly read at community worship, addressed to seven Churches in the Roman province of Asia (1:4-8). In a striking vision (1:9-20) John received his prophetic commission. One "in human form," the glorified Christ, walked among seven lampstands (the seven Churches) holding in his right hand—that is, in his power—seven stars: the heavenly counterparts of the Churches. He is no absentee landlord.

*Prophetic Messages* (Chs. 2–3). In the messages, each Church hears a verdict based on precise knowledge of its situation, both external (there are topical references) and spiritual. There is praise and blame—usually a mixture of both. Ephesus receives both censure and commendation. The tribulation and poverty of faithful Smyrna are noted, as well as that Church's special problem with Jewish hostility. The Church of Pergamum holds out bravely in a center of emperor-worship; but the Nicolaitans, John's bugbear, have made inroads. The community of Thyatira, otherwise exemplary, tolerates a Christian teacher—scathingly labeled "that Jezebel"—who proposes adaptation to the prevailing ethos, a proposal anathema to the prophet. This is "Nicolaitanism." The Church of Sardis is in poor shape; it lacks backbone. Philadelphia, a poor, humanly powerless community merits unstinted praise. On the other hand, the opulent Church in the prosperous town of Laodicea fares badly: about this community alone the heavenly scrutinizer has nothing good to say. These messages should be kept in mind throughout the visions that follow. Though John might seem to live in a fantasy world, his concern is focused on these troubled Churches. His purpose is firmly pastoral.

*The Scroll Vision* (Chs. 4–5). The opening vision of the throne of God (ch. 4) is manifestly inspired by several prophetical texts, notably the inaugural vision of Ezekiel. Before the throne, the "twenty-four elders" are heavenly counterparts of the earthly people of God; the "four living creatures" represent all aspects of created life. In a great liturgy the whole of creation sings praise of the Creator. In chapter 5 the "One seated on the throne" (designation of God throughout) handed over to the Lamb the sealed scroll which he held in his right hand: a transfer of power. The scroll contained God's redemptive plan for his world, a plan to be put into effect by the "Lamb who was slain." The heavenly hymns, in praise of the Lamb, serve to interpret the vision.

*The Seven Seals* (6:1–8:5). The breaking of the scroll-seals by the Lamb unleashed a series of plagues which follows the pattern of events in the synoptic apocalypse (Mark 13 parr.): war, strife among nations, famine, pestilence, persecution, cosmic phenomena. The first four seals (6:1-8) are the celebrated "four horsemen of the Apocalypse"—war and its attendant evils. The fifth and sixth seals introduce martyrs resting underneath the heavenly altar (6:9-11) and the traditional cosmic signs that presage the End (6:12-17). Before the breaking of the last seal the servants of God were sealed with the seal of the living God (7:1-8), sealed for protection *through* the great tribulation: 144,000, the Israel of God. In 7:9-17 they, beyond the tribulation, celebrate victory in a heavenly feast of Tabernacles. The seventh seal (8:1-5) marks an end which is also a beginning: it heralds a fresh series of plagues (8:6–11:19).

*The Seven Trumpets* (8:6–11:19). The trumpets, modeled on the plagues of Egypt, are presented in much the same manner as the seals: the first four are described in a few verses (8:7-13); the others unfold at greater length, interspersed with other visions. The fifth trumpet (or first woe) depicts a plague of demonic locusts (9:1-12); the sixth (second woe) shows vast demonic forces from beyond the Euphrates, bent on the destruction of Rome (9:13-21). These plagues strike one-third of the earth, just as the seals struck "a fourth of the earth." There will be no such qualification in the parallel plagues of bowls. Yet, even there, a prospect of repentance is still held out to "the inhabitants of the earth"—the enemies of God and of the Lamb.

Chapter 10 opens with a vision of a mighty angel holding a little scroll open in his hand: a fresh prophetic commission. It is an "open scroll": the time of waiting is over. Before morning comes the pre-dawn darkness of the final tribulation. Pagans will tread down the holy city for 1260 days (a variant of the three-and-a-half years of Daniel: a limited period of tribulation before final vindication) but the temple and those worshiping in it will be spared (11:1-2). The Church as such will stand; Christians must suffer the ordeal. Throughout the time of tribulation, the two witnesses (11:3-14), representing the Church, will exercise their prophetic ministry. Slain by the power of evil, they will be vindicated by God and restored to life. They mirror the destiny of the Lamb.

*The Woman and the Dragon* (Ch. 12). Chapters 12–13 offer a behind-the-scenes view of the power of evil at work in the present; chapter 14 will offer an anticipatory view of the victory of God in salvation and judgment. Chapter 12 combines a narrative describing an encounter between a pregnant woman and a dragon (vv. 1-6, 13-17) with a narrative depicting a heavenly battle (vv. 7-9). This sandwich-technique, reminiscent of Mark, indicates that the narratives must be understood in conjunction. The woman symbolizes the people of God bringing forth the Messiah; the dragon is the "ancient serpent" of Genesis 3. The woman's child was snatched, from the destructive intent of the dragon, to the throne of God: precisely by dying, Jesus defeated the dragon and was exalted to God's right hand. The expulsion of Satan—in his role of "accuser" of Christians—from heaven is the result of the victory of Christ on earth. Though defeated in heaven, evil still finds scope on earth. While the Church, as such, is under God's special care, the faithful are vulnerable.

*The Two Beasts* (Ch. 13). The two beasts of chapter 13, instruments of the dragon, are, respectively, Rome and the propagators of the imperial cult. John's first beast, emerging from the sea, is a composite of the four beasts of Daniel 7:2-8. To this beast the dragon (Satan) gave his power and authority. The beast is a parody of the Lamb; the healing of its mortal wound is reference to the Nero legend. It is not only enemy of God; it is enemy of humankind. The second beast (later called the "false prophet"), who induces all the "inhabitants of the earth" to worship the first beast, is the imperial religion in the service of Rome.

*Salvation and Judgment* (Ch. 14). In deliberate and striking antithesis to the beast and its followers stand the Lamb and his followers (14:1-5). Satan, the beasts and their followers ("the inhabitants of the earth"), the woman and her children, the Lamb and his companions—the dramatis personae of the eschatological struggle—have been introduced. Next comes the proclamation of the hour of judgment (14:6-13) which is, paradoxically, proclamation, too, of an "eternal gospel." This is followed by the proleptic harvest (14:14-16) and vintage (14:17-20) of the earth.

*The Last Plagues* (Chs. 15–16). The seven plagues "which are the last" are announced in chapter 15; the following chapter shows their execution. Modeled, like the trumpets, on the plagues of Egypt, the bowls follow the pattern of a rapid unfolding of the first four (16:1-9). This time, however, chastisement is universal and definitive: all followers of the beast are stricken. Moreover, they are already gathered at Armageddon, symbol of disaster (16:12-16), to await destruction (cf. 19:17-21). In chapter 16 the focus narrows from the cosmos to the representative of the world's rebellion against the Creator—Rome—leading to the climactic chapters 17–19.

*The End of Babylon* (17:1–19:10). Although the fall of Rome is proclaimed in 14:8, and is briefly described in 16:19, the end of the city, the great persecuting power, cannot be treated so casually. The whole of chapter 17 is given over to a description of Babylon—the goddess Rome—seated on the satanic beast. An *angelus interpres* lists the significant details of the vision: the woman, the beast, its seven heads and its ten horns. The beast is that of chapter 13. The angel offers a two-fold explanation of the seven heads: seven hills and seven emperors. The ten horns are ten kings, united in wholehearted support of the beast. Dramatically, at the close, beast and kings will devour the harlot: a vivid image of the self-destructive power of evil. The fall of Babylon is solemnly proclaimed in 18:1-8. Then follows a series of dirges (18:9-24) over Rome—self-interested laments of kings, merchants, and sea-farers who had battened on the extravagant wealth of Rome. A heavenly liturgy (19:1-10) celebrates the vindication of God's people.

*The End of Evil* (19:11–20:15). The passage 19:11-21 deals with the victory of Christ and his followers over the beast, the false prophet, and the kings of the earth. Victory is complete: the two beasts are cast into the "lake of fire"—symbol of final destruction—and their followers are slain. Victory is achieved by a majestic rider, wearing a cloak "dipped in blood," whose public name is "Word of God." It is victory of the slain Lamb. Now Satan alone is left.

In 20:1-10 we have two events juxtaposed: on the one hand is the overthrow of Satan, in two phases; on the other, a reign of a thousand years.

While Christ and his faithful reign, Satan will be powerless in their regard. The binding of Satan coincides with his downfall described in the parallel passage 12:7-12. He has no power over those who have "conquered him by the blood of the Lamb." The picture of the millennium is only one of John's ways of thinking about the End. It is wrong-headed to view it out of focus.

Inspired by Ezekiel, John (20:7-10) presents a picture of the final destruction of evil: Gog and Magog are larger-than-life antagonists of God. In order to participate in this mythical scene, the devil "must" be released to engage in his characteristic activity of "deceiving the nations." Then, defeated, Satan joins the two (symbolic) beasts in the lake of fire. The conquest of all powers hostile to God is followed by the general resurrection of the dead and the last judgment (20:11-15). With the total disappearance of evil, the present world order has come to an end.

*The New Jerusalem* (21:1–22:5). The former creation has been transformed and all evil has been wholly removed; now is the final phase of God's plan. The book closes with a magnificent vision of the new Jerusalem, the heavenly city, veritable kingdom of God. One of the seven angels of the bowls had shown John the great harlot (17:1); one of the seven now steps forward to show him the bride (21:9). The bride image is not developed but yields to that of the city "coming down out of heaven from God" (21:10). We might have expected the glowing description of the city (21:16-21) to be followed by a particularly stunning description of its temple (the Temple was the glory of the earthly Jerusalem). Instead—a brilliant touch—we learn that there is no temple, nor any need of one: God himself dwells there, and the Lamb (21:22). Consistently, the waters which in Ezekiel 47 (the model text) flow from the temple, here flow from "the throne of God and of the Lamb" (22:1). It is the river of the first paradise, and the tree of life is found again. There, the elect will look upon the face of God and of the Lamb and shall reign for ever and ever.

*Epilogue and Conclusion* (22:6-21). An epilogue (22:6-20) gives the closing words of the angel, the seer, and the Lord. John ends his work with the prayer of the early Christians, "*Marana tha*" ("Our Lord, Come!"), and with a parting blessing on all.

## Outline

I propose a flexible plan for Revelation which I shall follow in the commentary. The point has been made that, beyond some obvious indications (the septets, for instance) it is not possible to be sure of any structural intent of the author. My proposed outline is nothing more than a practical framework along reasonably discernible lines.

I. PROLOGUE, ADDRESS, AND INAUGURAL VISION (Ch. 1)
    Prologue (1:1-3)
    The Address (1:4-8)
    Vision of One Like a Son of Man (1:9-20)

II. THE MESSAGES TO THE SEVEN CHURCHES (Chs. 2–3)

III. THE SCROLL VISION (Chs. 4–5)
    The Heavenly Temple (Ch. 4)
    The Lamb and the Scroll (Ch. 5)

IV. THE SEVEN SEALS (6:1–8:5)
    The First Four Seals (6:1-8)
    The Fifth Seal (6:9-11)
    The Sixth Seal (6:12-17)
    The Sealing of the Faithful (7:1-8)
    Song of Victory (7:9-17)
    The Seventh Seal (8:1-5)

V. THE SEVEN TRUMPETS (8:6–11:19)
    The First Four Trumpets (8:6-13)
    The Fifth Trumpet (First Woe) (9:1-12)
    The Sixth Trumpet (Second Woe) (9:13-21)
    The Open Scroll (Ch. 10)
    The Temple Measured (11:1-2)
    The Two Witnesses (11:3-14)
    The Seventh Trumpet (11:15-19)

VI. THE WOMAN AND THE DRAGON (Ch. 12)
    The Woman and the Dragon (12:1-6)
    Victory in Heaven (12:7-12)
    Dragon and Woman (12:13-18)

VII. THE TWO BEASTS (Ch. 13)
    The First Beast (13:1-10)
    The Second Beast (13:11-18)

VIII. SALVATION AND JUDGMENT (Ch. 14)
    The Companions of the Lamb (14:1-5)
    Proclamation of Judgment (14:6-13)
    Harvest and Vintage (14:14-20)
      Harvest (14:14-16)
      Vintage (14:17-20)

IX. THE LAST PLAGUES (Chs. 15–16)
   Song of Moses and the Lamb (15:1-4)
   The Angels of the Bowls (15:5–16:1)
   The First Four Bowls (16:2-9)
   The Fifth Bowl (16:10-11)
   The Sixth Bowl (16:12-16)
   The Seventh Bowl (16:17-21)

X. THE HARLOT AND THE BEAST (Ch. 17)

XI. THE END OF BABYLON (18:1–19:10)
   The Fall of Babylon (18:1-8)
   Dirges Over Babylon (18:9-19)
   The Judgment of Babylon (18:20-24)
   Vindication of God's People (19:1-10)

XII. THE END OF EVIL (19:11–20:15)
   The End of the Beasts (19:11-21)
   The End of Satan (20:1-10)
   Satan Bound (20:1-3)
   Reign With Christ (20:4-6)
   End of the Dragon (20:7-10)
   The Last Judgment (20:11-15)

XIII. THE NEW JERUSALEM (21:1–22:5)
   The New Heaven and Earth (21:1-8)
   The New Jerusalem (21:9–22:5)

XIV. EPILOGUE AND CONCLUSION (22:6-21)

## VII. *Theological Perspectives*

Revelation is concerned with *thlipsis*, tribulation. It saw the light in an atmosphere of contrived crisis and in anticipation of consequent widespread persecution. John's message of hope will be heard by Christians who, in their measure, are experiencing tribulation. But, then, has Revelation anything to say to our Western world? The answer is, yes—if we reinterpret its symbols and permit them to speak, meaningfully, to our situation. We may find that John offers a challenge to our theology and our Christology, and beyond.

### God

In heaven, John saw a throne, and One seated on it. That One dominates Revelation. The Throne is the symbol of his Almighty power. He is Creator, and King of creation. He is the Creator who has total respect for his creation. And creation, in its fashion, unceasingly sings his praise. Yet, all is not well in his world, more particularly in his privileged world of humankind. He had, with calm deliberation, endowed humankind with freedom. He would honor human freedom with divine respect. He acknowledged, sadly, that "the imagination of man's heart is evil from its youth" (Gen 8:21). In John's perspective, humankind is set on a path of self-destruction. Evil is rampant in God's world. He is wholly sure that evil can never have the last word. God will act. He has acted. He had unsheathed the one weapon that would destroy evil, that had overcome evil: the Cross.

We know God through human perception of God. That perception will always be culturally conditioned; it will be colored by the human and historical situation. As a Christian, John saw his God revealed in the Lamb who was slain. That truth colored his vision of the One on the throne. He would not seek to describe that God, so far beyond any conception of human majesty. Yet, this was no aloof God. He was the God present in the Son. John had been loosed from sin in the blood of that Son. He had experienced the love of God. Never, for him, could God be a distant God. This awareness, indeed, was not something wholly new. As a Jew, sensitive to the prophetic tradition, he had been familiar with the reality of a transcendent God immersed in the life of his people. The Christ—the presence of God—who walks among John's Churches, plays the role that Yahweh had played through his prophets.

If God may not be seen or described, there is no veiling of the majesty of the One seated on the throne. The tone is set in the heavenly vision of chapter 4, with its hymn to the Lord God Almighty, the Creator. This is echoed in the victory song of 7:9-17, the praise of 11:15-19, and the song of Moses and of the Lamb in 15:3-4. In these instances, the Redeemer is being acknowledged. Divine sovereignty is manifest in another manner in the judgment of Rome (14:8; 18:1-9; 19:1-10). The arrogant throne of Caesar is no match for the throne that, at the last judgment, becomes the great white throne. God is all in all.

If the sovereignty of God is not in question, the exercise of that sovereignty does raise questions. There is, on the face of it, an unsavory side to the wielding of divine power. One might expect violence from the dragon; and there is the prospect of persecution of God's people. Instead, all-out conflict brings total disaster, not to others, but to the dragon and his followers. Violence comes from the One on the throne, and from the Lamb! The "wrath" of God is emphasized, a wrath poured out in a series of increasingly destructive plagues. There is a vindictiveness, underlined at the close of the vintage scene (14:17-20), with its vision of the "great winepress of God's wrath" and its river of human blood two hundred miles in spate. Or, again, the gruesome feast prepared for birds of prey (19:17-18) in a battle generalled by the Lamb! The Lamb—that should give us pause. And John has told us that the Lamb is he who reveals God. Can our God, then, be a God of wrath?

Before turning to John's portrait of the Lamb, it is well to advert to another aspect of divine sovereignty. When one looks at the plagues, one observes a recurring note, struck in the repetition of the verb *edothē* ("was given"). The Four Horsemen are "permitted" to wreak their havoc. A star fallen from heaven was "given" the key of the abyss in order to release the demonic locusts which were "given" destructive powers and were "told" and permitted to torment humankind (9:1-5). The false prophet was "allowed" to bring people to worship the beast, to cause those who refused to be killed, and to compel all to wear the mark of the beast (13:15-16). The role of the "ten horns"—ten kings—of the scarlet beast is especially noteworthy: "For God has put it into their minds to carry out his purpose," that is, the destruction of Rome (17:16-17). Finally, the dragon itself was not only seized and imprisoned, and again let loose (20:1-3), but let loose only to muster the nations for their and his final destruction (20:7-10). John's view is dualistic: a universe divided, in conflict, between good and evil. But there is never any doubt of the outcome. Evil, even in its most potent guise, is subject to the sovereign power of good—the One seated on the throne.

## The Lamb

The emergence of the Lamb is dramatic even in the context of this dramatic book. In his vision of the heavenly throne-room, John had been bidden to look for the Lion of the tribe of Judah. What met his gaze was "a Lamb standing as though it had been slain" (5:5-6). We ought not have been taken by surprise. After all, John's first characterization of Jesus Christ is as the one "who loves us and has loosed us from our sins with his blood" (1:5). Indeed, these words are now caught up in the heavenly canticle: "you were slain and by your blood you bought for God" people from every nation (5:9). "Lamb" is John's favorite title for Christ throughout. One may never forget that, from the outset, he is the Lamb who was slain. If John proceeds to paint the power and triumph of the Lamb, he is clear, and wants it understood, that the decisive victory of the Lamb was won on the Cross. He has made his own the conviction of Paul: "We preach Christ crucified . . . Christ the power of God and the wisdom of God. For the foolishnesss of God is wiser than men, and the weakness of God is stronger than men" (1 Cor 1:23-25). It is precisely in view of this "foolishness" of God that John hears the heavenly celebration of the slain Lamb as one worthy to receive all power (5:12), as one worthy of honor side by side with the One on the throne (5:13).

A distinctive feature of John's presentation of the Lamb is his assimilation of the Lamb to God. We have noted the Lamb's worthiness to receive honor together with God. Even the "wrath of God" is the "wrath of the Lamb" also (6:16). Surely, this must tell us something! The multitude of the saved attribute their victory to God "and the Lamb" (7:10). The heavenly Jerusalem has no temple ("its temple was the Lord God Almighty and the Lamb"), and the Lamb is the lamp of the heavenly city (21:22-23). When the throne appears for the last time, now in the new city-temple, it is "the throne of God and of the Lamb" (22:1, 3). Accordingly, the Lamb can declare of himself: "I am the Alpha and the Omega, the first and the last, the beginning and the end" (22:13), echoing the words of the One on the throne (21:6). The Lamb may speak as does the Johannine Jesus: "I and the Father are one" (John 10:30).

The parallel is instructive. The Johannine Jesus is one with the Father precisely because he is the one sent, the agent of the Father, and is thereby empowered to speak the words of God. John's Lamb is the "faithful witness" (1:5) who has received his revelation from God (1:1). It is because of his faithfulness to his witness-bearing, a faithfulness that brought him to the Cross, that he shares the throne of God. It is no less clear to the Lamb than it is to the Johannine Jesus that "the Father is greater than I" (John 14:28); the one sent and the faithful witness have this in common. They also share the declaration: "The one who has seen me has seen the Father" (John 14:9). "I and the Father are one . . . the throne of God and of the Lamb"—these tell us nothing of the "nature" of the Son/Lamb but tell us everything of the role of revealer that is the role of the Son/Lamb. For each John, Jesus is the one in whom God is fully present. God is the one who reveals himself wholly in Jesus.

The majestic, awesome One who sits on the throne is the same One who has revealed himself in the Lamb. It is this fact that makes acceptable the otherwise repellant, violent imagery of Revelation. John, like biblical writers in general, has to strive to convey, in inadequate human language, what limited human minds cannot comprehend in the first place. Our Creator God is a saving God. He is the God who desires to set humankind free from the tyranny of sin and evil. He is a God grieved by the ravages of evil—that is his "wrath." He cannot, he will not, ignore sin and evil. "The people of Israel groaned under their bondage . . . and God heard their groaning" (Exod 2:23-24). He will not turn a blind eye to oppression and to the travail of the oppressed. The violent imagery and language are designed to underline this truth. In human terms, there is retribution.

"Pay her back in her own coin, repay her twice over for her works.

In the cup she mixed, mix her a double draught!'' (Rev 18:6). The sentiment is human; God's "retribution" is divine. "God so loved the world that he gave his only Son" (John 3:16); "God shows his love for us that while we were yet sinners Christ died for us" (Rom 5:8). It is this God who is revealed in the Lamb who was slain. The decisive battle in God's war against evil will not be at Armageddon; it was fought on the cross. If war in heaven is a repercussion of that victorious battle (Rev 12:7-12), strife on earth is a reflection of it. This is the challenge to John's disciples and to all believers: "In the world you will have tribulation; but be of good cheer, I have overcome the world" (John 16:33). It is not easy to discern evident signs of God's total victory amid the manifest evils of our world. Faith must find ways of asserting it. But our human ways must always fall very short of painting the reality. It is helpful to recall the sage observation of Claus Westermann regarding Genesis 1:31, "And God saw everything that he had made, and behold, it was very good": "It was God's judgment that creation was good. It can never be our judgment, the fruit of our own experience. Our knowledge and experience are always limited by the unexplained and the incomprehensible. We can speak about creation then only with reference to the Creator for whom it presents no riddle" (C. Westermann, *Genesis 1-11. A Commentary*, trans. J. J. Scullion [Minneapolis: Augsburg, 1984] 174-75).

In relation to his own, the Lamb displays all the graciousness of God. He has liberated us from the evil deeds of our past. He has purchased from slavery, for God, at the cost of his blood, men and women of every nation, making of them a royal house of priests (Rev 5:9). The victors, who have come through the great tribulation, have won their victory in virtue of his: they have washed their robes in the blood of the Lamb (7:14). He is the shepherd who will guide them to the water of life (7:17). The victors share in the victory of the Lamb over the dragon: they have conquered him by the blood of the Lamb (12:10-11). They are the faithful ones, marked with the name of the Lamb and of his Father (14:1-5), who "follow the Lamb wherever he goes" (14:4). As firstfruits of the harvest of the world they represent the whole Church, all those ransomed from the earth. They are those who have been fondly harvested by the one "like a son of man," the gracious Lamb (14:14-16). The companions of the Lamb are the "armies of heaven" who accompany him, now as invincible rider on the white horse, as he rides out to final victory (19:11-21). One may see here the fourth evangelist's triumphal portrayal of the passion and death of Jesus pushed to the limit of apocalyptic imagery. There is the lovelier image of the marriage of the Lamb. The victors are invited to his marriage supper. In the exuberance of John's imagery, guests and bride are one and the same! (19:7-9). It is the consummation of the Lamb's—and so of God's—love affair with humankind. The imagery first put forward in Hosea 1–3 now, in Revelation, comes to full flowering. Truly, "God's dwelling is with humankind" (21:3).

No sketch of the Lamb would be complete without a glance at the Lord of the Churches. The title Lamb is not used of Christ in chapters 2–3, but he is that heavenly scrutinizer. As "one in human form" he is seen in striking majesty: he is *the* victor. John falls, in lifeless awe, at his feet, to hear the reassuring voice of the Jesus of the Gospel: "Do not be afraid." John realizes that here is no stranger. And he is no absentee landlord: he walks among the Churches. His message to each community is incisive and decisive. He looks at the state of each. He finds love, faithfulness even to death, patient endurance in face of intolerance and persecution. He also finds failure in love, a willingness to compromise with an inimical world, and the danger of betrayal. Always there is glowing promise to the victors, those who hold steadfast to the end.

There is not a little of John himself in all this, at least in the assessment of the condition of the Churches. He has no love for his theological rivals, the Nicolaitans; this Christ "hates their works" as John does (2:6). On the other hand, the gracious words, following hard on the harsh indictment of the Laodiceans (3:15-19), ring so true: "Here I stand knocking at the door; if anyone hears my voice and opens the door, I will come in and dine with such a one and that one with me" (3:12). Whether praise or blame, there is manifest pastoral concern. The flaming eyes of the Lamb see with the penetrating gaze of a caring God.

## The Symbolic World

*Angels.* God and Lamb evoke the heavenly world. Traditionally, angels are citizens of that world. "The revelation of Jesus Christ . . . he made it known by sending his angel" (1:1). An angel is mentioned in the very first verse of Revelation. For the rest, angels will appear, abundantly, on every page. There is no shortage of them: they number "myriads of myriads and thousands of thousands" (5:11). Belief in angels had grown considerably in later Judaism; they flourished in apocalyptic. A key function here is that of the *angelus interpres:* every heavenly vision or audition has to be interpreted; always, a heavenly figure is at hand to oblige. There are angels in charge of natural phenomena (e.g., Rev 16:5). Angels are heavenly counterparts of the earthly communities (chs. 2–3). And angels are, as we have noted, part of the population of heaven. In short, in Revelation, angels are omnipresent. Predominantly, they operate as messengers; it is their traditional role, indicated by the very name *angelos.* If at times they are clothed in majesty, that is but a reflection of the word or deed they speak or do at the divine bidding. They are, patently, symbols of God's variegated communication with his creation and, more particularly, with his world of humankind. Twice, John, overawed, falls in homage before an angelic visitor only to be sharply called to rights: "No, not that! I am a fellow servant with you and your brothers and sisters" (19:10; 22:8-9). Earlier, the author of Hebrews had put angels firmly in their place: "Are they not all ministering spirits sent forth to serve, for the sake of those who are to obtain salvation?" (Heb 1:14). Angels are pervasively part of the symbolic world of apocalyptic. In Revelation their role is that of literary mediators in the dramatic unfolding of God's plan for his world.

*The Dragon.* Over against the Lamb stands the beast, personification of Rome. Over against the One on the throne stands the dragon. Under the names of "the devil" and "the Satan" he appears, fleetingly, in the messages to the Churches. He is formally introduced in chapter 12. There the "great red dragon" threatens the woman and her child—the Messiah and Israel/Church mother. The "pre-history" of the dragon reaches back to ancient Near Eastern mythology: the chaos monster. It includes the Graeco-Roman story of the dragon Python. In John the dragon is also linked with the "serpent" of Genesis 3 as reinterpreted in Jewish tradition. As "devil" the dragon is "deceiver of the whole world" (12:9); as "the Satan" he is "the accuser" (12:10). This last characteristic is highly significant. It reflects the "prosecuting counsel" role of Satan in the Old Testament and in Jewish tradition. This is why he can be found in "heaven" (12:7-10). Exiled from this heaven as a result of Jesus' victory on the cross (12:10-11) he turns to earth in wrath, to wage war on the "children" of the woman (12:12-17). The instrument of his warfare is the beast (Rome) with its satellite beast (the imperial cult) (ch. 13). The dragon musters "the kings of the whole world" for the battle of Armageddon (16:12-16). His great army and the beasts will be totally destroyed by the rider on the white horse (19:17-21). That battle is described over again (20:7-10) in order, dramatically, to confirm the end of "the Satan," "the devil." The "lake of fire" is the final home of all symbols of evil: the beasts, Death, Hades, and the dragon (20:10, 14). The "lake of fire," the "second death," is annihilation: the absolute end of evil. Now there is a "new heaven and a new earth" (21:1) wholly free of evil. Then, God will be "all in all" (1 Cor 15:28).

John is heir to the figure of Satan that, during the intertestamental period, under the influence of Persian dualistic religion, emerged in Jewish tradition as personification of evil and implacable foe of God. His dragon, a malevolent presence, lurks in the background. In practice, John sees the power of evil embodied in the contemporary social structure, institutionalized in the empire (the beast). He finds it, too, in religious conflict within the community. When he speaks of Satan's activity, John consistently speaks in political terms (13:7; 18:3, 23; 20:7-8). In short, "Satan" is a powerful symbol for super-personal evil—"the sin of the world" (John 1:29), the collective burden of sin which weighs on humankind. There is a vast reservoir of evil which constantly threatens us, and which we are, by ourselves, helpless to dispel. The imagery must be taken very seriously. But, in the last resort, evil wears a human face. Our comfort is that "Satan" has been conquered. Victory is God's victory, by the power of the Cross. More precisely, the Cross is, for us, the definitive promise of final victory. We still stand in need of salvation. We are called to *hypomonē*—patient endurance.

## Liturgy

Revelation is explicitly designated for public reading in a liturgy (1:3), most likely a Eucharistic liturgy. From the heavenly celebration that met John's eyes and ears in chapter 4, there follows, throughout his book, one heavenly liturgy after another. Here the spatial dimension of transcendence, which is a feature of apocalypse, takes the shape of heavenly worship. It is, indeed, a distinctive aspect of the eschatology of the work, in that eschatological realities are made present in heavenly worship. And, because the Lamb appears in those scenes of heavenly worship, he thereby belongs in the world's present structure, for there is ongoing interaction between the heavenly and the earthly.

Worship unites heaven and earth. The object of worship is the One on the throne, and the Lamb. The voice of worship on earth blends with the sound of worship in heaven. Every creature "in heaven and on earth and under the earth and in the sea" sings praise (5:13); the souls of the martyred dead cry out (6:9-10); the prayers of God's people are presented to the Lamb (5:8). Worship breaks down all boundaries. In worship all are equal. Worship establishes what is true, what is real. It is response to the admonition of the Lord: "Seek *first* his kingdom and his righteousness . . ." (Matt 6:33).

Not alone by its liturgical setting, but also through a constant and insistent liturgical emphasis, Revelation makes its statement on the centrality of worship in Christian life. So central, indeed, is worship that the inimical "inhabitants of the earth" are also intent on worship: they are worshipers of the beast. John is making a thoroughly biblical point: human creatures are, as creatures, subject to some lordship. One must serve God or Mammon, whatever shape Mammon may assume. The choice is of fundamental importance. John is sure that idolatry corrupts the created order. Worship of God and of the Lamb prepares for and hastens the coming of the new heaven and new earth where righteousness dwells.

*Preaching*

One who is intent on understanding Revelation might begin by reading the whole of it at a sitting. The optimum would be to *listen* to the whole of it (well read, of course). The original recipients *heard* the letter read to them; it was specifically addressed to them. This does mean that it is not directly addressed to us. But it does carry a message for us who hold our Christian faith in common with our distant brothers and sisters of Asia.

When faced with a lectionary reading from Revelation, the average homilist blanches. How can one find anything meaningful to say on the basis of a text that means nothing to oneself? It is inescapably true that familiarity with its apocalyptic literary form is essential if one is to understand Revelation at all. There is no short-cut. It is worth the effort. It will be found that the book has much to offer; it is more challenging, and more encouraging, than one may have realized. There remains, however, the problem of the church congregation. Apocalyptic will be unfamiliar to it.

One recalls that Revelation was meant to be heard, and heard in a liturgical setting. Perhaps this is how the book should be presented today. It has a dramatic dimension. This was brought home to me when an appropriately abridged Revelation was presented with narrator, speakers, and choral singing of the hymns in a campus liturgy. Homilists will strive to do their best with the lectionary readings. One intent on getting across the whole message might seriously consider a para-liturgical setting—a liturgy focused exclusively on Revelation. Better still if Revelation were built into a Eucharistic liturgy. Then it would really speak in the setting John had envisaged. To facilate reading Revelation as a whole, I have provided in an appendix the entire text in English.

*Relevance*

If Revelation is seen as crisis literature, written in the stress of active persecution, it is not easy to see that it can have much to say to our Western Churches. We do not live in an atmosphere of apocalyptic crisis. We certainly do not experience or envisage violent persecution. But, if we regard Revelation, as one feels we should, as a reflection of John's assessment of his world, we may see how and where it does address us.

John was not coping with a situation of actual persecution. If there were to be "tribulation," it would be in response to a radical Christian rejection of the status quo. Here is where John's letter may nudge us to look critically on our world. Revelation does have something to say to

our Western world if, as said at the start, we interpret its symbols in relation to our situation. One may suggest some pointers.

The dragon is the oppressive weight of sin bearing on humankind.
It is many-faceted, but starkly manifest as greed in all its shapes, in particular, lust for power and control. In this line, the beasts may be rampant capitalism, so cruelly impersonal, and our consumer culture, so
shamelessly selfish. The slogan of unbridled affluence is: Who is like the
beast? (13:4).

A great contrast in Revelation is between the throne of God and the
throne of the beast, ultimately the throne of the dragon (13:14). The question is all about authority; more especially, the exercise of authority. God
is *Pantokratōr*, but his authority is visible in the Lamb. And Jesus had stated
his position, without ambiguity and with studied emphasis: "You know
that those who are supposed to rule over the Gentiles lord it over
them. . . . But it shall not be so among you. . . . For the Son of man
came not to be served but to serve, and to give his life as a ransom for
many" (Mark 10:42-45). The victory of God, his ultimate authority, is the
Cross of the Lamb. In light of that, John viewed any authority based on
power as demonic. We really must ask ourselves if the Christian Churches
have done as Jesus demanded or have followed the pattern of the Gentiles. We must discern and challenge the demonic in our ecclesiastical
structures. This is where a hearkening to John's message will be costly.
We need not doubt that challenge will bring *thlipsis*, tribulation. Faithfulness to this "revelation of Jesus Christ" demands that we take a stand
against power structures which distort the stark message of the Lamb,
the sword of his mouth: the word of the Cross.

In our reading of Revelation, the Lamb is the embodiment of the rule
of God. His voice is the cry of the poor and the afflicted, for the "rule
of God" is nothing other than God, a God bent on the salvation of humankind. The plagues can be viewed as the harvest of our sinning against
our environment. The new Jerusalem is the kingdom, the ultimate rule
of God, when God will be all in all. The One seated on the throne is the
God of justice; but the justice of our God is spelt mercy. Our God is manifest in the Lamb. Our prayer is *Marana tha*—"Come, Lord Jesus!"

Our prayer will be all the more hopeful and confident if we contem-
plate the optimistic word that speaks of a positive eschaton, and a positive eschaton *only*. God is God of life, who invites all to unending life
with him. The gates of the heavenly city stand invitingly open to welcome the nations and the splendor and wealth of the nations—everything
that is worthy of healed and whole humankind. God wills the salvation
of all. Appreciating something of the foolishness of God—and we glimpse
it throughout Revelation—one suspects that the names of all humans
will be read in the book of life. The Lamb has not broken for us the seal

on that scroll. It is enough to know that it is the scroll of God and of the Lamb.

FOR REFERENCE AND FURTHER STUDY

*Apocalypse*

Collins, J. J. "Apocalyptic Eschatology as the Transcendence of Death." *CBQ* 36 (1974).
_____. *The Apocalyptic Imagination.* New York: Crossroad, 1987.
_____, ed. *Apocalypse: The Morphology of a Genre. Semeia* 14. Missoula: Scholars Press, 1979.
Fiorenza, E. Schüssler, "The Phenomenon of early Christian Apocalyptic." In D. Hellholm, ed., *Apocalypticism,* 295–316.
Hanson, P. D. "Apocalypse, Genre" and "Apocalypticism." In *IDBSup,* 27–34.
_____. *The Dawn of Apocalyptic.* Philadelphia: Fortress, 1975.
_____, ed. *Visionaries and Their Apocalypses.* Philadelphia: Fortress, 1983.
Hartman, L. "Survey of the Problem of Apocalyptic Genre." In D. Hellholm, ed., *Apocalypticism,* 329–43.
Hellholm, D. "The Problem of Apocalyptic Genre and the Apocalypse of John." In *SBL 1982 Seminar Papers,* 157–98.
_____, ed. *Apocalypticism in the Mediterranean World and the Near East.* Tübingen: Mohr-Siebeck, 1983.
Koch, K. *The Rediscovery of Apocalyptic.* Naperville, Ill.: Allenson, 1972.
_____. "Vom profetischen zu apokalyptischen Visionsbericht." In D. Hellholm, ed., *Apocalypticism,* 413–46.
Minear, P. S. *New Testament Apocalyptic.* Nashville: Abingdon, 1981.
Morris, L. *Apocalyptic.* London: InterVarsity Press, 1973.
Rollins, W. G. "The New Testament and Apocalyptic." *NTS* 17 (1970–71) 454–76.
Rowland, C. *The Open Heaven: A Study of Apocalyptic in Judaism and Christianity.* New York: Crossroad, 1982.
Stone, M. E. *Scriptures, Sects and Visions.* Philadelphia: Fortress, 1980.

*Major Jewish Apocalypses*

Barr, J. "Jewish Apocalyptic in Recent Scholarly Study." *BJRL* 58 (1975) 9–35.
Carmignac, J. "Description du phénomène de l'Apocalyptique dans l'Ancien Testament." In D. Hellholm, ed., *Apocalypticism,* 163–70.
Charlesworth, J. H., ed. *The Old Testament Pseudepigrapha.* Vol. 1. New York: Doubleday, 1983.
Collins, J. J. *Daniel, 1 Maccabees, 2 Maccabees: With an Excursus on the Apocalyptic Genre.* Wilmington, Del.: Michael Glazier, 1981.
_____. *Daniel, With an Introduction to Apocalyptic Literature.* Grand Rapids: Eerdmans, 1984.
_____. "The genre Apocalyptic in Hellenistic Judaism." In D. Hellholm, ed., *Apocalypticism,* 531–48.

_____. "The Jewish Apocalypses." *Semeia* 14 (1979) 21–59.

_____. "The Sibylline Oracles." In J. H. Charlesworth, ed., *The Old Testament Pseudepigrapha*, vol. 1, 317–472.

Harrington, D. J. "Research on the Jewish Pseudepigrapha during the 1970s." *CBQ* 42 (1980) 147–59.

Nickelsburg, G. W. E. "The Apocalyptic Message of 1 Enoch 92-105." *CBQ* 39 (1977) 309–28.

_____. "The Books of Enoch in Recent Research." *RelSRev* 7 (1981) 210–17.

Sanders, E. P. "The Genre of Palestinian Jewish Apocalypses." In D. Hellholm, ed., *Apocalypticism*, 447–59.

Wilson, R. R. "From Prophecy to Apocalyptic: Reflections on the Shape of Israelite Literature." *Semeia* 21 (1979) 61–121.

*Literary Freedom*

Aune, D. E. "Intertextuality and the Genre of Apocalypse." In *SBL 1991 Seminar Papers* (Atlanta: Scholars Press, 1991) 142–53.

Barr, D. L. "The Apocalypse of John as Oral Enactment." *Int* 40 (1986) 243–56.

Ezell, D. *Revelations on Revelation: New Sounds from Old Symbols.* Waco: Word Books, 1977.

Linton, G. "Reading the Apocalypse as an Apocalypse." In *SBL 1991 Seminar Papers* (Atlanta: Scholars Press, 1991) 161–86.

Vorster, W. S. "Genre and the Revelation of John: A Study in Text, Context, and Intertext." *Neot* 22 (1988).

*Literary Form*

Aune, D. E. *Prophecy in Early Christianity and the Ancient Mediterranean World.* Grand Rapids: Eerdmans, 1983.

Blevins, J. L. "The Genre of Revelation." *RevExp* 77 (1980) 393–408.

Bloom, H., ed. *The Revelation of St. John the Divine: Modern Critical Interpretations.* New York: Chelsea House, 1988.

Boring, M. E. "The Apocalypse as Christian Prophecy: A Discussion of the Issues Raised by the Book of Revelation for the Study of Early Christian Prophecy." In *SBL 1974 Seminar Papers* (Missoula: Scholars Press, 1974).

Collins, A. Yarbro. *Crisis and Catharsis: The Power of the Apocalypse.* Philadelphia: Westminster, 1984.

_____. "The Early Christian Apocalypses." *Semeia* 14 (1979) 61–121.

Collins, J. J. "Pseudonymity, Historical Reviews and the Genre of the Revelation of John." *CBQ* 39 (1977) 329–43.

Corsani, B. "L'Apocalisse de Giovanni: Scritto apocalittico, o profetico?" *BibOr* 17 (1975) 253–68.

Fiorenza, E. Schüssler, "Apocalypse and Gnosis in the Book of Revelation and in Paul." *JBL* 92 (1973) 565–81.

_____. "Apokalypsis and Propheteia: The Book of Revelation in the Context of Early Christian Prophecy." In J. Lambrecht, ed., *L'Apocalypse johannique*, 105–28.

Hill, D. "Prophecy and Prophets in the Revelation of St. John." *NTS* 18 (1972) 401–18.

Kallas, J. "The Apocalypse—An Apocalyptic Book?" *JBL* 76 (1967) 69–80.

Karrer, M. *Die Johannesoffenbarung als Brief; Studien zu ihrem literarischen, historischen und theologischen Ort.* Göttingen: Vandenhoeck & Ruprecht, 1986.

Mazzaferri, F. D. *The Genre of the Book of Revelation from a Source-critical Perspective.* Berlin: Walter de Gruyter, 1989.

## Authorship and Date

Aune, D. "The Social Matrix of the Apocalypse of John." *BR* 26 (1981) 16–32.

Bell, A. A. "The Date of John's Apocalypse: The Evidence of Some Historians Reconsidered." *NTS* 25 (1979) 93–102.

Collins, A. Yarbro. *Crisis and Catharsis.* Philadelphia: Westminster, 1984, esp. 25–83.

──────. "Dating the Apocalypse of John. *BR* 26 (1981) 33–45.

Feuillet, A. *L'Apocalypse.* Paris: Desclee, 1962, esp. 75–90.

Kümmel, W. G. *Introduction to the New Testament.* Nashville: Abingdon, 1975, esp. 455–72.

Ulrichsen, H. "Die Sieben Haupter und die zehn Horner. Zur Datierung der Offenbarung des Johannes." *ST* 39 (1985) 1–20.

Wikenhauser, A. and J. Schmid. *Einleitung in das Neue Testament.* Freiburg: Herder, 1973, esp. 648–55.

## The Background

Collins, A. Yarbro. "Persecution and Vengeance in the Book of Revelation." In D. Hellholm, ed., *Apocalypticism,* 729–49.

──────. "The Political Perspective of the Revelation of John." *JBL* 96 (1977) 241–56.

Court, J. *Myth and History in the Book of Revelation.* Atlanta: John Knox, 1979.

Grant, R. M. *Early Christianity and Society.* New York: Harper & Row, 1977.

Habicht, C. "New Evidence on the Province of Asia." *JRS* 65 (1975) 65–91.

Johnson, S. E. "Asia Minor and Early Christianity." In J. Neusner, ed., *Christianity, Judaism and Other Greco-Roman Cults,* part 2, *Early Christianity* (Leiden: E. J. Brill, 1975) 77–145.

Keresztes, P. "The Jews, the Christians, and Emperor Domitian." *Vigiliae Christianae* 27 (1973) 1–28.

Malherbe, A. J. *Social Aspects of Early Christianity.* Philadelphia: Fortress, 1983.

Pleket, H. "An Aspect of the Emperor Cult: Imperial Mysteries." *HTR* 58 (1961) 331–47.

Scherrer, S. J. "Signs and Wonders in the Imperial Cult." *JBL* 103 (1984) 599–610.

Scott, K. *The Imperial Cult Under the Flavians.* New York: Arno, 1975.

Smallwood, E. M. "Domitian's Attitude towards the Jews and Judaism." *CP* 51 (1956) 1–13.

Thompson, L. L. *The Book of Revelation: Apocalypse and Empire.* New York and Oxford: Oxford University Press, 1990.

_____. "A Sociological Analysis of Tribulation in the Apocalypse of John."
    *Semeia* 36 (1986) 147–74.
Wilken, R. L. *The Christians as the Romans Saw Them.* New Haven: Yale University Press, 1984.


*The Purpose*

Bauckham, R. J. "The Worship of Jesus in Apocalyptic Christianity." *NTS* 27
    (1980–81) 322–41.
Blevins, *Revelation as Drama.* Nashville: Broadman, 1984.
Collins, J. J. "The Apocalypse—Revelation and Imagination." *Bible Today* 19 (1981)
    361–66.
Guthrie, D. *The Relevance of John's Apocalypse.* Grand Rapids: Eerdmans, 1987.
Thompson, L. "Cult and Eschatology in the Apocalypse of John." *JR* 49 (1969)
    331–50.
Vanni, U. *L'Apocalisse: Ermeneutica, exegesi, teologia.* Bologna: Dehoniane, 1988.
_____. "Gli apporti specifici dell' analisi letteraria dell' Apocalisse." *RivB*
    28 (1980) 319–25.


*Lines of Interpretation*

Boring, M. E. *Revelation.* Louisville: John Knox, 1989.
Krodel, G. A. *Revelation.* Minneapolis: Augsburg, 1989.
Kealy, S. P. *The Apocalypse of John.* Wilmington, Del.: Michael Glazier, 1987.
Hayes, Z. "Fundamentalist Eschatology." *New Theology Review* 1 (1988) 21–35.
Wikenhauser, A. and J. Schmid. *Einleitung in das Neue Testament.* Freiburg: Herder,
    1973.


*Text—Structure*

Barr, D. L. "The Apocalypse as a Symbolic Transformation of the World: A Literary
    Analysis." *Int* 38 (1984) 39–50.
Böcher, O. "Johanneisches in der Apokalypse des Johannes." *NTS* 27 (1981)
    310–21.
_____. "Das Verhältnis der Apokalypse des Johannes zum Evangelium des
    Johannes." In J. Lambrecht, ed., *L'Apocalypse johannique,* 289–301.
Boismard, M. É. " 'L'Apocalypse,' ou 'Les Apocalypses' de S. Jean." *RB* 56 (1949)
    507–39.
Bowman, J. B. "The Revelation to John. Its Dramatic Structure and Message."
    *Int* 9 (1955) 436–53.
Charles, C. H. *A Critical and Exegetical Commentary on the Revelation of St. John.*
    2 vols. Edinburgh: T. & T. Clark, 1920.
Collins, A. Yarbro. *The Combat Myth in the Book of Revelation.* Missoula: The Scholars Press, 1976.
Delobel, J. "Le texte de l'Apocalypse: Problèmes de méthode." In J. Lambrecht,
    ed., *L'Apocalypse johannique,* 151–66.
Fiorenza, E. Schüssler. "Composition and Structure of the Revelation of St. John."
    *CBQ* 39 (1977) 344–66.

_____. "The Quest for the Johannine School: The Apocalypse and the Fourth Gospel." *NTS* 23 (1977) 402–27.

Goulder, M. D. "The Apocalypse as an Annual Cycle of Prophecies." *NTS* 27 (1981) 342–67.

Lambrecht, J. "A Structuration of Revelation 4:1–22:5." In *L'Apocalypse johannique,* 77–104.

Mussies, G. *The Morphology of Koine Greek as Used in the Apocalypse of St. John: A Study in Bilingualism.* Suppl. NT 27. Leiden: Brill, 1971.

Porter, S. E. "The Language of the Apocalypse in Recent Discussion." *NTS* 35 (1989) 582–603.

Prigent, P. "L'Apocalypse: exégèse historique et analyse structurale." *NTS* 26 (1978) 127–37.

Spinks, L. C. "A Critical Examination of J. W. Bowman's Proposed Structure of the Revelation." *EvQ* 50 (1978) 211–22.

Vanni, U. *La Struttura Letteraria dell' Apocalisse.* Roma: Herder, 1980.

# GENERAL BIBLIOGRAPHY

## Commentaries

Allo, E. B. *Saint Jean: L'Apocalypse.* Paris: Gabalda, 1921².

Ashcroft, M. *Revelation.* Nashville: Broadman, 1972.

Barclay, W. *The Revelation of John.* Edinburgh: St. Andrew Press, 1960².

Beasley-Murray, G. R. *The Book of Revelation.* London: Marshall, Morgan & Scott; Grand Rapids: Eerdmans, 1974.

Beckwith, I. T. *The Apocalypse of John.* New York: Macmillan, 1919.

Böcher, O. *Die Johannesapokalypse.* Darmstadt: Wissenschaftliche Buchgesellschaft, 1975.

Boring, M. E. *Revelation.* Interpretation. Louisville: John Knox, 1989.

Bousset, W. *Die Offenbarung Johannes.* Göttingen: Vandenhoeck & Ruprecht, 1906.

Brutsch, C. *La Clarté de l'Apocalypse.* Geneva: Labor et Fides, 1966⁵.

Caird, G. B. *The Revelation of St. John the Divine.* London: A. & C. Black; New York: Harper & Row, 1966.

Cerfaux, L. and J. Cambier. *L'Apocalypse de Saint Jean lue aux Chrétiens.* Paris: Cerf, 1955.

Charles, R. H. *A Critical and Exegetical Commentary on the Revelation of St. John.* 2 vols. International Critical Commentary. Edinburgh: T. & T. Clark; New York: Scribner's, 1920.

Charlier, J. P. *Comprendre l'Apocalypse.* 2 vols. Lire le Bible 89–90. Paris: Cerf, 1991.

Collins, A. Yarbro. *The Apocalypse.* NTM 22. Wilmington, Del.: Michael Glazier, 1979.

_____. "The Apocalypse (Revelation)." *NJBC* (1990) 996–1016.

Corsini, E. *The Apocalypse: The Perennial Revelation of Jesus Christ.* Wilmington, Del.: Michael Glazier, 1983.

Ellul, J. *Apocalypse: The Book of Revelation.* New York: Seabury, 1977.

Farrer, A. *The Revelation of St. John the Divine.* Oxford: Clarendon Press, 1964.

Fiorenza, E. Schüssler. *Invitation to the Book of Revelation.* New York: Doubleday, 1981.

Ford, J. M. *Revelation: Introduction, Translation and Commentary.* Anchor Bible 38. New York: Doubleday, 1975.

Gonzalez Ruiz, J. M. *Apocalypsis de Juan: El libro del testimonio cristiano.* Madrid: Cristiandad, 1987.

Harrington, W. J. *The Apocalypse of St. John: A Commentary.* London: Chapman, 1969. [*Understanding the Apocalypse* (Washington: Corpus, 1969)].

Hughes, P. E. *The Book of Revelation: A Commentary*. Grand Rapids: Eerdmans, 1990.
Kealy, S. P. *The Apocalypse of John*. Wilmington, Del.: Michael Glazier, 1987.
Kiddle, M. *The Revelation of St. John*. London: Hodder & Stoughton, 1940.
Kraft, H. *Die Offenbarung des Johannes*. Tübingen: Mohr, 1974.
Krodel, G. A. *Revelation*. Minneapolis: Augsburg, 1989.
Ladd, G. E. *A Commentary on the Revelation of John*. Grand Rapids: Eerdmans, 1972.
Lohmeyer, E. *Die Offenbarung des Johannes*. Tübingen: Mohr, 1970[3].
Lohse, E. *Die Offenbarung des Johannes*. Göttingen: Vandenhoeck & Ruprecht, 1976.
Minear, P. S. *I Saw a New Earth: An Introduction to the Visions of the Apocalypse*. Washington: Corpus, 1968.
Morris, L. *Revelation*. Grand Rapids: Eerdmans, 1969.
Mounce, R. H. *The Book of Revelation*. Grand Rapids: Eerdmans, 1977.
Mulholland, M. R. *Revelation: Holy Living in an Unholy World*. Grand Rapids: Zondervan, 1990.
Müller, U. B. *Die Offenbarung des Johannes*. Gütersloh: Mohn, 1984.
Prigent, P. *L'Apocalypse de Saint Jean*. Geneva: Labor et Fides, 1988[2].
Richards, H. *What the Spirit Says to the Churches*. London: Chapman, 1967.
Rist, M. *The Revelation of St. John the Divine*. New York: Abingdon, 1957.
Roloff, J. *Die Offenbarung des Johannes*. Zurich: Theologischer Verlag, 1984.
Sweet, J. P. M. *Revelation*. Pelican Commentaries. London: SCM; Philadelphia: Westminster, 1979.
Swete, H. B. *The Apocalypse of St. John*. London: Macmillan, 1922[3].
Wikenhauser, A. *Offenbarung des Johannes*. Regensburg: Pustet, 1959[3].
Zahn, T. *Die Offenbarung des Johannes*. 2 vols. Leipzig: Deichert, 1922–26.

## Studies

Aune, D. E. *Prophecy in Early Christianity and the Ancient Mediterranean World*. Grand Rapids: Eerdmans, 1983.
Bloom, H. *The Revelation of St. John the Divine*. Modern Critical Interpretations. New York: Chelsea, 1988.
Charlesworth, J. H. *The Old Testament Pseudepigrapha*. Vol. 1. New York: Doubleday, 1983.
Collins, A. Yarbro. *The Combat Myth in the Book of Revelation*. Missoula: Scholars Press, 1976.
_____. *Crisis and Catharsis: The Power of the Apocalypse*. Philadelphia: Westminster, 1984.
Collins, J. J. *The Apocalyptic Imagination: An Introduction to the Jewish Matrix of Christianity*. New York: Crossroad, 1987.
Court, J. *Myth and History in the Book of Revelation*. London: SPCK; Atlanta: John Knox, 1979.
Feuillet, A. *The Apocalypse*. New York: Alba House, 1965.
Fiorenza, E. Schüssler. *The Book of Revelation: Justice and Judgment*. Philadelphia: Fortress, 1985.

Glasson, T. F., ed. *The Revelation of John*. Cambridge: University Press, 1965.

Guthrie, D. *The Relevance of John's Apocalypse*. Grand Rapids: Eerdmans, 1987.

Hanson, P. D. *The Dawn of Apocalyptic*. Philadelphia: Fortress, 1978.

——————, ed. *Visionaries and Their Apocalypses*. London: SPCK; Philadelphia: Fortress, 1983.

Hemer, C. J. *The Letters to the Seven Churches of Asia in their Local Setting*. Sheffield: JSOT, 1986.

Hellholm, D., ed. *Apocalypticism in the Mediterranean World and the Near East*. Tübingen: Mohr (Siebeck), 1989.

Hill, D. *New Testament Prophecy*. Atlanta: John Knox, 1979.

Lambrecht, J., ed. *L'Apocalypse johannique et l'Apocalyptique dans le Nouveau Testament*. Paris: J. Duculot; Leuven: University Press, 1980.

Laws, S. *In the Light of the Lamb: Imagery, parody, and theology in the Apocalypse of John*. Wilmington, Del.: Michael Glazier, 1988.

Minear, P. S. *New Testament Apocalyptic*. Nashville: Abingdon, 1981.

Ramsay, W. M. *The Letters to the Seven Churches*. London: Hodder & Stoughton, 1904. Reprint. Grand Rapids: Baker, 1963.

Rowland, C. *The Open Heaven: A Study of Apocalyptic in Judaism and Christianity*. London: SPCK; New York: Crossroad, 1982.

Thompson, L. L. *The Book of Revelation: Apocalypse and Empire*. New York and Oxford: Oxford University Press, 1990.

Vanni, U. *L'Apocalisse: Ermeneutica, esegesi, teologia*. Bologna: EDB, 1988.

# TRANSLATION, NOTES, INTERPRETATION

## I. PROLOGUE, ADDRESS, AND INAUGURAL VISION

### 1. *Prologue* (1:1-3)

1. The revelation of Jesus Christ, which God gave him to show his servants what must shortly come to pass. He made it known by sending his angel to his servant John, 2. who, in telling all that he saw, bore witness to the word of God and to the testimony of Jesus Christ. 3. Blessed is the one who reads aloud, and blessed are they who hear the words of this prophecy and heed what is written there, for the time of crisis is near.

#### NOTES

1. *revelation:* The term (*apokalypsis*) occurs only here in the book.

*of Jesus Christ:* Subjective genitive—a revelation from Jesus Christ. The full name, Jesus Christ, is found only in this chapter (1:1, 2, 5).

*which God gave to him:* God is the ultimate source—Revelation is "word of God." Yet, John's book is "the revelation of Jesus Christ" (see 22:2): God and Christ speak as one.

*his servants:* In the Old Testament "servant" means prophet (see Amos 3:7); here the term means the Christian communities (see Rev 2:20; 7:3).

*what must shortly come to pass:* Echoes Dan 2:28; that fulfillment should be "soon" is the expectation of apocalyptic (see Rev 22:6-7). John prepares his readers for an impending crisis, and for their salvation.

*angel:* The customary intermediary in apocalyptic.

*his servant John:* An otherwise unknown Christian prophet, most likely an itinerant prophet, and, probably, a Palestinian by birth. Revelation differs from other apocalypses in not being pseudonymous.

43

2. *all that he saw:* The whole book may be regarded as the testimony of Jesus Christ.

*bore witness . . . testimony (emartyrēsen . . . martyria):* In our translation, "bear witness" and "testimony" will consistently render verb and noun respectively.

*the word of God:* Here in the sense of Amos 3:7—the secret purpose of God. This word, attested by Jesus Christ, is seen by John in vision (or heard in audition). At a deeper level, Jesus is the "word of God," the one who definitively reveals God, who defines God.

3. *blessed:* The first of seven beatitudes in Revelation (1:3; 14:13; 16:15; 19:9; 20:6; 22:7, 14).

*the one who reads [aloud]:* The reader in public worship—the lector—who is to read faithfully (22:18-19). Reading and listening to Revelation is a liturgical act of the Christians of western Asia.

*hear . . . heed:* See Luke 11:18.

*the words of this prophecy:* An explicit claim that Revelation is prophetic. See 19:10.

*the time of crisis:* lit. "the time" (*kairos*)—the end; the time of deliverance and judgment, preceded by the "tribulation" (v. 9).

### INTERPRETATION

Revelation opens with a prologue (1:1-3) which is, in fact, an elaborate title. The author names himself: John—an otherwise unknown Christian prophet, for this apocalyptic *letter* (1:4; 22:21) is firmly characterized as "prophecy" (1:3; 22:7, 10, 18). He does not, like all other apocalyptists, need to resort to pseudonymity in respect of what is a "revelation of Jesus Christ" with God as the ultimate source (1:1), a revelation which, at the close, will be attested by Christ himself (22:6). John's intent is to prepare his Christian communities, the servants of God, for an imminent crisis, which he is willing to provoke. He is witness: eye-witness and ear-witness (because there will be auditions as well as visions). He bears witness to the secret purpose of God of which Jesus Christ is the prime witness. Indeed, God and Jesus testify to themselves.

Revelation is a pastoral letter to Christians in the Roman province of Asia, a letter to be read aloud in the worship services of the communities. John invokes a blessing on the reader—the lector—and on the community members who hearken to the word. These hearers come at the end of a chain of communication: God–Jesus–angel–reader–hearer. As a motive for hearing and keeping, he warns that the time of crisis is near. This motif of the nearness of the end threads through the writing. When John declares that the time is near, he means that, in his view, the End is soon. Was he, then, mistaken? In one sense, obviously yes. The end did not happen in his day, nor has it occurred nineteen centuries later. What we might learn from him is a sense of urgency, such as one finds also in Mark 9:1 and 13:30. For each of us, *our* time is the only time we have to fulfill our calling, and our death is the end for us on earth. Our span of years is important for us, and precious in the eyes of the Lord. (Boring, 68–74).

### FOR REFERENCE AND FURTHER STUDY

Bieder, W. "Die Sieben Seligpreisungen in der Offenbarung des Johannes." *TZ* 10 (1954) 13–30.

Dehandschutter, B. "The Meaning of Witness in the Apocalypse." In J. Lambrecht ed., *L'Apocalypse Johannique et l'Apocalyptique dans le Nouveau Testament* (Paris: Duculot; Leuven: University Press, 1980) 283–88.

Pesch, R. "Offenbarung Jesu Christi. Eine Auslegung von Apk 1:1-3." *BibLeb* 11 (1970) 15–29.

## 2. *The Address* (1:4-8)

4. John, to the seven Churches of Asia: Grace to you and peace, from him who is, who was, and who is to come, and from the seven spirits before his throne, 5. and from Jesus Christ, the faithful witness, the first-born of the dead, and ruler of the kings of earth. To him who loves us and has loosed us from our sins with his blood, 6. and has made us a royal house of priests to his God and Father—to him be glory and dominion for ever and ever. Amen.

7.     Behold, he will come with the clouds,
        and every eye will see him,
        even those who pierced him,
     and all the tribes of the earth
        will wail because of him.
     So be it. Amen.

8. "I am the Alpha and the Omega," says the Lord God, who is, who was, and who is to come, the Almighty.

### NOTES

4. *the seven Churches:* A symbolic number representing the whole Church of John's area. We know of at least three others besides the Churches listed in 1:11—Troas (2 Cor 2:12), Colossae (Col 1:1) and Hierapolis (Col 4:13).

*Asia:* A Roman province: the western part of Asia Minor (Turkey).

*grace . . . and peace:* The common greeting in Pauline letters.

*from him who is, who was, and who is to come:* In rabbinical literature a similar development of the divine name of Exod 3:14 was not uncommon. John may have been influenced by the Targums. Deut 32:39 in the *Targum of Pseudo-Jonathan* reads: "See now that I am he who is and who was and I am he who will be"; see Exod 3:14, "Thus shall you say to the children of Israel, 'I am who is and who will be has sent me to you.' "

*the seven spirits:* Suggested by the seven "angels of the face" (Tob 12:15; 1 Enoch 90:21) and by the seven lamps and seven eyes of Zech 4:2, 10—here a symbol of God's activity in the world.

5. *witness:* Originally meaning "witness," *martys* eventually moved to the meaning of "martyr," with the idea of death being uppermost, or absolute. "Witness" remains the dominant sense in Revelation, though death is also implied in 1:5; 3:14; 16:6 (A. A. Trites, "Martus and Martyrdom in the Apocalypse," *NovT* 15 [1973] 72–80).

   *the faithful witness, the firstborn of the dead, and ruler of the kings of the earth:* These three titles of Jesus Christ address directly the situation of John's readers: Jesus stood as faithful witness before Roman authority, a model for Christians in a parallel situation; his resurrection, as the "first fruits" of general resurrection (see 1 Cor 15:20; Col 1:18), holds out hope for Christians challenged to bear witness unto death; he, not Caesar, is the universal ruler (see Ps 89:27), "king of kings" (Rev 19:16).

   *who loves us and has loosed us:* A careful use of tenses: he loosed us (aorist) by his death; he loves us (present) eternally. Many manuscripts (mostly minuscules) read *lousanti* (washed); *lysanti* (loosed, freed), found only here in the NT, is better attested (p[18], Sinaiticus, A, C).

   *with his blood:* See Rom 3:24-25, "justified by his grace as a gift, through the redemption which is in Christ Jesus, whom God put forward as an expiation by his blood."

6. *a royal house of priests,* lit. "a kingdom, priests": See Exod 19:6, "You shall be to me a kingdom of priests and a holy nation." Christ has constituted his people as a royal house, sharing his authority (see 2:26; 3:21; 5:10; 20:6), and as mediators between God and the rest of humanity. John regards the Church as a prophetic, royal, and priestly community. This first (vv. 5b-6) of the many doxologies of the book, is addressed to Jesus Christ (see 5:13; 7:10; 2 Pet 3:18). It probably echoes an early baptismal formula.

7. The text is based on a combination of Dan 7:13 and Zech 12:10, a combination which occurs also in Matt 24:30. The passage of Zechariah is also found in John 19:37 in reference to the piercing of the side of the dead Jesus.

   *will come,* lit. "he comes": Present tense with future sense.

   *all the tribes of the earth:* Not in the pejorative sense of "the inhabitants of the earth"; rather, the enemies of Christ will lament in remorse.

*will wail because of him:* Despairing lament in view of impending condemnation, or repentant lamentation for what they had done to him? In Zech 12:10 the context is penitential grief, and this is the better sense here. "What John in fact says is that men will 'see' the pierced but triumphant Christ and will 'lament,' not for themselves but 'for him' " (Caird, 18). They will feel compunction for the wounds they have inflicted on him.

*So be it. Amen: Nai. Amen*—The Greek and Hebrew forms of the affirmative. A double affirmation is appropriate at this solemn moment. See 22:20.

8. The first of only two passages in Revelation (see 21:5-8) in which God is explicitly identified as speaker.

*I am (egō eimi):* Of four "I am" sayings, God is speaker in two (1:8; 21:6), and Jesus in two (1:17; 22:13). The close assimilation of God and Lamb (Christ) throughout Revelation is John's way of presenting God as the God who has revealed himself in Christ.

*the Alpha and the Omega:* The Greek rendering of a corresponding Hebrew expression, *aleph* and *tau* (the first and last letters of the alphabet in each language). God is the first and the last (Isa 44:6; 48:12), the beginning and the end (Rev 21:6).

*the Almighty: Pantokratōr*, a regular LXX rendering of "Yahweh Sebaoth," "lord of hosts," is John's favorite title for God (see 4:8; 11:17; 15:3; 16:7, 14; 19:6, 15; 21:22). God is the all-ruler, the sovereign Lord—a reminder to Christians that their God and his Christ (though the title "the Almighty" is never, in Revelation, formally attributed to Christ) hold supreme power, even over the arrogant "rulers of the earth."

### INTERPRETATION

After the titulary prologue, the letter opens with the customary epistolary formula: name of the sender (nominative) and name of the receiver(s) (dative). John's opening is reminiscent of Paul (see 1 Thess 1:1; 2 Thess 1:1-2); the wish, "grace and peace," occurs in almost all of Paul's addresses. Besides, John's address is elaborate (1:4-5) as Paul's tended to be (see 1 Cor 1:3; Gal 1:1-5; Rom 1:1-7). The letter addresses seven Churches—a symbolic number, meaning the Christian communities in general—in the province of Asia. The blessing of grace and peace issues from God, a God not remote but active in our world—the "seven spirits"—a God especially active and present in Jesus Christ. In this Christian apocalyptic letter the focus is on him. He is Jesus *Christ*, the Messiah. His titles speak to the situation of John's readers: fidelity unto death, victor over death, God's answer to Caesar's arrogance. He is the example and source of hope for Christians about to face the great persecution. They truly have reason for patient endurance.

Jesus' help is not only for the future; it is, more intimately, in the past and in the present. We were sinners: he liberated us from the evil actions and deeds of our past by dying on our behalf. Do we need further proof that he loves us? His generosity does not stop there. He not only liberated us from bondage, he has raised us to royalty: a royal house of priests, inheriting the privilege of the chosen people. Christians share the authority of the King of kings and stand as priestly mediators in the world of humankind. The "us" ("made us") is, obviously, inclusive: Christian women share the royal and priestly role as fully as their brothers. This generous Jesus is, indeed, worthy of honor and glory.

From the redemption wrought by Christ in time, John looks to his coming at the end. He will come, from the presence of the Father; none can hide from his presence. He will be manifest to all, even to those whose hostility numbers them with those who had brought about his death. If he appears as Judge, it will not be to condemn. The gracious mercy of this Judge touches hearts: the tribes of the earth will lament in remorse. To underline the seriousness of the promise, God himself speaks—he will speak again only at the close of this book (21:5-8). If he is the Almighty, the eternal, sovereign Lord, his might is present in the Lamb (5:5-6). He is ever the foolish God who displays his power in the cross of Jesus (see 1 Cor 1:23-25).

John's address is full of comfort. We are assured that our God is the everlasting, the Almighty. But we Christians meet this awesome God in the one who laid down his life for us. John puts, in his manner, what Paul had already declared: "God shows his love for us in that while we were yet sinners Christ died for us" (Rom 5:8). Once slaves of sin, we have been set free, with radical freedom: "if the Son makes you free, you will be free indeed" (John 8:36). Christian privilege brings its challenging obligation: priestly concern for the whole of humankind. But nothing less should inspire those who serve the God who is God of all.

Revelation was explicitly designed to be read aloud in the liturgy (1:3) and it is spangled with heavenly liturgies. It has been plausibly suggested that 1:4-8 might be read as a liturgical dialogue (Vanni, "Esempio di dialogo," 460f.).

*Lector*
(*ho anaginōskōn*)

Grace to you, and peace
from him who is, who was, and who is to come
and from the seven spirits before his throne;
and from Jesus Christ
the faithful witness,
the firstborn from the dead,
and ruler of the kings of the earth.

*Congregation*
(*hoi akouontes*)

To him who loves us
and has loosed us from our sins with his blood

and has made us a royal house of priests
to his God and Father—
to him be glory and dominion for ever and ever.
Amen.

*Lector*  Behold: he will come with the clouds,
and every eye will see him
even those who pierced him
and all the tribes of the earth will wail because of him.

*Congregation*  So be it. Amen.

*Lector*  I am the Alpha and the Omega
—says the Lord God—
who is, who was, and who is to come,
the Almighty.

## For Reference and Further Study

Bauckham, R. J. "The Role of the Spirit in the Apocalypse." *EvQ* 52 (1980) 452–66.

Filippini, R. "La forza della verita: Sul Concetto di Testimonianza nell'Apocalisse." *RivB* 38 (1990) 401–49.

Fiorenza, E. Schüssler. "Redemption as Liberation, Ap 1:5 and 5:9f." *CBQ* 36 (1974) 220–32.

Jeske, R. L. "Spirit and Community in the Johannine Apocalypse." *NTS* 31 (1985) 452–66.

Vanni, U. "Un esempio di dialogo liturgico in Ap 1:4-8." *Bib* 57 (1976) 453–67.

## 3. *Vision of One Like a Son of Man* (1:9-20)

9. I, John, your brother and sharer in the tribulation and sovereignty and endurance which are ours in Jesus, was on the island called Patmos on account of the word of God and the testimony of Jesus. 10. The Spirit came upon me on the Lord's day and I heard behind me a great voice like a trumpet, 11. which said, "What you see write in a scroll and send it to the seven Churches: to Ephesus, Smyrna, Pergamum, Thyatira, Sardis, Philadelphia, and Laodicea." 12. I turned to see whose voice it was that spoke to me, and having turned, I saw seven golden lamps, 13. and among the lamps one in human form dressed in a robe that came to his feet, with a gold girdle around his breast. 14. The hair of his head was white as snow-white wool, and his eyes flamed like fire; 15. his feet were like brilliant metal refined in a furnace, and his voice was like the roar of many waters. 16. In his right hand he had seven stars, and from

his mouth came a sharp two-edged sword; and his face was like the sun shining in its strength.

17. When I saw him, I fell at his feet as though I were dead. But he laid his right hand on me, and said, "Do not be afraid. I am the first and the last, 18. the living one who was dead, and I hold the keys of Death and Hades. 19. Write down therefore what you see, what now is, and what is to take place hereafter. 20. As for the secret of the seven stars you saw in my right hand: the seven stars are the angels of the seven Churches, and the seven lamps are the seven Churches."

## NOTES

9. *brother (adelphos):* Occurs five times in Revelation (1:9; 6:11; 12:10; 19:10; 22:9), always with an explicit ecclesial reference. John is brother of those to whom he writes, a fellow worker in the same religious society (see 2 Pet 3:15).

*sharer:* Shared Christian existence means, in particular, participation in Jesus' affliction.

*tribulation:* Sufferings (see 1 Pet 4:13; 5:1; 2 Cor 1:7; Phil 3:10; 4:14) suggesting persecution. Yet, for John, *thlipsis* is also an essential component of Christian living (see 2:9).

*sovereignty,* lit. "kingdom": A sovereignty based on endured suffering.

*endurance (hypomonē):* Patient endurance. The word occurs seven times in Revelation (1:9; 2:2, 3, 19; 3:10; 13:10; 14:12); it is the characteristic virtue of the persecuted, of those steadfastly enduring "tribulation." It is founded on faith in Jesus, the Lord who comes, and is inspired by the certainty of his love.

*in Jesus:* An expression found in Paul, characterizing Christian life as already participating in Christ; see Rev 14:13, "in the Lord."

*was on the island called Patmos,* lit. "I found myself (*egenomēn en*)": Patmos, a small (about ten miles long and five wide), barren island among the group of Sporades off the south-west coast of Asia Minor.

*on account of the word of God:* See 6:9; 20:4. It has been argued that John was there under judicial banishment (*relegatio in insulam*) following a sentence of the provincial governor. In light of the bland "I arrived on," John may simply have gone to preach on Patmos.

10. *the Spirit came upon me,* lit. "I was in (*egenomēn en*) the Spirit": Under the influence of the Spirit, referring to the gift of prophecy. See 4:2.

*the Lord's day:* Probably (but not certainly) Sunday. See Acts 20:7; 1 Cor 16:2; *Didache* 14:1. In the liturgical bent of Revelation it is probable that "the Lord's day" is the day of worship.

*a great voice like a trumpet:* See Ezek 3:12; the "trumpet" is an Old Testament cultic symbol.

11. *what you see:* All the visions of Revelation. The seven Churches are not listed haphazardly but in order: they were linked by a circular road that, from Ephesus, went north to Smyrna and Pergamum and then swung southwards to

take in the others. A messenger could carry the scroll to each of the Churches in turn, and by each it would be read and possibly copied (see Col 4:16).

12. *seven golden lamps:* Suggested by the seven-branched lampstand (*menorah*) (Exod 25:31-37; Zech 4:2) but here the lampstands (better, "lamps") are separate. The symbolism is explained in v. 20. For Rev 1:12-16 see Dan 10:5-6.

*I saw:* There is no reason, in principle, to doubt that John was recipient of real visions; ecstatic experience is a widely attested aspect of many religions. In their present form, the visions are literary compositions based on John's visionary experience. In some cases they may be solely literary; we have no way of knowing.

13. *one in human form,* lit. "like a son of man": Allusion to Dan 7:13—a heavenly being in human form (see Rev 1:7). In Daniel the one "like a son of man" is a symbolic figure, representing the saints of the Most High. But here "he is a real man who *died* and is *alive* (v. 18)" (Sweet, 69). Neither here nor in 14:14 does John use "son of man" as a Christological title.

*a robe that came to his feet:* The term *podērēs* ("robe") is found here only in the NT. See Josephus *Ant* 3.7.2, "the robe to the feet [*podērēs chitōn*] which [the priests] fasten at the breast." For the long priestly robe, see Exod 28:4; Wis 18:24.

*a gold girdle:* A girdle was part of the garb of the high priest (Exod 28:4; 39:29).

14. *white as snow-white wool:* See Dan 7:9, "his raiment was white as snow, and the hair of his head like white wool," said of the Ancient of Days (God).

15. *brilliant metal (chalkolibanos):* An unidentified alloy, probably a special product of Thyatira (2:18); recalls Ezekiel's vision of God (Ezek 1:27; 8:2).

*his voice:* The voice of the God of Israel (Ezek 1:24; 4:32); all the power of God is concentrated in his word.

16. *seven stars:* In v. 20 identified as "the angels of the seven Churches": the heavenly counterparts of the Churches.

*sword:* The word of God: see Isa 49:2; Wis 18:14-16; Heb 4:12. The only weapon of the exalted Christ is his word, Rev 19:15; see Isa 11:4; 49:2.

17-18. *fell at his feet:* The reaction of Daniel (Dan 10:7-9); see Rev 19:10; 22:8.

*I am the first and the last, the living one who was dead:* RSV reads: ". . . the living one; I died, and behold I am alive." Charles (1:31) rightly maintains that the text should be rendered as given in our translation.

*Death and Hades:* Hades here stands for the Hebrew *Sheol,* abode of the dead. These are powers rather than places. In 6:8 Death and Hades are clearly personified. See 1 Cor 15:26.

19. *what you see . . . now is . . . to take place:* A common formula to describe prophecy (van Unnik, "Prophecy," 86–94). Therefore, the whole of John's vision.

20. *secret (mystērion):* This is the inner meaning of a symbolic vision, as in Dan 2:47.

*angels:* The word *angelos* occurs frequently in Revelation, always in the sense of a heavenly being; the presumption is that it has the same meaning here. The "angels" are the heavenly counterparts of the earthly Churches.

## INTERPRETATION

In a striking vision, reminiscent of the inaugural visions of the prophets (see Isa 6; Jer 1; Ezek 1–3), John is commissioned to write what is to be revealed to him and to send the message to seven Churches of Asia. He writes to his brothers and sisters, stressing his solidarity with them, sharing not only their sufferings and their consistent resistance to inimical pressure but also the victory that will be theirs as reward of their endurance. John "found himself" on Patmos because of his preaching of the gospel and his loyalty to it in time of tribulation. On the Lord's day—most likely Sunday—John was touched by the prophetic Spirit. He heard a voice (audition rather than vision), which is clearly the voice of Christ. John is bidden to write—the book (*biblion*) is a papyrus scroll—and circulate his message. The Churches are symbolized by seven lamps (1:20). Now he sees a human figure dressed in priestly robes. This one "like a son of man" walks among the lamps (see 2:1): the heavenly Christ is no absentee landlord. He is present in his earthly communities; he knows their "works." It is in his name that John speaks his prophetic messages.

What is said of the Ancient of Days (God) in Daniel is here said of the one in human form. John, throughout, does not hesitate to use God-language of Jesus. "The use of such language is an expression of [John's] conviction that 'God' is to be defined as 'the one who has defined himself definitively in Jesus' " (Boring, 83). The Christ holds in his right hand (in his power) the seven stars which are the "angels," the heavenly counterparts, of the seven Churches. His only weapon is the sword of his mouth (19:21)—the word.

The overall effect of the vision is one of terrifying majesty: John's reaction is that of Daniel (Dan 10:8-9). Yet, this majestic figure remains the Jesus of the gospel, and John hears again his comforting "Do not be afraid" (see Mark 6:50; Matt 28:10). Just as descriptive details of the vision pointed to the assimilation of Christ to God, the words of the vision figure do likewise. He is "the first and the last" (Isa 44:6; 48:12), as the Lord God had said of himself in Rev 1:8. He is the living one, but the living one who died the death and now lives again. He is master of death and of the abode of the dead (see 20:13-14). John is bidden to write the whole of his vision. The obvious difficulty in v. 20, a verse which purports to explain the "mystery," the inner meaning of the seven stars, is the meaning of the "angels" of the Churches. It surely must be that *angelos* maintains here its meaning of heavenly being. Angels appear as the guardians of nations in Dan 10:13, 20, 21; 11:1; 12:1 in accordance with a view current in contemporary and later Judaism. Revelation itself speaks of "the angel of water" (16:4). Here, rather than guardians, they are, in keeping with apocalyptic thought, the heavenly counterparts of the earthly communities. The presence and authority of "the one in human form" are asserted: he walks amid the lamps, the earthly Churches, and holds in his power the stars or angels, the heavenly Churches.

This inaugural vision effectively brings out the oracular character of the first part of Revelation, for it is closely parallel to the inaugural visions of the Old Testament prophets. But where the latter proceeded to speak in the name of Yahweh ("thus says Yahweh"), John will make known the "revelation of Jesus Christ." And since, in his eyes, the symbolic seven reaches beyond the communities he addresses immediately, his message—the message of the Lord—has meaning for the Church until the end of time.

John's vision of the risen Lord is dramatic counterpart of the closing declaration of Matthew's Lord: "Lo, I am with you always, to the close of the age" (Matt 28:20). We, also, have the comfort of his presence in our midst. Comfort—but challenge, too, as the messages to the Churches will underline. We acknowledge this challenge as we worship him as our Lord. But never should we fear in his presence. He is the one who lifts from us even the deep-rooted fear of death, for he, the Living One, is victor over Death.

## For Reference and Further Study

Aune, D. E. "The Apocalypse of John and Graeco-Roman Revelatory Magic." *NTS* 33 (1987) 481–501.

Feuillet, A. "Jalons pour une meillieure intelligence de l'Apocalypse. Le prologue et vision inaugurale (chapitre 1)." *EspV* 85 (1975) 65–72.

Hartman, L. "Form and Message: A Preliminary Discussion of 'Partial Texts' in Rev 1–3 and 22:6ff." In J. Lambrecht, ed., *L'Apocalypse Johannique*, 129–49.

Kirby, J. T. "The Rhetorical Situations of Revelation 1–3." *NTS* 34 (1988) 197–207.

McNamara, M. *The New Testament and the Palestinian Targum to the Pentateuch.* Rome: Biblical Institute Press, 1966, esp. 192–99.

Rowland, C. "The Vision of the Risen Christ in Rev 1:13ff: The Debt of an Early Christology to an Aspect of Jewish Angelology." *JTS* 31 (1980) 1–11.

Saffrey, H. D. "Relire l'Apocalypse à Patmos." *RB* 82 (1975) 385–417.

Smith, C. R. "Revelation 1:19: An Eschatologically Escalated Prophetic Convention." *JETS* 33 (1990) 461–6.

Stott, W. "A Note on the Word KYRIAKH in Rev 1:10." *NTS* 12 (1965–66) 70–75.

Strand, K. A. "Another Look at 'Lord's Day' in the Early Church and in Rev 1:10." *NTS* 13 (1966–67) 174–81.

Thompson, L. L. "A Sociological Analysis of Tribulation in the Apocalypse of John." *Semeia* 36 (1986) 147–74.

van Unnik, W. C. "A Formula Describing Prophecy." *NTS* 9 (1963) 86–94.

Vanni, U. "Il 'Giorno del Signore' in Apoc 1:10, Giorno di Purificazione e di Discernimento." *RivB* 26 (1978) 187–99.

## II. THE MESSAGES TO THE SEVEN CHURCHES

### 4. *Message to Ephesus* (2:1-7)

1. To the angel of the Church at Ephesus write:
These are the words of the One who holds the seven stars in his right hand, who walks among the seven gold lamps: 2. I know your works—your toil and endurance. I know you cannot bear evil people and have put to the test those who call themselves apostles but are not, and you have found them to be false. 3. Endurance you have; you have borne up for my name's sake and have not grown weary. 4. But I have this against you: you have lost the love you had at first. 5. Be mindful, then, of how far you have fallen; repent, and do as you did before. If not, I will come to you and remove your lamp from its place, unless you repent. 6. You have this to your credit: you hate the works of the Nicolaitans, as I do.

7. You have ears—so listen to what the Spirit is saying to the Churches! To the victor I will grant the right to eat from the tree of life that stands in the paradise of God.

### Notes

1. *these are the words (tade legei):* An archaism, similar to the English "thus saith." It is a regular LXX rendering of *koh 'amar Yahweh* ("thus says Yahweh"), and also a Near Eastern epistolary prescript of royal edicts (D. E. Aune, *NTS* 36 [1990] 187f.).

   *The seven stars . . . gold lamps:* Because Ephesus was the most important Church of the province, the Lord appears under titles which express his relation to the Churches generally; see 1:13, 16, 20. He who is Lord of the Churches as spiritual entities is no stranger to the earthly Churches.

2. *I know:* As the God of the Old Testament prophets knows the situation of those to whom the prophecy was directed (e.g., Jer 48:30; Hos 5:2; Amos 5:12), so this Lord knows the situation of his Churches.

   *works:* As in Paul, "works" comprise responsible Christian conduct.

   *endurance (hypomonē):* "the 'consistent resistance' or 'staying power' of the saints" (Fiorenza, *The Book of Revelation*, 191).

   *apostles:* Itinerant charismatics who claimed authority and were acknowledged by some congregations. For John they are *false* apostles: he rejected their teaching and challenged them as rivals (see 2 Cor 11:13).

3. *borne . . . grown weary:* Word-plays: you have *borne* up, though you cannot *bear* evil people (v. 2); in spite of your "toil" (*kopos*, v. 2) you have not "grown weary" (*kekopiakes*).

4. *the love you had at first:* Has brotherly/sisterly love given way to censoriousness? Loss of love is a mark of the End (Matt 24:12; 2 Thess 3:14-15; 2 Tim 2:24-26). Contrast 2:19.

5. *be mindful . . . repent . . . do:* "Answer to three stages in the history of conversion" (Sweet, 27). The admonition holds an invitation.

   *remove your lamp:* Ephesus may lose its rank among the Churches, and may well disappear altogether. There appears to be topical advertance to a danger that the vigorous city and its Church might fall under the deadening sway of the temple of Artemis (the Artemesium) (Hemer, 56).

6. *Nicolaitans:* They are named again in 2:15; we learn more of them in 2:20-23.

7. *you have ears,* lit. "one who has an ear": This recalls a Synoptic saying of Jesus (Matt 13:9, 43; 11:15 parr.). The prophet John presents his message as that of Jesus.

   *the Spirit:* In v. 1 the speaker is the risen Jesus: Jesus and Spirit are equivalent in all the messages.

   *the victor,* lit. "one who conquers": To conquer is to prevail in battle, sport, or any contest; "conquering" is a key word in the book. In Revelation the battle is against Satan, waged by God, the risen Lord, and the faithful. Victory is won by "endurance" in face of "tribulation" (1:9). The promise to the Victor does not imply that John expected all Christians to suffer martyrdom; he did demand that all "endure."

   *the tree of life . . . in the paradise of God:* See Gen 2:8-9; Ezek 47:12; Rev 22:2, 14. "Tree of life" may have suggested the Cross to the original readers, as well as the sacred tree and asylum of Artemis. "The cross was the place of refuge for the repentant sinner in contrast with the tree which marked the asylum for the unrepentant criminal" (Hemer, 55). "Paradise" does not again occur in Revelation, nor does reference to eating from the tree of life. *(see, 22:14 )*

   *cf. p. 221,*

## INTERPRETATION

The messages to the seven Churches have the same literary characteristics as the properly apocalyptic part of Revelation and are the work of the same author. It has been argued that they might have existed independently of the rest and were added at a later stage of composition. But the links between these messages and the subsequent chapters, notably with the final chapters, are such that an independent existence of the former is unlikely. They are an integral part of the work from the start.

Each Church will hear a verdict based on a precise knowledge of its situation, both external (there are topical references) and spiritual. The Churches receive praise or blame (or both), usually with some qualifications, and in this there seems to be a definite plan or progression. Ephesus receives censure and commendation; Smyrna, Thyatira, and

Philadelphia (the even numbers) are praised, the last with marked warmth, while Pergamum, Sardis, and Laodicea are censured, the last very severely.

The seven messages follow a common plan. All open with the formula, "To the angel of . . . write." Next comes "These are the words of [*tade legei*] . . ."—the speaker is Christ, whose titles, mostly from the preceding vision, are relevant to the local situation in each case. His message always begins, "I know [*oida*] . . .", leading to an outline of virtues or faults, with corresponding praise or blame, and to a final recommendation. All close with the promise, "To the Victor . . .". The stereotyped formula, "You have ears—so listen to what the Spirit is saying to the Churches!" precedes the promise to the victor in the first three letters and follows it in the other four. The whole is redolent of Old Testament prophetic texts as this Christian prophet speaks, confidently, in the name of the Lord of the Churches.

The messages are crucial to an understanding of Revelation. John is not addressing an abstract "Church"; he speaks directly to communities of men and women, communities good, bad, and indifferent. The messages peg Revelation firmly to our world. It is a word of hope addressed to people who need hope, people who may falter. The messages, like so much of the New Testament, bring us encouragement. There never has been a perfect Christian community. Christians have been faithful and heroic, and they have been frail and vacillating. It is not enough for us to find comfort in the word to Philadelphia; we must also hearken to the word to Laodicea.

Ephesus, which lay at the mouth of the river Cayster, was the greatest city of the province of Asia. In Roman times it was populous, privileged, and wealthy, the chief port and market city of Asia. Because of extensive silting, the shoreline has receded and the ancient gulf is now a swampy plain. Ephesus was famed for its Artemesium—the temple of Artemis (Diana)—one of the seven wonders of the world. A feature of the temple is that it was recognized as an asylum, a place of refuge. From the time of Augustus the temple became associated with the imperial cult. Later, a temple to Domitian (81–96 c.e.) was established at Ephesus. Paul visited the city for the first time towards the close of 51 c.e. (Acts 18:19-21). He returned for a lengthy stay of about three years (53–58) (Acts 19–20). From there he sent disciples to other cities of Asia. It is not surprising that Ephesus stands first among the cities to which the messages are addressed.

Because he has seen with eyes that "flamed like fire" (1:14) the Lord "knows" the "works"—good (vv. 2–3, 6) and bad (v. 4)—of his Church. The praiseworthy works of this Church are its "toil" in resisting and overcoming false teachers and its "patient endurance," for the sake of Christ, in the labors and trials of the effort. Paul, too, had occasion to warn of "false apostles" (2 Cor 11:5-13). The difference is that Paul's "false a-postles" are Judaizers (that is, Jewish Christians who held that full observance of the Mosaic law was necessary for salvation; see Acts 15:1, 5) whereas, in our text, they are Nicolaitans (2:6). Paul had put forward the criterion of genuine apostleship: "The signs of true apostles were performed among you in all patience, with signs and wonders and mighty works" (2 Cor 12:12); measured by some such standard, the false apostles in Ephesus were shown in their true colors. Paul had foreseen that false teachers would seek to trouble the Ephesian Church (Acts 20:29-30). Ignatius, however, attests that the Ephesians had a reputation for their immunity to false teaching.

The Ephesian Christians had not emerged unscathed from their struggle with false teachers: they had maintained orthodoxy, but their love had waned. "Love" is *agape*— fraternal charity, a love which is self-giving, which seeks the good of others. Its source is God, who has first loved us (1 John 4:19) and who has given his Son in order to reconcile sinners to himself (John 3:16-17). "The love you felt at first": the admonition holds an invitation. But there is also a threat if the invitation is not heeded: Ephesus will lose its rank as first Church and may well disappear altogether.

Although the loss of their first love is grievous, the Ephesians still have in their favor that they hate the deeds which Christ also hates (see Isa 61:8; Zech 8:17). Did this zeal for truth push them too far and prove the cause of their failure to love? Sadly, later Christian history has too many instances of unholy zeal in the pursuit of "truth." Orthodoxy is no substitute for orthopraxis; it surely cannot replace the praxis of love.

The formula, "You have ears . . .", recalls a saying of Jesus found in the Synoptic Gospels: "he who has ears, let him hear" (Matt 13:9, 43; 11:15, parr.); each hearer of the message is called upon to appropriate the promises and warnings addressed to the Churches. "Victor" ("one who conquers") appears in all the letters. It is the one who "keeps my words until the end" (2:26), one who shares the victory of Christ (3:21). Elsewhere in the book the martyrs are those who have come out of the great tribulation; they are clothed in the white of victory for they have washed their robes in the blood of the Lamb (7:13-14). They have conquered Satan by the blood of the Lamb (12:11); they have been victorious over the beast and its image (15:2). Hence, in the messages, "the victor" is, first and foremost, the "martyr"—one who has won the victory as Christ did, by the laying down of life.

This is not to say that John expected all Christians to suffer martyrdom, or that he believed that only martyrs shared the blessedness of Christ. Always, the purpose of the book must be kept in mind. He writes to encourage his readers in what he perceives to be an hour of imminent peril.

Persecution looms and there will be victims: it is a threat that all must face. The martyr's reward is immortality (the "tree of life," see Gen 2:9) in the heavenly Jerusalem (22:2). It is perfectly natural that the earthly paradise of Genesis 2 should become a symbol of heavenly blessedness. One speaks of "martyrs" even though only in one text (17:6) does *martys* appear to carry the precise meaning of our *martyr*. The point is that John expects the *witness* to be faithful, at any cost.

## For Reference and Further Study

Enroth, A. M. "The Hearing Formula in the Book of Revelation." *NTS* 36 (1990) 598–608.
Gangemi, A. "L'Albero della Vita (Ap 2:7)." *RivB* 23 (1975) 383–97.
Strand, K. A. " 'Overcomer': A Study in the Macrodynamic of Theme Development in the Book of Revelation." *AUSS* 28 (1990) 237–54.

## 5. *Message to Smyrna* (2:8-11)

8. To the angel of the Church at Smyrna write:
    These are the words of the first and the last, who was dead and came to life again. 9. I know your tribulation and your poverty—yet you are rich—and the slander of those who claim to be Jews but are not: they are a synagogue of Satan. 10. Do not fear what you are about to suffer. For the devil will throw some of you into prison, to be put to the test, and for ten days you will suffer tribulation. Be faithful unto death, and I will give you the crown of life.
    11. You have ears—so listen to what the Spirit is saying to the Churches! The victor will not be harmed by the second death.

### Notes

9. *slander (blasphēmia):* Here, abuse or defamation; nevertheless, it is a strong term (13:1, 5-6; 17:3).

    *who claim to be Jews but are not:* Implies conflict over the title "Jew." Christians were claiming that they were the genuine "Jews," true heirs of the promises to Israel (see Rom 9:8); understandably, the ethnic Jews of Smyrna reacted angrily.

    *synagogue of Satan:* The sad overkill of polemic! See 3:9. The Jews, likely in response to the Christian claim, actively denounced Christians to Roman authorities. Jews took a prominent part in the martyrdom of the bishop of

Smyrna, Polycarp, c. 150 C.E. As in 2:15 ("Satan's throne") John may be suggesting that earthly conflict with synagogue and empire reflects a deeper conflict in the heavenly world.

10. *the devil (diabolos):* "Accuser," "slanderer"; identical with Satan, "the adversary." John reminds his readers of the ultimate source of their "tribulation."

   *prison:* Most likely, what is meant is detention pending trial.

   *to be put to the test:* Though it is "the devil" who has them cast into prison, the ordeal is a divinely ordained "test" of their faith.

   *ten days* (see Dan 1:12): Suggests a limited period, but a testing-time for all that.

   *unto death:* Mention of death underlies the seriousness of the "test" and of the response to it.

   *crown of life (stephanos):* "wreath"—an emblem pervasively present in Smyrna; a possible topical reference.

11. *the second death:* The expression occurs again in 20:6, 14; 21:8—it is the "lake of fire": annihilation, the final fate of the wicked. See Matt 10:28; Luke 12:4-5. See note at 20:6.

### INTERPRETATION

Smyrna, modern Izmir, lay thirty-five miles north of Ephesus, at the head of a splendid harbor. In Roman times it was one of the most prosperous cities of Asia. In 26 C.E. a temple to Tiberius was built there; the city was second only to Pergamum as a center of emperor cult. Smyrna had a considerable Jewish population by New Testament times. The pronounced antagonism of the Jews of Smyrna to the Church, prominent in the message, is documented in the later history of that Church.

The titles in 2:8, echoing 1:17-18, fit neatly in a message addressed to a "first" city which, destroyed about 600 B.C.E., had risen from its ruins about 300 B.C.E.; they are calculated to inspire and foster confidence within a Church threatened by persecution and death. The Christians are beset by trials and, in a wealthy city, are materially poor; but they are rich in spiritual goods, in faith. See Jas 2:5—"Has not God chosen those who are poor in the world to be rich in faith?" Christians were in conflict with the strong Jewish element in Smyrna. Jews had special, imperially acknowledged privileges and Judaism was a *religio licita*, officially recognized by the state. At first Christians, exclusively or predominantly Jewish as they were, would have sheltered under the Jewish umbrella. But, as the movement became increasingly Gentile, and distanced itself from Judaism, Jews might denounce Christians as members of an unauthorized cult. Christians did not improve the situation by claiming to be the true Israel (see Rom 9:8). Such a claim, by Gentiles, could not be stomached by ethnic Jews. And indeed, there is an arrogant ring to characterization of the synagogue as those "who claim to be Jews but are not." It is the perennial temptation of a religious group to make exclusive claims. And, John continues in polemic vein, the hostile Jews are agents of the devil—that "accuser of our brethren" (12:10)—who will use them to intensify the campaign against the Church. Delation to magistrates will lead to the arrest and imprisonment of some Christians; in prison they await trial which may well end in death. They are not to fear, because this persecution will not last, and because those who stand firm (even if it means death) will be rewarded. See Jas 1:12.

The "second death," identified with the lake of fire in 20:14 and 21:8, is also named in 2:11 and 20:6. In all cases it means annihilation (or, at very least, may justifiably be interpreted in that sense). The evidence of the Targums appears to stand in support. For instance, Jer 51:39, 57 warns that the inhabitants of Babylon, objects of divine chastisement, "shall sleep a perpetual sleep and not wake." Both times the *Targum of Jeremiah* renders the phrase: "they shall die the second death and shall not live in the world to come." This means exclusion from the resurrection; they will remain in the grave. All in all, then, it is reasonable to understand lake of fire/second death, in Revelation, as annihilation—the absolute end of anything, or anyone, not fit to be present in the New Jerusalem (see 20:11-15). See Matt 10:28; Luke 12:4-5. See note at 20:6.

FOR REFERENCE AND FURTHER STUDY

Gangemi, A. "La morte seconda (Ap 2:11)." *RivB* 24 (1976) 3–11.
Schrage, W. "Meditation zu Offenbarung 2:8-11." *EvT* 48 (1988) 388–403.

## 6. *Message to Pergamum* (2:12-17)

12. To the angel of the Church at Pergamum write:
These are the words of the One who has the sharp, two-edged sword. 13. I know where you dwell, where Satan has his throne—yet you hold fast to my cause. You did not deny your faith in me even in the days of Antipas, my faithful witness, who was slain in your city, where Satan dwells. 14. But I have a few things against you: you have there some who hold to the teaching of Balaam, who taught Balak to set a pitfall for the Israelites; he tempted them to eat meat sacrificed to idols and commit fornication. 15. In like manner you also have some who hold

to the teaching of the Nicolaitans. 16. So repent! Otherwise I will come to you quickly and make war on them with the sword of my mouth.

17. You have ears—so listen to what the Spirit is saying to the Churches! To the victor I will give some of the hidden manna; I will give to such a one a white stone, with a new name written on the stone, known only to the one who receives it.

## NOTES

12. *sword (romphaia):* The word of God; see Heb 4:12. This "sword" will serve a purpose, 2:16. John uses *machaira* for the literal sword (6:4; 13:10, 14). Pergamum "was pre-eminently the center of the imperial cult, and 'the sharp two-edged *rhomphaia*' is probably an allusion to the proconsular *ius gladii*" (Hemer, 71).

13. *I know where you dwell:* In the other messages Christ knows the "works" of a Church; here, uniquely, their situation.

    *where Satan has his throne:* Likely, a reference to the great altar of Zeus at Pergamum; but, perhaps, it may refer to Pergamum as center of emperor worship—the city "where Satan dwells."

    *you hold fast to my cause,* lit. "you hold fast my name": Christians refuse to give the divine title *kyrios* ("Lord") to Caesar. Domitian may have been addressed as *dominus et deus*—lord and god. See John 20:28.

    *Antipas, my faithful witness:* Here *martys* is "witness," not "martyr." See note at 1:5. The slaying of the faithful Antipas (of whom nothing further is known) suggests a specific persecution in which Christians of Pergamum had stood firm ("you did not deny"). It would seem that Antipas, arrested and interrogated by the Roman governor, had been executed (*ius gladii*). There is no suggestion that his death was related to emperor worship.

14. *the teaching of Balaam:* Jewish tradition, based on Num 31:16, presented Balaam (Num 22–24) as the man who had enticed the Israelites into idolatry and licentiousness, and as a covetous man (see Jude 11; 2 Pet 2:15). Like "Jezebel" (2:20), "Balaam" serves John in his polemic against the Nicolaitans.

    *to eat meat sacrificed to idols:* See 1 Cor 8:7-13; 10:20-30; Paul acknowledged that, *in principle,* Christians might eat idol-consecrated meat bought in the open market, and might participate in guild-feasts. In an emperor-worship environment, Pergameme Christians would have been under severe pressure; some seem to have rationalized the situation, rather like "the strong" at Corinth.

    *commit fornication (porneuein):* Everywhere apart from 9:21, John uses *porneuein* and *porneia* in a metaphorical sense (e.g., 17:2; 18:3, 9); one assumes that the meaning here is metaphorical. "The underlying issue is religious and cultural assimilation: What degree of exclusiveness does fidelity require and when does assimilation become idolatry" (A. Y. Collins, "*The Apocalypse,*" *NJBC*, 1002).

15. *Nicolaitans:* Their teaching is apparently identical with that of "Balaam" (v. 14).

16. *repent:* The "some" of the previous verses are the false teachers. The Christians of Pergamum had been remiss in harboring Nicolaitans.

    *make war . . . sword:* If they fail to repent, Christ will come as judge and smite them with the sharp sword of his word (v. 12); the threat is aimed at the Nicolaitans (see vv. 22-23).

17. *the hidden manna:* Reference to a Jewish apocalyptic tradition (see 2 Baruch 29:8) according to which the manna will reappear as food of the messianic kingdom (see 2 Macc 2:4-8).

    *a white stone:* While a *white* (color of victory and joy) stone is suitably given to the victor, its precise significance is obscure—perhaps an admission ticket to the heavenly banquet.

    *a new name:* The "new name" symbolizes new life (see Isa 62:2), here the new life given by Christ (see 3:12) to the victor, who alone can receive it (see 14:3).

### INTERPRETATION

Pergamum lay forty miles north of Smyrna. The city came under Roman control in 133 B.C.E.; in John's time it appears to have been the administrative headquarters of the province of Asia. Pergamum was a renowned religious center, at earlier times notable for the cults of Zeus and of Asclepius the god of healing. But John may perhaps be more concerned with the city as a center of emperor-worship. In 29 B.C.E. it had a temple dedicated to Rome (the *Dea Roma*) and Augustus—the first of the cities of Asia in which the imperial cult was established; it remained pre-eminently the focus of imperial cult in the province.

The Church of Pergamum was in a particularly difficult situation, though the nature of that situation is not entirely clear. Possibly it may have involved a special fervor of imperial cult. Whatever the pressure, the Christians there stood faithful. But, while the Church had withstood dangers from without, it had dealt less successfully with false doctrine within. We learn something more of the Nicolaitans (2:6). The point of comparison with Balaam is that as he, in Jewish tradition, seduced the Israelites by his counsel, so the Nicolaitans, by their teaching, entice the Churches to idolatrous practices. While *porneuein* in its literal sense means to fornicate, the metaphorical meaning (idolatry), common in the Bible, is the regular meaning in Revelation.

The Christians of Pergamum had been remiss in harboring Nicolaitans; they are bidden to repent: likely, to reject not only the teaching but the teachers as well. If they do not repent, Christ himself will be forced to act. Again, his only weapon is the sword of his mouth—the word (1:16;

19:13, 15). To the victor is promised the "hidden manna." There is abundant evidence, in later Jewish documents, of a popular expectation that in the latter days God would again provide manna. While a *white* stone (white being the color of victory and joy) is suitably given to the victor, its precise significance escapes us. The "new name" symbolizes new life (Isa 62:2). It might be, then, that the white stone is pledge of the divine favor which bestows participation in the life of the risen Christ. At any rate, it means reward of faithfulness.

The Church of Pergamum was under pressure of more than one kind. There was external opposition, as we have noted. Devotees of emperor-worship looked askance at these "disloyal" and subversive people. One of them had paid the ultimate price. To John's eyes, more serious was betrayal within, and in his view any compromise with the pervasive culture was betrayal. His was a typically radical prophetic stance, which must have looked extreme to those whom he scathingly likens to Balaam. But his prophetic word remains a challenge. It is a challenge that we, in our Western world, might well take to heart. For example: to many Western Christians the preferential option for the poor stressed in liberation theology seems extreme. But is it, after all, anything more or less than the gospel message? Cultural adaptation is all very well. Too readily, though, the Christian message can be made thoroughly "respectable."

### FOR REFERENCE AND FURTHER STUDY

Barrett, C. K. "Things sacrificed to idols." *NTS* (1965) 138–53.
Gangemi, A. "La manna nascosta e il nome nuovo." *RivB* 25 (1977) 337–56.

## 7. *Message to Thyatira* (2:18-29)

18. To the angel of the Church at Thyatira write:

These are the words of the Son of God whose eyes are like a flame of fire and whose feet are like brilliant metal: 19. I know your works: your love and faithfulness and service and endurance—indeed, your latest works are better than your earlier works. 20. But I have this against you: you tolerate that Jezebel, that woman who claims to be a prophetess, whose teaching lures my servants into fornication and eating meat sacrificed to idols. 21. I have given her time to repent, but she refuses to repent of her fornication. 22. So, I will throw her on a bed of pain, and throw those who commit adultery with her into great tribulation, unless they repent of her works. 23. And her children I will slay with pestilence. So all the Churches will know that I am the searcher of heart and mind, and that I will give to each of you what your conduct deserves. 24. But this I say to the rest of you in Thyatira, all who do not accept this teaching and have no experience of the deep secrets of Satan—as they call it—I do not lay upon you any further burden. 25. Only hold fast to what you have until I come.

26. To the victor, to the one who keeps my works until the end, I will give authority over the nations—as I myself received from my Father. 27. He will smash [rule] them with a rod of iron, as earthenware he will smash them to pieces. 28. And I will give him the morning star.

29. You have ears—so listen to what the Spirit is saying to the Churches!

## NOTES

18. *Son of God:* The only occurrence of the term in Revelation. But note 1:6; 2:27; 3:5, 21; 14:1 where God is spoken of as the Father of Christ.

    *brilliant metal (chalkolibanos):* "A refined alloy of copper and bronze with metallic zinc . . . *chalkolibanos* was a trade term whose meaning was familiar in Thyatira" (Hemer, 127).

19. *love:* In Thyatira *agapē* is not only present but comes first, and the fervor of this Church has continued to increase.

    *service:* For the service intended by *diakonia* see Rom 15:25, 31; 1 Cor 16:15; 2 Cor 8:4; 9:1; Heb 6:10.

20. *Jezebel:* Obviously a Nicolaitan, see 2 Kgs 9:22. As a "prophetess," this "Jezebel" is a prophet rival to John, with a notable following.

    *lures:* The verb *planan* ("deceives") is otherwise reserved for Satan and his imperial minions.

    *fornication (porneuein):* Metaphorical. This woman is named "Jezebel" after the Canaanite wife of Ahab who attempted to lead Israel into idolatry by introduction of the cult of Baal. Significantly, in 2 Kgs 9:22, Jehu speaks of the "harlotries and sorceries" (certainly referring to idolatrous practices) of Jezebel.

21. *time to repent:* Though she had been warned in the past (by John?) the woman had not changed her ways.

22. *bed (klinē):* Obviously a *double entendre* in view of "fornication," which here means religious infidelity. The suggestion is that some affliction will befall her.

    *those who commit adultery with her:* The punishment will be shared by her followers; these "children" are doomed like those of Ahab (2 Kgs 10:7).

    *tribulation:* Here *thlipsis* means punishment; it lacks the religious overtones it carries elsewhere.

23. *pestilence: Thanatos* means "death" or "pestilence."

    *all the Churches:* "Jezebel's" influence extended beyond Thyatira.

*I will give . . . .:* The concluding phrase of v. 23 recurs in a slightly different form in 22:12. See Matt 16:27.

24. *the rest:* Evidently, the majority (vv. 19-20).

    *the deep secrets of Satan:* Either an ironical retort to a claim to esoteric knowledge, or a contemptuous ("as they call it"!) response to knowledge of the "deep things of God" regarding the End (see 1 Cor 2:10): their vaunted wisdom comes not from God but from Satan.

25. *until I come:* Christ comes to reward his faithful ones, as he comes in judgment; see Acts 15:28.

26. *I will give authority over the nations:* A free rendering of Ps 2:8; the psalm was interpreted messianically as early as the first century B.C.E.; see *Pss. Sol.* 17:26-27. The victor will be rewarded by participation in Christ's authority over the nations—he "has made us a royal house" (1:6). See Matt 15:21, 28; 1 Cor 6:2; Rev 20:4; 21:5.

    *as I myself received from my Father:* In the manuscript tradition this phrase comes after v. 27; logically, it fits at the end of v. 26.

27. *he will smash them:* Poimainein is "to shepherd," "to govern." The Hebrew of Ps 2:9 runs: "You shall break them with a rod of iron, and dash them in pieces like a potter's vessel." It seems that John, like the LXX, assumed that *poimainein* could mean "to smash." Certainly, the context, that of a potter smashing a rejected vessel (see Jer 18:1-11), calls for this meaning here. "Pagan resistance will indeed be smashed, but God will use no other 'iron bar' than the death of his Son and the martyrdom of his saints" (Caird, 46).

28. *the morning star:* What the "morning star" means has never been satisfactorily determined. It may refer to Christ (22:16) and be akin to the assurance of shared authority (v. 26). In this message to Thyatira alone do we find a double promise (vv. 26, 28).

### INTERPRETATION

"The longest and most difficult of the seven letters is addressed to the least known, least important and least remarkable of the cities" (Hemer, 106). Thyatira stood in a broad valley, forty miles southeast of Pergamum. It was primarily a trading-center and was notable for the number of its trade guilds (with religious affinities), including those of metalworkers and dyers of wool. The first of Paul's converts at Philippi was "Lydia, from the city of Thyatira, a seller of purple goods" (Acts 16:14).

In contrast to Ephesus (2:4) *agapē* is not only found among the "works" of Thyatira, but heads the list (2:19). The one fault of the Thyatiran Church is that it tolerated the presence of "that Jezebel . . . who claims to be a prophetess." The livelihood of Christians in Thyatira depended on membership of the trade-guilds, and therefore pagan association. Already, in Corinth, Paul had had to deal with the problem of guild-feasts and the purchase of meat that had been offered in pagan temples (1 Cor 8:1-13; 10:20-30). John took a radical stance: there can be no compromise. Not all Christians shared his view. The Nicolaitans, whom he disparagingly likens to Balaam and Jezebel, saw the situation differently. In point of fact, "Jezebel," at Thyatira, was a prophetic rival to John, with a notable following. At stake was the question of assimilation: to what extent might Christians conform to the prevailing culture for the sake of economic survival or social acceptance? For John the only answer was: Not at all! Christians who decided otherwise had sold out. Apart from what he undoubtedly perceived as betrayal, John was profoundly concerned that the communities be steadfastly united in face of the all-out persecution he felt sure was at hand. This was no time for internal conflict.

Though she had been warned in the past, "Jezebel" had not changed her ways. John has to resort to threat: dire troubles will come upon her and her adherents. In the reaction to the Nicolaitans at Ephesus, Pergamum, and Thyatira, one is strongly reminded of the situation in the Johannine community reflected in 1 John. There the author is in polemic against "secessionists" who differed from him on theological (more precisely, Christological) grounds. He has not a good word for them. Among other things, they are "antichrists" (1 John 2:18-19), children of the devil (3:10), brethren of Cain (3:11). *Odium theologicum* is no more respectable than any other form of hate.

The Lord has no special task for the faithful ones of Thyatira; they are to hold fast to what they have (v. 19). The assurance, "I do not lay upon you any other burden" (v. 24) evokes an interesting parallel with Acts 15:28: "It has seemed good to the Holy Spirit and to us to lay upon you no greater burden . . . than that you abstain from what has been sacrificed to idols . . . and from *porneia*." The parallel is, however, fortuitous: the "decree" of Acts is concerned with getting Jewish and Gentile Christians into table fellowship.

The message closes with an exhortation to patient endurance sustained by a promise of generous reward at the coming of the Lord. At his coming he who had received his authority from his Father will share that authority with the victors. Here and now they are "smashing the nations," as the two witnesses will do (11:4-13). Here is the great paradox, the supreme irony, already present in the ambivalent *poimainein*: to smash and to shepherd. John Sweet asks an apposite question: "Does it all represent God's grace, brought to bear in the witness of Christ and his church, which is shepherd's crook to those who respond (see 7:17), iron bar to those who do not?" (96). Christ will give "the morning star" which (probably) is himself (22:16). The victor will not only win "the victory that overcomes the world" (1 John 5:4) by sharing Christ's triumph; the victor will possess Christ.

## FOR REFERENCE AND FURTHER STUDY

Gangemi, A. "La stella della mattino (Ap 2:26-28)." *RivB* 26 (1978) 241-74.

## 8. *Message to Sardis* (3:1-6)

1. To the angel of the Church at Sardis write:
These are the words of the One who has the seven spirits of God and the seven stars: I know your works—you have the name of being alive, though you are dead! 2. Wake up and put some backbone into what still survives—if only on the point of death. For I have found no work of yours perfect in the sight of my God. 3. Be mindful, therefore, of what you received and heard: heed it, and repent. If you do not wake up, I will come as a thief, and you will not know the hour of my coming. 4. Yet you have a few persons in Sardis who have not defiled their garments, and they will walk with me in white, for they are worthy.

5. The victor will likewise be robed in white. I will never strike the victor's name from the book of life, but will acknowledge that name before my Father and his angels.

6. You have ears—so listen to what the Spirit is saying to the Churches!

## NOTES

1. *the seven spirits of God and the seven stars:* See 1:4; 2:1. Echo of the "star" and "Spirit" of 2:28-29 just before.

   *your works:* For the first time in the messages, the "works" are not praiseworthy but, rather, merit severe censure (see 3:15).

2. *backbone:* lit. "strengthen."

   *what still survives,* lit. "the rest," "the things that remain": "Whatever remained at Sardis out of the wreck of Christian life" (Swete, 49).

   *on the point of death:* See Matt 8:22; Luke 15:24; John 5:25; Rom 6:13; 1 Thess 5:6; Rom 13:11. See especially Eph 5:14.

   *I have found:* To be taken with "in the sight of God."

   *no work of yours:* lit. "works of yours"—a sweeping indictment of the state of the Church.

3. *I will come as a thief:* Allusion to the two famous occasions when the citadel of Sardis had fallen through lack of vigilance—to Cyrus (586 B.C.E.) and to Antiochus the Great (218 B.C.E.). Their city had twice been taken by stealth: the Son of Man will come in the same manner (see Matt 24:43-44) unless they "heed and repent."

4. *persons*, lit. "names": the use of the word suggests a register or list; the allusion may be to the book of life.

   *worthy (axios):* In a positive sense this is elsewhere, in Revelation, predicated of God and Christ.

5. *victor:* The "victor" cannot be rigidly distinguished from the "few" of the previous verse.

   *robed in white:* In the Old Testament white apparel denotes festivity (Eccl 9:8), victory (2 Macc 11:8), the heavenly (Dan 7:9). All these associations meet in the "white garments" here and in the previous verse, but the emphasis is on victory. It may be that the "white garments" also symbolize the heavenly bodies after the resurrection (see 2 Cor 5:4). See 1 Enoch 62:15-16.

   *name:* The authentic personality. Word-play on "persons [names]," (v. 4) and "name"—reputation (v. 1).

   *the book of life:* This book—the divine register of people—is mentioned in the Old Testament (Exod 32:32-33; Ps 69:28; Isa 4:3; Mal 3:16); the "living" are the righteous. In Revelation the names are inscribed in the book "since the foundation of the world" (17:8). To be blotted out of this book meant death (Ps 69:28). In Rev 20:12 we read of "books" and the "book of life." These are, respectively, the books in which people's deeds are recorded and in the light of which they are judged, and the book of life which contains the names of the elect (20:15). In our verse we learn that election is conditional: while one cannot earn the right to have one's name in this book, one can forfeit it. The closing statement of the verse is a reminiscence of a saying of Jesus— Matt 10:32; Luke 12:8.

### INTERPRETATION

About thirty miles southeast of Thyatira lay Sardis, former capital of the Lydian kingdom of Croesus. Its citadel, thought to be impregnable, had never fallen to assault, but had twice been taken by stealth. In Roman times it was, like Ephesus, a commercial city, with a shrine to the goddess Cybele. It had an unusually prominent Jewish community. The city suffered a catastrophic earthquake in 17 C.E.

Here Christ is the one who has not only the seven stars but also "the seven spirits of God" (see 5:6): he is the one who possesses, and gives, the life-giving Spirit (see John 7:39). He alone can restore life to a dead Church. For the first time in these messages the "works" are not praiseworthy but rather meet with severe censure (see 3:15). The Christians of Sardis are either spiritually dead or in spiritual torpor. Note Eph 5:14, "Awake, O sleeper, and arise from the dead, and Christ will give you life," which is part of an early baptismal hymn. Life is not quite extinct after all; but these Christians must come fully awake and carefully tend the spark of life that does remain, lest it should really be extinguished. The lamentable state of the Church is displayed in its half-hearted living of the Christian life.

"Be mindful" (v. 3)—the same recommendation as to the Ephesians (2:5): let them look back to the time when they had willingly listened to the preaching of the gospel and had gladly come to believe. Let them cling now to that faith and promptly turn from their neglect. If they will not be urged, let them listen to warning. Their city had twice been taken by stealth: the Lord will come in the same way. See Matt 24:43-44. A faithful remnant remains, unsullied by the sin issuing from the religious and moral lassitude of the rest. For the first time, people other than the conqueror are explicitly promised blessedness. Clothed in white, symbol of holiness and victory, these faithful ones will dwell with Christ. Their names are indelibly inscribed in "the book of life" (see Dan 12:1; 1 Enoch 47:3): the register of citizens of the heavenly Jerusalem; it is "the book of life of the Lamb, slain since the foundation of the world" (13:8). Salvation is free gift; God's choice is not arbitrary. John warns that a name might be cancelled from the book (3:5). The closing statement of v. 5 is a reminiscence of a saying of Jesus: "Everyone who acknowledges me before people, I will also acknowledge before my Father who is in heaven" (Matt 10:32); ". . . the Son of Man also will acknowledge before the angels of God" (Luke 12:8).

## FOR REFERENCE AND FURTHER STUDY

Hemer, C. J. "The Sardis Letter and the Croesus Tradition." *NTS* 19 (1972) 94-97.

## 9. *Message to Philadelphia (3:7-13)*

7. To the angel of the Church at Philadelphia write:
These are the words of the holy One, the true One,
who has the key of David,
who opens and none may shut,
who shuts and none may open:
8. I know your works. Therefore, I have set before you an open door, which no one can shut. Though you have little power, yet you have kept

my word, and have not disowned my name. 9. Therefore, I will make those of the synagogue of Satan who claim to be Jews and are not, but lie; therefore, I will make them come and fall at your feet—they will know that I love you. 10. Because you have kept my word of endurance, I will in turn keep you safe through the hour of testing which is about to fall upon the whole world, to test those who dwell upon the earth. 11. I am coming soon; hold fast to what you have, and let no one rob you of your crown.

12. The victor I will make a pillar in the temple of my God, never to leave it. I will inscribe on the victor the name of my God, and the name of the city of my God, the new Jerusalem which comes down out of heaven from my God, and my own new name.

13. You have ears—so listen to what the Spirit is saying to the Churches!

## NOTES

7. This time the titles of Christ do not reflect details of the opening vision; they have relevance to the situation in Philadelphia.

*the holy One:* A divine title (Isa 40:25; Heb 3:3).

*the true One (alēthinos):* "Genuine"; in a Hebrew sense: "trustworthy."

*the key of David:* That Christ holds the key of David is especially relevant to this Church's relationship with the Jews. In Isaiah 22:22 the key entrusted to the steward Eliakim signified his control of the royal household; here it symbolizes the authority of the risen Christ, set over the house of God (Eph 1:22; Heb 3:6), exercising all authority in heaven and on earth (Matt 28:18) and over death and Hades (Rev 1:18). The title lends force to the promise of the following verse. "Such an assurance would be profoundly relevant to Christians faced with expulsion from the synagogue" (Hemer, 161).

8. *therefore,* lit. "behold" (*idou*): Occurs three times in vv. 8-9.

*an open door:* Promise of an open door which "none may shut" would be meaningful for Christians faced with expulsion from the synagogue; their present unjust rejection would be redressed in the future kingdom. See also Paul's "open door" (1 Cor 16:9; 2 Cor 2:12; see Col 4:3).

*have kept . . . not disowned:* Points to a time of trial, for the moment gone by; the following verse suggests conflict with Jews.

9. *synagogue of Satan* (see 2:9): As at Smyrna, opposition came from Jews; "synagogue of Satan" refers to a body of ethnic Jews who reject the claim of Christians to be the true Israel.

*come and fall at your feet:* Isaiah's prophecies of Gentile subjection to Israel are reversed (Isa 45:14; 49:23; 60:14). The promise is to be understood eschatologically: at the End the unbelieving Jews will see that the Church is the object of Christ's, and so of God's, love.

10. *my word of endurance,* lit. "the word of my endurance": Teaching centered on the endurance of Jesus—his self-revelation, characterized as endurance.

*keep you safe through (tēreso ek,* see John 17:15): God's people will receive special protection in the trial, rather than exemption from it. There is a word-play: "you have kept (*etēresas*) my word . . . I will keep (*tēreso*) you."

*the hour of testing (peirasmos):* Here with the meaning of eschatological tribulation for all. It is the only explicit reference in the messages to a worldwide ordeal, which is the theme of the rest of the book (Brown, "The Hour of Trial," 308–14).

*those who dwell upon the earth:* A recurring phrase (6:10; 8:13; 11:10; 13:8, 14; 17:8), meaning the unbelieving world. Compare a similar sense of *kosmos* in the Fourth Gospel and 1 John.

11. *I am coming soon:* In 2:16 Christ warned the Christians of Pergamum that he would "come to you quickly and make war on them" (the Nicolaitans); he will quickly come to Philadelphia too, but not as judge. His promised preservation of them during the "hour of testing" is both reward of their fidelity and assurance of the crown that awaits them.

*crown,* "wreath": "The use of the athletic metaphor was appropriate in Philadelphia, on whose inscriptions games and festivals are specially prominent" (Hemer, 165).

12. *a pillar in the temple:* "Pillar" and "temple" are metaphors; this text is not inconsistent with 21:22 where it is declared that there is no temple in the heavenly Jerusalem.

*never to leave it:* The promised stability has a special point in a town prone to earthquakes, from which people would flee for safety.

*of my God:* the remarkable reiteration (four times in the verse) emphasizes the certainty of the Lord's promise.

*the name:* The three names written on the "pillar" mark the victor as the property of God and of Christ and as a citizen of the heavenly city.

*the new Jerusalem:* To be related to the vision of chs. 21–22, especially to 21:2.

*which comes down out of heaven:* A permanent attribute of the new Jerusalem; see 21:2, 10.

*my own new name:* Promise of a full share in the revelation of Christ (see 2:17). Emphasis on "name" and "new name" may be an allusion to the name Neocaesarea given to Philadelphia.

## INTERPRETATION

Founded in the second century B.C.E., arguably as a center for the spread of Greek culture in Lydia and Phrygia, Philadelphia, a prosperous town, stood thirty miles southeast of Sardis. Like its neighbor, it was subject to earthquakes and had suffered disastrously in the great earthquake of 17 C.E. For a time afterwards, some of the inhabitants moved out of the city to the surrounding countryside. While there is no record of a Jewish community in the earlier years of Philadelphia, Jews were hostilely active there when Ignatius of Antioch (d. ca. 110 C.E.) wrote his letter to the Church, which he had previously visited.

As at Smyrna, a particular problem of Christians in Philadelphia was Jewish hostility. The "open door" of v. 8, in view of the explicit background of Isa 22:22, may have reference to an expulsion of Jewish Christians from the synagogues: Christ, not the Jews of Philadelphia, holds the key of David; it is he who unlocks the door to the household of the Lord. At the same time, "open door" is a Pauline metaphor: "a wide door for effective work has been opened to me" (1 Cor 16:9); "a door has opened for me in the Lord" (2 Cor 2:12; see Col 4:3)—in each case Paul means a favorable opportunity for missionary activity. Philadelphia will indeed be a center, for the spread not of Greek culture, but of the gospel. Since it is "he who has the key of David" who has opened the door, Philadelphian Christians are assured of efficacious preaching, especially in respect of the Jews in their midst (v. 9). The Church had little power, little influence (see 1 Cor 1:26) in Philadelphia, but Christ works through human weakness (2 Cor 12:9).

In contrast to the situation in Smyrna, there is promise of the conversion of the Jewish opposition in Philadelphia. John has turned prophetic declarations on Gentile homage to Israel into a promise of the homage of Jews to this small and weak but loyal Church (see Isa 60:14; 43:4). And here, for the first time in these messages, in relation to this little but faithful Church, we find explicit mention of the love of Christ: "I love you" (v. 9). Because they keep his word with the steadfastness which is marked by patient endurance, the Philadelphian Christians will reap their reward: they will be kept safe through the "great tribulation" (7:14), the persecution that is about to break on the Church. It is clear that Jesus will "keep safe" the Philadelphians not only because of their steadfastness but because they are little and weak and know it, thus letting Christ work through their weakness (v. 8). Even here the paradox is sustained, for safekeeping does not mean exemption from tribulation but efficacious support through it. The model is Gethsemane where "an angel from heaven"—divine help—strengthened a stricken Jesus (Luke 22:43) to face and bear the horror and agony of the Cross.

Christ had warned the Christians of Pergamum that he would come quickly and "make war on them" (2:16), that is, on those who held the teaching of the Nicolaitans. He comes here to Philadelphia, too, but not as judge. His promised preservation "through the hour of testing" is both reward for fidelity and an assurance of the crown that awaits: the "crown of life" (2:10). The victor will have a prominent and permanent place in the new temple of God. "Never to leave it"—for Jesus has kept all whom the Father has given him and none of them is lost (see John 17:12; 18:9).

## FOR REFERENCE AND FURTHER STUDY

Brown, S. "The Hour of Trial: Rev 3:10." *JBL* 85 (1966) 308–14.

## 10. *Message to Laodicea* (3:14-22)

14. To the angel of the Church at Laodicea, write:
    These are the words of the Amen, the faithful and true witness, the beginning of God's creation: 15. I know your works: you are neither cold nor hot. How I wish you were either cold or hot! 16. But because you are lukewarm, neither hot nor cold, I will spit you out of my mouth. 17. For you say, "I am rich, I have made my fortune, I have no need of anything," not realizing that you are a pitiful wretch, poor, blind, and naked. 18. I advise you to buy from me gold refined in the fire to make you rich, and white garments to put on to cover the shame of your nakedness, and ointment for your eyes so that you may see. 19. All whom I love I reprove and chasten; so, be zealous, and repent.
    20. Here I stand knocking at the door; if anyone hears my voice and opens the door, I will come in and dine with such a one and that one with me. 21. To the victor I will grant a seat beside me on my throne, as I myself was victorious and sat down with my Father on his throne.
    22. You have ears—so listen to what the Spirit is saying to the Churches!

### NOTES

14. *the Amen:* Christ is the "Amen," the one who is faithful to his word; only here in the New Testament is "Amen" an attribute of Christ. See Isa 65:16, "He who blesses himself in the land shall bless himself by the God of truth [lit., God of amen]."

    *the faithful and true witness* (see 1:5; 3:7): Spells out the meaning of "Amen": Christ is the witness whose testimony never falls short of the truth.

    *the beginning of God's creation:* The origin and principle of creation. See Col 1:15, 18: "[Christ] is the first-born of all creation . . . he is the beginning"; this passage may have been familiar to the Church of Laodicea (see Col 4:16). "Beginning" (*archē*) is also said of Christ in the concluding liturgical dialogue (22:13). See 2:8.

15–16. *neither cold nor hot:* "The water supply of Laodicea was warm, and a contrast with the hot medicinal waters of Hierapolis and the cold pure waters of Colossae. So the church was judged for its ineffectiveness rather than its spiritual temperature" (Hemer, 187). Water from the hot springs of Hierapolis, by that time become lukewarm, flowed over the cliff opposite Laodicea; the sulphurous water was nauseating. It seems that these factors lie behind and give further weight to these striking verses.

*I will spit:* "I am on the point of . . ."—the threat is made with a view to repentance.

17. *I am rich:* See Hos 12:9; 1 Cor 4:7-8.

18. *gold . . . white garments . . . ointment:* Topical references to business and products of Laodicea.

19. *all whom I love:* See Prov 3:12; Heb 12:5-7.

*be zealous: zēleuō* occurs only here in the New Testament. "Ephesus lacked *love*, Laodicea lacks *zeal* or passionate concern, which is a vital aspect of love in the biblical sense" (Sweet, 108).

20. *stand knocking . . . opens:* See Cant 5:2 [LXX]: "The voice of my beloved—he is knocking at the door: 'Open to me, my love. . . .' " Here the lover turns from the Church to the individual Christian. The true disciple will hear the voice of a friend (see John 10:3-4; 14:23; 18:37).

*dine (deipnein):* See 1 Cor 11:20, 25. "If any individual gives heed to the call of Christ and opens the door, Christ will enter the dwelling and exchange with such a one the fellowship of intimate communion in that endless feast of Love of which the Eucharist is the earnest" (Swete, 64).

21. *as I . . . was victorious:* See 5:5, 9. Here, explicitly, the victor is one who has shared the victory of Christ, one who has followed him along the road to victory, the way of the Cross. See Luke 22:28-30.

*throne:* This throne is reached through witness and death. "It is the profound and moving theme of the apocalyptic visions which follow that, in the agelong battle between God and Satan, God knows no other victory than that which is won by the Cross of Christ, faithfully proclaimed to the world in the martyr witness of his church" (Caird, 58).

*and sat down with my Father on his throne:* A stage in the progressive assimilation of God and Lamb; in 22:1, 3 we will read of "the throne of God and of the Lamb."

## INTERPRETATION

Laodicea, forty miles southeast of Philadelphia, in the valley of the Lycus, was founded by Antiochus II (261–246 B.C.E.) and developed under Roman rule into a major commercial city. It was a banking center, a manufacturer of clothing and carpets of the native glossy-black wool, and the seat of a medical school noted for "Phrygian powder" used in the making of eye salve. Laodicea was an opulent city and, after the disastrous earthquake of 60 C.E., it rose from its ruins without the aid of an imperial grant. It was geographically close to Hierapolis and water from hot springs in the plateau of Hierapolis flowed over a cliff in full view of Laodicea. Paul's disciple Epaphras, who had evangelized Colossae, also in the Lycus valley (Col 1:7), likely preached the gospel in Laodicea as well (Col 4:12). Letters to the Colossians and to the Laodiceans were to be exchanged (Col 4:16).

The material prosperity of Laodicea is reflected in the attitude of the Church which believes itself rich in spiritual possessions and in want of nothing (see 1 Cor 4:7-8). The rebuttal is emphatic: "You are the wretched (see Rom 7:24) and pitiable (see 1 Cor 15:19) one *par excellence.*" It is also "poor, blind, and naked"—ironic allusions to the banking business, eye-ointment, and clothing industry of Laodicea, objects of its self-complacency. The spiritual condition of the Laodiceans, as set forth in terms of poverty, blindness, and nakedness, is made the subject of an admonition calculated to heal their precarious state. Christ can give the true wealth: faith. See 1 Pet 1:7: "the genuineness of your faith, more precious than gold which though perishable is tested by fire." He can give them spiritual garments (see Rev 3:5), better than their own vaunted woolen products. See 2 Cor 5:4. He alone can give them the eye-ointment which can heal their tragic blindness. The severity of the rebuke, with its implied threat, is really a sign of Christ's concern, of his love (v. 19). He who loves the humble, faithful Philadelphians (3:9) loves also the self-sufficient, lukewarm Laodiceans. Though love is never cruel, it can be stern: it can inflict pain, but never hurt. These Christians must not only repent (see 2:5; 3:3), but "be zealous," shake themselves out of their lethargy.

The lover turns (v. 20) from the Church to the individual Christian and seeks an entry into the human heart. The true disciple will hear the voice of his or her friend. See John 10:3-4: "the sheep hear his voice . . . for they know his voice," the voice of the good shepherd; 18:37: "Every one who is of the truth hears my voice." And the friend will enter by the open door. See John 14:23: "If one loves me, one will keep my word, and my Father will love such a one, and we will come and make our home with that one" (see Eph 3:17). There is a Eucharistic flavor to the promise of a meal shared by Christ and the Christian, and also a look to the supper of the Lamb (Rev 19:9).

The promise to the victor (v. 21) finds a parallel in Luke 22:28-30 where, as here, enthronement follows immediately on mention of the heavenly feast: "You are those who have continued with me in my trials; as my Father appointed a kingdom for me, so do I appoint for you that you may eat and drink at my table in my kingdom, and sit on thrones judging the twelve tribes of Israel.'' As Christ through suffering entered into his glory, so the disciples, the companions of his trials, will share his glory; such is their reward. The victory of Christ is the victory of the Father who sent him, and the victory of the conqueror is the victory of Christ (see Rev 5:9-10; 7:14; 12:11).

The messages to the Churches are vitally important for a proper understanding of Revelation. While John seems to have his eyes fixed on heavenly realities, his feet are, all the while, firmly on the ground. The communities to and for whom he writes are communities of real men and women, of people who are coping, not always effectively, with difficult and painful situations. If the humble and faithful Philadelphians and the Christians of Smyrna earn unstinted praise, the self-sufficient Laodiceans, doubtless to their chagrin and incredulous surprise, hear only words of blame, and the Church at Sardis is more dead than alive. The Ephesians may have sustained orthodoxy, but at the price of intolerance. On the other hand, the situation in Thyatira and Pergamum warns that tolerance may be pushed too far.

Assessment and verdict are those of the Lord of the Churches, but filtered through the mind and words of the prophet. John's own temperament and uncompromising stance have colored his judgment and his words. Is ''that woman Jezebel'' quite as bad as he has painted her? Does she, perhaps, propose a way of Christian living which, though unacceptable to John, is not really incompatible with the gospel? Are the Jewish communities in the various cities really ''synagogues of Satan''? Still, if John displays a measure of intolerance, he has, as we shall see, a refreshing appreciation of the infinite stretch of God's mercy.

All in all, the challenge of the Way remains. There is an incompatibility between a wholehearted following of Christ and the standards of a world unenlightened by the gospel. The danger remains that Christians can settle, too readily, for a ''reasonable'' approach. It is the charism of a prophet to see to the heart of things. Only the starkest words can match his uncomplicated vision. The genuine prophet will speak a message of comfort, based on the faithfulness of God, but it will never be a comfortable message. John's messages to the Churches urge us to look to ourselves, to our contemporary Ephesus and Philadelphia and Laodicea. The ''beast'' in our world—at least in our Western world—is not as openly oppressive as the beast of John's world; it may be all the more dangerous, because more insidious.

Perhaps the relentless John is right after all: there is *no* compromise. At very least he should give us pause. And from these messages, too, we can draw a comfort that comes from a better grasp of the overall New Testament situation. We learn that our first brothers and sisters in the faith are no different from ourselves. They, as we, had, in human frailty, to live their faith in an unsympathetic, often hostile world. They, as we, had their doubts and their fears. They, as we, had to hear the warning, "In the world you have tribulation," and, despite every appearance to the contrary, to cling in hope to the assurance, "Be of good cheer, I have overcome the world" (John 16:33).

## FOR REFERENCE AND FURTHER STUDY

Rudwick, M. J. S. "The Laodicean Lukewarmness." *ExpTim* 69 (1957/58) 176–78.
Silberman, L. H. "Farewell to O AMHN: A Note on Rev III, 14." *JBL* 82 (1963) 213–15.

## FOR REFERENCE AND FURTHER STUDY, CHAPTERS 2-3

Aune, D. E. "The Form and Function of the Proclamations to the Seven Churches (Revelation 2–3)." *NTS* 36 (1990) 182–204.
Collins, A. Yarbro, "Vilification and Self-Definition in the Book of Revelation." *HTR* 79 (1986) 308–20.
Hemer, C. J. *The Letters to the Seven Churches of Asia in Their Local Setting.* Sheffield: JSOT, 1986.
Hubert, M. "L'Architecture des Lettres aux Sept Églises (Apoc 2–3)." *RB* 67 (1960) 349–53.
Leconte, R. "Les Sept Églises de l'Apocalypse." *BTS* 46 (1962) 6–14.
Muse, R. L. "Revelation 2–3: A Critical Analysis of Seven Prophetic Messages." *JETS* 29 (1986) 147–61.
Ramsay, W. M. *The Letters to the Seven Churches.* London: Hodder & Stoughton, 1904; Reprint. Grand Rapids: Baker, 1963.
Rife, J. M. "The Literary Background of Revelation II–III." *JBL* 60 (1941) 179–82.
Shea, W. H. "The Covenantal Form of the Letters to the Seven Churches." *AUSS* 23 (1983) 71–84.

# III. THE SCROLL VISION

## 11. *The Heavenly Temple* (Ch. 4)

1. After this I looked: a door stood open in heaven! And the voice that I had first heard speaking to me like a trumpet said: "Come up here, and I will show you what must take place hereafter." 2. At once, I fell into a trance. There in heaven stood a throne with One seated on it. 3. He who sat there was in appearance like jasper or cornelian; and round about the throne was a rainbow, bright as an emerald. 4. Round about the throne were twenty-four thrones, and on them sat twenty-four elders clothed in white garments, wearing gold crowns. 5. From the throne came flashes of lightning and peals of thunder, and burning before it were seven flaming lamps, the seven spirits of God, 6. and in front of the throne was what appeared to be a sea of glass, like crystal.

In the center, round the throne itself, were four living creatures, with eyes all over, front and back. 7. The first creature was like a lion, the second like an ox, the third had a human face, and the fourth was like an eagle in flight. 8. Each of the four living creatures had six wings, and eyes all over and inside them.

Day and night unceasingly they sing:

Holy, holy, holy is the Lord God Almighty,
who was, and is, and is to come!

9. Whenever the living creatures gave glory and honor and thanks to the One who sits on the throne, who lives for ever and ever, 10. the twenty-four elders fall down before the One who sits on the throne, and worship him who lives for ever and ever, and cast their crowns before the throne, saying:

11. Worthy are you, our Lord and God
to receive glory and honor and power;
for you created all things;
by your will they were created and came into being!

### NOTES

1. *after this I looked:* The phrase serves to introduce a fresh vision of special importance (see 7:1, 9; 15:5; 18:1; Dan 7:6). Verse 1 here signals a decisive turn to the future.

*a door stood open:* The conception of the opened heavens is found in Ezek 1:1, but the more precise idea of a door standing open reflects current apocalyptic phraseology (see 1 Enoch 14:15).

*heaven (ouranos):* Not simply the eternal abode of God, for it contains symbols of the world's evil (4:6; 12:7; 13:1), and will vanish like the old earth (20:1; 21:1).

*the voice:* That of 1:10—John forges a link between the messages and the rest of the book.

*come up here:* In the inaugural vision (1:10-20) the seer was on earth; now he is invited to heaven. See 2 Cor 12:2. The notion of a "heavenly tour" is common in apocalyptic; e.g., 1 Enoch 1-36; 2 Enoch.

2. *I fell into a trance,* lit. "I was in the Spirit": In a state of ecstasy, John was translated into heaven; see 2 Cor 12:2-4.

   *a throne with One seated on it:* The phrase, "One seated on the throne," occurs twelve times in Revelation; it is John's way of saying "God." The throne of God in heaven is frequently mentioned in the Old Testament (see 1 Kgs 22:19; Isa 6:1; Ezek 1:26; Dan 7:9). The description of the heavenly temple (vv. 2-8) is much influenced by the inaugural vision of Ezekiel 1. "Throne" is a political term, implying political polemic: a claim as to who *really* rules.

3. *in appearance:* There can be no immediate vision of God; see Ezek 1:26-28.

   *jasper or cornelian . . . emerald:* See Exod 28:17-21—three of the twelve jewels, representing the tribes of Israel, on the high priest's breastplate; here they evoke the radiance of God. Jasper (*iaspis*) recurs in 21:11, 18, 19 in relation to the New Jerusalem, as do cornelian (21:20) and emerald (21:19).

   *rainbow:* Immediately suggested by Ezek 1:28, it may also be a reminder of God's covenant with Noah (Gen 9:12-17): the judge mindful of his mercy. While precious stones are used to describe the New Jerusalem (Rev 21:11, 18-20), the breastplate of the high priest (Exod 28:17-20; 39:11), and the garden of Eden (Ezek 28:10-13), the use of precious stones in a description of the divine is not part of apocalyptic tradition.

4. *twenty-four elders:* These "elders" are not angels; they are human symbols (see 5:11). The number twenty-four may be suggested by the twenty-four classes of priests in 1 Chr 24:1-19; significantly, the elders of Revelation have a cultic role (4:9-10; 5:8-11; 11:16-18; 19:4). And they are kings, seated on thrones and wearing crowns. They fittingly represent the people of God, that "royal house of priests" (1:6). They are the heavenly counterpart of the earthly Church for, after their "Amen, Hallelujah" of 19:4, they are heard of no more; they are absent from the new Jerusalem.

5. *lightning . . . thunder:* Reminiscent of the theophany of Exod 19:16, a passage which had already inspired Ezek 1:13-14, John's immediate source.

   *seven flaming lamps, the seven spirits of God:* See Zech 4:2, 10. The burden of Zechariah's vision is that what is to be accomplished will be wrought "not by might, nor by power, but by my Spirit" (Zech 4:6). In Rev 5:6 the seven eyes of the Lamb are "the seven spirits of God sent out into all the earth," a manifest echo of Zech 4:10. And in Rev 1:4 the "seven spirits who are before his throne" symbolize the sevenfold Spirit. One should note, also, that the "seven flaming lamps" are the seven "angels of the face," the seven archangels of Jewish tradition (see 8:2). This is another instance of the multivalent imagery of John.

6. *a sea of glass:* The sea of glass like crystal may be the waters above the firmament of Gen 1:7; Pss 104:3. The immediate inspiration is current apocalyptic imagery. See 2 Enoch 3:3, "And they showed me [in the first heaven] a vast ocean, much bigger than the earthly ocean." It is natural to suppose that this "sea of glass" is the same as the "sea of glass mingled with fire" of Rev 15:2. "Sea" may also suggest the common mythological motif of the chaos monster; in this respect 21:1 is noteworthy: "and the sea was no more" in the new heaven.

*in the center (en mesō),* lit. "in the middle of" the throne: Suggesting, perhaps, that the living creatures are an integral part of the throne; see 5:6. It is not easy to follow John's description here (see Hall, "Living Creatures," 609–13).

*four living creatures:* Akin to the cherubim of Ezekiel; again, the immediate source is the apocalyptic tradition; see 1 Enoch 71:7; 39:12; 61:11-12; 2 Enoch 19:16. They are the four angels responsible for directing the physical world; therefore they symbolize the whole created cosmos. "Man is exalted among creatures, the eagle among birds, the ox among domestic animals, the lion among wild beasts; all of them have received dominion" (*Midrash Shemoth* R. 23 [Sweet, 120]).

*with eyes all over:* To the familiar cherubim and seraphim, the apocalyptic writers have added the *egrēgoroi,* who never close their eyes, and the *ophanim,* who are covered back and front, inside and out, with eyes. Typically, in his description, John has combined several of these elements. See 1 Enoch 39:12; 2 Enoch 19:6.

7. *lion . . . ox . . . human . . . eagle:* The cherubim of Ezekiel (inspired by the winged sphinx of the ancient Near East), human in form, have four faces—those of man, lion, ox, and eagle—four wings, and human hands. John has simplified the complicated imagery of Ezekiel. The identification of the "living creatures" with the four evangelists, apparently originating with Irenaeus, is wholly fanciful.

8. *six wings:* As the seraphim of Isa 6:2.

   *Holy, holy, holy:* Hymn to God the creator; Isa 6:3; 1 Enoch 39:12; 2 Enoch 19:6.

   *Almighty (Pantocratōr):* John's favorite title for God.

9. *glory and honor:* See Ps 29:1; 96:7 (LXX).

   *thanks (eucharistia):* A New Testament word. Swete observes that "while 'glory' and 'honor' have regard to the divine perfections, 'thanks' refers to the divine gifts in creation and redemption" (73).

   *who lives for ever and ever:* See Dan 4:34.

10. *fall down . . . and worship:* The elders, in keeping with their cultic role throughout Revelation, join in the cosmic worship of God.

    *cast their crowns:* As vassal kings removed their crowns when coming into the presence of the emperor, these kings lay their diadems of victory before their Lord: their victory and their glory were from him. The language reflects imperial court ceremonial.

11. *our Lord and God:* May be a retort to an alleged form of address to Domitian: *Dominus et deus noster.*

*to receive glory (doxa):* Only God and Lamb are worthy to receive glory (4:11; 5:12-13). "Glory" carries a liturgical and an eschatological significance.

*for you created all things:* God is worthy of glory, honor, and power because he is Creator.

*they were created and came into being,* lit. "they were, and were created": The word order is unexpected, but the idea of God's universal providence is clear. In 4:8-10 we discern an eschatological dimension to the heavenly worship of Revelation. Indeed, the eschatological realities are already present in the heavenly worship (L. L. Thompson, 63–69).

### Interpretation

In chapters 2–3 we have seen John, feet firmly planted in the ground, speak, in the name of the Lord, his prophetic messages to the flesh and blood communities of Asia. Now he is rapt to heaven and, for the rest of the work, he will be predominantly concerned with heavenly visions and auditions. Always, however, his concern will be with their earthly repercussion.

That same voice which had bidden John, "What you see write in a scroll and send it to the seven Churches" (1:11), now bids him, "Come up here, and I will show you what must take place hereafter." Compare what Paul says of his own experience: "I know a man in Christ who . . . was caught up to the third heaven" (2 Cor 12:2). John, however, gives the impression that he is left standing at the door. The first object that catches his eye is a throne. His whole vision will be dominated by this symbol of divine sovereignty. It will be the "great white throne" from which the Judge will pronounce sentence (20:11); in the final scene it is the "throne of God and of the Lamb" (22:1, 3). The "One seated on the throne" is John's favorite designation of God. He is making a political statement: here, and not in Rome, is where *real* authority is to be found.

It becomes clear in v. 3 that John had not really *seen* God; the one seated on the throne *appeared like* brilliant jewels. In his description he carefully avoids anthropomorphic details; he simply conveys the impression of dazzling light—brightness which at once shows and hides the presence of God. Ezekiel too (ch. 1) had sought to convey an impression of the invisible God. One need only compare texts to see how far John has surpassed his model.

The great throne does not stand alone but is surrounded by twenty-four other thrones. On these thrones sit twenty-four elders wearing the white robes of victory and crowned as kings. They are absorbed in the glorification of God and Lamb (4:9-10; 5:8-11, 14; 11:16-18; 19:4); they offer to God the prayers of the saints (5:8). Hence, they have a cultic role. As kings and priests they represent, in heaven, the "royal house of priests" (1:6) that is God's people. The living creatures are the four angels responsible for directing the physical world— they symbolize the created cosmos.

The canticle of v. 8 is based on Isa 6:3; it is the unceasing song of nature in praise of its Creator (see Ps 19:1-6). Whereas the living creatures addressed the Creator simply as "Lord God Almighty," the elders in their song (v. 10) see him as "our Lord," the Yahweh of revelation, and as "our God." The whole creation, animate and inanimate, hymns the Creator. The heavenly canticles in this chapter are the first of many in Revelation. Doubtless, all of them are modeled on, or reflect, early Christian hymns.

The great throne dominates Revelation: a constant reminder that God rules even in our chaotic world. He is the Creator-God, and in his immediate presence is humankind, the summit of creation. Human minds and tongues give shape and voice to the unceasing praise of animate and inanimate creation. The Creator is worthy of all honor; he deserves to be worshiped in our earthly liturgy. This vision might inspire us to more fitting celebration.

We may observe an ongoing interplay between the spatial transcendence of heavenly worship and the temporal transcendence of eschatological drama. Regularly, as shall be noted, eschatological drama arises in a liturgical setting and often climaxes in heavenly worship and liturgical acclamations (L. L. Thompson, 53–73). In our scene, God is worthy of glory, honor, and power because he is Creator. On the whole, chapter 4 is a celebration of creation, as chapter 5 will be a celebration of redemption.

### For Reference and Further Study

Bartina, S. "El toro apocaliptico lleno de ojos (Apoc 4:6-8; Ct 9:9)." *EstBib* 21 (1962) 329–36.

Brewer, R. R. "Revelation 4:6 and the Translations Thereof." *JBL* 71 (1952) 227–31.

Hall, R. G. "Living Creatures in the Midst of the Throne: Another Look at Revelation 4:6." *NTS* 36 (1990) 609–13.

Walker, N. "The Origin of the Thrice Holy, Apoc 4:8." *NTS* 5 (1958/59) 132–33.

## 12. *The Lamb and the Scroll* (Ch. 5)

1. Then I saw in the right hand of the One seated on the throne a scroll with writing inside and on the back, sealed with seven seals. 2. And I saw a mighty angel proclaiming in a loud voice: "Who is worthy to open the scroll and break its seals?" 3. But there was no one in heaven or on earth or under the earth able to open the scroll or to look inside it. 4. And I wept bitterly because no one was found worthy to open the scroll or to look inside it. 5. But one of the elders said to me: "Do not weep; the Lion from the tribe of Judah, the root of David, has won the right to open the scroll and its seven seals."

6. Then I saw between the throne and the four living creatures and among the elders a Lamb standing as though it had been slain; he had seven horns and seven eyes which are the seven spirits of God sent out into all the world. 7. Then he went and took the scroll from the right hand of the One seated on the throne. 8. And as he took the scroll, the four living creatures and the twenty-four elders fell down before the Lamb; each had a harp, and they held golden bowls full of incense, the prayers of God's people. 9. And they sang a new song:

> You are worthy to take the scroll and break its seals,
>> for you were slain
>> and by your blood you bought for God
>> those of every tribe, tongue, people, and nation;

10.
>> you have made them a royal house
>> of priests for our God,
>> and they [shall] reign on earth.

11. As I looked, I heard the voice of many angels round about the throne and the living creatures and the elders, myriads of myriads and thousands of thousands 12. proclaiming with a loud voice:

> Worthy is the Lamb who was slain
>> to receive power and wealth, wisdom and might,
>> honor and glory, and blessing!

13. Then I heard all creatures, in heaven and on earth and under the earth and in the sea, crying:

> Blessing and honor, glory and might,
>> to the One seated on the throne and to the Lamb
>> for ever and ever.

14. And the four living creatures said, "Amen"; and the elders fell down and worshiped.


### NOTES

1. *in the right hand:* The scroll, as God's property, is in his sole possession.
*a scroll with writing inside and on the back:* The contents had flowed onto the *verso* of the crowded papyrus, as in Ezek 2:10. This scroll (*biblion*) has been variously described as the book of life (see 3:5; 13:18, etc.); the revelation of

coming events throughout Revelation; the Old Testament (see Isa 29:11-12; 2 Cor 3:14-16). Here, it is more likely God's preordained plan for his world, to be revealed and carried through by the Lamb. Relevant is 1 Enoch 81:1-3: "So I looked at the tablet[s] of heaven, read all the writings [on them], and came to understand everything. I read that book and all the deeds of humanity and all the children of the flesh upon the earth for all the generations of the world." The sealed scroll of Revelation is a *Christian* book, closed to all except the slain Lamb and his followers.

*sealed with seven seals:* Official documents were sealed; a Roman prescription demanded that a will should be sealed with seven seals.

2. *a mighty angel:* See Dan 4:13-14; referred to again at 10:1; 18:21.

   *worthy:* Not only morally fit, but able to do so.

   *to open . . . and break:* Although the opening of the book necessitated a prior breaking of the seals, to be able to open the scroll is the first requisite and is mentioned first.

3. *in heaven or on earth or under the earth:* The threefold division embraces the whole of creation: no one at all can be found to open the scroll.

4. *I wept bitterly:* John's are not tears of frustration, as though seeing himself thwarted in his expectation of gazing into the future. In fact, the opening of the scroll means not only the revealing of God's purposes but the accomplishing of them. God's action is being postponed by lack of an agent through whom he may act. See 6:10.

5. *Lion from the tribe of Judah:* See Gen 49:9-10.

   *root of David:* See Isa 11:1-10; Rom 15:2. The texts point to the son of David who has dominion over the nations.

   *has won the right (enikēsen):* The verb *nikaō*, "conquer," "win," "triumph," "win the right," occurs very frequently in Revelation. See note at 3:21.

6. *I saw . . . a Lamb:* When John looks up to find the Lion of Judah, he sees a Lamb! From now on, "Lamb" is John's definitive title for Christ.

   *a Lamb standing as though it had been slain:* "John looks at the appointed place in the vision where the Lion was supposed to appear, and what he sees is a slaughtered Lamb. . . . This is perhaps the most mind-wrenching 'rebirth of images' in literature" (Boring, 108). "Lamb" (*arnion*), though diminutive in form, is no different in meaning from the usual *amnos*. While "Lamb" is John's definitive title for Christ, the significant factor is that he is the *slain* Lamb. "Lamb" might have been suggested to John by the morning and evening Temple sacrifice (Exod 29:38-42; Num 28:3-8), by the Passover lamb (Exod 12:1-27; Lev 23:5-6; Deut 16:1-7), and by the Servant (Isa 53:7). Yet, for him, "slain" does not appear to carry sacrificial overtones; elsewhere the verb *sphazō* is used of violent death (6:4; 13:3; 18:24).

   *seven horns:* Horn is a symbol of power; the seven horns of the Lamb speak of the fullness of his power as the victorious Christ, a victory achieved on the Cross ("slain"). See Matt 28:18; John 17:2.

*seven eyes . . . seven spirits:* The seven eyes of the Lamb stand for his fullness of knowledge (1:14). At the same time, the eyes are "the seven spirits of God sent out into all the world," like the "eyes of the Lord" in Zechariah. John's text not only echoes Zech 4:10 but recalls Isa 11:2—the sevenfold Spirit of the Lord resting on the root of Jesse (see v. 5). *Seven* spirits—P²⁴, Sinaiticus, and many minuscules; A and several minuscules omit "seven." In v. 6 images of power and awe (horns, eyes) mix with the image of death (redemptive death, as it will turn out).

7. *took the scroll:* A transfer of power.

8. *fell down before the Lamb:* The living creatures, whom we had heard worshiping God (4:8-10), here worship the Lamb; more and more, in Revelation, God and Lamb will be associated.

   *harp . . . bowls full of incense:* The elders, in keeping with their cultic function, hold harps (like the Levites of 1 Chr 25) and censers; and they exercise the priestly office of mediation, offering the prayers of the faithful to God. See Ps 141:2.

   *God's people,* lit. "the saints": God's faithful people; in the New Testament, effectively, Christians. In Judaism the office of presenting the prayers of the faithful before God is attributed to Michael and the archangels (see Tob 12:12, 15; Test Levi 3:5-6; 3 Bar 11). "Thus in our text the four and twenty Elders have definitely taken the part assigned in many circles of Judaism to the Archangels" (Charles, 1:145).

9. *a new song:* A "new song" is mentioned several times in Psalms (33:3; 40:4; 96:1; 98:1; 144:9; 149:1). Originally denoting simply a fresh song of praise, the phrase lent itself especially to the designation of songs composed for great occasions (see Ps 42:10; Jdt 16:13). "Newness" in character, purity, and permanence is a favorite theme in Revelation—newness not as regards time (*neos*), but as regards quality (*kainos*). See the "new name" (2:17; 3:12), the new heaven and the new earth (21:1), and the new Jerusalem (21:10).

   *for you were slain:* The Lamb is acclaimed because (*hoti*) he was slain and has redeemed through his blood people from every tribe and nation. In chapter 4 God is worthy of glory, honor, and power because (*hoti*) he is the creator (4:11). "The paralleling of God and the Lamb in the liturgies of chapters 4 and 5 conveys in subtle but unmistakable manner that creation and redemption are centre pieces of the whole work" (L. L. Thompson, 65).

   *by your blood:* Denoting a price (*en*): at the cost of your blood.

   *you bought: Agorazō* ("to ransom") is a Pauline word (1 Cor 6:20; 7:23; Gal 3:13; 4:5; see Rev 14:3-4; 2 Pet 2:1); the point of comparison is release from captivity.

   *those of every tribe . . . :* Based on a phrase which recurs in Daniel (3:4, 7; 5:19; 6:25), and found frequently in Revelation (5:9; 7:9; 11:9; 13:7; 14:6)—the order of the four terms varies.

10. *a royal house of priests:* See note at 1:6.

    *they [shall] reign:* The future (*basileusousin*) is the majority manuscript reading, referring, seemingly, to the millennial reign (20:4-6). The present (*basileuousin* A, 046, 1006 . . . ) "which is the hardest reading, is also the right reading" (Charles, 1:148). Christ "has bought" and "has made": the faithful already are a royal house of priests.

11. A new feature is introduced: praise of the countless host of angels (see Dan 7:10; 1 Enoch 40:1); their song is a response to that of vv. 9-10.

12. *worthy is the Lamb:* The doxology (see 1 Chr 29:11), addressed to the Lamb, is fuller than that which the elders have offered to the Creator (Rev 4:11); but in 7:12 the attributes of 5:12 are again found (though in a different order, and with "thanksgiving" instead of "wealth") in a doxology addressed to God.

13. *then I heard all creatures:* The whole of creation joins in praise of the Lamb. The threefold division of 5:3 now becomes fourfold, with the addition of the sea.

    *the One seated . . . the Lamb:* The conjunction of God and Lamb, which recurs in 7:10; 21:22; 22:1, 3 (see 3:21), represents an advanced Christology: the same worship is offered to God and Lamb, just as the throne of both is one and the same (22:3). This fact undergirds Boring's assertion, which he rightly affirms to be a datum of Christian faith, that "God is the one definitively revealed through Jesus Christ" (65). These scenes of heavenly worship (chapters 4 and 5 and elsewhere) concern realities which, if heavenly, are part of the world's present structure. The slain Lamb, acclaimed in heaven, belongs to our world, even when not acknowledged here.

## INTERPRETATION

When he turned again to the One on the throne, John saw a scroll lying on the open palm of that One's right hand. The apparent inconsistency that John can see the hand of one whom he could discern only through the effulgence of his glory (4:3) illustrates the proper approach to these visions: they are not meant to be visualized but, rather, to be interpreted intellectually. The "right hand" (as in 1:16) symbolizes the authority of the one concerned; the scroll, as God's property, is in his possession. The passage Ezek 2:1–3:9 provides not only the background to John's vision but also the key to the understanding of it. His vision of the scroll may well have been the inaugural vision of Ezekiel; at any rate, it maps out his mission. He is told: "Son of man, go, get you to the house of Israel and speak with my words to them" (3:4). The limits of his mission are drawn: "You are not sent to a people of foreign speech and a hard language, but to the house of Israel—not to many peoples" (3:5-6). In his free manner, John has taken up the mission which was forbidden to Ezekiel; for, the plan of God for his world, which begins to come into effect at the opening of the scroll, embraces the whole of God's creation—in particular, the whole of humankind.

It is a sealed scroll. The breaking of the seals not only discloses the contents of the scroll but brings them to pass: the breaking of the seals is a special, indeed an exclusive, task which the Lamb alone can perform. John has to learn that such is the case. "I wept bitterly": he weeps because there is no human agent to set God's purpose for humankind in train; he had understood that God will not dispense with an agent, such is his respect for humankind. One of the elders comforts John by assuring him that all is well. "Then one of the elders *said* to me . . . the Lion from the tribe of Judah . . . has won the right. . . . I *saw* . . . a Lamb standing, as though it had been slain" (5:5-6). In his vision John looked for the emergence of a Lion, and saw a slaughtered Lamb! What he learned, and what he tells his readers, is that the Lion *is* the Lamb: the ultimate power of God ("Lion") is manifest on the Cross ("Lamb"). This is why "Lamb" is John's definitive name for Christ. The Lamb, who enjoys fullness of power and knowledge, had won the right to break the seven seals. He went to the throne to receive the scroll: it is a transfer of power.

The mighty Lamb then receives the worship of the living creatures and the twenty-four elders, whom we had formerly heard worshiping God (4:8-10). They sang "a new song," a song for a great occasion. Here the occasion for the new song is the redemption wrought by Christ. The Lamb is worthy to be God's agent because he was slain (laid down his life); because he has purchased for God, at the cost of his blood, men and women of every tribe, tongue, people, and nation; because he has made them a royal house of priests. This time a countless host of angels joins in the heavenly praise. The doxology addressed to the Lamb (v. 12) is more fullsome than that earlier addressed to the Creator (4:11). Finally, the whole of creation, without exception, joins in the great canticle (v. 13). John hears the voice of the great acclamation; to it the four living creatures, heavenly representatives of the created universe, give their "Amen," and the elders worship as in 4:9-10. "Such is John's confidence in the universality of Christ's achievement that his vision cannot stop short of universal response" (Caird, 77).

The Almighty God has his plan and purpose for his world. In his dealing with the human world, he will not proceed without the co-operation of humankind. He sought his agent—and found him in the Lamb. This Messiah, scion of David, is the Lamb *who was slain*. Our Almighty God manifests his power on the Cross. In the Cross, in the blood of the Lamb, he offers forgiveness and holds out salvation to all. The Lamb, as the manifestation, as the very presence, of our gracious God, is worthy of our honor and worship. He is worthy precisely as the slain Lamb, as the crucified One. Like Paul and Mark, John, too, in his manner, proposes a *theologia crucis*. That comforting—if challenging—theme threads through his work.

## FOR REFERENCE AND FURTHER STUDY

Barrett, C. K. "The Lamb of God." *NTS* 1 (1954/55) 210–18.

Bergmeier, R. "Die Buchrolle und das Lamm (Apk 5 und 10)." *ZNW* 76 (1985) 225–42.

Fiorenza, E. Schüssler, "Redemption as Liberation: Apoc 1:5f. and 5:9f." *CBQ* 34 (1974) 220–32.

Ford, J. M. "The Divorce Bill of the Lamb and the Scroll of the Suspected Adulteress." *JSJ* 2, 2 (1971) 136–43.

Giesen, H. "Das Buch mit den sieben Siegeln." *BK* 38 (1984) 59–65.

Guthrie, D. "The Lamb in the Structure of the Book of Revelation." *VoxEv* 12 (1981) 64–71.

Hillyer, N. " 'The Lamb' in the Apocalypse." *EvQ* 39 (1967) 228–36.

Läpple, A. "Das Geheimnis des Lammes: Das Christusbild der Offenbarung des Johannes." *BK* 39 (1984) 53–58.

Müller, H. P. "Die himmlische Ratsversammlung: Motivgeschichtliches zu Apc 5:1-5." *ZNW* 54 (1963) 254–67.

Roller, O. "Das Buch mit sieben Siegeln." *ZNW* 36 (1938) 98–113.

van Unnik, W. C. " 'Worthy is the Lamb': The Background of Apoc 5." In A. Descamps and A. de Halleux, eds., *Melanges bibliques en hommage au R. P. B. Rigaux*, (Gembloux: Ducolot, 1970) 445–61.

## FOR REFERENCE AND FURTHER STUDY, CHAPTERS 4–5

Aune, D. E. "The Influence of Roman Imperial Court Ceremonial on the Apocalypse of John." *BR* 28 (1983) 5–26.

Feuillet, A. "Quelques énigmes des chapitres 4 à 7 de l'Apocalypse." *EspV* 86 (1976) 455–59.

Mowry, L. "Revelation 4–5 and Early Christian Liturgical Usage." *JBL* 71 (1952) 75–84.

O'Rourke, J. "The Hymns of the Apocalypse." *CBQ* 30 (1968) 399–409.

Surridge, R. "Redemption in the Structure of Revelation." *ExpTim* 101 (1990) 231–35.

Thompson, L. L. *The Book of Revelation: Apocalypse and Empire*. New York and Oxford: Oxford University Press, 1990, esp. 53–73.

Vanhoye, A. "L'Utilisation du livre d'Ezéchiel dans l'Apocalypse." *Bib* 43 (1962) 436–76.

## IV. THE SEVEN SEALS

### 13. *The First Four Seals* (6:1-8)

1. I watched as the Lamb broke the first of the seven seals, and I heard one of the four living creatures say in a voice like thunder, "Come!" 2. And there, as I watched, was a white horse, and its rider held a bow; he was given a crown and he rode out, conquering and to conquer.

3. When he broke the second seal, I heard the second creature say, "Come!" 4. And out came another horse, blood red. Its rider was given power to take away peace from the earth that people might slaughter one another; and he was given a great sword.

5. When he broke the third seal, I heard the third creature say, "Come!" And there, as I watched, was a black horse, and its rider held in his hand a pair of scales. 6. And I heard what sounded like a voice from among the four creatures say, "a quart of wheat for a denarius, and three quarts of barley for a denarius. But do not harm the oil and the wine!"

7. When he broke the fourth seal, I heard the fourth creature say, "Come!" 8. And there, as I watched, was a pale horse, and its rider's name was Death, and Hades followed with him. They were given power over a quarter of the earth, to kill by sword and famine, by pestilence and wild beasts.

#### Notes

1. *as the Lamb broke the first of the seven seals:* A symbolic action. For the first four plagues, John has turned to Zech 1:8-11; 6:1-8.

   *a voice like thunder:* This suits the lion character of the first creature (4:7). See 10:3-4.

2. *a white horse:* White is the color of victory (2:17; 3:5).

   *was given:* See note at v. 8.

   *a bow:* The imagery becomes more specific; mention of the bow points to the Parthians, the only mounted archers of the first century c.e. The Parthians, along the eastern frontier of the Empire, were the great contemporary threat to Rome (they are in mind again in 9:14 and 16:12). The first seal would suggest John's hope of a Parthian invasion signalling the beginning of the end of Roman sovereignty.

   *crown (stephanos):* Promise of victory. The image is that of triumphant warfare—the horseman rides on his career of conquest.

4. *blood red . . . great sword:* Like the first two woes of the Synoptic apocalypse (wars and international strife, see Luke 21:9-10), the first two horsemen are

not clearly distinguished. This second horse is the color of slaughter and his rider wields a great sword: warfare.

5–6. *held in his hand a pair of scales:* A denarius is the daily wage (Matt 20:2), and a quart of wheat the average daily consumption of a workman; barley provided poorer quality bread. These prices are eight times or more above normal: famine prices.

6. *do not harm the oil and the wine:* Wine and oil should not be regarded as luxury commodities since wheat, barley, oil, and wine were staple items in Palestine and Asia Minor. The conditions suggest famine, but not total famine (v. 8). It is possible that v. 6 may refer to a 92 C.E. edict of Domitian requiring half of the vineyards in the provinces to be cut down in favor of grain-growing. Our text may reflect, then, famine conditions and a remedy which threatened the vines (and, perhaps, the olive groves) of the region (Hemer, 158f.).

8. *a pale horse:* Symbol of pestilence as well as of death; *thanatos* ("death") can also mean "pestilence" (see 2:23; 18:8); this rider stands, too, as an epitome of the four plagues. *Pale,* lit. "green"—apparently meaning "sickly pale."
*Hades:* The abode of the dead (like Hebrew Sheol) swallows up the victims of the pestilence. Undoubtedly, Ezek 14:21 stands behind this verse.
*they were given,* lit. "it was given (*edothē*) to them": They are instruments of divine purpose (see 6:4; 9:1, 3, 5; 13:5, 7, 14, 15).
*a quarter of the earth:* An eschatological catastrophe: one-fourth of humanity is stricken; in 8:7-12 the plagues strike *one-third* of the earth.

### INTERPRETATION

The breaking of the seals unleashes a series of plagues (6:1–8:1), a series which follows the pattern of events in the Synoptic apocalypse (Mark 13 parr.): war, strife among nations, famine, pestilence, persecution, cosmic phenomena (earthquakes, eclipses, and so on). On the whole, John is closest to Luke who, unlike Mark and Matthew, lists pestilence and whose "distress of nations" (21:25) is the equivalent of Rev 6:15-17. On the other hand, Mark 13:24 and Matt 24:29 develop the "signs in the sun and moon and stars" (Luke 21:25) in much the same language as Revelation. Evidently, John is building on a tradition which also underlies the Synoptic passages.

Though John follows the pattern of the Synoptic apocalypse, he still quarries his descriptive material in the Old Testament. The four horsemen of Zech 1:8-11 (horsemen, because riders are implied in v. 11) are the angels who have surveillance of the world; their dispatch symbolizes judgment on the nations. In Zech 6:1-8 the four chariots presage the destruction of Babylon. They represent the messengers of God, going out from his heavenly council, traveling in different directions to patrol the earth. In 6:5 they are sent to the four destructive winds (see Rev 7:1).

Zechariah has suggested the horses and their colors, but John has altered their functions to suit his own purpose; typically, also, he has borrowed from two distinct visions.

The scroll had been sealed with seven seals and so, in fact, could not be unrolled until all the seals were broken. With fine dramatic effect, John presents the very breaking of a seal as a revelation: the loosing of the seals is a symbolic action. At first sight the fourfold "Come" (6:1-7) might seem to be no more than the summoning of the particular plague. However, it seems to anticipate the "Come" of the Spirit and the bride, of the hearer of the book, and of its writer (22:17, 20). There it is a liturgical response to the Lord's promise, "I am coming soon." Here is a heavenly parallel; the opening of the scroll is preceded by a solemn liturgy (5:8-14). The eschatological drama of seals flows from a scene of heavenly worship and will climax in the heavenly liturgy of 7:9-17. The breaking of the seals is the work of the Lamb; this work which he alone can do, will mean that things will be brought to pass, revealed. More precisely, the Lamb ("who was slain from the foundation of the world"), by breaking the first seal, unleashes the plagues, and not only these first plagues, for all three cycles—seals, trumpets, and bowls—are interconnected. This is a factor that tempers the violent imagery of the work.

Some have identified this rider on the white horse with the figure of 19:11-16, and have seen him as a symbol of the victorious course of the gospel. In fact, all that the two visions have in common is that the horse is white, the color of victory. It is evident that, in our passage, the four horsemen must be taken together. They represent war and its attendant evils—the war, strife, famine, and pestilence of the Synoptic apocalypse. The white horse signifies triumphant warfare; the horseman rides on his path of conquest. Though the rider is a symbolic figure, the Parthians, Rome's dreaded foe, are in mind, for John is going to focus on the fall of Rome—for him, *the* foe of the Church. As in the messages to the Churches, John's symbolic language can be topical.

The second horseman has been given power to take peace from the earth and to make men slaughter one another: the complementary sides of warfare. *Given* power—even destructive war serves a divine purpose! It is a forceful way of stressing that nothing, not even the most awful things that humans can do to one another, and to our world, can ever frustrate God's saving purpose. To speak of God "permitting" the deeds of human folly is, hopelessly, to misunderstand. God does not "permit." He respects, wholly, human freedom, freedom to do good and evil. He *grieves* over human folly and perversity.

War carries famine in its train: the rider on the black horse with his scales. Swete suggests that the voice from the midst of the living creatures is "the protest of Nature against the horrors of famine" (87). The rider on the pale horse is a symbol of pestilence. Hades, abode of the dead, swallows up the victims of the pestilence. If these plagues—"the beginning of birth pangs" (Matt 24:8)—strike a quarter of the earth, the trumpets will affect a third (8:7-12) and the bowls the whole (ch. 16). The plagues, while parallel, still mark inexorable progress towards the end.

Can we, in our decade, imagine that this "apocalyptic" picture is over-drawn? We have seen (on our television screens!) conquerors going out to conquer. We have seen death rain from the sky. We have seen the burnt corpses of a pathetic army. We have seen the sinister black pall from oil field fires, threatening our environment. Most harrowing of all, we have witnessed the agony of the Kurds. Their suffering, more than anything else, underlines the mindless folly of war—I saw a pale horse, and its rider's name was Death, and Hades followed with him! John does not glorify war. He unmasks its ugliness.

### FOR REFERENCE AND FURTHER STUDY

Bornkamm, G. "Die Komposition der Apokalyptischen Visionen in der Offen-barung Johannis." *ZNW* 36 (1937) 132–49.

Collins, A. Yarbro. "The Political Perspective of the Revelation to John." *JBL* 96 (1977) 241–56.

Dornseiff, F. "Die apokalyptischen Reiter (Apoc 6:1ff)." *ZNW* 38 (1939) 196–7.

Feuillet, A. "Quelques énigmes des chapitres 4 à 7 de l'Apocalypse." *EspV* 86 (1976) 455–59, 471–79.

Haapa, E. "Farben und Funktionen bei den Apokaliptischen Reitern." *TAiK* 73 (1968) 216–25.

Vanni, U. "Il terzo 'sigillo' dell' Apocalisse (Ap 6:5-6): simbolo dell'ingiustizia sociale?" *Greg* 59 (1978) 691–719.

Waldensberger, W. "Les chevaliers de l'Apocalypse (6:1-8)." *RHPR* 4 (1924) 1–31.

## 14. *The Fifth Seal* (6:9-11)

9. When he broke the fifth seal, I saw underneath the altar the souls of those who had been slaughtered for the word of God and for the testi-mony they bore. 10. They cried aloud, saying, "How long, Master, holy and true, must it be before you pronounce judgment and avenge our blood on the inhabitants of the earth?" 11. Then each of them was given a white robe, and they were told to rest for a little while longer until the number of their fellow-servants and brothers and sisters, who were to be killed as they themselves had been, was completed.

## NOTES

9. *underneath the altar:* The striking imagery is suggested by Lev 4:7, "The rest of the blood . . . he shall pour out at the base of the altar of burnt-offering"; and, since "blood is the life" (Lev 17:11), the "souls" of martyrs are where their life-blood is found.

*the souls of those who had been slaughtered:* The emergence of martyrs, Christians who will die in the great persecution that (in John's view) is about to begin.

*for the testimony they bore:* By sharing the fate of Jesus (see 1:9; 12:11, 17; 19:10; 20:4), which is his victory too.

10. *they cried aloud:* One may think of the blood of the martyrs crying out; see Gen 4:10 and Luke 11:50-51.

*How long?:* Echoes throughout the Old Testament (Ps 6:3; 13:1-2; 35:17; 74:9-10; 79:5; 80:4; 89:46; 94:3-4; Isa 6:11; Jer 47:6). See especially Zech 1:12. The slaughtered ones are eager for God's justice to be seen to be done.

*pronounce judgment and avenge our blood:* "pronounce judgment" (*krinō*) means "to vindicate." *Ekdikeō*, "avenge," means also to "procure justice for." The prayer is a call for God to reveal himself, to manifest his justice. See Ps 79:5-10; Rom 12:19; Luke 18:7-8.

*the inhabitants of the earth:* See Rev 3:10; 8:13; 11:10; 13:8, 12, 14; 17:2-8; throughout the book these are the enemies of God, the oppressors of God's people.

11. *a white robe:* Symbolizing victory and glorification (Dan 7:9). Charles (I. pp. 184–188) argues that, according to Jewish and early Christian literature, the *stolē leukē* signifies the spiritual bodies which were forthwith given to the martyrs, but not to the rest of the faithful departed until after the final judgment.

*to rest:* Not simply to "rest," but to enjoy repose. See 14:13.

*fellow-servants and brothers and sisters,* lit. "brethren": Both God's people in general and the martyrs in particular ("who were to be killed").

*until the number . . . was completed:* The idea that the end would come when the roll of martyrs is complete was current in later Judaism. A remarkable parallel is 4 Ezra 4:35-36: "Did not the souls of the righteous in their chambers ask about these matters, saying, 'How long are we to remain here? And when will come the harvest of our reward?' And Jeremiel the archangel answered them and said, 'When the number of those like yourselves is completed.'" "The death of the martyrs is the means by which God is to win his victory over the powers of evil, and only total victory can bring about the consummation of God's purpose" (Caird, 87). The meaning is not that there is a predetermined number of the saved. See Luke 18:7-8. Rather, the idea is that the death of martyrs brings the eschaton nearer.

## INTERPRETATION

At the opening of the fifth seal the slain righteous emerge; the pattern is still that of the Synoptic apocalypse (Matt 24:9-14; Mark 13:9-13; Luke 21:12-19). These martyrs are presented as sacrificial victims; underneath the heavenly altar they are safely in the presence of God (the heavenly throne-room has become a temple). It was a current rabbinical belief that the souls of the righteous were under the altar in heaven. These had been slain "for the word of God," for their fidelity to the one God and for their "testimony" to Jesus, by sharing his fate. Their *blood* called out to God ("The voice of your brother's blood is crying to me from the ground" [Gen 4:10]). There is, too, the remarkably apposite text of Luke 11:50-51, ". . . that the blood of all the prophets, shed from the foundation of the world, may be required of this generation" (see Matt 23:35-36). Surely the author of Hebrews has a more sensitive perception when he speaks of "the sprinkled blood [of Jesus] that speaks more graciously than the blood of Abel" (Heb 12:24). One should keep such a text in mind in this call for "vengeance" here. For what is the shape of a "vengeance" to be wreaked by the Lamb who was slain?

The martyrs do call for vindication. The words of their prayer assert the principle of divine retribution, which forbids the exercise of personal revenge. So, Paul in Rom 12:19 (referring to Lev 19:18 and Deut 32:35): "Beloved, never avenge yourselves, but leave it to the wrath; for it is written, 'Vengeance is mine, I will repay, says the Lord.'" See Luke 18:7-8: "Will not God vindicate his elect, who cry to him day and night? Will he delay long over them? I tell you he will vindicate them speedily." God will vindicate the martyrs by demonstrating clearly and unmistakably that evil has not won. It will be evident to all that these helpless victims are the true, the only victors.

These martyrs have already received the white robe of victory, and they are bidden to rest a little longer. Here we meet with an assertion that is subsequently made several times and in various ways: martyrs are at peace from the moment of their martyrdom (see 7:9-17; 12:10-11; 14:1-5, 13-14; 15:2-4; 19:4; 20:4-6). In later Judaism there was a view that the end would come when the number of righteous was complete. John is not thinking of a predetermined number of saved; his point is that there will be many more martyrs. The great tribulation will wreak havoc and yet will fail, miserably. The martyrs are God's "shock-troops."

John, in view of the great tribulation which he expects imminently to break, has to put before the Christians of his concern a prospect of violent death. Their *hypomonē*, "patient endurance," may—most likely will—demand faithfulness unto death. He takes care, then, to stress the blessedness of such fidelity. The faithful will pass, immediately beyond death, into their heavenly rest. All very well, but the oppressor cannot emerge unscathed. The blood of the victims must be avenged. Justice must prevail. "How long . . . before you pronounce judgment?" This is a human sentiment; but it does underline the truth that, in God's world, evil must not, cannot, prevail. The "how long" betrays understandable human impatience with a situation in which evil does seem to win the day. Our longing and our prayer will not spur God to violent action against evil. He has already taken the action that underwrites the total rout of evil. His deed is the Cross. We are back to the Lamb.

### FOR REFERENCE AND FURTHER STUDY

Feuillet, A, "Le premier cavalier de l'Apocalypse." *ZNW* 57 (1966) 229–59.
van den Eynde, P. "Le Dieu du desordre. Commentaire synthétique d'Apocalypse 6:9-11." *BVC* 74 (1967) 39–51.

## 15. *The Sixth Seal* (6:12-17)

12. I watched as he broke the sixth seal. There was a great earthquake; the sun turned black as a hairy sackcloth, and the moon all red as blood; 13. the stars in the sky fell to earth as a fig tree shedding its unripe figs when shaken by a gale; 14. the sky was torn apart like a scroll being rolled up, and every mountain and island was dislodged from its place. 15. Then the kings of the earth, the nobles and the commanders, the rich and the powerful, and every slave and freeman, hid themselves in caves or under the mountain crags; 16. and they cried to the mountains and to the crags, "Fall on us and hide us from the One who sits on the throne and from the wrath of the Lamb; 17. for the great day of their wrath has come, and who can stand?"

### NOTES

12. *a great earthquake:* The cosmic earthquake is a regular feature of the traditional apocalyptic scheme (see Ezek 38:19; Isa 2:19; Rev 8:5; 11:13; 16:18). And, also in line with traditional imagery, the earthquake is followed by cosmic upheaval. See Joel 2:31; Isa 13:10; 34:4.

12-13. *sun . . . moon . . . stars:* Joel 2:31, "The sun shall be turned into darkness, and the moon to blood, before the great and terrible day of the Lord comes"; Isa 13:10, "For the stars of the heavens and their constellations will not give their light; the sun will be dark at its rising and the moon will not shed its light." See *Assumption of Moses* 10:4-5.

*hairy sackcloth:* Made of the hair of black goats.

13. *fig tree . . . scroll:* Isa 34:4: "All the host of heaven shall rot away, and the skies roll up like a scroll. All their host shall fall, as leaves fall from the vine, like leaves falling from a fig tree."

14. *mountain and island:* For the removal of mountain and island, see Rev 16:20.

15–16. *the kings . . .:* See Ps 2:2. All classes of society will be terror-stricken by the cosmic portents: kings, magistrates, military authorities, wealthy, strong, slaves, and free. Social distinctions will be forgotten in the frantic attempt to escape. See Isa 2:19, "And men shall enter the caves of the rocks and the holes of the ground from before the terror of the Lord"; Hos 10:8, "And they shall say to the mountains, 'Cover us' and to the hills 'Fall upon us.' " Also Luke 23:30.

16. *the wrath of the Lamb:* "This phrase is a deliberate paradox. . . . Neither literally nor as a metaphor for self-sacrificing love is a lamb naturally associated with 'wrath'. . . . For the victory by which 'the Lamb' won the right to open the scroll was the Cross" (Caird, 90f.).

17. *the great day of their wrath:* Zeph 1:14-15, "The great day of the Lord is near . . . a day of wrath is that day"; Nah 1:6, "Who can stand before his indignation? Who can endure the heat of his anger?"; see Joel 2:11; Mal 3:2. The verse expresses the alarm of the conscience-stricken inhabitants of the earth; it is a proleptic reference to the final battle against the kings of the earth. "Their wrath": the wrath of the One seated on the throne *and* of the Lamb; here the Lamb is again assimilated to the Father; see 5:13; 22:1.

INTERPRETATION

At the breaking of the sixth seal the cosmic phenomena appear. Close parallel with the Synoptic apocalypse is maintained, but the Old Testament has provided the imagery of the common tradition which depicts the end of history and the end of the world. How aesthetically pleasing are the images of the fig tree with its winter fruit and the sky vanishing like a rolled-up scroll! No one, great or small, can escape the "wrath." Above we have remarked the irony of the contrast: "Lo, the Lion . . . I saw a Lamb" (5:5-6); here we have the conscious paradox, "the wrath of the Lamb." For, though this Lamb is the one to whom judgment has been given (ch. 5), and though he will appear as the rider on a white horse terrible to his enemies (19:11-21), his victory was won on the cross (12:11). "With one exquisitely paradoxical phrase John calls before the imagination of his hearer-readers both the terror of the coming judgment and the glad tidings that the judge is the One who has already paid the supreme penalty on behalf of the world. Though it is no less wrath for being so, the wrath is 'the wrath of the lamb'" (Boring, 127).

The martyrs had called for vindication (6:10). God has unleashed his "wrath." He is not, nor ever could be, a vindictive God. He is not aloof to injustice and the human suffering it involves. He has his own way of coping with it. His answer is the Lamb. His "wrath" is written on the Cross. We should read his message and act accordingly—act for justice and peace in our world. That way of facing and overcoming evil is the way of "the wrath of the Lamb."

## For Reference and Further Study

Bauckham, R. J. "The Eschatological Earthquake in the Apocalypse of John." *NovT* 19 (1977) 216–25.

## 16. *The Sealing of the Faithful (7:1-8)*

1. After this I saw four angels standing at the four corners of the earth, holding back the four winds of the earth so that no wind should blow on land or sea or on any tree. 2. Then I saw another angel ascend from the rising of the sun, holding the seal of the living God, and he cried aloud to the four angels who had been given power to devastate land and sea: 3. "Do not devastate land or sea or trees until we have set the seal of our God on the foreheads of his servants." 4. I heard how many had been marked with the seal—a hundred and forty-four thousand from all the tribes of Israel: 5. twelve thousand from the tribe of Judah, twelve thousand from the tribe of Reuben, twelve thousand from the tribe of Gad, 6. twelve thousand from the tribe of Asher, twelve thousand from the tribe of Naphtali, twelve thousand from the tribe of Manasseh, 7. twelve thousand from the tribe of Simeon, twelve thousand from the tribe of Levi, twelve thousand from the tribe of Issachar, 8. twelve thousand from the tribe of Zabulon, twelve thousand from the tribe of Joseph, twelve thousand from the tribe of Benjamin.

## Notes

1. *after this I saw:* Introducing a fresh vision of special importance. See note on 4:1.
   *four angels:* The notion that angels (of the lower orders) guarded elemental

forces was current. See Rev 14:18, "the angel who has power over fire," and 16:5, "the angel of water": personifications of natural forces.

*four corners:* The author assumes that the earth is four-cornered; see Isa 11:12; Ezek 7:2.

*four winds:* In Jewish tradition the winds that blew from the four angles or corners of an earth square in shape (as distinct from the winds that blew from the sides) were harmful. Besides, it was expected that a great storm would usher in the end. See Matt 24:31. The winds which will hurt the earth are restrained until God had sealed his elect.

2. *another angel,* see 10:1: Representing the divine will.

*from the rising of the sun:* There may be a reference to Ezek 43:2—the glory of God coming from the east. The Messiah was expected from the east (Matt 2:1-2). In Rev 16:12 danger comes from the east.

*the seal of the living God:* The divine signet ring, like that of an oriental monarch (see Gen 41:42; Esth 3:10; 8:2, 8, 10; Dan 6:17; 1 Macc 6:15) which marked the sealed as his property. See 2 Tim 2:19. This "seal" involves a word-play with the seven "seals." The four angels who are in charge of (or represent) the destructive winds are themselves depicted as devastators of land and sea.

3. *on the foreheads of his servants:* Ezek 9:4-6: "The Lord said to him [the angel scribe], 'Go through the city, through Jerusalem, and put a mark on the foreheads of the men who sigh and groan over all the abominations that are committed in it.' And to the others [six destroying angels] he said in my hearing, 'Pass through the city after him and smite . . . but touch no one upon whom is the mark.' " In Revelation the sealing of "God's servants" does not symbolize protection from tribulation and death but means being sustained in and through tribulation.

4-8. *I heard how many:* John has not witnessed the sealing, but he hears the number of the sealed and their description.

*a hundred and forty-four thousand:* A thousand signifies an immense number and 144 is the square of 12. The 144,000 (to be identified with the group in 14:1-5) is symbolic Israel; in early Christianity "Israel" represents the Church as the continuation of Israel (see Rom 9–11; Gal 6:16; Eph 2:11-22; 1 Pet 2:9). Here, then, we have the twelve tribes of the old Israel and the twelve apostles of the new Israel (21:12-14). A multitude of 144,000 conveys the idea of a vast throng beyond reckoning—in fact, quite the same as the "great multitude" of 7:9. See the 10,000 talents of Matt 18:24—a well-nigh unimaginable sum.

*from all the tribes of Israel:* John portrays the Church as the Israel of God. The solemn (rather tedious) enumeration is typical of apocalyptic (see Rev 21:12-13, 19-20). Judah comes first in the list because the Messiah hailed from that tribe (see 5:5). The list includes both Joseph and Manasseh (whereas one might have expected either Joseph or Ephraim/Manasseh), so another tribe has to go: Dan has been dropped. We cannot say why the list should have taken just this form.

INTERPRETATION

Before the last seal was broken, the servants of God were signed with the seal of the living God, 144,000 of them. The opening of the last seal will unleash the plagues of trumpets (8:6–11:19), which are modeled on the plagues of Egypt. The sealing of the elect recalls the immunity of the Israelites to the plagues that struck the Egyptians. John's unexpected twist is that his servants will be sealed for protection *through* the great tribulation. They achieve their victory, yes, but in the only Christian manner: "love of life did not bring them to shrink from death" (12:11).

The four chariots of Zechariah went forth to "the four winds of heaven" (Zech 6:5). John had previously utilized the image of the chariots (transformed into horsemen); here he makes use of the reference to the four winds. In the context of a vision of destruction, he adverts to divine concern: the Lord does know his own. See 2 Tim 2:19, "God's firm foundation stands, bearing this seal: 'The Lord knows those who are his.'" John's message is that to be a bearer of the seal of God is costly. The seal of God is the seal of the Lamb, the Lamb "who was slain from the foundation of the world" (13:8). John is never a purveyor of cheap grace.

One should keep in mind that, for John, the victors are those who "loved not their lives even unto death" (12:11). The "sealing," assurance of divine concern, will entail no "rapture" for the elect. They will be "caught up" indeed, but caught up in the tribulation, helpless victims—helpless as their Lord on his cross. For them, as for him, there will be no legion of angels. We must look for no miracle, apart from the abiding miracle of our God's loving care.

FOR REFERENCE AND FURTHER STUDY

Geyser, A. "The Twelve Tribes in Revelation: Judean and Judeo-Christian Apocalypticism." *NTS* 28 (1982) 388–99.

Smith, C. R. "The Portrayal of the Church as the New Israel in the Names and Order of the Tribes in Revelation 7:5-8." *JSNT* 19 (1983) 111–8.

## 17. *Song of Victory* (7:9-17)

9. After this I looked, and there was a vast throng, which no one could count, from all nations and tribes and peoples and tongues, standing before the throne and the Lamb, robed in white and with palm branches in their hands. 10. They were shouting aloud, Victory to our God who sits on the throne, and to the Lamb! 11. All the angels who stood round the throne and the elders and the four living creatures fell on their faces before the throne and worshiped God, crying: 12. Amen! Praise, glory and wisdom, thanksgiving and honor, power and might, be to our God for ever and ever. Amen.

13. Then one of the elders spoke to me and asked, "These people robed in white—who are they and where have they come from?" 14. I answered, "My lord, it is you who know." He said to me, "They are those who have passed through the great tribulation; they have washed their robes and made them white in the blood of the Lamb.

15.   That is why they stand before the throne of God and worship him
day and night in his temple,
and he who sits on the throne will be their tabernacle.

16.   They shall not hunger anymore, or thirst anymore;
never again shall the sun strike them, nor any scorching heat.

17.   For the Lamb who is at the center of the throne will shepherd them,
and will guide them to the springs of the water of life;
and God will wipe away every tear from their eyes."

### NOTES

9. *a vast throng:* Not distinct from, but the same group as that of vv. 4-8 viewed under a different aspect: it is the Church triumphant in heaven. "The first vision [vv. 4-8] shows the church on earth *before the last day*. It is being sealed. . . . The second vision [vv. 9-17] shows the church at worship before the throne *after the last day*" (Krodel, 180).

*which no one could count:* In effect, 144,000 is also a countless multitude.

*before the throne:* As in chs. 4 and 5, the heavenly throne-room. The countless host of peoples from every nation and language stands before the throne of God and Lamb, celebrating a heavenly feast of Tabernacles.

*palm branches:* A symbol of victory and of rejoicing after war (see 1 Macc 13:51; 2 Macc 10:7). The feast of Tabernacles was celebrated in the seventh month, after the harvest; it was an occasion of great rejoicing (see Lev 23:33-36; Neh 8:13-18) when palm branches were carried and booths raised on the flat rooftops. In Zech 14:16-19 Tabernacles is set in the messianic era. The symbolism is clear; in our terms we might depict these martyrs as celebrating, in heaven, a perpetual Christmas.

10. *victory (sōtēria),* lit. "salvation": See 12:10; 19:1. "Here one theme only is dwelt on—victory, deliverance, salvation—by those who have just emerged in triumph from the strife. . . . They know and proclaim that the victory, the deliverance (*hē sōtēria*), is not their own achievement, but that of God and of the Lamb" (Charles, 1:211). Again, the association of God and Lamb.

11. *all the angels:* See 5:11

12. The wording of this doxology, with its seven features, is very like the angelic praise of the Lamb in 5:12.

13–14. *one of the elders:* As in 5:5, an elder intervenes to interpret the vision. For the form of the dialogue see Zech 4:4-5; 6:4-5.

   *My lord, it is you who know:* See Ezek 37:3.

   *the great tribulation:* See Dan 12:1; Mark 13:19; Matt 24:21. For John, the tribulation through which Christians come triumphantly is imminent persecution (3:10; 13:7-10) sparked by their faithfulness to the Lamb.

   *have washed . . . made them white:* Theirs is not a merely passive role: by the shedding of their blood they have joined their sacrifice to that of the Lamb; ultimately, it is their association with his death that has won their victory. Only those who have washed their robes have place in the New Jerusalem (22:14). There are very close parallels between the heavenly scene of 7:13-17 and the description of the New Jerusalem (21:2–22:5).

15. *worship (latreuousin):* The idea is of a vast worshiping congregation rather than of an exclusive priesthood (*leitourgein*). Explicit mention, in a liturgy, of *worship* of God (and Lamb), is found here and 22:14 only.

   *will be their tabernacle (skēnōsei):* In the heavenly feast of Tabernacles, as God will dwell with his people in the New Jerusalem (21:3). There is reference, too, to the *shekinah*, the immediate presence of God among his people.

16–17. *not hunger . . . or thirst:* Isa 49:10, "They shall not hunger or thirst, neither scorching wind nor sun shall smite them, for he who has pity on them will lead them, and by springs of water will guide them." Isa 25:8, "The Lord God will wipe away tears from all faces." In the New Jerusalem God will give "water from the spring of the water of life" (21:6) and wipe away all tears (21:4).

### INTERPRETATION

This "vast throng" is not a group distinct from the 144,000 (itself a "great throng"): it is the same group now viewed beyond the great tribulation. In keeping with John's consistent outlook, these are presented as happy here and now; they stand before God and Lamb, celebrating a heavenly feast of Tabernacles. As martyrs—the ideal representatives of God's people—they have come triumphantly through the tribulation: the vision is proleptic. The angels, the countless host of 5:11, join in the heavenly liturgy, first by adding their "Amen" to the prayer of the martyrs, and then with their own prayer. This heavenly liturgy forms the climax to the opening of the seals.

The victors, robed in white, have passed through the "great tribulation." This echoes Dan 12:1, "And there shall be a time of trouble, such as never has been since there was a nation till that time," and reminds one of Matt 13:9, "For in those days there will be such tribulation as has not been from the beginning of creation which God created until now, and never will be." A "great tribulation" was expected to precede the end; for John, the tribulation through which these martyrs come triumphantly is imminent persecution (see 3:10; 13:7-10). These are the victors of the messages (2:7, etc.). The striking paradox (made *white* in the *blood* of the Lamb) has a haunting beauty; and, as beauty, it speaks truth. It expresses God's and the Lamb's definition of victory: they have won by suffering death, not by inflicting hurt.

In their priestly role (1:6) these faithful ones join the heavenly choir, as is their right. In their feast of Tabernacles they have no need to build their own booths: God himself will be their tabernacle. The texts of Isaiah (49:10; 25:8) which refer to the happy return from the Exile, find their fulfillment in the shepherding of the Lamb who leads his own sheep to the unfailing fountains of life (see John 10:27-28). For, in startling and lovely paradox, the Lamb has become a shepherd.

"Was it not necessary that the Christ should suffer these things and enter into his glory?" (Luke 24:26) is the rebuke of the risen Lord to the uncomprehending Emmaus disciples. John pictures the glory of the victors beyond their tribulation. They have triumphed, but not on their own. Victory is theirs because, and only because, the Lamb had first conquered. It is a conviction shared by the fourth evangelist, "apart from me you can do nothing" (John 15:5), and by Paul, "I can do all things in him who strengthens me" (Phil 4:13). It is a lesson we need to take to heart. A glorious destiny awaits us, yes; but precisely as faithful followers of the Lamb. If we cannot share John's expectation of imminent eschatological tribulation, we may well be failing to discern a more insidious and pervasive challenge. John saw through the empire of his day, discerned its distorted standard of values. We have become so much part of our contemporary empire, the lifestyle of the Western world, that we may no longer be stirred, excited, by prospect of heavenly joy.

## For Reference and Further Study

Comblin, J. "La rassemblement du peuple de Dieu. Ap. 7:2-4, 9-14." *AsSeign* 66 (1973) 42–9.

Draper, J. A. "The Heavenly Feast of Tabernacles: Revelation 7:1-17." *JSNT* 39 (1990) 111–18.

Feuillet, A. "Les martyrs de l'humanité et l'Agneau égorgé. Une interpretataion nouvelle de la prière des égorgés en Ap 6:9-11." *NRT* 99 (1977) 189–207.

Wolff, G. "Die Gemeinde des Christus in der Apokalypse des Johannes." *NTS* 27 (1981) 186–97.

## 18. *The Seventh Seal* (8:1-5)

1. When the Lamb broke the seventh seal, there was silence in heaven for about half an hour. 2. I saw the seven angels who stand before God, and they were given seven trumpets.

3. Then another angel came and stood at the altar, holding a golden censer. He was given much incense to offer with the prayers of all God's people on the golden altar before the throne, 4. and the smoke of the incense went up before God with his people's prayers from the angel's hand. 5. The angel took the censer, filled it with fire from the altar, and threw it down on the earth; and there came peals of thunder, flashes of lightning, and an earthquake.

### NOTES

1. *silence in heaven:* May be an echo of a Jewish tradition of a primeval silence preceding the first day of creation. See 4 Ezra 7:30-33. More aptly, given Revelation's close linking of heavenly worship and eschatological drama, the opening of the seventh seal brings liturgical silence in heaven. It is a ritual anticipation of the plagues of trumpets, which will be introduced by heavenly worship in 8:3-4 (L. L. Thompson, 66–68).

2. *the seven angels:* These are the "angels of the presence" (see Isa 63:9, "the angel of his presence"), the seven "archangels" (see 1 Enoch 20:1-8) of Jewish tradition who serve in the immediate presence of God, namely, Michael, Gabriel, Raphael, Uriel, Raguel, Sariel, and Remiel. See Tob 12:15; and Luke 1:19, "I am Gabriel, who stand in the presence of God."

   *seven trumpets:* In the Old Testament, the trumpet announces God's judgment (see Joel 2:1; Zeph 1:16; Isa 27:13). In the New Testament, trumpet blasts, sounded by angels, proclaim the final judgment (Matt 24:31; 1 Cor 15:52; 1 Thess 4:16).

3-4. *another angel:* This angel (see 7:2; 10:1; 14:6, 8-9; 18:1) took his place at the altar—this time the altar of incense and not the altar of holocausts (6:9); in 14:18 this angel is "the angel who has power over fire." It may be, however, that John visualizes a single, dual purpose altar. See Luke 1:11.

5. *fire from the altar:* See Exod 10:2. John has changed the prophet's scattering of burning coals over Jerusalem to the casting of fire on the earth. See Wis 19:13.

*peals of thunder . . .:* See 11:19; 16:18. "Each of the septets concludes with the *son et lumière* proper to the divine throne (4:5)" (Sweet, 160).

## INTERPRETATION

The seventh seal would suggest the end. Instead there is silence—a liturgical pause of half an hour. Because the seals blend, evidently, into the trumpets, the "silence in heaven" is a dramatic literary device. Thereupon, the seven "angels of the face" emerge. The involvement of these, the angelic "top brass," underlines the solemnity of the moment. Yet, not even they are independent actors. They were given (*edothēsan*) trumpets: all the plagues come from God. Before they can sound their sinister trumpets, another angel appears on the scene, one who officiates as priest in the heavenly temple, and offers the incense. In Rev 5:8 we read of "the golden bowls full of incense, which are the prayers of the saints." But the metaphor is not quite the same; here the prayers of the saints are apparently the live coals on which the grains of incense fall. It appears that the prayers are represented by the coals on the altar of holocausts, that is, they are the prayers of the martyrs of 6:9-10.

While Revelation never directly refers to the worship of the earthly Church, Christians would surely recognize their prayers in this incense rising before the heavenly throne. The martyrs had prayed: "How long must it be before you vindicate us?" (6:10); now their prayer, which had gone up to God (8:4), returns to the earth, causing things to happen on earth. The thunder, lightning, and earthquakes sound in heaven (see 4:5; 11:19): they are the warning signs of a great visitation. See Wis 19:13, "The punishments did not come upon the sinners without prior signs in the violence of thunder."

In his parable of the widow and the judge (18:1-8), Luke has Jesus ask a question: "And will not God vindicate his elect, who cry to him day and night?" He answers the question firmly: "I tell you, he will vindicate them speedily" (18:7-8). God is never impervious to suffering, least of all to the pain of the innocent and the oppressed. He will have the last word; his justice will prevail. "Speedily"—God's time-scale may seem slow to us. The author of 2 Peter had faced that problem: "Do not ignore this one fact, beloved, that with the Lord one day is as a thousand years, and a thousand years as one day" (2 Pet 3:8). We, on our pilgrimage, will pray our "How long?" perhaps with human impatience. Our faith should assure us that the kingdom, the reign of God, will come. Our daily prayer, "Thy kingdom come," is efficacious prayer, because God it is who will bring about that rule: salvation for humankind.

# V. THE SEVEN TRUMPETS

## 19. *The First Four Trumpets* (8:6-13)

6. Then the seven angels who held the seven trumpets prepared to blow them.

7. The first blew his trumpet; and there came hail and fire mixed with blood cast upon the earth. A third of the earth was burnt up, a third of the trees were burnt up, and all the green grass was burnt up.

8. Then the second angel blew his trumpet; and what looked like a great mountain flaming with fire was cast into the sea. A third of the sea was turned to blood, 9. a third of the living creatures in it died, and a third of the ships were destroyed.

10. Then the third angel blew his trumpet; and a great star fell from the sky, blazing like a torch, and it fell on a third of the rivers and springs of water. 11. The name of the star was Wormwood; and a third of the water turned to wormwood, and many people died from drinking the water because it had become bitter.

12. Then the fourth angel blew his trumpet; a third of the sun was struck, a third of the moon, and a third of the stars, so that a third part of them turned dark, and a third of the day did not appear, and likewise the night.

13. Then I looked, and I heard an eagle [vulture] crying aloud as it flew in mid-heaven: Woe, woe, woe to the inhabitants of the earth because of the remaining trumpet blasts which the three angels are about to blow.

### NOTES

7. *hail and fire mixed with blood:* See Exod 9:23-26 (seventh plague). The combination of fire and blood in a context of judgment is found in Joel 2:30; see Acts 2:19. In Jewish imagination the mingling of hail and fire in Exod 9:23-24 is a miracle within a miracle; Wis 16:15-24.

*a third . . . all the green grass:* A good example of John's literary freedom, this switch from "a third" to "all."

8–9. See Exod 7:20 (first plague).

*a great mountain flaming with fire:* Probably suggested by a tradition attested in 1 Enoch 18:13, "And I saw there [in the deep pit] the seven stars [which] were like great, burning mountains"; "and there I saw seven stars of heaven bound together in it, like great mountains, and burning with fire" (21:3). Note v. 10 here—the "great star" fallen from heaven. It is an apocalyptic dramatization of the first plague of Egypt. A text of Jeremiah may be in mind as well, where Babylon is likened to a "destructive mountain" which the Lord will turn into "a burnt-out mountain" (51:25). If Rome be "Egypt" (the plagues motif), it is also "Babylon." The burning, red-hot mass turns the waters of the sea into blood. Again, destruction is limited to *one-third* of the ocean.

10. See Exod 7:20 (first plague). The Exodus text describes the turning of the Nile waters into blood—a single plague. In vv. 8-9 and 10-11, John has transformed it into two plagues; whereas above he had spoken of the ocean, now he turns to rivers and springs.

*a great star:* Like the burning mountain of v. 8, a burning star (see 1 Enoch 18:13) destroys a third of the fresh water supply. Babylon may be in mind. Note the dirge for the king of Babylon: "How are you fallen from heaven, O Day Star, son of Dawn!" (Isa 14:12).

11. *wormwood:* The plant wormwood (*artemisia absinthiaca*) has a bitter taste. Wormwood is metaphor for divine punishment in Jer 9:15; 23:15; Lam 3:15, 19, and for disaster in Prov 5:4. The plague is the reverse of the miracle of Marah (Exod 15:23-25). In Amos 5:6-7 and 6:12 "wormwood" stands for perversion of justice. "Wormwood is the star of the new Babylon which has 'poisoned' by its idolatry the 'springs' of its own life" (Caird, 115).

12. See Exod 10:21-23 (ninth plague).

*sun . . . moon . . . . stars:* Note the disturbance of the heavenly bodies in Amos 8:9 and Joel 3:15.

*a third:* Strictly speaking, this would cause a partial darkness (a lessening of light), not a shortening of day and night as the second half of the verse suggests. John seeks to produce an effect and to emphasize the partial character of the visitation.

13. *I looked, and I heard:* John saw a vision and heard a voice as at 5:11 and 6:1.

*an eagle:* A messenger of coming judgment appears in the zenith, where the sun stands at midday. Likely, for "eagle" (*aetos*—4:7; 12:14) we should read "vulture." Thus, in Luke 17:37, *aetoi* should be translated "vultures" rather than "eagles": "Where the body is, there the vultures will be gathered together." A vulture is an obvious symbol of doom and in Hos 8:1 the presence of a vulture (LXX, *aetos*) calls forth the trumpet alarm: "Set the trumpet to your lips, for a vulture is over the house of the Lord."

*woe, woe, woe:* Reference to the three remaining trumpet-blasts.

*the inhabitants of the earth:* See 3:10; 6:10; 11:10; 13:8, 14; 14:6; 17:8. In 14:6 these "inhabitants of the earth" will hear "an eternal gospel."

INTERPRETATION

For his plague series of trumpets and bowls, John has looked, in large measure, to the plagues of Egypt (Exod 7–10). He has managed his source with customary aplomb.

| Trumpets | Plagues of Egypt | Bowls |
|---|---|---|
| 1. Rev 8:6-7 Hail, fire, blood | Seventh: Exod 9:13-25 | 7. Rev 16:17-21 Thunder, hail |
| 2. Rev 8:8-9 Sea into blood | First: Exod 7:14-25 | 2. Rev 16:3 Sea into blood |
| 3. Rev 8:10-11 Waters bitter | First: Exod 7:14-25 | 3. Rev 16:4-7 Water to blood |
| 4. Rev 8:12 Darkness | Ninth: Exod 10:21-23 | 5. Rev 16:10-11 Darkness |
| 5. Rev 9:1-11 Locusts | Eighth: Exod 10:12-20 [Joel 1:6-2:5] | |
| | Sixth: Exod 9:8-12 | 1. Rev 16:2 Ulcers |
| | Second: Exod 8:2-6 | 6. Rev 16:12-16 Frogs |
| 6. Rev 9:13-21 (Euphrates) | | 6. Rev 16:12-16 (Euphrates) |
| | | 4. Rev 16:8-9 Burning heat |
| 7. Rev 11:15-19 Heavenly worship | | |

The angels of the presence had been waiting for the heavenly signal: now they make ready to sound their trumpets. The plagues, triggered by the trumpet blasts, strike one-third of earth and heaven—contrast the "fourth of the earth" of the seals. It is the second act of the drama: the first act repeated with more dramatic intensity. In his series of plagues John is not indulging in tiresome repetition; he is building up to a dramatic climax. He is leading to the ultimate battle, the decisive conflict of good and evil. He will not plunge into that final battle; he will move, stage by painful stage. As ever, he is realistic. His readers face the prospect of the great tribulation. He is not prepared to comfort them by assurance of a short travail. The ordeal will be soon, and it will not go on for ever, but, for the victims, it will be all too long. His three series of plagues serve a pastoral purpose, effectively underlining the dire choice: "You cannot *serve* God and Mammon."

John has modeled his plagues of trumpets (and bowls) on the plagues of Egypt. One must assume that his plagues, like the Egyptian plagues, are not the vindictive punishment of human sin but rather the result of human rejection of God's invitation. The plagues of Egypt were not punishment of Pharaoh; they were designed to procure the liberation of God's people: "Let my son go" (Exod 4:23). Just as the appeal to Pharaoh was vain, so, John believes, God will continue to encounter human intransigence.

The triple woe (v. 13) refers to the three remaining trumpet-blasts or, more precisely, to the visitations called forth by them. Earth and sea have been stricken by the former plagues; now is the turn of the inhabitants of the earth. We should note, however, 14:6 where the same "inhabitants of the earth" will hear the proclamation of an "eternal gospel." "The plagues are not God's primary will but the fruit of its rejection" (Sweet, 165).

God offers salvation—but on what terms? On no terms but his. This is not being dictatorial; quite the contrary. His offer of salvation is based on his radical refusal to dominate. The kingdom of God is the free kingdom of wholly liberated women and men. Revelation, like every Scripture text, is a text for humankind. "Plagues" are God's reaction to evil and sin, a reaction envisaged and depicted in human mode. His will is always salvation.

### FOR REFERENCE AND FURTHER STUDY

Casey, J. "The Exodus Theme in the Book of Revelation Against the Background of the New Testament." *Concilium* 189 (1988) 85–95.
Müller, H. P. "Die Plagen der Apokalypse: Eine formgeschichtliche Untersuchung." *ZNW* 51 (1960) 268–78.

## 20. *The Fifth Trumpet (First Woe)* (9:1-12)

1. Then the fifth angel blew his trumpet; and I saw a star fallen from heaven to earth, and he was given a key to the shaft of the abyss. 2. He opened the shaft of the abyss, and smoke came up from the shaft like smoke from a great furnace, and the sun and the air were darkened by the smoke from the shaft. 3. Out of the smoke came locusts over the earth, and they were given the powers of earthly scorpions. 4. They were

told to do no harm to the grass of the earth or to any green plant or any tree, but only to those people who did not have God's seal on their foreheads; 5. they were not permitted to kill them, but only to torment them for five months; and their torment was like the torment of a scorpion when it stings. 6. In those days people will seek death but will not find it; they will long to die, but death will elude them.

7. In appearance the locusts were like horses equipped for battle. On their heads were what looked like gold crowns; their faces were like human faces. 8. and they had hair like women's hair and teeth like lions' teeth. 9. They had chests like iron breastplates; the sound of their wings was like the sound of many chariots with many horses charging into battle. 10. They had tails like scorpions, with stings, and in their tails lay their power to harm people for five months. 11. They had as their king the angel of the abyss, whose name in Hebrew is Abaddon and in Greek Apollyon.

12. The first woe has passed; but there are still two woes to come.

## NOTES

1-2. *a star:* A "fallen star" is a fallen angel. For the tradition of "fallen angels" see 1 Enoch 6–13—a legend based on Gen 6:1-4. See Luke 10:18, "I saw Satan fall like lightning from heaven."

*the abyss:* The usual LXX rendering of *tĕhôm* (Gen 1:2; 7:11; Ps 105:9; 107:26); also applied to Sheol (Job 41:22-23; Rom 10:7). In Revelation, "abyss" is the provisional abode (or jail) of Satan and the fallen angels (see 9:1-2, 11; 11:7; 17:8; 20:1, 3). See Luke 8:31, "And they [many demons] begged him not to command them to depart into the abyss." John pictures the abyss as entered by a shaft whose mouth was kept under lock and key; a (fallen) angel was permitted (*edothē*) to unlock it.

2. *smoke:* See Exod 19:18, "the smoke of it [Mount Sinai] went up like the smoke of a kiln." "Fallen angels" and "abyss" are not to be taken any more literally than other of John's symbols. Behind his symbolic language throughout is his conviction that evil has its origin in human sin.

3-5. See Exod 10:12-15 (eighth plague); Joel 1:6-7, 15; 2:1-11.

*they were given (edothē):* The locusts are instruments of God's purpose.

*scorpions:* Creatures proverbially hostile to humans; see Luke 10:19.

4. *do no harm to the grass:* These are no natural locusts.

5. *to torment them:* A scorpion sting, though exceedingly painful, is not usually fatal; these "locusts" are commissioned to torture, not to slay.

*five months:* A short period; see "ten days" (2:10). Perhaps reflects the locust's life-span of five months.

6. *will seek death:* See Job 3:20-21, "Why is light given to him that is in misery . . . who longs for death, but it comes not"; Jer 8:3, "death shall be pre-

ferred to life by all the remnant that remains of this evil family." See Rev 6:15-17.

7-10. *the locusts:* This description of the locusts owes much to Joel 2:1-11.

*like horses:* The heads of locusts resemble those of horses.

*crowns:* The semblance of crowns suggests their invincibility.

*human faces:* The human dimension of evil; evil is fruit of human rebellion against God.

8. *like women's hair:* Long-haired Parthians may be in mind (see 6:2). Throughout vv. 3-10 John may have been influenced by the Book of Wisdom's midrashic treatment of the plagues of Egypt. See Wis 12:8-9, "But even these you did spare, since they were but humans, and did send wasps as forerunners of your army. . . . You were not unable to destroy them at a blow by dread wild beasts."

11. *king:* See Prov 30:27, "the locusts have no king, yet all of them march in rank." But these "locusts" are demonic beings, and they have a king. It is noteworthy that "king" (*basileus*) was used of the Roman emperor ("their emperor, the angel of the Abyss" [NJB]). This "angel of the abyss" is not the angel of v. 1.

*Abaddon:* The Hebrew word *'abaddôn*, "destruction," is found almost exclusively in the Wisdom literature (Job 26:6; 28:22; 31:12; Prov 15:11; 27:20; Ps 88:11) as a name for the region of the dead, synonym of Sheol or Hades. See Rev 6:8.

*Apollyon:* This Greek word, "destruction," is equivalent to the Hebrew *'abaddôn*. There may be an intentional pun, if Domitian had affected the divine name Apollo. More to the point, John wants his readers to understand that he is warning them of "the destroyers of the earth" (11:18).

12. *first woe . . . two woes:* See 8:13; 9:12; 11:14; 12:12; 16:17.

### INTERPRETATION

As in the case of the seals (6:1-8) the first four trumpets were treated briskly (8:7-12). The fifth and sixth trumpets are given in more detail and represent an intensification of the eschatological tribulation.

The fifth trumpet blast ushers in an Egyptian-style plague of locusts already greatly embellished by Joel. John, in his turn, not only outdoes the prophet but explicitly presents his locusts as a demonic plague. Their hurtful power is similar to that of the scorpion, a creature, like the serpent, proverbially hostile to humans and readily taken as a symbol of evil forces. So Luke 10:19, "I will give you authority to tread upon serpents and scorpions, and over all the forces of the enemy." Since these are not natural locusts, they do not harm vegetation; their target is "the inhabitants of the earth," those who do not bear the mark of God (see

7:2-3). These demonic locusts had human faces (v. 7). "Evil may take many sinister forms and ramify far beyond the immediate implications of individual sin; but in the last analysis it has a human face, for it is caused by the rebellion of human wills against the will of God" (Caird, 120).

There is, in our world, an oppressive burden of evil. Awful things happen every day. It is tempting to look to forces beyond humankind; indeed, such has been the human propensity. Perhaps just here is the truly "demonic" dimension of evil. To look to an influence beyond ourselves, and an influence, for that matter, more malignant and more powerful than we, is to evade our responsibility. It is more honest, and potentially more healing, to acknowledge our responsibility. There is an influence, true, that weighs upon us, but it is the inherited burden of human perversity.

"The imagination of man's heart is evil from his youth" (Gen 8:21): evil is within humanness, not outside of it. For evil is not only the absence of good; it is, more precisely, the absence of everything human. But it is something within humanness. Satan is a powerful symbol, representing the whole gamut of evil and its infectious presence in the human race. The Christian hope is the restoration of all things in Christ—meaning not only that humanness will be purged of evil but also the absolute end of evil itself. The "lake of fire" consumes even "the dragon" (Rev 20:10, 14).

## 21. *The Sixth Trumpet (Second Woe) (9:13-21)*

13. Then the sixth angel blew his trumpet; and I heard a voice coming from the horns of the golden altar before God. 14. It said to the sixth angel who held the trumpet: "Release the four angels held bound at the great river Euphrates!" 15. So the four angels were released: they had been held in readiness for this very hour, day, month, and year, to kill a third of humankind. 16. The number of the troops of cavalry was twice ten thousand times ten thousand; I heard their number. 17. This is how I saw the horses and the riders in my visions: they wore breastplates, fiery red, dark blue, and sulphur yellow; and the horses had heads like lions' heads, and from their mouths came fire, smoke, and sulphur. 18. By these three plagues—the fire, the smoke, and the sulphur that came from their mouths—a third of humankind was killed. 19. The power of the horses lay in their mouths and in their tails; for their tails are like serpents—they have heads, and with them, they wound.

20. The rest of humankind, who were not killed by these plagues, still did not renounce the gods their hands had made, nor give up worshiping demons, and the idols of gold and silver and bronze and stone and wood, which cannot see or hear or walk; 21. nor did they repent of their murders, their sorceries, their fornication, or their robberies.

## NOTES

13. *I heard a voice:* What John hears (vv. 13-16) interprets what he is going to see (v. 17).

   *golden altar:* The altar of incense (8:3); the "voice" is the voice of the prayers of the saints (8:4); the "horns" are the raised corners of the altar. The passage harks back to 8:2-5.

14. *four angels:* Instruments of divine "wrath" (see 1 Enoch 66:1); akin to the four angels of 7:1.

   *held bound:* Allusion to the myth of fallen angels.

   *Euphrates:* The Euphrates marked the eastern frontier of Rome; John utilizes the paranoic Roman fear of a Parthian threat from beyond the river.

15. *in readiness for this very hour:* The ministers of wrath are set free to carry out their task. The fixing of their time of release, down to the very hour, emphasizes the truth that all is happening in accordance with a divine plan; or, better phrased, that nothing happens outside the divine purpose. Anticipation of 16:12-16.

   *a third:* Again the scope is limited but, this time, a third of humankind will be *killed*; a third, that is, of "those who did not have God's seal on their foreheads" (9:4).

16. *the number:* Note the locust swarms of Exodus and Joel (Exod 10:14; Joel 2:2-11).

   *I heard their number:* Why John draws attention to the number as he does escapes us.

17. *breastplates:* The color of the riders' armor, fiery red, smoky blue, and sulphurous yellow, matched the colors of the fire, smoke, and sulphur breathed out of the horses' mouths. See Job 41:19-21.

18-19. *these three plagues:* For the limitation of their scope, see v. 15. As background, see Wis 11:17-18.

   *the power of the horses:* Verse 19 is modeled on 9:10.

20-21. *the rest of humankind:* That is, the two-thirds of the unsealed (9:4) who had not been slain by the plague of the sixth trumpet (9:15, 18). See Ps 115:4-5, 7; Dan 5:23.

   *did not renounce the gods:* See Zech 1:4. Wis 14:22-26 gives a list of the vices and crimes that flow from idolatry and explicitly states in 14:27 that "the worship of idols not to be named is the beginning and cause and end of every evil." See Rom 1:20-32. There are similar lists of vices in Rev 21:8 and 22:15.

21. *nor did they repent:* Repentance is always God's object—ultimately, *metanoia,* radical conversion. See Wis 12:10, 19-21; Rom 2:4-5. "Like Paul in Romans 1, John believes that moral evils . . . are not the fundamental sin, but only the symptom of man's idolatry, his refusal to accept his own creaturely status and his dependence on his Creator" (Caird, 123).

### INTERPRETATION

The four angels of 9:14 are instruments of divine "wrath," God's reaction to sin and evil. The Euphrates marked the eastern frontier of the Roman Empire; beyond it lay the Parthians, the dreaded and mysterious enemy of Rome. John has the topical situation in mind, but his "cavalry" are not the Parthians but another presentation of the demonic locusts of 9:3-11. Besides, the great powers, Assyria and Babylon, which had devastated Israel, had come from beyond the Euphrates: an invasion from the east was an obvious symbol of woe for Jerusalem. See Isa 8:7, "Behold, the Lord is bringing up against them the waters of the River [Euphrates], mighty and many, the king of Assyria and all his glory." John transforms this into a symbol of woe for Rome.

The ministers of vengeance are set to carry out their task, they are ministers of a divine purpose. The vast forces at the disposal of the destroying angels numbered two hundred million: a host as great as the locust swarm of Exodus and Joel. The deadly power of the visitation lay in the three plagues—the fire, the smoke, and the sulphur—that issued from the mouths of the demonic horses. They could also wound with the bite of their serpent tails. This last detail may well be a reference to the Parthians; their mounted archers fired a volley on the charge and another, backwards, as they immediately retired. But, for John, these serpent-like horses are emissaries of Satan, "that ancient serpent" (12:9). See Wis 11:17-18, "For your all-powerful hand . . . did not lack the means to send upon them . . . newly created unknown beasts full of rage, or such as breathe out fiery breath, or belch forth a thick pall of smoke, or flash terrible sparks from their eyes." There are other indications that John may have known the Book of Wisdom.

The motivation of the plagues is not vindictiveness; they are a summons to *metanoia.* But, as with Pharaoh, this purpose was not achieved: humankind did not repent. See Wis 12:20, "You used such care and such indulgence even in punishing your children's enemies who deserved to die, granting them time and opportunity to win free of their wickedness"; Rom 2:4-5, "Do you presume upon the riches of his kindness and forbearance and patience? Do you not know that God's kindness is meant to lead you to repentance?"

The biblical view is that idolatry is the root of all evil. The first temptation is to be like God; the first sin is to act accordingly. The human being
is creature and can never be other. Our destiny—the glorious status of
children of God—is achieved only with God, never in defiance of him.
The generous Father, who yearns for our salvation, summons us to
*metanoia*. This means, above all, turning from our "idolatry," from our
vain endeavors to go it alone. We become what our God wants us to be
in his way and together with him, not otherwise.

## 22. *The Open Scroll* (Ch. 10)

1. Then I saw another mighty angel coming down from heaven, wrapped
in a cloud, with a rainbow over his head: his face was like the sun, and
his legs like pillars of fire. 2. He held in his hand a little scroll which
was open. He set his right foot on the sea and his left on the land. 3.
Then he gave a great shout like the roar of a lion; and when he shouted
the seven thunders spoke out. 4. When the seven thunders had spoken, I was about to write, but I heard a voice from heaven saying, "Seal
up what the seven thunders have said; do not write it down." 5. Then
the angel I saw standing on the sea and the land raised his right hand
towards heaven, 6. and swore by him who lives for ever and ever, who
created heaven and everything in it, earth and everything in it, sea and
everything in it, that there would be no more delay. 7. When the time
comes for the seventh angel to blow his trumpet, the hidden purpose
of God will have been accomplished, as he proclaimed to his servants
the prophets.

8. Then the voice which I had heard from heaven was speaking to
me again and saying, "Go, take the scroll which is open in the hand
of the angel who stands on the sea and the land." 9. I went to the angel
and asked him to give me the little scroll. He said to me: "Take it, and
eat it. It will turn your stomach sour, but in your mouth it will taste sweet
as honey." 10. I took the little scroll from the angel's hand and ate it,
and it was sweet as honey in my mouth, but when I swallowed it my
stomach turned sour. 11. Then I was told: "Once again you must
prophesy over many peoples and nations and tongues and kings."

## NOTES

1. *then I saw:* John is no longer in heaven (4:1) but on earth; he saw an angel
   "coming down from heaven."

   *another mighty angel:* That is, not one of the seven trumpet angels, nor any
   of the four of 9:14 (see 7:2; 14:6, 8-9, 15, 17-18). For "mighty" see Dan 4:13;

Rev 5:2; 18:21. Significantly, the "mighty angel" of 5:2 is the one who issued the challenge to open the sealed scroll. Only three angels are called "mighty" (5:2; 10:1; 18:21).

*cloud . . . rainbow . . . sun:* Cloud is the heavenly vehicle (see Dan 7:13; Ps 104:3; Rev 1:7; 11:12; 14:14). Rainbow, from the sun-brightness of his face against the cloud (see Ezek 1:28), evokes God's promise to Noah (see 4:3). In 1:16 the face of the "one in human form" shone like the sun. The angel bears the delegated attributes of deity but is also the angel of Jesus Christ.

*pillars of fire:* Dan 10:6; the description may contain a reference to Exod 14:19, 24. In short, this mighty angel, reflecting the divine glory, is spokesperson of God's saving purpose.

2. *a little scroll (biblaridion):* The diminutive, though found three times in the chapter (vv. 2, 9, 10), is not significant; it is used interchangeably with *biblion* in v. 8.

*which was open:* Here is the real contrast with the sealed scroll of 5:1 (see Ezek 2:9).

*sea . . . land:* A message for the whole earth—"sea and land."

3. *like the roar of a lion:* Because a "loud voice" is commonplace in Revelation, the voice of this mighty angel has to be expressed in more impressive terms. His call was a signal, at once answered by the call of the "seven thunders."

*seven thunders:* The voice of God. See Ps 29:3, "The voice of the Lord is upon the waters; the God of glory thunders"; Jer 25:30, "The Lord will roar from on high . . . against all the inhabitants of the earth"; see John 12:28-29.

4. *seal up . . . :* See Dan 8:26, "Seal up the vision, for it pertains to many days hence." John is bidden, by a heavenly voice (see 14:2, 13; 18:4), to seal the message communicated to him, a message concerning events yet in the future. The purpose of the sealing of the message of the seven thunders is not immediately clear. It may be to insist that John, though he provides a revelation of Jesus Christ (1:1), is not privy to the whole of divine knowledge. Alternatively, it seems that, in this context, the "seven thunders" might be understood to speak a message of doom; the command to "seal up" means that God has cancelled the doom. See Jonah 3:10; Mark 13:20.

5. *raised his right hand towards heaven:* The angel, already standing on sea and land, now raises his right hand to heaven (standard gesture in oath-taking); he touches the three parts of the universe because he is going to swear by him who created them. See Dan 12:7; Deut 32:40.

6. *who created . . . :* God is ever Creator; his secret purpose must be in harmony with his overall purpose for creation.

*no more delay:* The declaration stands in conscious contrast to Dan 12:7, "that it would be for a time, two times, and half a time" before all should be accomplished. Or it might be John's reinterpretation of the text. He wrote to warn of "what must shortly come to pass" (1:1). There had been the delay of the seals and the trumpets, with God giving opportunity of repentance (see 2 Pet 3:9); now "the hidden purpose of God" is to be accomplished.

7. *hidden purpose of God,* lit. "mystery": See Rev 1:20; 17:5, 7. The sounding of the seventh trumpet will herald the end (11:15-19).

   *proclaimed to his servants the prophets:* See Amos 3:7, "Surely the Lord God does nothing without revealing his secret to his servants the prophets." God "proclaimed," lit. "evangelized (*euēngelisen*)" the mystery to the prophets. This refers to the "gospel (*euangelion*)" of 14:6; we shall see that the passages correspond. John, of course, envisages Christian prophets—"martyrs" in effect.

8. *Go, take the scroll (biblion):* Again (see 1:1) John is commissioned; his mission unfolds in chs. 12–22.

9. *take . . . and eat:* Inspired by Ezek 3:13, a prophetic investiture; eating the scroll symbolizes the prophet's digesting of the message which he has to transmit. In Ezekiel, though the book was sweet in the mouth, its contents, with regard to Israel, were full of "dirges and laments and words of woe" (2:9-10).

10. *mouth . . . stomach:* For Ezekiel (3:1-3) his mission of prophet of judgment was congenial—"in my mouth as sweet as honey." For John, the task is bittersweet. This, however, may be implicit in Ezekiel; see 3:14, "I went in bitterness . . . the hand of the Lord being strong upon me." See Jer 15:16-18. Every word of God, even the proclamation of judgment, is at once word of grace and of challenge. "Every person who struggles to preach and teach the word of God knows this taste, this satisfaction, and this sickness in the stomach" (Boring, 142).

11. *I was told,* lit. "they say to me" (*legousin moi*): A plural of indefinite statement.

    *once again you must prophesy:* The renewed commission to prophesy (vv. 8-10) is made explicit. He is to "prophesy over" (*epi*): "The Seer was not sent to prophesy in their presence . . . nor against them . . . but simply with a view to their several cases" (Swete, 132).

    *peoples . . . nations . . . tongues . . . kings:* See 3:4; 6:25; 7:14; see Rev 5:9; 14:6. The "kings" are especially those mentioned in 17:10, 12 (Charles, 1:269). Contrast Ezek 3:11, "Go . . . to your people."

## INTERPRETATION

Traditionally, this scroll has been designated the "little scroll." True enough, it is called a *biblaridion* (v. 2); yet, by verse 8, it has become a *biblion.* More to the point, it is an *open* scroll. In 5:2 the invitation of a "mighty angel" led to the opening of the sealed scroll: there is a parallel between angels and scroll of chapter 5 and chapter 10, but the differences are marked. The angel of chapter 10, with traits also of the "son of man" of Daniel (Dan 7:13), is more majestic than the other; of gigantic stature, he stands on sea and land (see Exod 20:4, 11; Ps 69:34) because his message is for all of humankind. Significantly, the angel who is entrusted with the open scroll is by far the most impressive angelic figure of this angel-studded book. This scroll has an importance beyond its size. Where the visions of the first, sealed scroll are obscure and veiled, the visions to follow are more forcefully depicted and in greater detail—it is an *open* scroll.

In apocalyptic, visions which are sealed are messages, communicated by God, which will be fulfilled only in the distant future. That is precisely why we read in Rev 22:10, "Do not seal up the words of the prophecy of this book, *for the time is near*"; this message is about to be fulfilled. On the other hand, in 10:4, as in Daniel, John is bidden, by a heavenly voice (see 14:2, 13; 18:4), to seal the message communicated to him. It is typical of John's paradoxical style that the seer is instructed to seal up what he had not written. Always, it is the idea that mattters—but the idea here is not immediately clear. The observation of G. B. Caird is provocative: "Treated as an integral part of its context, the sealing has a weighty theological meaning. If God's prophet is ordered not to write down what he has heard the seven thunders say, but to seal it away, this can only mean that God had canceled the doom of which they were the symbol. . . . Humanity must be stopped forthwith from endlessly producing the means of its own torment and destruction. 'If the Lord had not cut short the time, not a living creature could have escaped' (Mark 13:20)" (126f.).

In Rev 10:5-7 the angel solemnly swears that "there shall be no more delay." Dan 12:4-9 provides a key. Daniel was ordered to seal up the revelations he had received, and the angel swore by the Creator that they would be accomplished after a certain delay ("a time, two times, and half a time," that is, three and a half years, the time of tribulation). John, in contrast, will proclaim the contents of the scroll (v. 11): the earlier situation has been transformed.

The heavenly voice which had ordered John not to seal the message of the seven thunders now bids him take the open scroll from the angel. The angel's words are inspired by Ezek 3:1-3, a prophetic investiture; the eating of the scroll symbolizes the prophet's digesting of the message which he has to transmit. This message is bitter-sweet: sweet because it proclaims the triumph of the Church, bitter because it must include the sufferings of Christians.

This marks a new prophetical investiture, distinct from that of 1:9-20. John must "again" prophesy, and this time about "many peoples and nations and tongues and kings." In other words, he is called to a fresh mission: he must prophesy as he had not done up to now. Where the mission of Ezekiel had been restricted to the house of Israel (Ezek 3:4-5), John's mission breaks out of this restriction and is more like that of Jeremiah, who stands as the prophet to the nations (see Jer 1:10).

The command to John, "Seal up what the seven thunders have said," may be akin to the divine declaration after the Flood: "I will never again curse the ground because of men, neither will I ever again destroy every living creature as I have done" (Gen 8:21). In the Flood story we see the holy God's radical incompatibility with evil—his grief over human sin. On the other hand, he has decided to put up with humankind's tendency to evil, "for the imagination of man's heart is evil from his youth" (Gen 8:21). His forbearance will wear down that resistance to his love.

To be a witness to Christ is a life-long task. To be a prophet, Christ's spokesperson, is a challenging task. There is, indeed, the privilege of service, but the cost is high. Every person who strives to preach and teach the word of God knows at once fulfillment and frustration. There is no more worthwhile service. But one must feel the pain that ripples through the pages of the New Testament, the pain of the preachers of the good news: that the word is not heeded.

FOR REFERENCE AND FURTHER STUDY

Bergmeier, R. "Die Buchrolle und das Lamm (Apk 5 und 10)." *ZNW* 76 (1985) 225–42.
Michael, J. H. "The Unrecorded Thunder-Voices (Apc 1:3)." *ExpTim* 36 (1924–25) 424–27.

## 23. *The Temple Measured* (11:1-2)

1. Then I was given a cane to use as a measuring rod, and was told: "Go and measure the temple of God and the altar and those who worship there. 2. But leave out the outer court of the temple and do not measure it; for it has been given over to the Gentiles, and they will trample over the holy city for forty-two months."

### NOTES

1. *a cane to use as a measuring rod:* See Ezek 40:3; Zech 2:1-2. "Cane," lit. "reed," serves as a surveyor's rule; Ezechiel's reed was of six cubits, about nine feet. The measuring of the temple is the first exercise of the fresh prophetic investiture (9:8-11).

*temple (naos):* Stands for the whole of the temple precincts, except for the outer court, the court of the Gentiles.

*those who worship there:* the measuring of worshipers is patent symbolism.

2. *the outer court:* In parallel fashion, this outer court also includes people. Not measured = left unprotected.

*leave out (ekbale exōthen),* lit. "cast out": "Temple" and "outer court" represent, respectively, the Church in its inward being (analogous to "the woman" of 12:6) and the Church in its earthly, empirical existence (see 12:17).

*the holy city:* Here, the earthly Church, which yet, as the heavenly Jerusalem (21:2-4) will also be "measured" (21:15).

*trample . . . for forty-two months:* This "forty-two" months is nothing else than the "time, two times and half a time" of Dan 7:25, that is, three and a half years, the approximate duration of the persecution of Antiochus IV, and hence a symbol of a time of trial (see Rev 11:3; 12:6, 14; 13:5).

### INTERPRETATION

The episode of the measuring of the temple is not unlike the sealing of the servants of God (7:4-8). John himself becomes an actor in the drama he witnesses and is bidden measure the temple he sees in vision. What is thus measured is under God's special protection, as in Ezekiel and in Zechariah. In Revelation protection means support in and through suffering and death (see 7:1-8). The measuring not only of temple and altar but also of worshipers underlines the fact that we are dealing with symbols. "Temple" is the Christian community who worships God; see 1 Cor 3:16-17. The "measuring" of the temple is a variant of the "sealing" of the Church in 7:1-8.

In contrast, the "trampling" of the holy city is the great tribulation. So we have the paradox that, on the one hand, the community will be sheltered and, on the other hand, the unprotected community will be trampled. The disciple is not greater than the master. The triumph of Jesus occurred through suffering and death. Again we are reminded that the slain Lamb, who yet lives, is the Christological focus of the book and the model of its ecclesiology.

The passage offers a salutary warning that the firm promise of the endurance of the Church in face of any and every assault, even the most insidious assault of apathy, does not cover the vulnerability of Christians. Harassed Christians will have reason to ask, accusingly, as did the disciples in Mark's storm-tossed boat, "Teacher, do you not care if we perish?" (Mark 4:38). Christians may feel that the Lord has no care for them, has abandoned them, and the Church may seem to be at the mercy of the forces pitted against it. One might argue that Revelation was written to meet just such a situation, written to bolster the encouraging declaration of Christ, "Have confidence, I have overcome the world" (John 16:33).

## For Reference and Further Study

Feuillet, A. "Essai d'interprétation du chapitre xi de l'Apocalypse." *NTS* 4 (1957–58) 183–200.
Giblin, C. H. "Revelation 11:1-13—its Form, Function and Contextual Integration." *NTS* 30 (1984) 433–59.

## 24. *The Two Witnesses* (11:3-14)

3. And I will commission my two witnesses to prophesy for those one thousand two hundred and sixty days, dressed in sackcloth.

4. These are the two olive-trees and the two lamps that stand before the Lord of the earth. 5. If anyone tries to harm them, fire comes out of their mouths and consumes their enemies; so shall be killed anyone who tries to harm them. 6. They have power to shut up the sky so that no rain may fall during the time of their prophesying; and they have power to turn water into blood and to strike the earth with every kind of plague as they wish.

7. But when they have completed their testimony, the beast that comes up from the abyss will wage war on them and will overcome them and kill them. 8. Their corpses will lie in the street of the great city which is figuratively called Sodom and Egypt, where also their Lord was crucified. 9. And people from every nation and tribe and tongue and race will stare at their corpses for three and a half days and will not permit their corpses to be placed in a tomb. 10. The inhabitants of the earth gloat over them; they celebrate and send gifts to one another, for these two prophets were a torment to the inhabitants of the earth. 11. But after the three and a half days, a breath of life from God came into them, and they stood up on their feet, and a great dread fell upon those who beheld them. 12. Then they heard a loud voice from heaven saying to them, "Come up here!" And they ascended to heaven in a cloud, in full view of their enemies. 13. And in that hour there was a great earthquake, and a tenth of the city fell. Seven thousand people were killed in the earthquake; the rest were terrified and gave glory to the God of heaven.

14. The second woe has passed; but the third is coming soon.

## Notes

3. *I will commission* (lit. "I will give to") *my two witnesses:* The speaker is Christ; see 2:13; 21:6. *Two* witnesses springs from Deut 19:15. In v. 10 they become "two prophets": their mission is to prophesy, and their prophetic mission

will involve their death (v. 7). The two witnesses appear abruptly; the passage 11:3-13 is unlike anything encountered hitherto.

*one thousand two hundred and sixty days:* The duration of the ministry of the two prophets (forty-two lunar months) is the same as the duration of the time of the Gentiles (11:20), the whole time of the Church (12:6, 14). These witnesses represent the Church in its function of witness-bearing; see Acts 1:8, 22; 2:32.

*sackcloth:* A reference to the rough costume of ancient prophets (see 2 Kgs 1:8; Mark 1:6), a sign that the witnesses were to preach a message of repentance (*metanoia*).

4. *olive-trees . . . lamps:* See Zech 4:2-3, 11-14. In Zechariah the lampstand is Israel and the olive trees are Zerubbabel the Davidic prince ("king") and Joshua the high priest, the "two anointed ones who stand by the Lord of the whole earth" (Zech 2:14).

5-6. The two witnesses are symbolic figures based on Old Testament models: the "two olive trees" of Zechariah (Rev 11:4), and here Moses and Elijah. In late Judaism it was believed that Elijah and Moses (the "prophet-like-Moses," Deut 18:15-18) would usher in the eschatological age. It was a view assimilated by early Christianity (see Mark 9:2-13; Luke 1:15-17; 4:25-26; 7:11-17; John 1:21); our text follows this line.

*fire comes out of their mouths:* See Num 16:35; 2 Kgs 1:10. It is noteworthy that Jesus rebuked James and John for desiring to emulate Elijah, calling down destructive fire from heaven (Luke 9:54-55). One suspects that Jer 5:14 may be more immediate to John: "Behold, I am making my words in your mouth a fire, and this people wood, and the fire shall devour them." Even more apposite is Ben Sira: "Elijah, a prophet like fire, whose word flamed like a torch" (Sir 48:1).

*power to shut up the sky . . . to turn water into blood:* Obvious references to Elijah (1 Kgs 17:1) and Moses (Exod 7:14-25).

*during the time of their prophesying:* That is, three and a half years (v. 3). The drought proclaimed by Elijah is for "three years" (1 Kgs 17:1). Revelation reflects a tradition also found in Luke 4:25 and Jas 5:17.

7. *when they have completed their testimony:* "Completed"—"fulfilled" (*telesōsin*).

*the beast that comes up from the abyss:* Abruptly introduced here (a stylistic trait of John) and explained in 13:1-8. "Coming up from the abyss" is a permanent characteristic of the beast.

*kill them:* The witnesses are "two lamps" out of the seven (1:20): John did not expect all loyal Christians to die in the great tribulation. The "two witnesses" are the "victors" of the messages.

8. *their corpses will lie:* The bodies will lie unburied (see Jer 8:2; Tob 1:17; 2 Macc 5:10) in the street of the "great city" (v. 9). A recollection of the "dishonorable" burial of Jesus (Mark 15:46)? "Corpses" (*ptōma*)—singular as in v. 9a; perhaps the collective singular, viewing the witnesses as a corporate entity; v. 9b, however, has *ptōmata*—plural.

*which is figuratively called Sodom and Egypt,* lit. "allegorically" (*pneumatikos*): John has gone out of his way to underline the symbolic character of the "great city," which can only be Rome (16:19; 18:10, 16, 18-19, 21; see 14:8; 16:19; 17:5; 18:2).

*where also their Lord was crucified:* Points to Jerusalem, but an "allegorical" Jerusalem. It is noteworthy that in Isa 1:10; 3:9, Jerusalem is called Sodom, and in Wis 19:14 Sodom is linked with Egypt. Paul asserts that Jesus was crucified by "the powers that ruled the world" (1 Cor 2:6-8). "The city is heir to the vice of 'Sodom,' the tyranny of Pharaoh's 'Egypt' and the blind disobedience of 'Jerusalem' " (Caird, 138). This sweeping designation of the "great city" might well alert us to the subtlety and fluidity of John's imagery throughout.

9. *people from every nation:* Another indication that the "great city" is not histori-cal Jerusalem but Rome; witness had been borne by the symbolical "two wit-nesses" throughout the Empire.

   *for three and a half days:* In place of three and a half years: a brief triumph. Recalls the "three days" of Jesus before resurrection; see v. 11.

10. *gloat . . . send gifts:* "The delight of the spectators is represented as at once fiendish and childish" (Swete, 138). John 16:20 speaks of the joy of "the world" at Jesus' death; *kosmos* (in a pejorative sense) is, in the Fourth Gospel and 1 John, equivalent to "the inhabitants of the earth" in Revelation.

    *torment:* Compare Elijah "troubler of Israel" (1 Kgs 18:17; 21:20)—the role of the prophet/witnesses in the eyes of those who reject them. See Wis 2:12-20: the just man is "a living condemnation of all our way of thinking. The very sight of him is an affliction to us" (2:14-15).

11. *a breath of life from God:* See Ezek 37:10, "So I prophesied as he commanded me, and the breath came into them, and they lived and stood upon their feet." John thinks of the "resurrection" of Ezekiel 37 but, beyond it, he has in mind the "Lamb standing as though it had been slain" (5:6), "the firstborn of the dead" (1:5). The beast will not have the last word over the witnesses, any more than the dragon had over their Lord (12:5). Note, too, the "first resur-rection" of 20:4-6. See 1 Thess 4:16-17.

    *a great dread:* Gloating quickly turns to consternation. See Matt 28:4.

12. *a loud voice:* Summoned by a heavenly voice (surely that of their Lord) they receive the recompense of their faithful witness.

    *they ascended to heaven in a cloud:* As it was for their Lord, the resurrection of the witnesses is followed by their ascension; and, like the Lord, "they went up to heaven in a cloud" (see Acts 1:9). We are to recall that Elijah "went up by a whirlwind into heaven" (2 Kgs 2:11) and that, according to Jewish tradition, Moses was removed from the sight of his followers by a cloud (see Josephus, *Ant.*, 6. 8. 48).

13. *a great earthquake:* See 6:12; Ezek 38:19-20—a familiar symbol of divine punish-ment. Here, unlike the earthquake of 6:12-14, the chastisement is mitigated: a tenth of the city fell. Caird observes intriguingly: "the death and vindica-

tion of the martyrs is itself the earthquake shock by which the great city is overthrown'' (139).

*seven thousand people:* The number is surely symbolic; the Elijah background may suggest a key. In 1 Kgs 19:18 the faithful are seven thousand; John, ironically, has seven thousand false witnesses die. Both the visible triumph of the two witnesses (''in full view of their enemies,'' v. 12) and this mitigated punishment were meant to bring people to their senses.

*were terrified (emphoboi):* Hopeless terror, or repentance? The passages 14:7 and 15:4 firmly indicate the positive alternative.

*gave glory to the God of heaven:* The phrase expresses repentance regularly in the Old Testament.

14. *second woe . . . third woe:* The second woe is the sixth trumpet (9:13-21); the third woe is never clearly identified.

### INTERPRETATION

The two witnesses—who emerge abruptly here, and are not mentioned again after this passage—represent the Church in its function of witness-bearing; see Acts 1:8, ''You shall be my witnesses in Jerusalem . . . and to the ends of the earth.'' Acts describes the preaching to Israel: the apostles are witnesses to Christ who must proclaim the events of his life from the baptism of John to the ascension of Jesus, especially the crowning event of the resurrection (Acts 1:22; 2:32). Their preaching is accompanied by ''signs'' (Mark 16:17; Acts 4:30; 5:12; 8:6-8). They meet with hostility (Acts 4:2-3; 5:17-18) like the Old Testament prophets (Luke 11:47-50; Acts 7:51-52), but they are aided by the Holy Spirit (Acts 4:27-31) and even miraculously delivered from death (5:19-21; 12:1-17). All of this is verified in the ministry of the two witnesses. ''The number 'two,' like the number seven, symbolizes the whole community and recalls the principle of two witnesses (Deut 19:15) as well as two functions of the church, priesthood and kingship'' (Krodel, 223).

John freely adapts the text of Zechariah 4: now the two olive trees and two lamps (Zechariah, ''seven lamps'') represent his two witnesses. ''King'' and ''priest,'' both ''anointed ones,'' represent the Church, a ''royal house of priests'' (Rev 1:6; 5:10). As ''two lamps'' out of the ''seven lamps'' of the universal Church (1:20), these witnesses are those faithful Christians whose faithfulness will entail the shedding of their blood. The witnesses cannot be silenced as long as their ministry lasts; those who try to stifle them will bring destruction on themselves. Like the Lamb (1:16), the word is the only weapon they hold and wield.

The witnesses are protected and immune from danger as long as their allotted time of office lasts, that is, for three and a half years (11:13), the duration of the Church right up to the moment of the great final assault.

Their death (and glorification) is to occur at the end of the present epoch. The "beast that comes up from the abyss" is the great persecuting power, instrument of Satan. That this verse (11:7) is best understood in terms of the final assault on the Church is seen from its close correspondence with 20:7-8, "When the thousand years are ended, Satan will be let loose from his prison, and he will come out to deceive the nations." Rev 20:7-9 depicts the final Satan-inspired rebellion of the nations against "the camp of God's people and the beloved city"; but the enemy forces are destroyed by fire from heaven (20:9; see 11:5). In ch. 20 the assault is followed by judgment (20:11-15); the last judgment also figures in 11:18.

As an added indignity, the witnesses' bodies will remain unburied and will be left to lie in the street of "the great city." In the context of Revelation this can only be Rome, here "allegorically" designated Sodom, Egypt, and, by implication, Jerusalem. "The great city in Revelation is . . . not a geographic location but a symbolic place. Its essential characteristic lies in the allegorical label of 'Sodom and Egypt.' . . . In short, Jerusalem, Babylon, and Rome are fused by John into one single entity, 'the great city' " (Krodel, 226). The whole empire will rejoice, but exultation of the beast and his followers is ephemeral. The beast will not have the last word over these witnesses any more than the dragon had over their Lord (12:5).

The number of people killed in the earthquake (seven thousand) is surely symbolic. Both the visible triumph of the two witnesses and this mitigated punishment were meant to bring people to their senses. If the survivors were "terrified," this "terror" nudged them to repentance. All in all, v. 13 does suggest that the faithful witness unto death of the witness-prophets achieved what the punitive plagues had failed to bring about. Rightly so, because the only Christian victory is the Cross (7:14). The only weapon of the Lamb is the word, the "sword of his mouth" (1:16; 19:15). As Paul came to understand, that "word of the cross" is the very "power of God" (1 Cor 1:8).

"Jesus Christ, the faithful witness" (1:5) bore courageous witness before Jewish religious authority and Roman procurator—and paid the price. The "two witnesses" stand for his faithful ones who are prepared to walk his way and, like him, pay the price. They earn the hatred of "the beast that comes up from the abyss." We, as Christians, are urged to be witnesses in our turn. In our Western world at least (it is not so elsewhere) we may have little fear that we will be summarily slaughtered and our bodies left to lie where we fall. By and large, our witness is so discreet that "the inhabitants of the earth" are not troubled. We, for the most part, blend decently into the background of our culture; we are wholly respectable. John would not rate our Christian witness very highly. Nor, one fears, does he who walks among the lamps!

FOR REFERENCE AND FURTHER STUDY

Considine, J. S. "The Two Witnesses, Apoc 11:3-13." *CBQ* 8 (1946) 377–92.
Reddish, M. G. "Martyr Christology in the Apocalypse." *JSNT* 33 (1988) 85–95.
Robinson, B. P. "The Two Persecuted Prophet-Witnesses of Rev 11." *ScrB* 19 (1988) 14–19.
Seng, H. "Apk 11:1-14 im Zusammenhang der Johannesapokalypse: Aufschluss aus Lactantius und Hippolytos." *VetChrist* 27 (1990) 111–21.
Strand, K. A. "The Two Witnesses of Rev 11:3-12." *AUSS* 19 (1981) 377–92.

## 25. *The Seventh Trumpet* (11:15-19)

15. Then the seventh angel blew his trumpet, and there were loud voices in heaven saying, The sovereignty of the world has passed to our Lord and to his Christ, and he shall reign for ever and ever. 16. The twenty-four elders, who sit on their thrones before God, fell on their faces and worshiped God, 17. saying,

> We give you thanks, Lord God Almighty,
>> who are and who was,
>>> because you have assumed your full power and entered on your reign.

18.     The nations rose in wrath,
> but your wrath has come.
> Now is the time for the dead to be judged
>> and for rewarding your servants the prophets,
>> and your people, and those who fear your name,
>> both small and great,
>> and to destroy the destroyers of the earth.

19. Then God's sanctuary in heaven was opened, and the ark of the covenant was seen in his sanctuary; and there came flashes of lightning and peals of thunder and an earthquake and heavy hail.

### NOTES

15. *loud voices in heaven:* Contrast the liturgical silence of 8:1; this heavenly liturgy (vv. 15-18) corresponds to that of 7:9-12. It closes the eschatological drama of the trumpets.

*the sovereignty of the world,* lit. "the kingdom of the world": In John 14:30 Satan is "the ruler of this world."

*he shall reign:* Singular, although the sovereignty has passed to "the Lord and his Christ," see 12:10; 19:6, 16. Another instance of the assimilation of

Lamb to God; the rule of God and Christ is one. "The rightful sovereign of the universe who has always been king *de iure,* has now become king in fact" (Boring, 148).

17. *who are and who was:* See 1:4, 8; 4:8. But now there is no "who is to come": God *has* taken his power and begun to reign.

18. *rose in wrath . . . wrath (ōrgisthēsan . . . orgē):* Word-play—the futile violence of humans is answered by the effective judgments of God. See Ps 2:1.

    *the time for the dead to be judged:* This proleptic judgment-scene (vv. 15-18) anticipates the final judgment (20:11-15). The nations "who rose in wrath" are those of Ps 2.

    *destroyers of the earth:* See 19:15-21; 20:9-10. King of the demonic hosts is Abaddon/Apollyon—"the destroyer" (9:11). The ultimate "destroyers" are the beast and the dragon. At the End, they will be destroyed (19:17-21; 20:7-10).

19. *God's sanctuary in heaven:* Not only the heavenly temple but its holy of holies is thrown open: the ark of the covenant is visible to all! But, note Rev 15:8.

    *the ark:* The ark, symbol of God's presence, disappeared in the destruction of Solomon's Temple by Nebuchadnezzar in 587 B.C.E. A Jewish legend, reflected in 2 Macc 2:4-8, represents Jeremiah as having hidden both ark and altar of incense against the day of Israel's restoration. He declared that the hiding-place was to remain unknown "until God gathers his people together again and shows his mercy, And then the Lord will disclose these things, and the glory of the Lord will appear" (2:7-8).

    *flashes of lightning . . . .:* Typically, cosmic phenomena accompany a theophany. Each plague septet ends with similar cosmic manifestations: see 8:5; 11:19; 16:17-21.

### INTERPRETATION

The seventh trumpet which follows, without delay, the announcement of the third woe (v. 14) may, perhaps, be that third woe. In point of fact, unlike the other two, the "third woe" is nowhere clearly designated. After a typical liturgical introduction (11:15-19), the trumpet signals what is, ostensibly, Satan's final triumph—in reality his downfall. In contrast to the silence that followed the opening of the seventh seal (8:1), the sound of the last trumpet is answered by loud voices of praise in heaven—the voices not only of elders, living creatures, and angelic choirs (4:8; 5:11-12) but also, surely, of the "vast throng" (7:9-10). The canticle of 11:17-18 is put in the mouth of the twenty-four elders. These elders thank and glorify God who has at last manifested his almighty power: the kingdom of God has come. Until now God is he "who is, who was, and who is to come" (1:4, 8; 4:8). But here there is no "who is to come" (see 16:5): he has come, his reign has begun.

The close of the second prophetic part of Revelation, a scene of final judgment (20:11-15), corresponds to the proleptic judgment-scene of 11:15-18. The time has come for judging, for rewarding, and for destroying. Three classes receive reward: the prophets, God's faithful people, and those who fear God's name. In view of v. 13 it would appear that these last are or at least include those who finally repented and did homage to God. The "destroyers of the earth" are not to be confused with the "inhabitants of the earth," who are human dupes of the *destroyers:* the dragon and the beasts. The "wrath" of God is aimed primarily at the "destroyers"; it is only when they are at last removed that humankind can finally be at rest.

Again in proleptic vision, the holy of holies of the heavenly temple is thrown open and the ark of the covenant is visible to all. The fulfillment will come in the new Jerusalem when God will dwell with humankind (21:3). In the meantime we will find, in 15:8, that the sanctuary will be closed during the unleashing of the final plagues. But here, as assurance to the faithful, the open temple finds a remarkably apposite parallel in Heb 10:19: "Therefore, brothers and sisters, we have confidence to enter the sanctuary by the blood of Jesus." Christians have full confidence to "draw near to the throne of grace" (Heb 4:16). That assurance, in Hebrews no less than in Revelation, is founded on "the Lamb who was slain." The ark is visible, the glory of the Lord has appeared (see 2 Macc 2:7-8). Now is the end: the kingdom has come. The glory of the Lord has appeared, not for Israel's restoration, but in universal sovereignty.

"Our God reigns!" That is our Christian conviction. We sing our faith in the teeth of an incredulous world. Our claim is not triumphalist, or ought not be. The kingdom of God "is a new world in which suffering is abolished, a world of completely whole or healed men and women in a society where peace reigns and there are no master-servant relationships" (E. Schillebeeckx, *Church: The Human Story of God* [London: SCM, 1990] 116). Can we honestly claim, given this definition of the kingdom, a description faithful to the subversive message of Jesus, that God reigns in our Church—quite apart from his status in the "world" in which we live?

## VI. THE WOMAN AND THE DRAGON

### 26. *The Woman and the Dragon* (12:1-6)

1. A great sign appeared in heaven: a woman robed with the sun, with the moon under her feet, and on her head a crown of twelve stars. 2. She was with child, and she cried out in her pangs of birth, in anguish to be delivered. 3. Then a second sign appeared in heaven: a great red dragon with seven heads and ten horns and seven diadems on his heads, 4. and his tail swept down a third of the stars of heaven and hurled them to the earth. The dragon stood before the woman who was about to give birth, so that when her child was born he might devour it. 5. And she gave birth to a son, a male child, who is destined to rule all the nations with a rod of iron; but her child was snatched up to God and to his throne. 6. The woman fled into the desert, where she had a place prepared by God that there she might be sustained for twelve hundred and sixty days.

### NOTES

1. *a great sign:* A new vision described as a *sēmeion* ("sign," "portent"), a term proper to this second part of Revelation (12:1, 3; 13:13-14; 15:1; 16:14; 19:20).

   *a woman:* This woman is surely the bride, the heavenly Jerusalem (19:7-8; 21:9-10), antithesis of the harlot (Rome) (17:14; 18:16).

   *sun . . . moon . . . stars:* Attributes of the high goddess of ancient mythology—John's background is complex. The mother goddess, queen of heaven, was worshiped in the cities of Asia. John may be suggesting that the Woman here is the true Queen of Heaven.

2. *with child:* See Gen 3:16; Isa 66:7-8; Mic 4:10.

3-4a. *a great red dragon:* See Gen 3; Wis 2:24. The dragon is "fiery red" (see 6:4), the color of bloodshed and murder. See John 8:44.

   *heads . . . horns . . . diadems:* Many-headed monsters are mentioned in Ps 74:13-15; ten horns are worn by the fourth beast of Dan 7:7. In contrast to the "diadems" here are the "many diadems" of the rider on the white horse (19:12)—the Christ who is truly "King of kings and Lord of lords" (19:16).

   *a third of the stars of heaven:* A loose rendering of Dan 8:10, "It [the little horn = Antiochus IV] grew great even to the host of heaven; and some of the host of the stars it cast down to the ground, and trampled upon them."

4b-5. *the dragon stood before the woman:* As in the retelling of Genesis 3, the woman and serpent/dragon are face to face.

*he might devour it:* See Jer 51:34, "[The inhabitants of Zion] say, 'Nebuchadnezzar the king of Babylon has devoured me, he has crushed me; . . . he has swallowed me like a monster.'"

*a son, a male child:* See Isa 66:7 (LXX): the Messiah, explicitly identified by reference to Ps 2:9.

*to rule all the nations: poimainein,* "to shepherd," can also mean "to smash"; see 2:27. Ps 2:9, "You shall break them [the nations] with a rod of iron, and dash them in pieces like a potter's vessel." For John, the rule of the Lamb is a shepherding. See 7:17.

*snatched up to God:* Reference to the ascension (see Acts 1:9, "he was lifted up"; 2:33-35) and the triumph of Christ, which will bring about the fall of the dragon.

6. *the woman fled into the desert:* In the Old Testament, wilderness is a traditional place of refuge for the persecuted (Exod 2:15; 1 Kgs 17:2-3; 19:3-4; 1 Macc 2:29-30); more immediately, John has the Exodus in view (see v. 14). "Desert" is an excellent example of the ambivalence of symbols, for it too regularly has a negative significance.

*sustained,* lit. "fed," "nourished" (*trephein*): Recalls the manna. See also Elijah (2 Kgs 17:4).

## INTERPRETATION

Revelation 12 is based on two sources: a narrative describing the conflict between a pregnant woman and a dragon (vv. 1-6, 13-17) and a narrative depicting a battle in heaven (vv. 7-12)—a sandwich-technique reminiscent of the style of Mark.

Many parallels may be found in the Old Testament and other Jewish texts to individual elements of chapter 12. The closest parallel, however, to the narrative of the woman and the dragon is a Graeco-Roman version of the legend of Apollo's birth. Leto had become pregnant by Zeus. The dragon Python foresaw that this child, a son, would replace him as ruler over the oracle at Delphi. He sought to kill the child at birth. Zeus commissioned the North wind and the sea-god Poseidon to aid Leto. She gave birth to Apollo and Artemis; Apollo slew the dragon Python. John adapted the story to describe the birth of the Messiah (Collins, "The Apocalypse," *NJBC*, 1008). But it is not his only source. He glances back at the ancient myth of the perennial threat of chaos, as well as to a current reading of Gen 3.

The woman, though first seen in a setting of splendor, is with child and close to delivery. Her birth-pangs may be those of Eve (Gen 3:16); they are, more immediately, the birth-pangs of travailing Israel. See Mic 4:10, "Writhe and groan, O daughter of Zion, like a woman in travail." In rabbinical literature "the birth-pangs of the Messiah" is a familiar phrase. Verses 5-6 identify the woman more closely. Whatever his background, and whatever the later use of the text (in Mariology), for John this woman is the heavenly Israel, depicted in terms of the woman of Gen 3. She is faced by Satan, the ancient serpent (Gen 3:1); she brings forth in anguish (3:16); her child will suffer attack by Satan (3:15). She is, all the while, the people of God who gives birth to the Messiah and the messianic age.

In stark contrast to the woman stands another sign: a great red dragon. Much earlier than the Python image is that of dragon or sea-serpent as a mythic symbol of chaos. Babylonian and Canaanite texts mention a serpentine monster with seven heads. In his text, John links the "dragon" with the "serpent" of Gen 3. Already, in a retelling of the Genesis story, the *nāḥāš* ("snake") had become "the devil" (Wis 2:24). In his reference to the sweeping down of "a third of the stars" John seeks to depict the colossal reach and vast strength of the monster. In Dan 8:10, which he surely has in mind, the "stars" are angelic representatives of pagan powers. John's text has nothing to do with a legendary "fall" of angels. It is worth observing that a reading of Gen 6:1-4 in the sense of angelic "fall" is not biblical. It goes back to 1 Enoch 6–13.

The dragon seeks to destroy the child of the woman. Her "male child" is the Messiah, explicitly identified as such by the invocation of Psalm 2. The reference is significant. The anointed king of the Psalm is addressed by God not at his birth but at his enthronement: "You are my son, today I have begotten you" (Ps 2:7). See Acts 13:33, "This he has fulfilled . . . by raising Jesus; as also it is written in the second psalm, 'Thou are my son, today I have begotten thee' "; the text is applied to the resurrection (see Rom 1:4). By the "birth" of the Messiah John does not mean the nativity but the Cross—the enthronement of Jesus. Interestingly, the idea behind this passage of Revelation is thoroughly Johannine: the death of Jesus, which is his glorification, is also the moment of the assault of Satan and of his defeat. Precisely by dying on the cross, Jesus defeated the dragon and was exalted to God's right hand. The Fourth Gospel has no temptation story at the beginning of the ministry: Satan makes his bid at its close. It is he who instigated Judas' betrayal (John 13:2, 27; see Luke 22:3). In his final discourse Jesus declared: "I will no longer talk much with you, for the ruler of this world is coming. He has no power over me" (John 14:30). Luke, who has many contacts with the Johannine tradition, reflects the same viewpoint. After the temptation story he adds, "And when the devil had ended every temptation, he departed from him until an opportune time" (Luke 4:13); the moment indicated by the "opportune time" is the moment of the passion (22:3, 53).

Meanwhile the woman—the people of God of the Old Testament who, having given Christ to the world, thereby became the Christian Church—

found refuge in the desert where God cared for her for 1,260 days. This is the equivalent of forty-two months or three and one-half years—the earthly duration of the Church. By "desert" John seems to have in mind more than an unspecified traditional place of refuge; v. 14 surely has the Exodus in view. Wilderness suggests the Sinai wandering: the desert was the place of freedom and safety after Egyptian bondage, the oppression of the dragon/Pharaoh. Besides, God's care, described as sustainment, or nourishing, recalls the manna.

To John the Church appears as a woman, pregnant with the Messiah, a woman who will become bride of the Lamb. In the here and now she is protected from the malignant design of the dragon. Jesus had spoken to Peter of "*my* Church," promising that the "gates of Hades" would not prevail against it (Matt 16:18). We share that assurance. But we must also expect that the Church will ever be an *ecclesia pressa*, a Church under fire. The dragon will be around until the end.

## 27. Victory in Heaven (12:7-12)

7. Then war broke out in heaven. Michael and his angels fought against the dragon. The dragon with his angels fought back, 8. and he did not prevail, nor had they place any more in heaven. 9. The great dragon was thrown down, that ancient serpent, who is called Devil and the Satan, the deceiver of the whole world; he was thrown down to the earth, and his angels with him.

10. And I heard a loud voice in heaven proclaim:
> Now is the salvation and power and sovereignty of our God,
> and the authority of his Christ;
> for the accuser of our brothers and sisters is driven out,
> he who accused them day and night before our God.

11. They have conquered him by the blood of the Lamb
> and by the testimony they bore,
> for love of life did not bring them to shrink from death.

12. Rejoice, then, you heavens
> and you that dwell in them!
> But woe to you, earth and sea,
> for the devil has come down to you in great fury,
> knowing that his time is short!

### NOTES

7. *Michael and his angels:* Michael, an archangel (Jude 9), captain of the angelic hosts and champion of God's people (Dan 10:21; 12:1); in Jewish tradition,

the most powerful figure after God. Here his initiative is really the initiative of God himself. Michael had come to be angelic representative of the power of goodness in the strife with evil; as such, he fights with Satan (see Jude 9). In Daniel, Michael is the protector of Israel, and struggles with the angel protector of the Persians (Dan 10:13, 21; 12:1).

*the dragon with his angels:* Not a reference to a "fall" of angels; rather, it marks the end of the adversarial role of Satan, "the accuser."

8. *nor had they place any more in heaven,* lit. "nor was their place found any more in heaven": Until now, they had a proper place in heaven. This "heaven" is the "first heaven," not the "new heaven" (Rev 21:1).

9. *thrown down:* In biblical tradition Satan appears in heaven (see Job 1:6-12; 2:1-7; Zech 3:1-5); now his role of "accuser of our brothers/sisters" (v. 10) is ended.

    *that ancient serpent:* Reference to Gen 3, heavily reinterpreted. While in Gen 3:1 the snake is a mischievous wild creature, in Wis 2:24 it has become "the devil," source of spiritual death.

    *Devil (diabolos):* "Informer," "slanderer"—"deceiver of the whole world."

    *Satan,* lit. "adversary": This is the role of Satan in Job 1–3 and Zech 3:1-5. "By identifying the 'dragon' with Satan, the devil, the ancient serpent, John shows that he intends to symbolize all the anti-God forces from Eden on, whatever they may be called" (Boring, 155).

    *deceiver of the whole world:* Satan's role is henceforth on earth (vv. 12-13). His work of deception is documented: 16:14; 20:7-8; 2 Thess 2:9-12; John 8:44.

10. The heavenly hymn (vv. 10-12) serves as a commentary on the preceding narrative. This is not Michael's victory—it is the Lord's!

    *accuser of our brothers and sisters,* lit. "the accuser of our brethren": See Job 1:6; Zech 3:1-2. Note Luke 22:31, "Simon, Simon, behold Satan demanded to have you that he might sift you like wheat." Satan demanded to have Simon as he had sought to ruin Job. Our text reflects the "prosecuting counsel" role of Satan current in the Old Testament and in Jewish tradition. The victory of Christ has brought this role to an end. Job and Zechariah testify to the role of "the Satan": to challenge the sincerity and the truth of human obedience to God. Satan has no further access to God. "Brothers/sisters" are some of the "rest of the offspring" of the woman (v. 17).

11. *they have conquered:* See 2:7; Christian victory comes through "patient endurance" in the "tribulation."

    *by the blood of the Lamb:* They ("our brothers/sisters") are those "who have come out of the great tribulation" and "have washed their robes . . . in the blood of the Lamb" (7:14). They have conquered Satan "by the blood of the Lamb": his victory is their victory too (see 5:9-10; 7:9-17). The assimilation of the martyrs to Jesus is particularly clear here and in 20:4-6.

    *love of life:* See John 12:25; Rev 2:10.

12. *rejoice:* Heaven is free of the oppressive presence of Satan.

    *woe to you, earth and sea:* Because of the establishment of the kingdom of the beast (13:1-10). Is this the third woe? See 11:14. Though "the inhabitants of the earth" will gladly follow and worship the beast (13:4), this is their path to ultimate destruction (14:9-11), a plague more terrible than any other.

*in great fury:* Smarting from his humiliating defeat, and knowing that his days are numbered, he will redouble his efforts on the stage and in the time left to him.

*his time is short:* It is the "time, and times, and half a time" of 12:14 (see v. 6).

## INTERPRETATION

The fall of the dragon is dramatized in 12:7-15 (an elaboration of vv. 4-5); and although here Michael is represented as casting Satan out of heaven, it really is the victory of Christ. Victory over Satan was won by Christ *on the cross.* The hymn of vv. 10-12 is a commentary on the narrative of vv. 7-9, 13-17. Everything that John sees in heaven is the counterpart of some earthly reality. When the victory is being won in heaven, Christ is on earth on the cross. Because he is part of the earthly reality, he cannot at the same time be part of the heavenly symbolism. Here, in fact, John has reversed the standard heaven-earth relationship. Normally, heaven is the "real" world with earth a reflection of it. In our case, the victory is won, by Jesus, in this world, a victory that brings about the defeat of evil forces in the heavenly world. Fittingly, then, in Rev 12:11 "the heavenly chorus explains that the real victory has been won 'by the life-blood of the Lamb.' Michael's victory is simply the heavenly and symbolic counterpart of the earthly reality of the cross. Michael, in fact, is not the field officer who does the actual fighting, but the staff officer in the heavenly control room, who is able to remove Satan's flag from the heavenly map because the real victory has been won on Calvary" (Caird, 154).

This story, it should be said, is not concerned with the origin of "Satan" and has nothing to do with a legendary fall of angels. The story reflects the general apocalyptic view that what takes place in heaven is reflected in events in this world. Though defeated in heaven, Satan still finds scope on earth. The story is, in fact, a dramatic presentation of the defeat of Satan by the death of Jesus. The best comment on it is provided by two gospel texts. In Luke 10:18 Jesus declares, "I saw Satan fall like lightning from heaven": Satan has been dismissed from his prosecutor's role in the heavenly court (see Job 1:6-12; 2:1-7); Jesus and his disciples are the effective challenge to evil. In John 12:31 we read, "Now is the judgment of this world, now shall the ruler of this world be cast out [or, variant, 'cast down']." Jesus had just said (John 12:23) that the hour of his death (his glorification) had come; v. 31 describes it as the hour of judgment on the hostile world, the hour when Satan would be cast out (or cast down from his "place" in heaven). Thus we discover the meaning of our Revelation passage: through his glorification, fruit of his ministry and death, the Messiah has won a first and decisive victory over Satan. The latter's power is thus basically broken; it is limited in regard to place (to the earth, v. 9) and time ("his time is short," v. 12). Although in John's thought the dragon is Satan, the prince of evil spirits, and the implacable enemy of God, the place of Satan in heaven reflects another strand of biblical tradition. In Job 1:6-12; 2:1-7, Satan ("the adversary") is one of the angels in the heavenly court: he is the heavenly prosecutor whose function it is to test the genuineness of human virtue. Satan is likewise accuser in Zech 3:1-2 and 1 Chr 21:1; and the same idea is vaguely present in 1 Pet 5:8; Jude 9; 1 Tim 3:6. But he can no longer exercise this office. He has lost his last case: "Now is the judgment of this world, now shall the ruler of this world be cast out" (John 12:31). See Rom 8:1.

The heavenly hymn (vv. 10-12) extols the saving power of God, manifest in the victory of Christ. Significantly, it is "our brothers and sisters," object of his accusations, who have conquered Satan. Their victory, won "by the blood of the Lamb," comes through the laying down of their lives. Despite the bellicose language and imagery of Revelation, John maintains that the war against evil was fought and won on the cross. The brothers and sisters have "conquered" indeed; but to conquer, in the case of Christ and Christians, is to die. "Conquer" never designates vindictive action against the enemies of Christ or Christians. Jesus, silent before the Roman procurator, faithful unto death, won his victory. He conquered through suffering and weakness rather than by might. There can be no other Christian victory. Thus the heavenly defeat of the dragon is signalled as a victory of the "brothers/sisters"—faithful Christians. The victims become victors. This factor tempers the violent imagery of the work.

"War broke out in heaven"—does this, somehow, underwrite our human propensity for strife and war? It has been too easy for us to conjure up the concept of "just" war; we have not shrunk from the notion of "holy" war. John has already painted, in somber colors, the hideous reality of war (6:1-8). And, throughout his book, Christians are never the perpetrators, always the victims, of violence. After all, it is the Lamb, by breaking the first seal, who unleashes the plagues, the Lamb "who was slain from the foundation of the world." There is no human violence against evil. There is resistance—something quite different. *Costly* resistance: "love of life did not bring them to shrink from death."

## 28. Dragon and Woman (12:13-18)

13. When the dragon saw that he had been thrown down to the earth, he went in pursuit of the woman who had given birth to the male child. 14. But the woman was given two great eagle's wings so that she could fly to her place in the desert where she was to be sustained for a time, times, and half a time, away from the serpent. 15. Then the serpent spewed a flood of water after the woman, to sweep her away in its flood. 16. But the earth came to the assistance of the woman, and opened its mouth and swallowed the river which the dragon spewed from his mouth. 17. So the dragon was furious with the woman and went off to wage war on the rest of her offspring, those who keep God's commandments and have the testimony of Jesus. 18. And he took his stand on the seashore.

### NOTES

13. *he went in pursuit of the woman:* The dragon's attempt to destroy the woman, implicit in 12:6, is described in vv. 13-16.

14. *two great eagle's wings:* The Exodus background is evoked (see Exod 19:4; Deut 32:11-12; Isa 40:31).

    *for a time, times, and half a time:* Dan 12:7; see Rev 11:2-3; 12:6. This is also the period during which the beast is allowed to wage war against God's people (13:5). The Church, as such, is under God's special care during the time of tribulation.

15. *the serpent spewed a flood of water:* The dragon is now the "serpent," that is, the "ancient serpent" (v. 9). This flood of water is probably borrowed remotely from Mesopotamian mythology; the dragon (Leviathan, Rahab) has some relation to the cosmic serpent, symbol of the power of evil and darkness.

16. *the earth . . . opened its mouth and swallowed:* The earth had opened to swallow the rebels in the desert (Num 16:30; 26:10; Deut 11:6). The earth ("nature") is the good creation of God and is on the side of God's people.

17. *to wage war on the rest of her offspring,* lit. "the rest of her seed (*sperma*)": A clear reference to Gen 3:15—"woman" and "ancient serpent" are in conflict. See 12:4.

    *those who keep . . . .:* The "seed" of the woman, her faithful children, "keep God's commandments" (see Rev 14:12) and bear witness to Jesus by being partners in his steadfast testimony (1:9; 19:10; 20:4).

18. *and he took his stand:* The variant, "and I stood" would link the sentence with 13:1. However, the former reading receives overwhelming support from the best manuscripts.

    *on the seashore:* The sea is the abyss (11:7).

INTERPRETATION

The dragon sought to destroy the woman, but she is protected for "a time, times, and half a time" (vv. 6, 14): the Church, as such, is under God's special care throughout its historical duration. The "two great eagle's wings" recall the Exodus background and are a symbol of the speed and effectiveness of the divine help. See Deut 32:11-12, "Like an eagle . . . spreading out its wings, catching them, bearing them on its pinions, the Lord alone did lead them"; Isa 40:31, "They who wait for the Lord . . . shall mount up with wings like eagles."

The flood of water spewed by the dragon is a flood of evil which would engulf the woman (see Ps 18:4; 32:6; 124:4-5; Isa 43:2). Besides, in view of the Exodus typology, the flood may have been suggested by the crossing of the Red Sea; in Ezek 29:3; 32:2-3, Pharaoh is "like a dragon in the sea," a water monster. The dragon, frustrated in his attempt to destroy the Messiah (vv. 4-5), is further enraged when he discovers that he cannot harm the mother of the Messiah: the Church as such is beyond his reach (see Matt 16:18). The faithful on earth, however, are vulnerable: Satan, through his instruments, can make war on them; they will be persecuted and put to death. They are "brothers and sisters" of the Messiah (Rom 8:29) and children of the Church; see Gal 4:26, "But the Jerusalem above is free, and she is our mother." The dragon, intent on his warfare against the offspring of the woman, is about to conjure up the terrible beasts of chapter 13, instruments of his malignant purpose.

The woman is sheltered by God, out of range of the dragon. But "the rest of her offspring" are vulnerable. Divine assurance that the Church will survive does not guarantee the permanence of any local Church; almost all the New Testament Churches vanished centuries ago. In our day we witness a change in focus as the European Church is, grudgingly, yielding its pivotal role. The Church, though firmly situated in our world of place and time, is not tied to any place nor bound by any particular culture. It is *katholiē*—universal.

FOR REFERENCE AND FURTHER STUDY, CHAPTER 12

Cerfaux, L. "La Vision de la Femme et du Dragon de l'Apocalypse." *ETL* 31 (1955) 21-33.
Ernst, J. "Die 'himmlische Frau' im 12. Kap. der Apk." *TGl* 58 (1968) 39-59.
Feuillet, A. "Le chapitre XII de l'Apocalypse: Son caractère synthétique et sa richesse doctrinale." *EspV* 88 (1978) 674-83.
_____. "Le messie et sa mère d'après le chapitre XII de l'Apocalypse." *RB* 66 (1959) 55-86.

Gollinger, H. "Das 'Grosse Zeichen': Offb. 12—das Zentrale Kapitel der Offenbarung des Johannes." *BK* 39 (1967) 401–16.

Michl, J. "Die Deutung der apokalyptischen Frau in der Gegenwart." *BZ* 4 (1959) 301–10.

Minear, P. S. " 'Far as the Curse is Found': The Point of Revelation 12:15-16." *NovT* 33 (1991) 71–7.

Montagnini, F. "Le 'signe' d'Apocalypse 12 à la lumière de la christologie du Nouveau Testament." *NRT* 89 (1967) 401–16.

Prigent, P. *Apocalypse 12. Histoire de l'exégèse*. Tübingen: Mohr, 1959.

Saffrey, H. D. "Relire l'Apocalypse à Patmos." *RB* 82 (1975) 385–417, esp. 410–17.

Shea, W. H. "The Parallel Literary Structure of Revelation 12 and 20." *AUSS* 223 (1985) 37–54.

Vanni, U. "Il 'grande segno': Ap 12:1-6." In *L'Apocalisse*, (Bologna: Dehoniane, 1988) 227–51.

# VII. THE TWO BEASTS

## 29. *The First Beast* (13:1-10)

1. Then out of the sea I saw a beast rising, with ten horns and seven heads; on its horns were ten diadems, and on each head a blasphemous name. 2. The beast I saw was like a leopard, but its feet were like a bear's and its mouth like a lion's mouth. The dragon conferred on it his own power, his throne, and great authority. 3. One of its heads was wounded, as it seemed, unto death, yet its mortal wound was healed. And the whole world gazed with wonder after the beast; 4. they worshiped the dragon because he had conferred his authority on the beast, and they worshiped the beast, saying, "Who is like the beast? Who can fight against it?"

5. It was allowed to mouth boasts and blasphemy and it was given permission to exercise authority for forty-two months. 6. It opened its mouth in blasphemies against God, blaspheming his name and his dwelling, that is, those who dwell in heaven. 7. It was allowed to wage war on God's people and conquer them; and it was given authority over every tribe, people, tongue, and nation. 8. All the inhabitants of the earth will worship it, all whose names have not been written in the book of life of the Lamb, slain since the foundation of the world.

9. If you have ears, hear then! 10. Whoever is for captivity, to captivity he goes; whoever is to be slain by the sword, by the sword must he be slain. This calls for the endurance and faith of God's people.

## NOTES

1. *out of the sea:* "Sea" is a hostile element, fitting home of evil. See Dan 7:2-8; 4 Ezra 11:1; 12:11; 1 Enoch 60:7-10; 2 Baruch 29:4.

   *with ten horns and seven heads:* Like the dragon (12:3); note the many-headed Leviathan of Ps 74:14.

   *ten diadems:* Symbol of kingly power (the ten horns of Daniel's fourth beast are ten kings, Dan 7:24). The seven heads stand for the fullness of might—a totalitarian state. The further significance of beasts and horns will be explained in 17:9-14; they identify the power as the Roman Empire.

   *on each head a blasphemous name:* The divine titles affected by the emperors, e.g., *kyrios* (Lord), *sebastos* = *Augustus* (worthy of reverence), *divus* (divine), *dominus et deus* (Lord and God).

2. *leopard . . . bear . . . lion:* The beast of v. 1, like the fourth beast of Dan 7:7, is now described in terms of the other three beasts of Dan 7:4-6. More or less contemporaneously with Revelation, 4 Ezra sees Rome in Daniel's fourth beast: "The eagle which you saw coming up from the sea is the fourth kingdom which appeared in a vision to your brother Daniel" (12:11).

   *power . . . throne . . . authority:* "Throne" is a symbol of God's authority throughout Revelation (e.g., 4:2; 20:11); the dragon, with his "throne," is a parody of God.

3. *wounded, as it seemed, unto death,* lit. "slain unto death": Parody of the Lamb that was slain (5:6, 12; 13:18).

   *its mortal wound was healed:* Nero's suicide in 68 c.e. was followed by a year of civil war which threatened the existence of the empire; with Vespasian, the beast came to life again. Though, in the New Testament, the term "antichrist" is found only in the Johannine letters (1 John 2:18, 22; 4:3; 2 John 7), the beast is an antichrist figure, adversary of Christ and of God.

   *gazed with wonder,* lit. "and the whole world wondered after the beast": John is very conscious of the seductive appeal of Rome; see chs. 17–18.

4. *they worshiped the dragon:* Emperor-worship is really worship of Satan. See 1 Cor 10:20, "I imply that what pagans sacrifice they offer to demons [and not to idols which are nothing]."

   *conferred his authority (edōken):* Perhaps a parody on the "it was given" throughout; elsewhere it means the working out of a divine plan.

   *who is like the beast?:* Parody of Exod 15:11, "Who is like thee, O Lord." There may be a touch of irony: in Rev 12:7-9 Satan is defeated by Michael, whose name signifies "Who is like God?"

   *who can fight against it?:* The seeming invincibility of the Empire.

5. *it was allowed . . . it was given (edothē):* Passive of divine action. Mysteriously, even the activity of the beast falls within a divine plan.

   *boasts and blasphemy:* See Dan 7:8, 20. The blasphemous claims of the emperors echo those of Antiochus IV (the "little horn" of Daniel).

*forty-two months:* The beast's power endures as long as the time of the Gentiles (11:2), as long as the prophesying of the two witnesses (11:3), as long as the woman's abode in the wilderness (12:6, 14).

6. *blasphemies:* See Dan 7:25; 11:36. Likewise "the man of lawlessness" (Antichrist) of 2 Thess 2:4 "opposes and exalts himself against every so-called god or object of worship, so that he takes his seat in the temple of God, proclaiming himself to be God."

   *his dwelling, that is, those who dwell in heaven:* John's "dwelling," his temple, is a people, not a place; see 11:1; 3:12. Some manuscripts read "his dwelling *and* those who dwell in heaven." Our translation renders the much better attested text—also the more difficult, a strong point in its favor.

7. *to conquer them:* See Dan 7:6, 21. This conquering involved killing (v. 15); the Lamb and his followers conquer by dying (5:5; 12:11).

   *was allowed . . . was given: edothē* twice as in v. 5—even in this destructive warfare against his people God, mysteriously, is still sovereign. "Here is another example of the realism of John. He holds out no false hope of rescue from death for those who remain faithful" (Boring, 160).

   *authority over every tribe . . . :* The authority of the beast covered the inhabited world, the *orbis Romanus.* The mission of the two witnesses had been equally widespread (11:9).

8. *whose names . . . book of life:* See 3:5; 20:12, 15. See note at 3:5. "We must not read more into John's doctrine of predestination than he intends. . . . His doctrine springs from the thoroughly biblical idea that salvation is from start to finish the unmerited act of God" (Caird, 168).

   *slain since the foundation of the world:* The saving death of the Lamb was part of God's plan from the beginning. See Acts 2:23, "This Jesus, delivered up according to the definite plan and foreknowledge of God." And 1 Pet 1:18-20, "You know that you were ransomed . . . with the precious blood of Christ, like that of a lamb without blemish or spot. He was destined before the foundation of the world but was made manifest at the end of times for your sake."

9. *if you have ears, hear then!:* An admonition found at the close of each of the messages to the Churches. John is again turning directly to Christians with a special admonition to them. As in 2:7, 11, 17 this call for serious attention points ahead to the following proclamation.

10. *whoever is for captivity:* John is inspired by Jeremiah's oracle against Jerusalem: "Those who are for pestilence, to pestilence, and those who are for the sword to the sword; those who are for famine, to famine, and those who are for captivity, to captivity" (Jer 15:2).

    *whoever is to be slain by the sword:* This is the reading of Alexandrinus. The widely attested reading, "if any one slays with the sword" (1828, versions) is, likely, influenced by Matt 26:52, "All who take the sword will perish by the sword." Charles asserts, emphatically, that A alone is right; the purpose of the text is to enforce an attitude of loyal endurance.

*this calls for the endurance and faith,* lit. "here the endurance": A salutary reminder of what is entailed in opposing the beast and refusing to worship it: captivity and death face the Christians who will not associate with "the inhabitants of the earth." Christian endurance is a sharing in the passion of Christ; faith sees there the only true victory.

## INTERPRETATION

In Daniel 7:2-8 four beasts, representing world empires, emerged from the "great sea"; John also sees his beast, a composite of Daniel's four, come up out of the sea. In 4 Ezra we have a close parallel: "Behold, there came up from the sea an eagle that had twelve feathered wings and three heads" (11:1); "The eagle which you saw coming up from the sea is the fourth kingdom which appeared in a vision to your brother Daniel" (12:11). "Sea" has something of the sense of the *tĕhôm,* the "deep" or "abyss" of Gen 1:2 (in Rev 11:7 the beast came "from the abyss"); and the "sea" will be excluded from the new order (21:1). It is a hostile element and, fittingly, home of monsters. In v. 11 John will describe another beast "which rose out of the earth." He follows an apocalyptic tradition that, on the fifth day (see Gen 1:21), God had created two mythological creatures, Leviathan and Behemoth, one to inhabit the sea and the other the land. See 4 Ezra 6:49-52: "Then you kept in existence two living creatures, the name of one you called Behemoth and the name of the other Leviathan. . . . And you gave Behemoth one of the parts which had been dried up on the third day, to live in it . . . but to Leviathan you gave the seventh part, the watery part." See 1 Enoch 60:7-10; 2 Bar 29:4. John had ample precedent for his beasts.

Already 4 Ezra had seen Rome in Daniel's fourth beast. John follows the same line, and he describes his beast in terms of the other three of Daniel—a fine example of his free use of sources. To the beast the dragon gave his own power, throne, and authority. Satan (though cast down from heaven) is still "the ruler of this world" (John 12:31) for a short time (Rev 12:12). He can still declare: "To you I will give all this authority and their glory; for it has been delivered to me, and I give it to whom I will" (Luke 4:6). John regards the empire as the agent of Satan, and the persecuting emperors as his vassals.

The beast is a parody of the Lamb (see 5:6). One of its heads had received a mortal wound, and the healing of a *mortal* wound is nothing less than return from the dead. Yet John is more precise. A "head" of the beast is an emperor. The head whose mortal wound was healed is the beast "that was, and is not, and is to ascend from the abyss" (17:8-11); he has in mind the legend of *Nero redux*—Nero returned (from exile, or death). The "whole world" gaped in wonder on this beast and its restored head (see 17:8); the world is amazed to see Nero return from the abyss. A presence more sinister than Nero is here: emperor-worship is really worship of Satan. "Who can fight against it?" points to the motive that prompted the worship of the beast: not moral greatness but invincible power. Yet, God is the ultimate source of all authority and power; even Satan's activity falls mysteriously within the divine purpose, which is always a saving purpose. And the beast, in one form or other, will survive as long as the earthly duration of the Church. Already, though, this beast senses failure. His frustrated rage ("blasphemy" in a broad sense) is aimed at God's "dwelling"—this is to say "those who dwell in heaven" (v. 6), the martyrs who rejoice at the fall of Satan (12:12).

The beast is the dragon's instrument in his warfare against the seed of the woman (12:17), and his authority covered the New Testament world, the *orbis Romanus*. His worshipers are "the inhabitants of the earth" (see 3:10; 6:10; 8:13; 11:10), the enemies of God; here they stand out clearly in contrast to the followers of the Lamb, whose names are in the book of life. John does not thereby assert that the worshipers of the beast are predestined to damnation. He is clear that salvation is a free and unmerited gift of God (see 3:5).

At this point, John turns with a special admonition to Christians. The day of persecution is at hand. Christians will be saved through the tribulation, not from it. Captivity, exile, death: such may be the fate of the faithful Christian. Again there is a summons to *hypomonē*, patient endurance. It is precisely this suffering without resistance that calls for patient endurance and faith (see 1:9; 14:12). Caird's illuminating comment opens up a wider perspective: "When one man wrongs another, the other may retaliate, bear a grudge, or take his injury out on a third person. Whichever he does, there are now two evils where before there was one; and a chain reaction is started, like the spreading of a contagion. Only if the victim absorbs the wrong and so puts it out of currency, can it be prevented from going any further. And this is why the great ordeal is also the great victory" (170).

A great power, notably a totalitarian power, may seem to have an impressive permanence and a seeming invincibility. Yet, historically, empires have collapsed with dramatic suddenness. In our day we are witnessing the eclipse of a "superpower." But one empire may also succeed another. The "beast" may assume many guises. Assault on God's people—arising from the nature of the beast—may not be brutal; it may be an insidious infiltration, a weakening of the nerve of the Church. If John calls for endurance and faith in face of active persecution, he calls for no less endurance in face of what he regards as the threat of an alien culture—witness his messages to the Churches. This may well be the challenge to us in our Western world.

FOR REFERENCE AND FURTHER STUDY

Beale, G. K. "The Influence of Daniel upon the Structure and Theology of John's Apocalypse." *JETS* 27 (1984) 413–23.

Collins, A. Yarbro. "The Political Perspective of the Revelation to John." *JBL* 96 (1977) 241–56.

Hanhart, K. "The Four Beasts of Daniel's Vision in the Night in the Light of Rev 13:2." *NTS* 27 (1981) 576–83.

Minear, P. "The Wounded Beast." *JBL* 72 (1953) 93–102.

Prete, B. "Il testo di Apocalisse 13:9-10: una minaccia per i persecutori o un'esortazione al martirio?" *SBFLA* 27 (1977) 102–18.

Reicke, B. "Die jüdische Apokalyptik und die johanneische Tiervision." *RSR* 60 (1972) 181–92.

## 30. *The Second Beast* (13:11-18)

11. Then I saw another beast rising out of the land; it had two horns like a lamb's, but spoke like a dragon. 12. It wielded all the authority of the first beast in its presence, and made the earth and its inhabitants worship the first beast, whose mortal wound had been healed. 13. It worked great miracles, even making fire come down from heaven to earth in the sight of people. 14. By the miracles it was allowed to perform in the presence of the beast it deceived the inhabitants of the earth, telling the inhabitants of the earth to set up an image to the beast which had received the sword-wound and yet lived. 15. It was allowed to give breath to the image of the beast, so that the image of the beast might even speak, and to cause those who would not worship the image of the beast to be killed. 16. It caused everyone, small and great, rich and poor, free and slave, to have a mark put on the right hand or on the forehead, 17. and no one was allowed to buy or sell unless one had the mark, the name of the beast or the number of its name.

18. This calls for wisdom. Let anyone who has intelligence figure out the number of the beast, for it is the number of a human being; and its number is six hundred and sixty-six.

### NOTES

11. *another beast:* In 1 Enoch 60:7-10 and 4 Ezra 6:51 Behemoth is a land monster; here, likewise, this second beast arises out of the land. Perhaps a more immediate reference is the fact that whereas in Daniel's vision the four beasts "come up out of the sea" (Dan 7:3), in the interpretation of the vision they "arise out of the earth" (Dan 7:11).

12. *all the authority of the first beast:* Which, in its turn, is authority of the dragon (v. 4).

    *made the earth . . . worship:* If the first beast is a political symbol, it is the business of the beast from the land to promote the worship of the first; it is a religious symbol. It appears that the imperial religion in the service of Rome is principally in mind (v. 14); in Asia, cultic officials required that religious honors be addressed to the emperor.

13. *it worked great miracles:* As a false prophet (16:13; 19:20; 20:10) the second beast can work miracles. See Mark 13:22, ''False Christs and false prophets will arise and show signs and wonders, to lead astray, if possible, the elect''; see 2 Thess 2:9-10. Early Christian tradition expected that prodigies would precede the coming of Antichrist.

    *making fire come down from heaven:* Aping the sign of the prophet Elijah (1 Kgs 18:38; 2 Kgs 1:10) and of the two witnesses (Rev 11:5).

14. *it was allowed (edothē) to perform:* Mysteriously, even the beast operates within a divine plan; God is wholly sovereign.

    *it deceived the inhabitants of the earth:* As a tool of Satan, ''the deceiver of the whole world'' (12:9).

    *to set up an image to the beast:* Reference to statues of emperors set up in temples of Rome and of the empire, to which divine honors were rendered. Even if, in practice, the emperor in the imperial cult was subordinated to the gods, for Christians imperial cult was one with the worship of the traditional gods, and, as such, unacceptable.

15. *allowed (edothē) to give breath:* Contrast ''the breath of life from God'' that brought about the resurrection of the witnesses (11:11); see Ezek 37:10.

    *so that the image of the beast might even speak:* Speaking statues were engineered in various ways, e.g., by hiding somebody in a hollow statue or by use of ventriloquism. John suggests that the voices could be used to instigate violent action against those who refused to comply with the Caesar-cult (see Dan 3:5-6). Though this is our only evidence that the fraudulent practices of pagan cults were features of imperial cult, John's claim is entirely credible.

    *to be killed:* Underlines the solemn warning of v. 10.

16. *it caused everyone:* See 6:15; 11:18; 19:5, 18; 20:12—the whole population of the empire.

    *a mark: Charagma* is an official stamp, as well as the impress of the emperor's head on coins (see v. 17). The mark of the beast (14:11; 16:2; 19:20) is surely in contrast to the seal of the Lamb (7:3; 14:1). Servants of the beast are marked with the ''stamp'' of the beast—a travesty of the seal of God upon the servants of God (7:2-3). In neither case does John envisage a a literal brand or tattoo.

17. *no one was allowed to buy or sell:* Economic pressure; note the problem of guild membership in Pergamum (2:13-16). There, Christian artisans who wished to earn a livelihood by practice of their trade, would have had to join pagan

guilds. More generally, the "mark" could allude to coins of the realm bearing the image, name, and insignia of the emperor. John may be calling on his readers to avoid using Roman coins—thus effectively ruling out buying and selling (Collins, *Crisis and Catharsis*, 126f.).

18. *this calls for wisdom*, lit. "here (*hōde*) is wisdom": The shrewdness that can interpret this riddle; see 17:9.

*the number of the beast:* The number of the beast stands for its name, which can be discovered by the process of gematria, that is, by the addition of the numerical value of the letters of a name—in Hebrew and Greek, in place of numerals, the letters of the alphabet were given a numerical value. The snag is that the name must be known beforehand if it is to be identified with certainty. A Pompeii graffito reads, "I love her whose number is 545"—the girl and her friends would recognize the name.

*it is the number of a human being*, lit. "it is the number of a man": In other words, the beast (the Roman Empire) is here represented by an individual emperor (just as in Dan 2:27-28 Nebuchadnezzar stands for the Babylonian Empire). It is reasonable to believe that the emperor is Nero, much in mind throughout Revelation. It is scarcely coincidental that the Greek *Nerōn Kaisar*, transliterated into Hebrew script (*nrwn qsr*), gives 666. It is noteworthy that the Latin form *Nero Caesar* (in Hebrew script *nrw qsr*) gives 616, which occurs as a variant reading. One may not rule out a generic significance in the number 666. If seven is the perfect number, then six is the penultimate, incomplete number—"six-six-six" being emphatically negative. In contrast, *Iēsous* gives 888 (*Sib. Or.* 1. 324–29).

### INTERPRETATION

This second beast (called the "false prophet" in 16:13; 19:20; 20:10), with the horns of a lamb, is a parody of the Lamb—for, when it speaks, it is the voice of the dragon that is heard: a wolf in sheep's clothing (see Matt 7:15). This beast, who wields the authority of the first beast, and—false prophet—induces all the "inhabitants of the earth" to worship the beast, is the imperial religion in the service of Rome. It is the interpreter and servant of the beast and, as false prophet, can work miracles. This beast still had to operate within a divine plan: "it was allowed." True sovereignty belongs solely to the One on the throne.

The false prophet causes all (see 6:15; 11:18; 19:5, 18; 20:12) of those who adopted the imperial cult to wear the mark of the beast. John is not thinking of a literal mark. We have seen that the servants of God receive his seal upon their foreheads (7:3), and the followers of the Lamb have his name and his Father's name written on their foreheads (14:1). So, too, the servants of the beast are marked with the "stamp" of the beast: it is a travesty of the seal of the living God (7:2). In each case the wearers of the seal are under patronage: divine or satanic according to their allegiance. It seems that v. 17 envisages an economic boycott against those who stand aloof from the imperial cult. A totalitarian regime, especially in a sycophantic atmosphere, has many ways and means of bringing pressure to bear. The yellow star, which Jews were compelled to wear in Nazi Germany, victimized them. Christians in Asia, if not in quite the same manner, could be efficiently marginalized.

The beast—that is, the first beast—is effectively named. The empire-beast is represented by an emperor; all indications are that Nero is the emperor in question. For John, the second beast represented false religion—specifically, the imperial cult. Historically, even religion that is "authentic" has too often worn aspects of the beast. The word of Jesus stands as perennial challenge: "The sabbath was made for man, not man for the sabbath" (Mark 2:27). Religion is for men and women; men and women are not meant to be slaves of religion. The beast "made" people to do, "caused" people to do things. Can we honestly claim that religion, even our Christian religion, has not been tyrannical, that it does not still, in some measure, dominate? We have it on the authority of Jesus that we ought not only to reject, but actively to oppose, this abuse of religion. To take such a stand may cost us dearly. Jesus paid his price.

### For Reference and Further Study

Beale, G. K. "The Danielic Background for Revelation 13:18 and 17:9." *TynBul* 31 (1980) 163–70.

Oberweis, M. "Die Bedeutung der neutestamentlichen 'Rätselzahlen' 666 (Apk 13:18) und 153 (Joh 21:11)." *ZNW* 77 (1986) 226–41.

Prigent, P. "Au temps de l'Apocalypse II, Le Culte imperial au 1er siècle in Asie Mineure." *RHPR* 55 (1975) 227–33.

Scherrer, S. J. "Signs and Wonders in the Imperial Cult: A New Look at a Roman Religious Institution in the Light of Rev 13:13-15." *JBL* 103 (1984) 599–610.

# VIII. SALVATION AND JUDGMENT

## 31. *The Companions of the Lamb* (14:1-5)

1. Then I looked, and there on Mount Zion stood the Lamb, and with him 144,000 who had his name and the name of his Father written on their foreheads. 2. I heard a sound from heaven like the sound of many waters, like the sound of mighty thunder; the sound I heard was like harpists harping on their harps. 3. They were singing a new song before the throne and the four living creatures and the elders, and no one could learn the song except the 144,000 who were redeemed from the earth. 4. These are they who have not defiled themselves with women, for they are virgins; these follow the Lamb wherever he goes. These have been redeemed from humankind as first fruits for God and the Lamb. 5. No lie was found on their lips: they are without blemish.

### NOTES

1. *on Mount Zion stood the Lamb:* In 11:18 and 12:5 (see 2:27) John has made use of Psalm 2; he has the same psalm in mind here. Note: "I have set my king on Zion, my holy hill" (Ps 2:4); yet, John sees not a warrior king but the Lamb (see Lion and Lamb in 5:5-6).

   *144,000:* Those who were sealed in 7:1-8; they are the victors of the messages (2:3, etc.). It is a military roll-call: the "thousands of Israel."

   *his name and the name of his Father:* Note the promise to the victor of 3:12. The 144,000 stand in sharp contrast to those who carry the mark of the beast (13:16-17).

2. Much of the phraseology of the verse occurs elsewhere in Revelation. "I heard a sound from heaven" (10:4; 14:15; 18:4); "like the sound of many waters" (1:15; 19:6); "like the sound of mighty thunder" (19:6); "harps" are mentioned in 5:8; 15:2.

   *I heard a sound:* What John hears interprets what he sees.

3. *a new song:* In 15:3-5 the conquerors of the beast will sing the "song of Moses" (Exod 15:1-2) which celebrated deliverance from Egypt; this "new song" of Rev 5:8-10 (see 7:9-10) celebrates the new deliverance of God's people.

   *redeemed from the earth:* "Earth" (see "inhabitants of the earth") here corresponds to the "world" (*kosmos*) of the Fourth Gospel and 1 John: it is the unbelieving world.

4. *these are they who have not defiled themselves with women, for they are virgins:* There seem to be two main lines of interpretation. (1) The 144,000 here are the "armies of heaven" of 19:14. After the emergence of the beasts and their followers (ch. 13), we are poised for holy war. In holy war soldiers were re-

quired to preserve ceremonial purity (Deut 20; 23:9-10; see 1 Sam 21:5; 2 Sam 11:11). There is, too, the matter of priestly service (see Lev 15:18). "Defilement," in this context, has the meaning and purpose of insulating the mysterious power of sex from the sacred ministries of priesthood and war. (The Scriptures were said "to defile the hands" because study of them is apart from other tasks.) Perhaps "holy war" is the dominant metaphor. "These virgins are the ritually pure soldiers around the military Lamb-Lion" (Ford, *Revelation*, 234). (2) The designation "chaste" (lit. "virgins") should be understood in a metaphorical sense. The Old Testament prophets, especially Hosea, Jeremiah, and Ezekiel, had represented the covenant relationship as a marriage of God with his people (see Hos 1-3; Jer 2:1-4; Ezek 16; 33); therefore, all idolatry was regarded as adultery or fornication (and, in fact, Canaanite worship did involve ritual prostitution). In Revelation, the Church is the bride of the Lamb (19:7; 21:2-9), while Rome is presented as a harlot (17:4-6; see 14:8). The 144,000 are contrasted with the followers of the beast because they have refused to worship the beast and have remained faithful to the Lamb. In not giving themselves to the cult of the beast they have kept their virginity (Boismard, "Notes," 161-172). It must be acknowledged that others would take the text at its face value. Thus, A. Yarbro Collins: "It is likely that this characterization of an ideal group reflected and reinforced tendencies toward the practice of sexual continence" ("The Apocalypse [Revelation]," *NJBC*, 1010).

*these follow the Lamb wherever he goes:* See Mark 8:34; John 21:19; Luke 9:57, "I will follow you wherever you go." The victors have indeed followed the Lamb; they had shared his suffering and now share his glory (see Luke 24:26).

*first fruits:* Jesus is the first fruits of the dead, of those who belong to him (1 Cor 15:20-23); these redeemed are the first fruits of the harvest of salvation.

5. *no lie was found on their lips:* See Zeph 3:13; 1 Pet 2:22, "He committed no sin; no guile was found on his lips" (see Isa 53:9). Here the lie would consist in acknowledging the claims of the beast; see "all liars," Rev 21:8.

*without blemish (amōmos):* "Unblemished" is in the LXX a Levitical term for appropriate sacrifices; the 144,000 are sacrificially perfect.


## INTERPRETATION

In deliberate and striking antithesis to the beast and his followers stand the Lamb and his companions, bearing on their foreheads the name of the Lamb and of his Father (14:1-5). The 144,000 are the "army" of the Lamb, his faithful earthly followers, now "redeemed from humankind" (v. 4). Mount Zion is the heavenly counterpart of the earthly Jerusalem; John hears the sound of a heavenly liturgy. This time the words of the hymn are not given: only the 144,000 could "learn" (that is, hear and understand, see John 6:45) the new song. This is because the "new song" celebrates their deliverance; see the "song of Moses" (15:3-4).

The characterization of the Lamb's companions as "they who have not defiled themselves with women" sounds offensive, even when one interprets the phrase symbolically. The two approaches indicated in the Notes are not incompatible: both understand John's language metaphorically. The 144,000 represent all the redeemed, women and men. Male terminology is part of the military imagery: the "army" of the Lord ranged against the horde of the beast. In John's mind, this "army" can be represented as a community of chaste "virgins." Their "warfare" is precisely in resisting the "fornication" of idolatry, through unshakable fidelity to the Lamb. One recalls that, in Revelation, the Church is "bride" of the Lamb (21:9). Likewise for Paul, the Corinthian community is a "pure bride" betrothed to Christ (2 Cor 11:2).

The 144,000 "follow the Lamb wherever he goes." They have indeed followed: they have shared his suffering and now share his glory. They are first fruits of the harvest of the world—the harvest of God and of the Lamb. They are "virgins" in their attachment to the Lamb and truthful in "holding fast his name" (2:13). Like the sacrificial offerings of the temple, they are unblemished because they have kept themselves undefiled from idolatry. And, if they have been faithful unto death, then they have joined the Lamb as unblemished victims. For, elsewhere in the New Testament, Jesus himself is so described: "You have been ransomed with the precious blood of Christ, like that of a lamb without blemish or spot" (1 Pet 1:19); "Christ . . . offered himself without blemish to God" (Heb 9:14). In this, too, the victors are true followers of the Lamb.

John characterizes as "virgins" the dedicated followers of the Lamb. They are not "liars" (see 21:8; 22:15): they resist the claims and blandishments of the beast. They are worthy sacrificial victims, prepared for death if faithfulness demands it. Here is a thought-provoking pattern for any follower of the Lamb. It is no more than Jesus had demanded: "If anyone would come after me, let one deny oneself and take up one's cross and follow me" (Mark 8:34).

## FOR REFERENCE AND FURTHER STUDY

Boismard, M. É. "Notes sur l'Apocalypse." *RB* 59 (1952) 161–72.
Fiorenza, E. Schüssler. "The Followers of the Lamb: Visionary Rhetoric and Social-Political Situation." *Semeia* 36 (1986) 123–46.
Ford, J. M. "The Meaning of Virgin." *NTS* 12 (1965–66) 293–99.
Skrinjar, A. "Virgines Enim Sunt (Apoc 14:4)." *VD* 15 (1935) 136–52.

## 32. *Proclamation of Judgment* (14:6-13)

6. Then I saw another angel flying in mid-heaven, with an eternal gospel to proclaim to the inhabitants of the earth, to every nation, tribe, tongue, and people. 7. He cried in a loud voice: Fear God and give him glory; for the hour of his judgment has come. Worship him who made heaven and earth, the sea and the springs of water.

8. Another angel, a second, followed, saying,
> Fallen, fallen is Babylon the great,
> who has made all nations drink
> the wine of the wrath of her fornication!

9. And another angel, a third, followed them, saying in a loud voice, "Whoever worships the beast and its image and receives a mark on his forehead or hand, 10. shall also drink the wine of the wrath of God, poured undiluted into the cup of his anger, and shall be tormented with fire and brimstone before the holy angels and before the Lamb." 11. The smoke of their torment will go up for ever and ever; there will be no respite day or night for those who worship the beast and its image and whoever receives the mark of its name. 12. Hence the endurance of God's people, those who keep the commandments of God and the faith of Jesus.

13. Then I heard a voice from heaven, saying, Write this: Blessed are the dead who die in the Lord henceforth. Yes—says the Spirit— that they may rest from their labors; for their works go with them.

### NOTES

6. *another angel:* Rev 14:6-20 is wholly proleptic, that is, it anticipates events yet to come and summarizes the coming judgment. Each of the angels who now appear in quick succession is designated "another angel" (14:6, 8, 9, 15, 17-18); the first of them is thus distinguished from the angel of the seventh trumpet (11:15), the last-mentioned angelic being.

*flying in mid-heaven:* See 8:13. The angel flies in mid-heaven because his proclamation is of universal import.

*with an eternal gospel to proclaim* (lit. "to evangelize"): His "eternal gospel" which must be "evangelized" recalls 10:1-2, 7. The "little scroll," which contains the good news of the mystery of God revealed to the prophets (10:7), is this "eternal gospel" now to be proclaimed to "the inhabitants of the earth."

*to every nation . . . :* See 10:11; 11:9-10: the invitation is addressed to "all."

7. *he cried in a loud voice:* The proclamation is made to pagans, and so the terms resemble those of the proclamation addressed by Barnabas and Paul to the pagans of Lystra: "We bring you good news, that you should turn from these vain things to a living God who made the heaven and the earth and the sea and all that is in them" (Acts 14:15; Exod 20:11).

*the hour of his judgment has come:* Even judgment is gospel, good news. See John 12:31-32, "Now is the judgment of this world, now shall the ruler of this world be cast out; and I, when I am lifted up from the earth, will draw all to myself." The fact remains that God wills the salvation of all (see 1 Tim 2:4).

8. *fallen is Babylon the great:* See Isa 21:9, "Fallen, fallen is Babylon"; Dan 4:30. The chastisement of the "great city" will form the subject of 17:1-9. As in 1 Pet 5:12 "Babylon" stands for Rome. Babylon was depicted by the Old Testament prophets as the ungodly power *par excellence,* as an oppressive force, and as a symbol of idolatry and immorality. See Isa 21:9; Jer 51:7-8.

*the wine of the wrath of her fornication:* Brings together two phrases round separately elsewhere: "the wine of the wrath of God" (14:10); "the wine of her fornication" (17:2). The rather strange word *thymos* ("wrath") can also indicate strong feeling akin to madness and may be suggested by Jer 51:7: "Babylon was a golden cup in the Lord's hand, making all the earth drunken; the nations drank of her wine, therefore the nations went mad."

9-10. *whoever worships the beast:* People are not compelled to follow the beast to destruction; the third angel proclaims that God's wrath is aimed at those who *worship* the beast (see 13:4, 16-17).

*the wine of the wrath of God:* See Jer 25:15; Isa 51:7; Ps 75:8. The "wrath" or "anger" of God does not mean a feeling or attitude of God towards humankind but an inevitable process of cause and effect; "wrath" is the effect of human sin.

*tormented with fire and brimstone:* The "lake of fire and brimstone" (19:20; 20:10) is the ultimate fate of the wicked (21:8). The image comes from the destruction of Sodom and Gomorrah (Gen 19:24-26), colored by Isa 30:33, "For a burning has long been prepared for you . . . the breath of the Lord, like a stream of brimstone, kindles it" (see Ezek 38:22).

*before the holy angels and before the Lamb:* John cannot be said to share the view of some apocalypticists who believed that the sight of the torments of the damned would add to the bliss of the redeemed (see 1 Enoch 27:3; 48:9; 4 Ezra 7:36); the "Lamb who was slain" is unlikely to gloat!

11. *the smoke of their torment:* The smoke rising "for ever and ever" (a liturgical phrase) is from the doomed city; the fate of humans is depicted in terms of the fate of the city.

*no respite day or night:* See 4:8: the four living creatures "rest not day and night, saying, 'Holy, holy, holy' "; here we have a parody of worship.

*those who worship the beast:* In John's view, even Christians might be seduced by Roman culture—note the messages to the Churches.

12. *hence the endurance of God's people,* lit. "here (*hōde*) the endurance": See 13:10, 18; 17:9. God's people is being summoned to face up with fortitude to the crisis, the tribulation.

13. *a voice from heaven:* It requires a heavenly voice to proclaim this new beatitude, assuring the faithful ones that they are about to enter into rest.

*who die in the Lord:* These share not only the death but also the resurrection of the Lord. See 1 Cor 15:8.

*henceforth (ap'arti):* Better taken with the words which precede it.
*yes, says the Spirit:* The Spirit speaks, as in the messages to the Churches.
*that they may rest:* See Matt 11:28.
*their works go with them:* See Matt 25:31-46; Rev 20:12.

## INTERPRETATION

Satan, the two beasts, and their followers (the "inhabitants of the earth"), the woman and her children, the Lamb and his companions—the dramatis personae of the great eschatological drama—have all been introduced. Now comes the proclamation of the hour of judgment.

The first of three angels who appear in quick succession flies in mid-heaven—the zenith—because his proclamation is of universal import. He proclaims a "gospel": *euangelion* can only mean "good news." The invitation is addressed to all of humankind, including "the inhabitants of the earth." They are urged to "fear God and give him glory" (see 11:13)—they are being called to repentance, to *metanoia* (see Mark 1:14-15). "If the angel carries a 'gospel' which has 'eternal' good news 'to every nation, tribe, tongue and people,' it is hard to see how it could differ from *the* gospel" (Caird, 182). The angel proclaims that the time of salvation is at hand; the call to repentance and offer of salvation are addressed to *all* humankind. Even the declaration, "the hour of his judgment has come," is gospel, good news, because it will take the form of removal of the destroyers of the earth (11:18)—not the "inhabitants of the earth," but the beasts and the dragon, which are symbolic figures (19:17-21; 20:7-10).

The second angel proclaims that the hour of judgment will involve the fall of Babylon (Rome), already judged by God and marked down for destruction. She is condemned for the dire effects of the "wine of her fornication." Already, the picture of the "great harlot" (17:1-6) is suggested—familiar Old Testament imagery. So, Nahum, in reference to Nineveh, speaks of "the countless harlotries of the harlot . . . who betrays nations with her harlotries" (Nah 3:4); similarly, Tyre is a harlot (Isa 23:16-17), and even Zion can deserve the title: "How the faithful city has become a harlot" (Isa 1:21). Rome, instrument of the dragon in his warfare against humankind, has led the world astray by its pagan religion, by its emperor-worship, and by its extravagant wealth. Rome has driven the nations mad.

The third angel proclaims that God's wrath is aimed at those who *worship* the beast (see 13:4, 16-17). Inveterate worshipers of the beast will be given to drink of the undiluted wine of God's wrath. They will be tormented for ever and without respite in the presence of the angels and of the Lamb. What is one to make of such language and imagery? We must recall that, in John's view, even Christians (so the messages to the Churches) may become worshipers of the beast, and John is writing to *Christians*. His book is pastoral in purpose. He is conscious of the seductive side of Rome. His terrible picture of eternal torment is meant to alert his readers, to awaken them, brutally, to what he perceives to be a deadly threat. "As objectifying language about what will happen to our enemies, it is cruel beyond imagination; as confessional language, intended not to describe the fate of outsiders but to encourage insiders to remain faithful, it functions precisely like the language of Jesus in the Gospels (Matt 10:28; 25:30, 46)" (Boring, 170f.).

Following on the lurid threats, God's people is summoned to face up with fortitude to the crisis, the tribulation. The description of judgment in vv. 9-11 is an incentive to John's readers to "keep the commandments of God and the faith of Jesus"—the faithfulness that Jesus displayed. In John 12:31-32 the hour of judgment is the hour of "glorification" of Jesus—the hour of his death; so, too, the judgment described here will involve the passion of the saints, the death of martyrs. See Rev 1:2; 2:13; 12:17. And as the death of Jesus, though judgment on the world, was in order to draw all to him (John 12:31-32), so the suffering of Christians is a salutary witness to the world. Note the reaction to the death and glorification of the two witnesses (Rev 11:12-13).

If, today, we find wholly unacceptable a God who can callously, and almost casually, exterminate those who will not "conform," we may not presume that our first-century brother was less sensitive than we. Apart from anything else, he, too, had read his Book of Wisdom: "For all things are dear to you and you hate nothing that you have created—why else would you have made it? How could anything have continued in existence, had it not been your will? How could it have endured unless called into being by you? You spare all things because they are yours, O Lord, who loves all that lives" (Wis 11:24-26). Yet, the author of Wisdom has some blood-curdling words of judgment on the wicked (see Wis 3:10-12; 16:15-16; 18:9-19). Jesus himself, in words of warning, did not pull his punches. We are faced with a God foolishly bent on the salvation of humankind, and a humankind foolishly bent on "autonomy." Human "wisdom" could only envisage the whipping of "rebellion" into submission. God is "greater than our hearts." He does not come to destroy.

After the "stick" of vv. 9-12, John now produces a "carrot." If the tribulation calls for patient endurance, a voice from heaven, surely the voice of their Lord (see 11:12; 16:15), assures the faithful ones that they are about to enter into rest. Those "who die in the Lord" are, primarily, the martyrs, the firstfruits of the redeemed (14:4), but the beatitude, in the widest sense, applies to all who die in Christ. The Spirit speaks, as in the messages to the Churches; for the beatitude is addressed to Christians who find themselves on the verge of the great tribulation. The labors of the faithful are over, but their works abide and go with them (see Matt 25:31-46; Rev 20:12). They have entered upon the fullness of rest promised by Jesus: "Come to me all you who labor and are heavy-laden, and I will give you rest" (Matt 11:28).

God has not given up on humankind. To the end, even "the inhabitants of the earth" will hear the challenge of the good news. God alone knows if even they will, indeed, resist to the bitter end—and God is God of salvation. He is a God who cannot and will not condone injustice and oppression: evil must, somehow, be totally defeated. Rome, as symbol of oppression, has a debt to pay. But human oppressors are dupes of evil forces. Oppressors stand in more dire need of salvation than the oppressed.

John's grim picture of retribution is a pastoral warning to his hearer/readers. They may be shaken by persecution or seduced by the glamour of the empire. He seeks to bring home to them just how terrible would be a turning from the following of Christ. Faithfulness to him is the path of life; any other way is a road to death. Yet, death in faithfulness to him is "rest," rest that is the beginning of new life. Good deeds will win their reward. As Christians, they had been given the challenge and the promise: "love your enemies, and do good, and lend, expecting nothing in return; and your reward will be great, and you will be children of the Most High" (Luke 6:35).

## FOR REFERENCE AND FURTHER STUDY

Altink, W. "I Chronicles 16:8-36 as Literary Source for Revelation 14:6-7." *AUSS* 22 (1984) 187–96.
Cerfaux, L. "L'Évangile Éternal (Apoc 14:6)." *ETL* 39 (1963) 672–81.

## 33. *The Harvest* (14:14-16)

14. Then I looked, and there appeared a white cloud, and sitting on the cloud one like a son of man, with a gold crown on his head and a sharp sickle in his hand. 15. Another angel came out of the temple and called in a loud voice to him who sat on the cloud: Put in your sickle, and reap, for the hour to reap has come, for the harvest of the earth is fully ripe. 16. So the one who sat on the cloud swung his sickle over the earth, and the earth was reaped.

NOTES

14. *sitting on the cloud one like a son of man:* See 1:7, "Behold, he comes with the clouds" (see Dan 7:13); here the figure is seated on a cloud. "One like a son of man" = a human figure; neither here nor in 1:13 is "son of man" a title. This "son of man" comes between two groups of three angels: 14:6, 8, 9 and 14:15, 17, 18. While it is not certain that the "son of man" is Christ, this distinction from angels, and the passages 1:7, 13-16; 19:11-16, would suggest as much. The "one like a son of man" in 1:13 is, unquestionably, Christ.

*gold crown (stephanos):* Suggesting royalty and victory. See 19:12.

*a sharp sickle in his hand:* The one like a son of man came not to conquer but to reap. In Mark 13:26 the coming of the Son of Man on the clouds is the beginning of judgment. More significant is Rev 1:7: all the tribes of the earth lament in remorse at the coming, with the clouds, of the glorified Christ.

15. *another angel came out of the temple:* The "one like a son of man" waits for the word of the Father. See Mark 13:32, "But of that day or hour no one knows, not even the angels in heaven, nor the Son, but only the Father." See John 5:27.

*put in your sickle and reap:* For reaping as an image of judgment, see Isa 17:5; 27:12; Jer 51:33; Joel 3:13; Matt 13:30, 39. It is noteworthy that in Matthew both "wheat" and "weeds" grow to harvest; then, angel harvesters will gather the "weeds" out of the kingdom while the "wheat" "will shine like the sun in the kingdom of their Father" (13:41-43).

*the harvest of the earth is fully ripe:* Caird observes that in the LXX *therismos*, "harvest," and *therizō*, "to harvest," are used for gathering in, not for a mowing down of enemies (190).

16. *the earth was reaped:* The harvest and vintage of 14:14-20 are proleptic. The last judgment comes in 20:11-15, where all the dead stand before the throne; all are judged, not only those whose names are "written in the book of life." Here "the earth" must have the same inclusive meaning.

INTERPRETATION

This vision of harvest and vintage is based on Joel 3:12-13, the extermination of the pagan nations: "Let the nations bestir themselves, and come up to the valley of Jehoshaphat; for there I will sit to judge all the nations round about. Put in the sickle, for the harvest is ripe. Go in, tread, for the wine press is full. The vats overflow, for their wickedness is great." Undoubtedly, for Joel, harvest and vintage are parallel images of judgment. Precisely on this basis it has been regularly maintained that John's harvest and vintage must be taken, together, in the same sense. What we must realize is that John, in his customary manner, has reacted freely to the source and has developed, differently (harvest = salvation, vintage = judgment), each part of the Joel couplet. John's own text, not the Joel passage, should determine our interpretation.

One "like a son of man"—a human figure—makes his appearance. In 1:13 the "one like a son of man" is Christ. Surely the figure who arrives in the heavenly vehicle (cloud) and wears a gold crown of royalty and victory, is that Christ. Bearing a sickle, he comes not to conquer but to reap. In Mark 13:26-27 the Son of Man (there a Christological title) comes "in clouds" to "gather his elect," to harvest them. In Revelation the "one like a son of man" waits for the word of God, who alone knows the hour of judgment (see Mark 13:32). Now "the hour of his judgment has come" (Rev 14:7); in its manner, as we have noted, this is good news. The angel who issues from the temple comes from the presence of God—a herald who conveys to the reaper the commission of the Lord. The harvest is ripe; the wheat is gathered into the heavenly barn (see Matt 13:41-43). One is reminded of an early Irish hymn: *Ag Críost an síol, ag Críost an fómhar, in iothlainn Dé go dtugtar sinn*—"Christ is the sower, Christ is the harvester: we yearn for the barns of God."

Mark's farewell discourse (ch. 13) has a gracious picture of the parousia of the Son of Man (13:24-27). Formerly, in 8:38, Jesus had warned that only those who, here and now, in this vale of tears, are not "ashamed" of a suffering Son of Man will rejoice in his glorious coming. For the faithful ones that coming will be joy indeed. The Son of Man will not come to execute judgment. The purpose of his appearing will be to gather together the scattered people of God. Though John's "one like a son of man" is not a Christological title, as "Son of Man" is in Mark, he, too, pictures Christ as the harvester. While we cannot share Mark's view (13:30), nor John's, that the end is very near, we do share their faith in God's victory in Christ. And, for each of us, the "parousia" will be our meeting with the Son of Man when we pass out of this life into the life of God. It should be our Christian hope that we stand among the elect, to be harvested and fondly welcomed home by him.

## FOR REFERENCE AND FURTHER STUDY

Feuillet, A. "La moisson et la vendage de l'Apocalypse (14:14-20). La significa-
    tion chrétienne de la révélation johannique." *NRT* 94 (1972) 113–32, 225–50.
van Schaik, A. P. "*Allos angelos* in Apk 14." In J. Lambrecht, ed., *L'Apocalypse
    Johannique*, 217–28.

## 34. *The Vintage* (14:17-20)

17. Then another angel came out of the heavenly temple, and he also had a sharp sickle. 18. And another angel, one who has authority over fire, came out from the altar, and he called to the one who had the sharp sickle, saying, Put in your sharp sickle and gather the clusters of the vine of the earth, for its grapes are ripe. 19. So the angel swung his sickle over the earth and gathered the vintage of the earth and threw it into the great winepress of God's wrath. 20. The winepress was trodden outside the city, and blood flowed from the winepress up to the horses' bridles for a distance of sixteen hundred stadia.

### NOTES

17. *another angel:* The passage 14:17-20 is a preview of 19:11-21. In the Synoptic Gospels angels are ministers of the Son of Man at the judgment; see Matt 13:39, 41-42.

18. *who has authority over fire:* This angel "came out from the altar"; the verse recalls 6:9-10 and 8:3-5. In 8:5 an angel (called in 8:3 "another angel") cast down on the earth coals from the altar, coals which represented the prayers of the martyrs of 6:9-10. Now, the roll of the martyrs is complete, see 6:11. "The harvest of the earth is fully ripe" (14:15); its "grapes are ripe" (v. 18).

19. *the great winepress of God's wrath:* The background is Isa 63:1-6; see Rev 19:11-16. See Targum Gen 49:11. The same passage of Isaiah stands behind Rev 19:11-21 where Christ executes bloody judgment, as an angel does here. Sweet asks, pertinently: "Can John be simply echoing the OT? Can Christ finally conquer in the manner of the beast?" (232).

20. *outside the city:* The destruction of the pagan nations was expected to take place in the course of their final assault on the holy city (see Joel 3:12; Zech 14:2-3, 12-13; Ezek 38-39; Rev 20:9). For John the "city" is the new Jerusalem. However, he would have been aware that "outside the city" was the place of the crucifixion of Jesus; see Luke 20:15; Matt 21:29; Heb 13:12-13. Again he insinuates that the judgment of the world was achieved on the cross.

    *up to the horses' bridles:* This gruesome picture of a river of human blood, first imaged in Isa 63:1-6, is more immediately suggested by the apocalyptic tradition. See 1 Enoch 100:1, 3: "In those days the father will be beaten together with his sons until a stream shall flow with their blood. . . . The horse shall walk through the blood of sinners up to his chest; and the chariot shall sink down up to its top"; see 4 Ezra 15:35. The 1 Enoch passage has to do with the self-destruction of sinners!

    *for a distance of sixteen hundred stadia* (approximately two hundred miles): The number is symbolic, a square number (40 x 40): judgment of the whole earth (see 19:11-21).

### INTERPRETATION

There is another side of judgment: the fate of those "whose names have not been written in the book of life of the Lamb" (13:8). It is still the judgment of God: the second angel, carrying a sickle, comes from the temple in heaven, from the divine presence. As with the one like a son of man, the angel of judgment receives a commission, this time from the angel "who has authority over fire," who comes from the "altar." Now is the time for judgment on the persecutors of God's people.

The whole passage of Isa 63:1-6 (see Rev 19:11-16) suggests the great winepress of the wrath of God. John, following tradition, sets the destruction of the "nations" at their assault on the "beloved city" (20:9)— for him the new Jerusalem. But there is more to it than that. "That the winepress was trodden 'outside the city' suggests both the place of the shedding of Jesus' blood at the crucifixion, an element of the story of the cross that had already been traditional, and the suffering of Christians with Christ (see Heb 13:11-13). The rebirth of images of 19:13-15 shows that Christ's conquering cannot finally be by brute force, that his judgment must finally be the expression of his love. Such reflections do not take the edge off the terrors of the judgment of the holy God; they may make it possible to take them seriously by readers who also affirm the ultimately redemptive purpose of God expressed elsewhere in the Bible, including elsewhere in Revelation" (Boring, 171f.). John insinuates yet again that the judgment of the world was achieved on the cross.

The violent imagery of Revelation is traditional—not an invention of John. It does not follow that John, with his genial creativity, employs that imagery in its original sense. One must keep in mind his pastoral intent of summoning his readers to what he firmly believes to be a life or death decision. He seeks to counter, as vehemently as he can, the seduction of the beast. A witness to the rightness of his Christian instinct is the fact that he has threaded through his visions the prospect and promise of universal salvation. His God is Father of the Lamb who was slain.

God is patient, but he cannot ignore evil, he will not condone oppression. There is place for his "wrath," his radical incompatibility with evil. He copes with evil in *his* way. His answer to the worst that humankind can perpetrate is the answer of the Cross. The great river of blood from the winepress of his wrath is a warning that innocent blood cannot be shed with impunity. God is not vindictive. God does not punish. The problem for humans—and it is a humanly insoluble problem—is to maintain faith in the long-suffering of God, faith in the infinitely forgiving love of God and, at the same time, to grasp, and find some way to express, his abhorrence of evil and sin. Our human imagery and language are inadequate. Unhappily, we too readily end up presenting an unsavory image of our gracious God.

# IX. THE LAST PLAGUES

## 35. *Song of Moses and the Lamb* (15:1-4)

1. Then I saw another portent in heaven, great and astonishing: seven angels with seven plagues, the last, for with them the wrath of God is spent.

2. And I saw, as it were, a sea of glass mingled with fire and, standing beside the sea of glass, holding harps of God, were those who had been victorious against the beast and its image and the number of its name. 3. They were singing the song of Moses, the servant of God, and the song of the Lamb:

> Great and marvelous are your works,
>   Lord God Almighty;
> Just and true are your ways,
>   O King of the nations.
> 4.   Who shall not fear you, Lord,
>   and do homage to your name?
> For you alone are holy.
> All nations will come
>   and worship before you,
>   for your righteous deeds have been revealed.

## NOTES

1. *another portent:* Looks back to 12:1, 3. This opening verse is a heading to the chapter. In v. 6 we are told that the seven angels come out of the temple, thus really appearing for the first time.

   *seven plagues:* See Lev 26:21, "If you walk contrary to me, and will not hearken to me, I will bring more plagues upon you, sevenfold as many as your sins."

   *the last:* The seven plagues are explicitly designated "the last": another, final, Mosaic series of seven plagues will be poured out on the city figuratively called Egypt (11:8).

   *with them the wrath of God is spent:* This is so even though the end is described in chs. 18–20; for the fact is that these chapters will develop, in dramatic fashion, what is already present in the plagues of bowls.

2. *a sea of glass:* The sea of glass is that of 4:6; the seer is once more in heaven.

   *those who had been victorious:* They are the sealed of 7:1-8 and the 144,000 of 14:1-5. They are also the victors, the faithful members of the seven Churches.

   *harps of God:* Consecrated to the service of God (see 1 Chr 16:42; 2 Chr 7:6; Rev 14:2).

**3-4.** *the song of Moses:* See Exod 15:1, "Then Moses and the people of Israel sang this song to the Lord." As with the previous plagues, the seven bowls are introduced through heavenly worship.

*Moses, the servant of God:* As in Heb 3:5, Moses is called God's servant and is set in contrast to the Son: "Now Moses was faithful in all God's house as a servant . . . but Christ was faithful in all God's house as a son." The deliverance of the Israelites from Egypt was the type of the deliverance of God's people from the beast; thus the "song of Moses" is also, and principally, the "song of the Lamb" because they who worship have won their victory by the blood of the Lamb (7:14; 12:11). The canticle itself is a mosaic of Old Testament phrases: Ps 111:2; 139:14; Amos 4:13; Ps 145:17; Deut 32:4; Jer 10:7; Ps 86:9; Mal 1:11; Ps 98:2.

*O King of the nations:* The reading *ethnōn*, "nations," (Sinaiticus, A), is preferable to *aiōnōn*, "ages" (P⁴⁷, Sinaiticus*). See Jer 10:7.

*all nations will come and worship before you:* "God's acts of judgment have salvation and worship as their ultimate goal" (Krodel, 279).

*your righteous deeds (dikaiōmata),* lit. "judgments": The dominant nuance is positive; this is the meaning in 19:8, which speaks of "the righteous deeds *(dikaiōmata)*" of God's people.


## INTERPRETATION

The seven plagues which are the last (15:1)—and thus distinct from the plagues of seals and trumpets—are announced in chapter 15; the following chapter shows their execution. The vision that presents the angels of the bowls, while modeled on the presentation of the archangels of the trumpets (8:2-6), is also a development of it: the seven are announced, a liturgical interlude follows, and then the seven act.

The seven plagues are the last because "with them the wrath of God is completed." The seer is once more in heaven and sees again the "sea of glass" of 4:6—but, this time, a sea "mingled with fire": symbol of God's judgment. In view of the Exodus background, "sea" evokes the Red Sea: redemption for Israel, judgment on Egypt. Beside the sea stand the victors: the faithful ones "who have not defiled themselves" with the fornication of emperor worship. They have been victorious against the beast—a dramatic reversal because the beast "was allowed to wage war on God's people and conquer them" (13:7; see 13:15). They have won the victory in the same manner as the "Lamb who was slain" (5:6; 3:21).

The victors chant their victory song. Though termed the "song of Moses," their song, unlike the song of Exodus, is not one of triumph over their enemies: it is solely praise of God. Again we are challenged to question John's alleged vindictiveness. All the more so because the second part of the song (v. 4) holds out hope that the nations, in view of the righteous deeds of the Lord, will fear him—that is, acknowledge him—and render him homage and worship. In other words: God is king of the nations and the nations will come to acknowledge him as their King. Our God, even in judgment, is always in the business of salvation, bent on the salvation of humankind. "We must accept this optimism as an essential part of John's theology. There are a few passages like this in his book where he speaks unequivocally and without the cloak of symbol, and, instead of ignoring them or treating them as erratic and inconsequent intrusions, we ought to allow them to control our interpretation of his symbolism" (Caird, 199).

## 36. *The Angels of the Bowls* (15:5–16:1)

5. After this, as I looked, the sanctuary of the heavenly Tent of Testimony was opened, 6. and out of the sanctuary came the seven angels with the seven plagues. They were robed in fine linen, pure and shining, and had golden girdles round their breasts. 7. Then one of the four living creatures gave the seven angels seven golden bowls full of the wrath of God who lives for ever and ever. 8. And the sanctuary was filled with smoke from the glory of God and from his power, so that no one could enter the sanctuary until the seven plagues of the seven angels were completed.

16:1. Then I heard a loud voice from the sanctuary say to the seven angels: "Go and pour out the seven bowls of God's wrath on the earth."

### NOTES

5. *after this, as I looked:* The formula (see 4:1; 7:1, 9; 18:1) serves to introduce a new vision of special importance.

*the sanctuary of the heavenly Tent of Testimony,* lit. "the temple of the tent of the testimony": A strange designation. What John has in mind is the heavenly tabernacle, archetype of the earthly tent of witness. See 11:19, "Then God's sanctuary in heaven was opened." See Exod 29:9, "According to all that I show you concerning the pattern of the tabernacle . . . so you shall make it"; Acts 7:44; Heb 8:5, "They [the Levitical priests] serve a copy and shadow of the heavenly sanctuary."

6. *out of the sanctuary came the seven angels:* The angels of v. 1 now make their appearance: these actors in the eschatological drama come forth from the cultic place.

*fine linen:* These angels are clothed like the bride (19:8) and the armies of heaven (19:14).

*golden girdles:* The one like a son of man of 1:3 wore a "gold girdle around his breast."

7. *one of the four living creatures gave the seven angels:* Note the similar role of the living creatures in 6:1-8.

   *the wrath of God:* See Rom 1:18; Heb 10:31.

   *who lives for ever and ever:* See 4:9; 10:6.

8. *filled with smoke . . . glory . . . power:* See Exod 40:35; Isa 6:4; Ezek 10:4; 1 Kgs 8:10-11—traditional details of a theophany, to emphasize the solemnity of the hour.

   *no one could enter the sanctuary:* As Moses (Exod 40:35) and the priests (1 Kgs 8:11) could not enter tent or temple because of the cloud of the Lord's glory. Perhaps John means that the time for intercession is over: it is the hour of judgment. "No one may interfere during the execution of his wrath" (Krodel, 280). See 11:19.

16:1. *a loud voice:* This time the "loud voice" coming from the temple which "no one could enter" (15:8) may be that of God (see v. 17).

   *the seven bowls of God's wrath:* See 15:1, 7.

   *pour out . . . on the earth:* The first four plagues (vv. 2-9), like the plagues of Egypt, are aimed at the four elements of the physical world; they are natural plagues.

INTERPRETATION

John sees the heavenly sanctuary standing open, and seven angels, bearers of the seven last plagues, in priestly robes, come forth in solemn procession from the divine presence (see 14:15, 17-18). In ch. 6 the four living creatures, each in turn, signaled the appearance of each of the four horsemen (the first four seals); here, one of the living creatures hands to the seven angels the bowls of God's wrath. In 5:8 the twenty-four elders held golden bowls full of the incense of the saints' prayers; but the golden bowls of our text are full of "the wine of God's wrath" (14:10). Again we are back to the divine "wrath." The author of Hebrews declared in solemn warning, "It is a fearful thing to fall into the hands of the living God" (Heb 10:31), into the ambit of his "wrath." I have long thought that a perceptive observation of C. H. Dodd, apropos of Rom 1:26, 28, has, once for all, put God's "wrath" in proper perspective: " 'It is an awful thing,' says the Epistle to the Hebrews (10:31) 'to fall into the hands of the living God.' Paul, with a finer instinct, sees that the really awful thing is to fall out of his hands, and to be left to oneself in a world where the choice of evil brings its own moral retribution" (*The Epistle of Paul to the Romans* [London: Collins, 1959] 55). Increasingly, I believe that John would add his "Amen."

Surely John has invited us to view the seven plagues about to be unleashed (15:5-8) against the background of a God who thinks only in terms of salvation (15:3-4). For a Christian can there be any other God than this God? Otherwise, what could one make of a God who did not spare his own Son? What does one make of the folly of the Cross? John is faced with the enigma of an infinitely gracious God face to face with human perversity. His problem—which is our problem—is to face that riddle within our grossly limited human perspective. From a simply human point of view the situation might seem uncomplicated. There is right and there is wrong, and wrong calls for punishment. That human view is too simplistic. In his time, David had made the wise decision: "Let us fall into the hands of the Lord, for his mercy is great; and let me not fall into the hands of men" (2 Sam 24:14). John's problem was how to make his Christians measure up to the tribulation he foresaw. He felt he had to jolt them into awareness of crisis—hence the bite of his imagery and language. We might ask ourselves how well we Christians perform in a largely post-Christian world. John perceived that the current ethos of his day was out of step with the message of Jesus. He was prepared to put forth his view, without remainder and without apology. Have we the courage to do as much?

## FOR REFERENCE AND FURTHER STUDY

Hanson, A. T. *The Wrath of the Lamb.* London: SPCK, 1957.

## THE SEVEN BOWLS (16:2-21)

### 37. *The First Four Bowls* (16:2-9)

2. So the first went and poured out his bowl on the earth, and foul and grievous sores broke out on the people who had the mark of the beast and worshiped its image.

3. The second poured out his bowl on the sea; and it turned to blood, like the blood from a dead body, and every living thing in the sea died.

4. The third poured out his bowl on the rivers and springs of water, and they turned to blood. 5. And I heard the angel of the waters say,

> Righteous are you,
>> who are and who was, O Holy One,
>> because you have thus passed judgment;

6.       for they shed the blood of your people and your prophets,
> and you have given them blood to drink.
> They have their desserts!

7.     And I heard the altar say.
> Yes, Lord God Almighty,
>> true and righteous are your judgments.

8. The fourth poured out his bowl on the sun; and it was allowed to scorch people with its flame. 9. They were scorched with a scorching heat, and they blasphemed the name of God who had the power to inflict such plagues, but they did not repent and give him glory.

## NOTES

2. The bowls (like the trumpets) are modeled on the plagues of Egypt. This time, however, chastisement is universal and definitive: all the worshipers of the beast and persecutors of Christians are stricken. Moreover, they are already gathered at Armageddon (16:14, 16) to await destruction (19:17-21).
See Exod 9:8-12 (sixth plague). See Deut 28:35.
*foul and grievous sores:* Through their attack on the physical world, the plagues strike the human world too, specifically, "the inhabitants of the earth": explicitly in bowls one and four, indirectly in two and three.

3. See Exod 7:20-21 (first plague). See the second trumpet, Rev 8:8-9.
*like the blood from a dead body,* lit. "blood as of a dead man": Suggests the picture of a murdered man sweltering in his blood (Swete, 201).
*every living thing:* See Gen 1:21; total destruction, and not just of a third of marine creatures as in Rev 8:9.

4. See Exod 7:20-21 (first plague). As in the trumpets (8:8-11), John has made two plagues of the first Egyptian plague. Here, again, there is no restriction (see 8:10-11)—all fresh water was turned to blood.

5-6. *the angel of the waters:* For the notion of an angel in charge of the elements, see 7:1; 14:8; also 9:11. See 1 Enoch 66:1-2, "After this he showed me the angels of punishment who are prepared to come and release all the powers of the waters which are underground to become judgment and destruction unto all who dwell upon the earth . . . for they were the angels who were in charge of the waters." Swete (202) observes that the words of the angel "form a sort of antiphon to the canticle of 15:3-4; they illustrate the divine 'righteousness' and 'holiness' proclaimed in that Song."
*who are and who was:* As at 11:17, God is no longer "he who is to come" (see 1:4).
*they shed the blood . . . blood to drink:* The principle is that of Wis 11:16: "that they might learn that one is punished by the very things by which one sins."

*your people and your prophets:* As in 11:18; 18:24. In 17:6 Babylon is "drunk with the blood of God's people and with the blood of the witnesses [martyrs] of Jesus."

*they have their desserts!:* Repeats sarcastically the same phrase, *axioi eisin*, of 3:4, where it means "they are worthy."

7. *I heard the altar say:* That is, either the angel of the altar (14:18) or the altar of 6:9; 8:3-5 personified. In either case, it is the voice of the martyrs of 6:9-11; their prayer has been answered. The words are an echo of 15:3; see 19:2.

8. *it was allowed (edothē) to scorch people with its flame:* Contrast the promise to the vast throng at 7:16, "never again shall the sun strike them, nor any scorching heat." Again the principle is that of Wisdom: "For through the very things by which their enemies are punished, they themselves receive benefit in their need" (Wis 11:15).

9. *they blasphemed the name of God:* Like their master (13:1, 5-6; 17:3) they blasphemed God whom they blamed as cause of their suffering (see 11:10; 16:11, 21). For cursing (blaspheming) the name of God, see Rom 2:24; 1 Tim 6:1; Jas 2:7.

*they did not repent:* See 9:20-21; 16:11. Contrast 11:13 where there is repentance.

*give him glory:* See 11:13; 14:7; 19:7—the solemn proclamation of 14:7 has gone unheeded.

### INTERPRETATION

The first three of the seven angels (15:1) pour out their bowls in quick succession. The plagues are adaptations of the first and sixth plagues of Egypt, the first being again split into two plagues as in Rev 8:8-11. We meet once more (v. 5) the notion of an angel in charge of the elements: the "angel of the waters." This angel invokes the *lex talionis:* it is just and meet that those who have shed innocent blood should have blood for their drink. The plague of the fourth trumpet (a plague of darkness) struck the sun (8:2); here, too (16:8), the sun is struck, but with different effect: not darkness but excessive heat. Not even these final plagues deny an opportunity to repent, but the worshipers of the beast are obdurate.

### FOR REFERENCE AND FURTHER STUDY

Collins, A. Yarbro. "The History-of-Religion Approach to Apocalypticism and the 'Angel of the Waters' (Rev 16:4-7)." *CBQ* 39 (1977) 367–81.

Staples, P. "Rev XVI 4-6 and its vindication formula." *NovT* 14 (1972) 280–93.

## 38. *The Fifth Bowl* (16:10-11)

10. The fifth poured out his bowl on the throne of the beast, and its kingdom was plunged in darkness. People gnawed their tongues in pain, 11. and blasphemed the God of heaven for their pains and sores, and did not repent of their works.

### Notes

10. See Exod 10:21-22 (ninth plague). See Rev 8:12; 9:1-12. The bowl-plagues five to seven are aimed directly at the worshipers of the beast.

    *the throne of the beast:* See 13:2, "the dragon conferred on it his own power, his throne, and great authority." The throne of the beast is Rome.

    *people gnawed their tongues in pain:* Wisdom 17 paints a vivid picture of the terrors of the plague of darkness.

11. *and blasphemed the God of heaven:* In vv. 9, 11, 21 John's declaration that people blasphemed God points to those who had wholly taken on the character of the false god they served, the beast who is the great blasphemer (13:1, 5-6; 17:3).

    *for their pains and sores:* The effects of the earlier plagues (vv. 2, 8-9) persist.

    *did not repent:* See v. 9.

### Interpretation

The fifth angel poured his bowl on the throne of the beast, that is, on Rome. This plague assailed the very seat of the world-power and covered the whole empire ("its kingdom"). It is a grim prelude to definitive judgment. As with Pharaoh, the plague only served to harden the hearts of worshipers of the beast.

## 39. *The Sixth Bowl* (16:12-16)

12. The sixth poured out his bowl on the great river, the Euphrates, and its water was dried up, to prepare a way for the kings from the sunrise. 13. Then I saw coming from the mouth of the dragon, from the mouth of the beast, and from the mouth of the false prophet, three foul spirits like frogs. 14. For they are demonic spirits, able to work miracles, who go out to the kings of the whole world, to muster them for battle on the great day of God the Almighty. 15. Behold, I come like a thief! Blessed is he who stays awake and keeps his garments by him, so that he does

not walk naked and his shame be seen. 16. And they mustered them at the place which is called in Hebrew Armageddon.

## NOTES

12. *the great river, the Euphrates:* See 9:14.

    *the kings from the sunrise:* The sixth bowl dries up the Euphrates to open their way. See Exod 14:21; Jos 3:17; Jer 50:38; 51:36-37. John thinks of a Parthian invasion; see 9:14.

13-14. See Exod 8:5-6 (second plague); Rev 9:1-11. These plagues are directed against the latter-day Egypt—Rome.

13. *dragon . . . beast . . . false prophet:* See ch. 13—a "satanic trinity."

    *the false prophet:* The second beast of 13:11; see 19:20.

    *three foul spirits, like frogs:* Quite like the locusts of the fifth trumpet (9:1-11), these frogs are demonic beings. See Zech 13:2, "On that day, says the Lord of hosts . . . I will remove from the land the prophets and the unclean spirit." "Demonic [foul] spirits," see Mark 1:23; Matt 10:1; etc. These spirits, from the mouths of the satanic trinity, are lying spirits which deceive humankind (13:14) and lead people to their doom. See Deut 13:1-2; Mark 13:22; 2 Thess 2:9-12.

14. *the kings of the whole world (oikoumenēs):* The kings of the empire, the civilized world, as distinct from the "barbarian" kings of v. 12.

    *to muster them for battle:* John is thinking of the legend of *Nero redux* (or *redivivus*), the popular belief that Nero would return, at the head of a Parthian army, to destroy his enemies and regain his throne (see 13:3; 17:11). The demonic spirits summoned "the kings of the whole world" to join the Eastern invaders. See Ps 2:2, "The kings of the earth set themselves . . . against the Lord and his anointed"; see Rev 17:13-14; 19:19.

    *the great day of God the Almighty:* See Joel 2:11, "For the day of the Lord is great and very terrible; who can endure it?"; 2:30, "before the great and terrible day of the Lord comes"; see Rev 6:17.

15. *Behold, I come like a thief:* See 3:3-4, 18. The voice is the voice of Jesus (see 14:13), again calling for watchfulness (Matt 24:43; Luke 12:39; see 1 Thess 5:2). This is one of the seven beatitudes in Revelation (see 1:3; 14:13; 19:9; 20:6; 22:7, 14). The warning is not really out of place, though many commentators have judged it so.

    *so that he does not walk naked:* See the admonition to the Church of Laodicea: they are advised to buy from the Lord "white garments to put on to cover the shame of your nakedness" (3:18). The present subjunctive tenses *walk naked* and *be seen* point to a habitual situation. "The danger is of being caught not momentarily but habitually off guard—not, to put it crudely, with trousers down, but without trousers at all" (Sweet, 249).

16. *Armageddon:* The name means "the mountain of Megiddo." Megiddo, situated on a plain near Mount Carmel, dominated the strategic pass from the coast to the plain of Jezreel. Its situation made it the scene of many battles. Since the defeat and death of Josiah at Megiddo (2 Kgs 23:29-30) it had become a symbol of disaster.

## INTERPRETATION

In Rev 9:14 we read: "Release the four angels held bound at the great river Euphrates." Then the vision of the sixth trumpet went on to describe the invasion of a demonic army from beyond the river, whose objective was the killing of a "third of humankind" (9:15-19). The sixth bowl dries up the Euphrates to open a path for "the kings from the sunrise." Here, more obviously than in the demonic army of 9:15-19, the Parthians are in mind—Rome's mysterious and dreaded foe, typifying all foreign invaders. The kings from the East are ready to move westward as soon as passage has been opened for them. A concerted assault of kings of the East and "kings of the whole world" (v. 14) is not only on Rome. Because they are deluded instruments of the beast, it is ultimately against the Lamb. The nations are marshalled for the eschatological battle; this is the breaking of the day of the Lord.

At this point John throws in a pastoral warning: "I come like a thief!" Jesus had warned his disciples that the end of Jerusalem would come unexpectedly, brooking no delay on the part of those who would escape: "Let him who is on the housetop not go down nor enter his house, to take anything away; and let him who is in the field not turn back to take his mantle" (Mark 13:15-16). Now he warns his followers to be prepared for the last days of "Babylon"; they must discern his coming in that event. He comes "like a thief" because both the hour of his coming and its manner in the events of history are hidden from them.

Like the number 666 (13:18), the significance of the name Armageddon would have been apparent to John's readers; it soon became a puzzle. It seems that John thinks of Megiddo as symbol of disaster: it spells the destruction of the assembled armies (see 19:11-21). Armageddon is figure of the eschatological battle—wherever it may be.

## FOR REFERENCE AND FURTHER STUDY

LaRondelle, H. K. "The Biblical Concept of Armageddon." *JETS* 28 (1985) 21-31.

## 40. *The Seventh Bowl* (16:17-21)

17. The seventh poured out his bowl on the air; and out of the sanctuary there came from the throne a loud voice saying, "It is done!" 18. And there were flashes of lightning and peals of thunder, and a violent earthquake, so violent that its like had not been since humankind appeared on earth. 19. The great city was split in three, and the cities of the nations fell. And Babylon the great was remembered before God and made to drink the cup of the wine of the fury of his wrath. 20. Every island vanished, and not a mountain was to be found. 21. Huge hailstones, weighing over a hundredweight, fell from the sky on humankind; and they blasphemed God because of the plague of hail, because that plague was exceedingly great.

### NOTES

17. *It is done!:* Already the seventh seal and the seventh trumpet signaled the end; here the "end" is final! See 10:6-7; 11:15; 15:1.

18. *lightning . . . thunder . . . earthquake:* See 8:15; 11:19. These are the traditional accompaniments of a great visitation. See Dan 12:1; Exod 9:24; Mark 13:19. Mention of "earthquakes" (disasters all too familiar to inhabitants of Asia) in 8:5 and 11:19 allude to the Sinai theophany and build up to the climactic earthquake of the last plague (16:18). "Rev 16:18 both alludes to whatever John's readers were accustomed to recall as the greatest earthquake ever, and projects that experience into the apocalyptic future which will surpass any known disaster" (R. J. Bauckham, *NovT* 19 [1977] 231).

19. *the great city . . . Babylon the great:* Rome (14:8).
    *remembered before God:* God will not forever countenance wickedness; the oppressed will be vindicated.

20. *every island . . . mountain:* Disappearance of islands and mountains is an apocalyptic sign of the end. See *Assumption of Moses* 10:4, "And the high mountains shall be made low, and the hills shall be shaken and fall."
    *huge hailstones:* See Exod 9:23-24 (seventh plague).
    *they blasphemed God:* Those stricken by the fifth plague had likewise blasphemed (vv. 10-11).

### INTERPRETATION

This final plague is of cosmic range; so the seventh angel poured his bowl "into the air." The same voice which had sent the angels on their mission (16:1) (coming from "the throne," the voice is, more surely than at v. 1, the voice of God) now declares that their work is accomplished (see 21:6): these plagues are indeed "the last" (15:1). Fittingly, at the close of the last plague of all, the traditional earthquake is of unprecedented violence. This "violent earthquake" brings about the splitting apart of the "great city" and the downfall of "the cities of the nations"—political catastrophe across the Empire. God had seemed to overlook the wickedness of Rome as she went her proud way, mistress of the earth. But his justice will not be flouted and the hour of her retribution has come. She who "made all the nations drink the wine of the wrath of her fornication" (14:8) must now, herself, drink the wine of God's wrath (see 14:10).

The final verses (20-21) describe the further effects of the outpouring of the seventh bowl. Traits of the seventh Egyptian plague already appeared in v. 18, but the central scourge of hail is emphasized here. John, with his hailstones "heavy as a hundredweight," merely makes more impressive the "very heavy hail" of Exodus. As in vv. 9 and 11 the result of this plague, too, is to harden the hearts of "the inhabitants of the earth." Despite the total devastation of vv. 18-20, humankind is still present to blaspheme! The story is not ended.

The seven plagues of bowls are "the last." As the plagues of Egypt were to bring Pharaoh to relent, to "let my people go," these plagues of bowls are a last effort to bring people to repent. Alas, evil is pervasive and deeply engrained. But, is evil ultimately resistant to the persistent love of God? It would seem that, as one looks more deeply, John did not believe so. If he has to show, in a wholly unambiguous manner, that God does not countenance wickedness and oppression—"it grieves him to his heart" (Gen 6:6)—he will not hide the depth and range of God's forgiving and saving will.

The word of Jesus in v. 15 underlines the pastoral intent of the plague sequences. John's hearer/readers are left in no doubt that their God is wholly alive to the evil world in which they live. He seeks to warn them that evil may be, to some extent, veiled and seductive. They need to be ever alert. Because we are not victims of persecution or discrimination on religious grounds, we are more vulnerable than were John's people to threats to our Christian standards. Their experience of intolerance, if not incipient persecution, conditioned them to measure their world by a "hermeneutic of suspicion." Our danger is that we become too receptive, even gullible. We may readily accept current values as normative, not recognizing that they will not stand the scrutiny of the gospel. It would be well to ponder on the warning to Laodicea (3:15-19).

FOR REFERENCE AND FURTHER STUDY

Bauckham, R. J. "The Eschatological Earthquake in the Apocalypse of John." *NovT* 19 (1977) 224-33.

# X. THE HARLOT AND THE BEAST

## 41. *The Harlot and the Beast* (Ch. 17)

1. And one of the seven angels who held the seven bowls came and spoke to me: "Come," he said, "I will show you the verdict on the great harlot, enthroned on many waters, 2. with whom the kings of the earth have committed fornication, and the inhabitants of the earth have made themselves drunk on the wine of her fornication." 3. He carried me away in spirit into a wilderness, and I saw a woman mounted on a scarlet beast which was covered with blasphemous names and had seven heads and ten horns. 4. The woman was clothed in purple and scarlet and bedecked with gold and precious stones and pearls. In her hand she held a gold cup full of obscenities and the filth of her fornication; 5. and on her forehead was written a mysterious name: "Babylon the great, the mother of harlots and of all obscenities on earth." 6. I saw that the woman was drunk with the blood of God's people and with the blood of the martyrs [witnesses] of Jesus. At the sight of her I wondered greatly.

7. Then the angel said to me: "Why do you wonder? I will tell you the mystery of the woman and of the beast she rides, with the seven heads and the ten horns. 8. The beast you saw was and is not and is to rise from the abyss; and it goes to perdition. The inhabitants of the earth, whose names have not been written in the book of life since the foundation of the world, will be astonished to behold the beast that was and is not and is to come. 9. This calls for a mind with wisdom. The seven heads are seven hills on which the woman sits enthroned. They are also seven kings: 10. five have fallen, one now is, and the other has not yet come, and when he comes he must stay for a short while. 11. And the beast that was and is not is also an eighth, yet he is one of the seven and he goes to perdition. 12. The ten horns you saw are ten kings, who have received no kingdom as yet; but for one hour they are to receive royal authority with the beast. 13. They have a single purpose and will yield their power and authority to the beast. 14. They will wage war on the Lamb, and the Lamb will conquer them, for he is Lord of lords and King of kings, and those who are with him are called, and chosen, and faithful."

15. Then he said to me: "The waters you saw, where the harlot sat enthroned, are peoples and multitudes and nations and tongues. 16. And the ten horns which you saw, and the beast, they will come to hate the harlot and will make her desolate and naked; they will devour her flesh and will burn her with fire. 17. For God has put it into their minds to carry out his purpose by being of one mind, and by yielding their sovereignty to the beast until God's words are fulfilled. 18. The woman you saw is the great city that holds sway over the kings of the earth."

NOTES

1. *the verdict:* The execution of the verdict on Rome, already twice proclaimed (14:8; 16:9), is to be described at length in chs. 17–18.

   *the great harlot:* In Ezek 16 Jerusalem is a harlot and in Ezek 23 Jerusalem and Samaria, sisters, are a pair of harlots; see Isa 23:15-17; Nah 3:4. "The personification of the city as female and the image of prostitution for idolatry and excessive wealth have roots in Hebrew tradition. . . . In the twentieth century such images may not be used uncritically because, e.g., their ill effects on the lives of women have been recognized" (Collins, "The Apocalypse [Revelation]," *NJBC*, 1012).

   *enthroned on many waters:* See Jer 51:13, in reference to Babylon: "O you who dwell by many waters, rich in treasures, your end has come, the thread of your life is cut." The description does not, literally, fit Rome; John has simply borrowed it from Jeremiah and has applied it to his "Babylon." In v. 15 the "waters" are interpreted as Rome's vassals.

2. *the kings of the earth:* See v. 18; 16:14; 18:9-10; to be distinguished from the "kings" of 17:12. The "kings of the earth" are the rulers who have purchased the favor of Rome; the "inhabitants of the earth" are the enemies of God and the infatuated worshipers of the beast.

3. *He carried me away in spirit into a wilderness:* See 1:10. While wilderness or desert (*erēmos*) can be a haunt of demons (Isa 13:20), it may, here, have a positive connotation—John's vantage-point.

   *a woman mounted on a scarlet beast:* This woman is the antithesis of the one in ch. 12. The beast is the one of ch. 13, now arrayed in scarlet (*kokkinos*) (reflecting the fiery red [*pyrros*] dragon of 12:3), and wearing blasphemous names all over, not only on his seven heads (13:1). It is the empire, the woman being the goddess Rome (*Dea Roma*), sustained by the great empire. "She is in fact riding a tiger" (Sweet, 254).

4. *purple and scarlet:* Decked in imperial colors and making a display of finery, i.e., extravagant wealth; the bride, in contrast, is clothed in the fine linen of righteous deeds (19:8).

   *a gold cup:* See Jer 51:7, "Babylon was a golden cup in the Lord's hand, making all the earth drunken."

   *full of obscenities (bdelygmata):* The same expression as the "abomination" of Dan 9:27; 11:31; 12:11 (see Mark 13:14): the altar of Zeus set up in the Jerusalem temple by Antiochus IV; therefore it means idolatry.

5. *on her forehead . . . a name:* It is frequently stated that Roman prostitutes displayed their names on their foreheads; there does not seem to be sufficient evidence to support such a claim (Ford, *Revelation*, 279). Perhaps the observation catches up, in parody, 14:1.

   *a mysterious name,* lit. "a name of mystery (*mystērion*): The name is not to be taken literally (see 11:8); Babylon is a mystical name for Rome.

6. *drunk with the blood of God's people:* We may find here an allusion to the bloody persecution of Nero (see 17:10). Rome is guilty of the double crime of idolatry (v. 4) and of murder (v. 6); Ezekiel had accused Jerusalem of these same crimes (see Ezek 16:36-38; 23:37, 45).

*blood of the martyrs* [witnesses]: Here only in Revelation *martys* seems to have the sense of "martyr"; see 16:6; 18:24; 19:2. There appears to be no difference between "God's people" and "the martyrs of Jesus."

*I wondered greatly,* lit. "I wondered with great wonder": The marveling of the seer in the face of a vision is a feature of apocalyptic (see Dan 7:15).

7. *the angel said to me:* In apocalyptic, angels commonly fill the role of interpreter (see Dan 7:15, 28; 8:15-26).

8. *the beast you saw was and is not and is to rise:* See 13:3, 12, 14. A parody on the divine title "who is and who was and who is to come" (1:4). Nero *was* (he ruled Rome), he is *not* (he is now dead), he *is to rise* (he will return to regain power).

*is to rise from the abyss:* A permanent characteristic of the beast, just as the permanent characteristic of the Lamb is "as though it had been slain" (5:6).

*and it goes to perdition:* A second permanent attribute of the beast (Caird, 216).

9. *this calls for a mind with wisdom,* lit. "here is the mind that has wisdom": Note the similar phrase in 13:18. Here, too, the point is not to find a key to a puzzle but, rather, to discern the true character of Babylon/Rome.

*seven hills . . . seven kings:* The city on the seven hills was a traditional description of Rome. The "kings" are Roman emperors. The historical emperors are as follows: Julius Caesar (d. 44 B.C.E.), Augustus (31 B.C.E.–14 C.E.), Tiberius (14–37), Gaius (37–41), Claudius (41–54), Nero (54–68), Galba, Otho, Vitellius (68–69), Vespasian (69–79), Titus (79–81), Domitian (81–96), Nerva (96–98), Trajan (98–117). We have no way of knowing how John handles the list. Does he begin with Julius Caesar, or with Augustus? Would he have ignored the three rival claimants of 68–69? More to the point is that the number seven is symbolic; John is not concerned with the exact number of emperors who ruled after Nero. He seeks to emphasize that the last monstrous emperor will emerge very soon.

11. *yet he is one of the seven:* The author plays on the number seven. By means of the Nero legend he can make his eighth emperor (a *Nero redux*) one of the seven: Nero all over again, he is "antichrist."

12. *ten kings:* See Dan 7:24; Rev 13:1. These ten kings belong to the future; they will receive authority for one hour with the beast, that is, at his appearing. As part of the beast (v. 3) they are distinct from the "kings of the sunrise" (16:12) who muster for the battle of Armageddon.

13. *a single purpose:* The kings are unanimous in their wholehearted support of the beast.

14. *will wage war on the Lamb:* See 16:14; 19:19.

*Lord of lords and King of kings:* See Deut 10:17; Ps 136:3; Dan 2:47; 2 Macc 13:4; 1 Tim 6:15; Rev 19:16.

*those who are with him:* The faithful followers of the Lamb will share his triumph.

*called, and chosen, and faithful:* See Matt 22:14, "For many are called, but few are chosen." This is the only occurrence of *klētos*, "called," and *eklektos*, "chosen," in Revelation.

15. *the waters you saw:* The "many waters" of 17:1, a feature borrowed from Jeremiah's description of Babylon (Jer 51:13), are now said to represent the mixed and teeming peoples of the empire.

16. *the ten horns:* The horns grow from the heads of the beast, (v. 3) who cynically uses them to destroy the harlot; they are the "ten kings" of v. 12. See Ezek 16:39, 41; 23:25-29.

17. *for God has put it into their minds:* After all, these kings, and the beast itself, are instruments of God's purpose (see Isa 7:18; 45:1).

   *God's words:* The words of God which must be fulfilled are his decree against Rome (14:8; 16:19; 18:8).

18. *the woman you saw:* In John's vision the woman sat enthroned on seven hills (v. 9).

   *the kings of the earth:* Rome's vassals (see 18:9); they are to be distinguished from the "ten kings" who are allies of Antichrist (v. 12).

## INTERPRETATION

Although the fall of Rome is proclaimed in 14:8 and is briefly described in 16:19, the end of that city, the great persecuting power, cannot be treated so casually. The whole of chapter 17 is given over to a description of Babylon—the goddess Rome—seated on the satanic beast; the fall of Rome is solemnly acclaimed in 18:1-8. Then follow a satirical lament (18:9-24) and a triumphant liturgy in heaven (19:1-10).

The plagues of bowls were the last; what follows fills out the details of these plagues. This is why one of the seven angels of the bowls now serves as John's guide. In the prophetic literature idolatry is termed "fornication" and a city given to idolatry is termed a "harlot." Also, in Rev 18:3 the excessive wealth of Rome is "wantonness." In terms that refer better to historical Babylon, John depicts the worldwide political influence of Rome and its vast trade through its port of Ostia. Rome appears as the great harlot because of her idolatrous religion and excessive wealth. With idolatry went vices of every kind, and Paul has painted a lurid picture of the vices of paganism (Rom 1:24-32). The "kings of the earth" are the rulers who have purchased the favor of Rome; the "inhabitants of the earth" are the infatuated worshipers of the beast, enemies of God.

John, fallen into a trance, was transported by his angel guide into a wilderness. Desert is an ambivalent symbol: it is a place of demons and temptation, but also a place of God's protection (as in chapter 12 where the woman rests secure). While desert, as abode of evil, might appear to be a fitting setting for the great harlot, it seems more likely that John does not intend us to regard the desert as the location of the woman (Babylon/Rome); rather, from that place of security and detachment, John could see the city in its true colors. Indeed, ch. 18 would suggest that he was conscious of the fascination of the empire.

The woman was proudly decked in imperial purple and scarlet and made a display of costly finery. Yet, all her magnificence pales before the shining splendor of the woman of 12:1 and before the simple beauty of the bride of the Lamb (19:7-8). Her mysterious name is perhaps a parody of the mysterious name of the rider of 19:12. The harlot holds a golden cup full of "the wine of the wrath of her fornication" (14:8) which the nations have drunk (18:3). John saw that the woman was drunk, but drunk with blood. The slain people of God are evidently martyrs; the repetition ("God's people," "witnesses") may serve to enhance the guilt of Rome.

Despite himself, John is impressed by the grandeur of Rome. Besides, he had been invited to witness God's judgment on Babylon, yet no ruined city met his gaze. Instead, he had seen a bejewelled woman on a scarlet beast. He needs an interpreter.

An *angelus interpres* lists the significant details of the vision: the woman, the beast, his seven heads, and his ten horns. In his explanation, he takes the beast first (17:8-17) and briefly mentions the harlot last of all (v. 18). In ch. 13 the beast was said to have recovered from a deadly wound (13:3, 12, 14). Again, John bends the Nero legend to his purpose. Here the beast is said to have died of its wound ("is not") and gone to the abyss (see 11:7), and has returned again but only to go to final doom (see 19:20). As in 13:3, people will stand in awe of the beast, amazed at its vitality. But now the "whole world" of 13:3 is made more specific: it includes only "the inhabitants of the earth," whose names were not found in the Lamb's book of life (13:8; 20:12, 15)—they are the worshipers of the beast (16:2). A permanent characteristic of the beast is that it rises from the abyss—home of demonic beings—and goes to perdition: it carries the stamp of ultimate destruction. "When it appears, it is already on the way out. John is afraid his fellow Christians will surrender to an enemy already defeated. His revelation is to remove the cover (the literal meaning of *apocalypse*) and let them see the reality of things" (Boring, 181).

At this point the angel calls for special attention: "This calls for a mind with wisdom." What follows is enigmatic, like the number of the beast (13:8). The angel offers a twofold explanation of the seven heads of the beast. In the first place, the heads stand for seven hills; Rome was widely known as the city on the seven hills—not much need for "wisdom" in this respect. But the heads have a further significance: they are kings—without doubt, Roman emperors. We are told that "five have fallen" and that "one is"—the sixth, in whose reign the book is thus set. The reign of his successor, the seventh, will be short. Then comes the last emperor, the eighth, who is also one of the seven, and who wears the stamp of doom. We cannot really be more specific and, with any confidence, name the emperors John may have had in mind. For that matter, the obviously symbolic bent of his "seven" would suggest that he did not mean to be more precise.

The ten horns of the beast are ten kings. As part of the beast, they are distinct from the kings from the East (16:12) who muster for the battle of Armageddon. They are united in their wholehearted support of the beast; and when they have, with him, brought about the downfall of Rome (17:12, 16-17), they follow him in war against the Lamb. But the beast has arisen only "to go to perdition" (17:8, 11): he and his followers will be conquered by the Lamb; the battle will be described in 19:11-21 (see 16:13-16). The faithful followers of the Lamb will participate in his victory. They "have conquered him by the blood of the Lamb and by the testimony they bore" (12:11); they are the victors who have been given "authority over the nations" (2:26). They are not only called and chosen, but have sealed their call and election by their fidelity; they are those "who follow the Lamb wherever he goes" (14:14).

The ten kings who had so wholeheartedly supported the beast (vv. 12-14) now turn on the harlot. "The savaging of the whore by the monster and its horns is John's most vivid symbol for the self-destroying power of evil" (Caird, 221). Logically, this destruction of the harlot should precede war on the Lamb, war which will end in the total destruction of kings and beast (v. 14). John is never inhibited by something as unimportant as logic! Ironically, kings and beast serve God's purpose as they implement his verdict on Rome. Although his earlier indications are already sufficiently clear, John takes care to spell out the identity of the harlot. The closing verse (v. 18) is bitingly sarcastic: this city thinks herself to be absolute mistress of the kings of the earth, the very kings destined to destroy her.

Our Western civilization has much that is admirable. But is it really as healthy as it seems? It is founded on capitalism, an economic system that is defensible only within limits. In practice, the greed of our consumer-oriented society oversteps the borders of justice. Ask the Third World! The great business corporations are motivated almost solely by profit: they oppress, directly and indirectly. Pollution of the environment, result of an unbridled exploitation of natural resources, itself spurred by pursuit of gain, is a cancer at the vitals of our planet. Nations, even the more wealthy and powerful nations, do not have the political will to face a dire situation with courage. Greed is a particularly nasty form of evil. John's striking image of kings and beast consuming the Great City holds a message for us. He depicts the civilization of his day as being fatally threatened from within itself. It is not difficult to diagnose a malaise at the heart of our world. Is it too late to save the patient?

### For Reference and Further Study

Beale, G. K. "The Danielic Background for Revelation 13:18 and 17:9." *TynBul* 31 (1980) 163–70.

_____. "The Origin of the Title 'King of kings and Lord of lords' in Revelation 17:14." *NTS* 31 (1985) 618–20.

Bruns, J. E. "The Contrasted Women of Apocalypse 13 and 17." *CBQ* 26 (1964) 459–63.

Cambier, J. "Les images de l'A. T. dans l'Apocalypse." *NRT* 77 (1955) 113–23.

Dyer, C. H. "The Identity of Babylon in Revelation 17-18." *Bibliotheca Sacra* 144 (1987) 305–16, 433–49.

Strobel, A. "Abfassung und Geschichtstheologie der Apokalypse, 17:9-12." *NTS* 10 (1964) 433–45.

## XI. THE END OF BABYLON

### 42. *The Fall of Babylon* (18:1-8)

1. After this I saw another angel coming down from heaven; he had great authority and the earth was lighted up by his splendor. 2. With a mighty voice he proclaimed:
　　　　Fallen, fallen is Babylon the great!
　　　　　She has become a dwelling for demons,
　　　　　a haunt for every unclean spirit,
　　　　　a haunt for every unclean and loathsome bird.
3.　　　For all the nations have drunk of the wine of the wrath of
　　　　　her fornication;
　　　　　the kings of the earth have committed fornication with her,
　　　　　and the merchants of the earth have grown rich
　　　　　on the strength of her wanton luxury.
4. Then I heard another voice from heaven saying:
　　　　Come out of her, my people,
　　　　　that you may have no part in her sins,
　　　　　and that you do not suffer her plagues;

5.     for her sins are piled high as heaven
         and God has remembered her crimes.
6.     Pay her back in her own coin,
         repay her twice over for her works!
         In the cup she mixed, mix her a double draught!
7.     To match her pomp and wanton luxury,
         mete out to her torment and grief!
         She says to herself:
         "I sit here as queen!
         No widow am I, no mourning will I see!"
8.     Therefore in a single day will her plagues come,
         pestilence, mourning, and famine,
         and she will be burnt to the ground;
         for mighty is the God who has condemned her.

### NOTES

1. *another angel:* John sees an angel of great authority—not his guide of ch. 17—come down from heaven. He has come forth from the presence of God and reflects the divine splendor (see 10:1). See Ezek 43:2.

2. *with a mighty voice:* The focus is on the speech of the angel. In form a dirge, the speech here is a proclamation of judgment.

   *Fallen:* The fall of Babylon has been accomplished by the final plague (16:17-19; see 14:8; Jer 51:8; Isa 21:9). John's description of the ruined city echoes Old Testament prophetic texts: Isa 13:15-22; Jer 50:39; Isa 34:11-15; Zeph 2:13-14.

3. *the wine of the wrath of her fornication:* Here, "fornication" is not only idolatry but wanton luxury.

   *kings . . . merchants:* The lament of the "kings of the earth" is given in vv. 9-10 and that of the merchants in vv. 11-16.

   *wanton luxury:* The extravagant wealth of Rome.

4. *another voice from heaven:* See 10:4, 8; 11:12; 14:2, 13—not the voice of God, who is named in the third person in vv. 5 and 8.

   *come out of her, my people:* The invitation is an echo of Jer 51:6, 45: "Flee from the midst of Babylon, let every man save his life. . . . Go out of the midst of her, my people!" See Isa 48:20; 52:11. Compare the admonition to flight in the Synoptic apocalypse (Mark 13:14-28; Matt 24:16-20).

5. *piled high as heaven:* See Jer 51:9.

   *God has remembered:* See 16:19; the time has come "for destroying the destroyers of the earth" (11:18).

6. *pay her back . . . repay:* See Jer 50:15, 29. The command is addressed to the ministers of divine justice: the angels of the plagues and the unsuspecting

instruments of 17:16-17. Vengeance is the prerogative of God (Deut 32:35; Rom 12:19; Heb 10:30).

*in her own coin*, lit. "as she has rendered": The *lex talionis*; but the payment is given "twice over," see Isa 40:2; Jer 16:18; 17:18—it is full retribution.

*in the cup she mixed:* See 14:8, 10; 17:4; 18:3.

7. *torment and grief:* See Isa 9:5; 14:10-11. "The aim of the plagues is to pierce the blindness of affluence and power" (Sweet, 269).

*I sit here as queen:* See Isa 47:7 (declaration of Babylon): "I shall be mistress for ever." Compare the complacency of the Laodiceans, 3:17.

8. *pestilence, mourning, and famine:* See 6:5-8.

*burnt to the ground*, lit. "burnt with fire": See v. 18 ("the smoke of her burning")—because the city will be destroyed in war by an invading army (17:16).

### INTERPRETATION

In the proleptic vision of 14:8 the fall of Babylon had been proclaimed; the seventh bowl (16:17-21) had brought its destruction. John lingers over the fate of Rome. He had devoted chapter 17 to a description of "Babylon," ending with assurance of its destruction. Now he develops that oracle of doom against the "great city."

An angel of great authority comes, mirroring the divine splendor, from the presence of God. The fall of Babylon is presented as an event of the past because it has been accomplished by the final plague. The terms of John's description of the ruined city were readily available to him in the Old Testament prophets. The reason for Babylon's punishment is, in the first place, her idolatry. But there is also the luxury of the city. The traders of the empire grew rich by pandering to the extravagant tastes of the capital.

Another voice from heaven invites: "Come out of her, my people." John has in mind texts of Jeremiah and Isaiah which urge the chosen people to flee Babylon before that city reaps its punishment. Now Christians are bidden to flee Rome lest they become involved in her sin and chastisement. But the Christians of *Asia* are John's immediate pastoral concern; he speaks metaphorically. They "come out" of Rome by resisting the culture and values of the empire. Caird has a provocative observation: "The only inhabitants now left in the great city are those who, through all the premonitory plagues, have obdurately refused to repent (10:20; 16:9, 11). Yet even at this late hour it is still possible for men to prove themselves God's 'people' and to escape their share in Babylon's 'plagues' by disassociating themselves from 'her sins.' To the bitter end the miracle of grace remains open, and God never refuses to say 'My people' to those who before were not his people (Hos 2:23; Rom 9:25-26;

1 Pet 2:10)'' (224). John goes on to declare that the sins of Rome are piled high as heaven (see Jer 51:9) and that God's justice has taken stock of her crimes. The "great city" will be the supreme example of the operation of the *lex talionis*. Rome, oblivious of her nemesis, proclaims: "I sit here as queen"—the arrogant self-assurance of its invincibility typical of every great empire. Verses 7-8 develop the idea of proportionate retribution: let her share of misery match her arrogance. The words of the mighty God must be fulfilled (17:17).

### For Reference and Further Study

Klassen, W. "Vengeance in the Apocalypse of John." *CBQ* 28 (1966) 300–11.
Strand, K. A. "Some Modalities of Symbolic Usage in Revelation 18." *AUSS* 24 (1986) 37–46.

## 43. *Dirges Over Babylon* (18:9-19)

[The kings' lament]
9. The kings of the earth who committed fornication with her, and lived wantonly with her, will weep and wail over her, as they watch the smoke of her burning. 10. Standing far off in terror at her torment, they will say:
> Alas, alas, great city,
> mighty city of Babylon!
> In one hour your doom has come!

[The merchants' lament]
11. And the merchants of the earth will weep and mourn for her, because no one buys their cargoes any more, 12. cargoes of gold and silver, precious stones and pearls, fine linen and purples, silk and scarlet; all sorts of scented woods and every type of ivory work and all kinds of objects in costly wood, bronze, iron, or marble; 13. cinnamon and spice, incense, myrrh, and frankincense; wine, oil, fine flour and wheat, cattle and sheep, horses, chariots, slaves, and human livestock.

14.   The fruit for which your soul longed is gone from you
> and all your luxuries and splendors are lost to you,
> never to be found again.

15. The merchants of these wares, who were made rich through her, will stand far off in terror at her torment, weeping and mourning, 16. and saying,
> Alas, alas, for the great city
> that was robed in fine linen and purple and scarlet,
> adorned with gold and precious stones and pearls.

17.    In one hour so much wealth laid waste!
[The seafarers' lament]
    Then every sea-captain and seafarer, sailors and those who make a
living from the sea, stood far off. 18. and cried out as they watched the
smoke of her burning: Was there ever a city like the great city? 19. They
threw dust on their heads, and cried out, wailing and mourning, saying,
        Alas, alas for the great city,
            where all who had ships at sea grew rich from her wealth.
        In one hour she has been laid waste!

## Notes

The kings' lament

9–10. *the kings of the earth:* See 17:2; 18:3; Ezek 26:16-17. The passage 18:9-19 echoes
Ezekiel's lamentation over the fall of Tyre (Ezek 26-27).

*standing far off:* "With a touch of grim humor John paints them as standing
at a safe distance from the conflagration, and contenting themselves with idle
lamentations" (Swete, 231).

*in one hour:* Repeated in vv. 17, 19. See 17:12: the ten kings with the beast
receive authority "for one hour" in order to destroy Rome.

The merchants' lament

11–13. See Ezek 27:2-3, 12-13, 22; Isa 23:1-12.

*because no one buys their cargoes:* The self-interest of the merchants is pronounced.

*and human livestock,* lit. "and human souls": See Ezek 27:13, "they exchanged
the persons of men and vessels of bronze for your merchandise"—an oracle
against Tyre. "Human livestock" would refer to slaves destined for the amphi-
theatre or for prostitution.

14. Several commentators feel that this verse is out of place and would fit better
in the context of 18:22-23. It is, however, not unlike 18:16, 19. The desired
ripe autumn fruit will never be gathered: Rome will reap the harvest which
her deeds have merited. Her luxury and her splendor have vanished forever.

15–17a. *the merchants:* Self-interest is the merchants' only concern; see v. 10.

*so much wealth laid waste:* Doom had fallen on Babylon "in one hour"; but
the merchants' prime concern is the loss of so much wealth.

The seafarers' lament

17b–19. *every sea-captain and seafarer:* The tenor of the lament is the same as the
others. See Ezek 27.

*they threw dust on their heads:* Ezek 27:30.

## INTERPRETATION

The fall of Rome finds dramatic expression in the three dirges chanted over her conflagration by the kings, the merchants, and the shipowners and sailors of the world. The whole passage is manifestly inspired by Ezekiel's dirge over Tyre (Ezek 27–28).

### The kings' lament

These vassal kings deplore the fate of the city whose luxury as well as whose idolatry they had shared. John, ironically, underlines their self-interest by stressing their fastidious care not to be involved in the fate of the "mighty city."

### The merchants' lament

The self-interest of the merchants is, not surprisingly, even more pronounced: they mourn for their vanished trade and not for Babylon. We know that Rome's commerce was vast; the long list of imports vividly depicts its range and the exotic nature of the products. The list, which ranges through precious metals and stones, costly textiles, rare fabrics, cosmetics, foodstuffs, and livestock reaches its climax with traffic in slaves. The merchants, like the kings (v. 10), will stand well clear of the stricken city. Their dirge opens with the words of the previous lament (v. 10). But, while the kings address the "mighty city," the merchants look only to her wealth and splendor, which they describe in terms reminiscent of 17:4, the description of the harlot. We find a similar, but more explicit, fluctuation between woman and city (bride and new Jerusalem) in 21:9-10.

### The seafarers' lament

Like the merchants, the shipowners and sailors find that their interests, too, have suffered a dire blow. In Ezekiel 27 the downfall of the island city of (ancient) Tyre is, with dramatic appropriateness, portrayed as a shipwreck; and though Rome was not, like Tyre, a seaport (Rome's port was Ostia) the capital of the empire was the focus of world trade. The attitudes and words of these latter mourners are similar to those of the others (see vv. 10, 15-16). In 17:1 John had pictured the harlot (Rome) "enthroned on many waters"—Jeremiah's description of Babylon (Jer 51:13). He is concerned, not with geography, but with the symbolism of "Tyre" and "Babylon."

## FOR REFERENCE AND FURTHER STUDY

Collins, A. Yarbro. "Revelation 18: Taunt-Song or Dirge?" In J. Lambrecht, ed., *L'Apocalypse Johannique,* 185–204.
Vanhoye, A. "L'Utilisation du livre d'Ézéchiel dans l'Apocalypse." *Bib* 43 (1962) 436–76.

## 44. *The Judgment of Babylon* (18:20-24)

20. Rejoice over her, heaven, and God's people, and apostles, and prophets, for God has given judgment for you against her.

21. Then a mighty angel lifted up a stone like a great millstone and hurled it into the sea, saying,

> Thus will Babylon, the great city,
> be hurled down with violence,
> never to be seen again!

22.    The sound of harpers and minstrels,
> flute-players and trumpeters,
> will be heard in you no more;
> and any craftsman of any trade
> will be found in you no more;
> and the sound of the mill
> will be heard in you no more;

23.    the light of the lamp
> will be seen in you no more;
> and the voice of the bridegroom and bride
> will be heard in you no more.
> For your merchants were the great ones of the earth
> and through your sorcery were all nations led astray.

24.    And in her was found the blood of prophets and of God's people,
> and of all who have been slain on earth.

## NOTES

20. *rejoice over her, heaven:* An echo of 12:12a which celebrates the Christian victory over Satan; v. 12b then goes on to warn of the devil's wrath now vented on the earth.

*God has given judgment,* lit. "God has judged your judgments from her": *krima,* "judgment," here has overtones of a lawsuit or court case: God has passed sentence on Babylon, the very sentence of death she had passed on God's people. "For you"—your judgment—links up with 6:9-11. See 13:7, 15; 18:24.

21. *a mighty angel:* See 5:2; 10:1. The symbolic action of the angel, and his words, are reminiscent of Jer 51:63-64. Jeremiah had commissioned Seraiah to read aloud Jeremiah's sentence on Babylon, then tie a stone to the scroll and throw it into the Euphrates, declaring: "Thus shall Babylon sink, to rise no more." *never to be seen again:* See Ezek 26:21.

22-23.  See Jer 25:10, "I will banish from them the voice of mirth and the voice of gladness, the voice of the bridegroom and the voice of the bride, the grinding of the millstones and the light of the lamp"; Ezek 26:13, "I will stop the music of your songs, and the sound of your lyres shall be heard no more"; see Isa 24:8; 23:8.

   *will be heard in you no more:* A refrain that poignantly and effectively underscores the total eclipse of Rome and its world.

23. *your merchants:* Proud and self-sufficient in their wealth, they were effective propagandists of the "sorcery" of Rome. See 18:11-16.

   *your sorcery:* See 2 Kgs 9:22; Isa 47:12; Nah 3:4. *pharmakia* is "magic," "sorcery" (see 9:21), here used in the wider sense of idolatry and luxury. The *Sibylline Oracles* inveighed against the great wealth of Rome. See *Sib. Or.* 3:350-55; 4:145-48; 8:9-11, 17-18, 33-36, 95-99 (Collins, *Crisis and Catharsis*, 90–94).

24. *in her:* She, the "great city," "represents all human arrogance, all suppression of witness to higher authority, from Cain to Nero" (Sweet, 276).

   *the blood of prophets:* See Jer 51:49, "Babylon must fall for the slain of Israel, as for Babylon have fallen the slain of all the earth"; Luke 11:50, "that the blood of all the prophets, shed from the foundation of the world, may be required of this generation"; Matt 23:35.

   *slain:* Like the Lamb (5:6) and those whose souls rested beneath the altar (6:9).

### INTERPRETATION

   Verse 20, which anticipates the canticle of 19:1-8, introduces the symbolic judgment (v. 21) and the heavenly lament (vv. 22-24). "God's people and apostles and prophets," who have come triumphantly through the great tribulation engineered by Satan, now join in the heavenly rejoicing. Their suffering has made the heavenly victory an earthly reality. The symbolic gesture of the "mighty angel" is reminiscent of Jer 51:63-64: it symbolizes the complete submergence, the final disappearance, of imperial Rome; it rounds off the proclamation of 18:1-3. The solemn repetition of the phrase "will be . . . no more" gives an air of pathetic finality to the fate of Rome. All the arts of civilized life have come to an end. The bright festive lights will shine out no more and the sounds of joy are stilled for ever. The ruined city has become the abode of wild beasts and of demons (18:2).

   The last verse (v. 24) gives the chief reason for Rome's destruction. She is guilty of the blood of God's people (see 16:6; 17:6; 18:20), not only those slain in Rome but also those who have suffered throughout the empire.

The dirges of kings and merchants and seafarers over Rome are instructive. Self-interest is the name of the game. With the fall of Rome, the economic bottom had fallen out of their world. Up to now, they had been captains of commerce, manipulating and controlling world trade, and battening on it. The empire was the source of Rome's wealth.

We too, in our Western world, are jealous of our standards and lifestyle. The *Sibylline Oracles* document widespread unrest at taxation and exploitation. In our day there is concern that the First World owns or controls the great bulk of our earth's resources. A minority of the earth's inhabitants enjoy a lifestyle denied the rest.

In the face not only of affluence but, to an unacceptable degree, of excessive wealth, there is far too much grinding poverty. Justice demands that we of the First World be prepared to share. But that is not enough. We should come to realize just how far our prosperity is achieved and maintained at the cost of the poverty of others. We are being challenged to turn from self-interest.

As Christians we are being challenged by the gospel of Jesus Christ. Jesus taught and lived that the reality of God is revealed in the realization of more humanity between fellow human beings—giving drink to the thirsty, feeding the hungry, welcoming the stranger. Matthew's story of judgment (25:31-46) is focused on purely human concerns. The emphasis is on the needy person, the one in distress. What is at stake is an attitude towards the little ones, the humble and the needy. The criterion is not the standard of religion or cult; it is, starkly: has one helped those in need?

As Christians, we might heed and hearken to the invitation, "Come out of her, my people." We might begin by looking critically at the values of *our* world; we might measure it by the standard of the gospel. A painful task. And, if we try to follow up on our findings, a costly task. Princes of commerce, mighty corporations, will not take kindly to challenge, will not welcome lower profit-margins. John tells us that greed, exploitation, and oppression are a cancer that will undermine and destroy every empire.

## 45. The Vindication of God's People (19:1-10)

1. After this I heard, as it were, the shout of a vast throng in heaven:
   Hallelujah!
   Victory and glory and power belong to our God
2.        for true and just are his judgments.
   For he has condemned the great harlot
      who corrupted the earth with her fornication,
      and has avenged on her the blood of his servants.

3. And again they shouted: Hallelujah! The smoke from her goes up for ever and ever! 4. And the twenty-four elders and the four living creatures fell down and worshiped God who sits on the throne, saying, Amen! Hallelujah!

5. Then came a voice from the throne, saying,
      Praise our God, all you his servants
      you who fear him, small and great.

6. And I heard, as it were, the sound of a vast throng, like the sound of many waters and as the sound of mighty thunder peals, saying,
   Hallelujah!
      For the Lord God the Almighty has entered on his reign.
7.        Let us rejoice and be glad and give glory to him,
      for the marriage of the Lamb has come.
   His bride has made herself ready,
8.        and it is granted to her to attire herself in fine linen,
      shining and clean—
      for the fine linen is the righteous deeds of God's people.

9. And he said to me, "Write this: blessed are those who are invited to the marriage feast of the Lamb." And he said to me, "These are the very words of God." 10. And I fell at his feet to worship him. But he said to me: "No, not that! I am a fellow servant with you and your brothers and sisters who hold the testimony of Jesus: worship God. For the testimony of Jesus is the spirit of prophecy."

### NOTES

1. *after this I heard:* Introduces a new scene; see 4:1; 7:1, 9; 15:5; 18:1. Vv. 1-4 respond to 18:20.

*the shout of a vast throng:* Seemingly the vast throng of 7:9-10, chanting a victory ode.

*Hallelujah:* Transliteration of a Hebrew phrase meaning "Praise Yahweh" and found in many of the psalms. It was used in synagogue worship and figured early in the Christian liturgy. In the New Testament it occurs only in Revelation.

*victory and glory and power belong to our God:* See 4:11; 5:12; 7:10, 12; 12:10. *Sōtēria*, "salvation," is here properly rendered "victory."

2. *corrupted:* She has brought moral ruin upon the earth.

   *the blood of his servants:* See 2 Kgs 9:7, "That I may avenge on Jezebel the blood of my servants the prophets, and the blood of all the servants of the Lord."

3. *the smoke from her goes up for ever and ever:* See Isa 34:14; Rev 14:11: the destruction is definitive; Babylon will "never be seen again" (18:21).

4. *elders . . . and living creatures:* These were last mentioned in 14:3; as nearest the throne, they add their "Amen" to the canticle of the angels (see 5:14).
   *Amen! Hallelujah!:* See Ps 106:47. The passage 19:4-6 shows a close correspondence with the seventh trumpet (11:15-19); both passages refer to the end. We find a declaration of divine sovereignty (11:15, 17; 19:4, 6), the "servants who fear your name, both small and great" (11:18; 19:5), and the thunder peals (11:19; 19:6).

5. *praise our God:* See Ps 113:1; 134:1; 135:2—the Hallel psalms.

6. *the sound of a vast throng:* In 11:17 the heavenly choir had celebrated the divine sovereignty; here the vast throng of victors catches up the hymn.
   *many waters . . . mighty thunder peals:* So sounded the mighty hymn of praise (1:15; 14:2; 6:1; 10:3-4).

7. *let us rejoice and be glad:* See Matt 5:12, "Rejoice and be glad, for your reward is great in heaven."
   *give glory to him:* See 11:13; 14:7; 16:9.
   *the marriage of the Lamb has come:* Israel as bride of Yahweh is a prophetic theme (Hos 2:16; Isa 54:6; Ezek 16:7-8). Jesus is represented as referring to himself as bridegroom (Mark 2:19-20; see Matt 22:1); Paul transferred the prophetic imagery to Christ and the Church (2 Cor 11:2). The theme is further developed in Ephesians and Revelation: Eph 5:25, "Christ loved the church and gave himself up for her"; in Revelation those who form the bride of Christ have been redeemed "by the blood of the Lamb" (5:9; 7:14; 14:3-4).
   *his bride:* It is quite in John's style to introduce the bride of the Lamb abruptly (see 11:7; 14:18); the image will be explained in a later scene (21:9-14).
   *has made herself ready:* The bride has donned her wedding gown. In Eph 5:26-27 Christ has prepared his bride by washing her in the bath of baptism and by making her immaculate. Here the situation is quite the same.

8. *it is granted (edothē) her to attire herself:* Her wedding gown is gift. In Eph 5:26 Christ "sanctified" his bride; here she "is given" the white bridal dress of holiness. Always, her sanctity is his achievement.
   *fine linen (byssos):* The fine, costly linen of Egypt.
   *shining and clean:* See 15:6. John explains that this fine linen is the holy lives of God's people—*dikaiōmata*, "judgments," or, as here, "righteous deeds."

9. *invited to the marriage feast:* See 16:15. "Marriage feast" is a common figure of the kingdom (Matt 7:11; 22:1-14; 25:1-13; 26:29).
   *these are the very words of God:* A paraphrase of *Amen.*

10. *I fell at his feet to worship:* See Dan 8:17, "When he [the angel] came near, I was frightened and fell upon my face." Though *proskynein* may have a wider sense (see 3:9), the angel chooses to interpret John's gesture as a form of worship. The admonition, "No, not that!," repeated in the parallel situation in 22:9, may be meant as a warning against angel worship, a practice not unknown in Asia Minor. See Col 2:18, "Let no one disqualify you, insisting on self-abasement and worship of angels." See Heb 1:5-14: angels do not outrank Christians; in worship, humans and angels are equal and subordinated to Jesus as God's Son.

*fellow servant (syndoulos):* See 22:9, "fellow servant with you and your brothers the prophets." Like John, the angel plays a prophetic role—hence the reference to prophecy at the close of the verse.

*who hold the testimony of Jesus: echō,* "to have," here means to possess, and faithfully preserve, Jesus' witness. In the parallel passage, 22:9, the prophets "keep the words of this book."

*worship God:* A firm command. To worship God alone (and the Lamb) is the ultimate answer to the idolatry John has confronted throughout.

*for the testimony of Jesus is the spirit of prophecy:* "Of Jesus" is subjective genitive (as in 1:2, 9; 12:17); it refers to the witness he has borne in his life, teaching, and death. The Christian prophet bears witness to Jesus by speaking his word.

### INTERPRETATION

Though we have a fresh scene, 19:1-4 is a recapitulation: catching up and developing the theme of 18:20, responding to the invitation of the seer there. The occasion of the heavenly victory song is stressed: execution of judgment on Babylon for her crimes of idolatry and blood-guilt. The great harlot, who had seduced the whole earth and had become drunk with the blood of martyrs (17:1-6), has met her just deserts.

The elders and living creatures (last mentioned in 14:3) add their "Amen" to the canticle of the angels (see 5:14). A voice from the throne summons all servants of God to praise the Lord: the vast throng of victors takes up the hymn. They rejoice that their often repeated prayer— "Your kingdom come"—has been answered: the Lord reigns! (see 11:15). This is the perspective so evident in Daniel: when the enemy of God has been overthrown, then God's kingdom will appear.

The victors are invited guests at the marriage feast of the Lamb. His bride has made herself ready, although her wedding gown is his gift. And yet it is woven of the righteous deeds of God's people. We need to remind ourselves of the fluidity of John's images. So, it appears that while the bride is the Church, the wedding guests are the members of the Church, and their deeds are her bridal dress. Similarly, in chapter

12, the woman is the Church (12:1-6), and yet Christians can be described as "her children" (12:17); and in 7:17 the Lamb is also a shepherd. In all cases the symbolism is clear; John simply manages his imagery with complete freedom. Only three female figures appear in the visions of Revelation: the woman "robed with the sun" of chapter 12, the woman "clothed in purple and scarlet" of chapter 17, and the woman "attired in fine linen" of chapter 19. The first and third represent the Church; the other is her great adversary.

Another beatitude (19:9) carries the beatitude of 14:13 a step further: the "rest" of those who die in the Lord has turned into the joy of the Lamb's marriage festival. The solemn confirmation, "These are the very words of God," reaches back over the series of revelations. John would assure his readers yet again that the apparent triumph of the enemies of God is indeed illusory. The final, desperate assault of evil can only serve to hasten the victory of God, of the Lamb, and of the faithful.

John, overwhelmed by a vision that bore the seal of divine authority, spontaneously fell at the feet of the angel. The admonition, "No, not that!," seems to be a warning against angel worship. This angel firmly declares himself a fellow-servant: angels do not outrank Christians. The author of Hebrews is splendidly dismissive: "Are they not all ministering spirits sent forth to serve, for the sake of those who are to obtain salvation?" (Heb 1:14). Angels, like Christians, are servants, sharing a like authority—their fidelity to the witness that Jesus bore. John, throughout, has vehemently opposed any form of idolatry—not alone worship of the beast, but the idolatry of compromise, as in the case of the Nicolaitans. In the context of 19:10 the worship of God alone is urged by the witness of Jesus, and the message put in the mouth of a Christian prophet is the word of God attested by Jesus. Caird translates: "The testimony of Jesus is the spirit that inspires the prophets."

"Thy kingdom come!" is the daily prayer of God's people. Heaven rejoices in justice. We must not forget that, for God, justice is vindication. His justice is the removal of all that is injustice, the removal of oppression in any guise.

A common image of future blessedness was that of the messianic feast. For John, in Christian terms, it is more specifically the marriage feast of the Lamb. He has occasion to remind his Christians, firmly, not only that they are invited guests at the marriage feast but that they are, at once, the bride herself and her bridal dress. The seeming jumble of John's imagery here holds a salutary reminder. "The Church" is bandied about so readily, and means many different things. Commonly, one thinks of the Church as an abstraction. Indeed, John might be said to share this view: he has the woman sitting secure in the wilderness (12:6, 14). Yet we should always respect the subtlety of his imagery. Here, at least, he makes clear that he is not dealing in abstractions. He reminds us that the Church has no existence apart from the living community (a living community, too, beyond death) of Christian men and women. It is we, all of us together, who form the bride of Christ; it is our righteous deeds that clothe her. The Church is not some entity "out there" or "up there." It is not represented by a hierarchy; leaders in the Church have a servant role, not a representative role (see Mark 9:35; 10:42-45). It is, simply, the people of God—"*all* who fear him, small and great."

Angels are pervasive in Revelation: traditional features of an apocalyptic scenario. Here (19:10) and in 22:8-10 John seems to feel that an embarrassment of angels might mislead. Like the author of Hebrews (Heb 1:14) he decides to put them firmly in their place.

### FOR REFERENCE AND FURTHER STUDY

Boring, M. E. "The Theology of Revelation: 'The Lord Our God the Almighty Reigns.' " *Int* 40 (1986) 257–69.
Fekkes, J. " 'His Bride Has Prepared Herself': Revelation 19–21 and Isaian Nuptial Imagery." *JBL* 109 (1990) 269–87.
Ford, J. M. " 'For the Testimony of Jesus is the Spirit of Prophecy' (Rev 19:10)." *ITQ* 42 (1975) 284–91.

## XII. THE END OF EVIL

### 46. *The End of the Beasts* (19:11-21)

11. And I saw heaven wide open, and behold, a white horse; its rider's name was Faithful and True and in righteousness he judges and makes war. 12. His eyes flamed like fire, and on his head were many diadems; written on him was a name known to none but himself; 13. he was clothed in a cloak dipped in blood, and he was called the Word of God. 14. The armies of heaven followed him on white horses, clothed in fine linen, white and clean. 15. From his mouth came a sharp sword with which to smite the nations, for it is he who will rule them with a rod of iron, and it is he who treads the winepress of the wine of the fury of the wrath of God the Almighty. 16. On his cloak and on his thigh was written the title: King of kings and Lord of lords.

17. Then I saw an angel standing in the sun, and he cried aloud to all the birds that fly in mid-heaven: "Come, gather together for the great

banquet of God, 18. to eat the flesh of kings and flesh of captains and flesh of warriors, the flesh of horses and their riders, and the flesh of all, the free and the slave, the small and the great." 19. And I saw the beast and the kings of the earth with their armies, mustered to do battle with the rider and his army. 20. The beast was captured, and along with him the false prophet who had worked miracles in its presence, by which he deluded those who had received the mark of the beast and worshiped its image. These two were thrown alive into the lake of fire with its sulphurous flames. 21. And the rest were slain by the sword of the rider on the horse, the sword which came out of his mouth, and all the birds gorged themselves on their flesh.

## NOTES

11. *I saw heaven wide open:* See Ezek 1:1. In 4:1 John saw an open door in heaven, and in 11:19 the temple in heaven was thrown open (see 15:5); now heaven is wide open and "God breaks out into the world in the form of a *white horse* and him who *sat upon it*" (Sweet, 282). The "parousia" of Christ is God's word of the Cross which confounds the world.

    *a white horse,* lit. "behold: a white horse and he who sat upon it": The words are repeated from 6:2. In both cases, "white" is the symbol of victory—but there the resemblance ends. The rider here is not the personification of victorious warfare of 6:2; he is the Word of God (19:13).

    *Faithful and True:* See 3:14, "the Amen, the faithful and true witness." See 1:5; 3:7; Isa 11:3-5; Ps 96:13; Ps. Sol 17:23-31.

    *in righteousness he judges:* He "judges" (*krinei*) might be taken in the sense of handing down a condemnatory sentence. Rather, John has in mind Isa 11:4, "with righteousness he will judge the poor, and decide with equity for the meek of the earth." To be noted, too, is the king (who could be interpreted messianically) of Ps 45:4, who is to "ride forth victoriously for the cause of truth and to defend the right."

    *makes war:* On the beast and his followers: 16:14; 17:14.

12. "Every phrase in the description of the Rider adds something important to our understanding of his character and function" (Caird, 241).

    *his eyes flamed like fire:* See 1:14; 2:18. Like the "faithful and true" of the previous verse, this offers a cross-reference to the messages.

    *many diadems:* The dragon wears seven diadems (12:3) and the beast ten (13:1); the "many diadems" of the rider represent a royalty beyond any earthly sovereignty—he is King of kings and Lord of lords (v. 16). See 11:15.

    *written . . . a name:* The harlot had a name written on her forehead (17:5); note the name written on the foreheads of the 144,000 (14:1).

    *known to none but himself:* In Semitic thought the "name" stands for the person. No one can "know," that is, fully understand, who the rider is, except himself (see 2:17). See Luke 10:22, "No one knows who the Son is except the Father, or who the Father is except the Son.'' This name is not that of v. 13, nor is it contained in the titles of v. 16.

13. *clothed in a cloak dipped in blood:* See Isa 63:1-3; Wis 18:14-16. A variant, well-attested, is ''sprinkled'' (*errantismenon*), reflecting Isa 63:3; ''dipped'' (*bebammenon*), is preferable, and is supported by the image of treading the winepress (v. 15).

   *the Word of God:* The ''stern warrior'' of Wis 18:15—God's ''all-powerful word'' leaping down from heaven to slay the first-born of the Egyptians.

14. *the armies of heaven:* While, at first sight, it might appear that ''the armies of heaven'' are the angelic hosts (see Matt 26:53), they are, in reality, the ''called and chosen and faithful'' of 17:14—the companions of the conquering Lamb.

   *clothed in fine linen, white and clean:* See v. 8, ''the fine linen is the righteous deeds of God's people.''

15. *from his mouth came a sharp sword:* This sharp sword (see 1:16; 2:12) is the sword of the prophetic word (Isa 49:2; see Heb 4:12; Eph 6:17).

   *rule them with a rod of iron: poimainein,* lit. ''shepherd''; see 2:27; 12:5.

   *it is he who treads:* As in ''it is he who will rule,'' *autos* is emphatic.

   *the winepress of the wine of the fury of God the Almighty:* This combines the figures of the winepress (14:19) and the cup of wrath (14:10).

16. *on his cloak and on his thigh:* Probably means ''on the cloak and that most exposed part of it which covers the thigh'' (Swete, 255).

   *King of kings and Lord of lords:* See 17:14. The title is obviously not that secret name of v. 12. It challenges the claim of the emperor.

17. *standing in the sun:* See Ezek 39:17-20. See ''in midheaven,'' 8:13; 14:6; this, too, is a proclamation of universal import: this is the final battle.

   *come, gather together . . . .:* In Ezekiel, the destruction of the forces of Gog, king of Magog, is pictured as a sacrificial feast (Ezek 39:17-20).

19. *the kings of the earth:* Those of 1:5; 17:2; 18:3.

   *mustered:* This is the assembly for Armageddon (16:16).

20. *the beast was captured:* Victory is immediate (see 17:14) and total. See 2 Thess 2:8, ''Then the lawless one will be revealed, and the Lord Jesus will slay him with the breath of his mouth and destroy him by his appearing and his coming.''

   *the beast . . . the false prophet:* The captured leaders of the assault (see 13:11-17) are not cast into the bottomless pit, a place of detention (9:1-2; 20:1-3) but into the ''lake of fire.''

   *the lake of fire:* The place of final punishment (see 14:10; 20:10, 14). See Dan 7:11; Num 16:30. See note at 20:10.

21. *the rest were slain:* The followers of the two beastly leaders, slain by the sharp sword of the rider on the white horse (v. 15), await, in Sheol, the final judgment (20:12-13). Then they, too, will be thrown into the lake of fire (20:15).

*the sword which came out of his mouth:* See Isa 49:2, "he made my mouth like a sharp sword."

## INTERPRETATION

This passage deals with the victory of Christ and his followers over the beast, the false prophet, and the kings of the earth, an episode already described proleptically in 14:14-20; 16:12-16; 17:12-14.

John sees heaven thrown wide open for the parousia of the "one like a son of man" (1:13). He comes forth majestically, riding a white horse of invincible victory. His very name declares him to be upholder of faithfulness and truth: his word and life and death are testimony to faithfulness and truth. He comes as judge, but his righteousness is vindication of the poor and the meek of the earth (Isa 11:4). He comes as warrior but his war will be against the destroyers of the earth—the dragon and the beasts. None can escape his scrutiny; all are subject to his authority. He bears a mysterious name distinct from the name of v. 13 and the titles of v. 16. John, ardent follower of the Lamb, knows that, ultimately, the Lamb is as wondrously mysterious as the gracious God he images.

The rider wears a cloak "dipped in blood"; his public name is "Word of God." There can be no doubt that John has in mind Isa 63:1-3: "Who is this that comes from Edom, in crimsoned garments from Bozrah. . . . Why is thy apparel red, and thy garments like his that treads in the winepress? 'I have trodden the winepress alone, and from the peoples no one was with me; I trod them in my anger and trampled them in my wrath; their lifeblood is sprinkled upon my garments, and I have stained all my raiment' "; see Wis 18:4-16. This is Third Isaiah's violent portrayal of God's victory over Edom—over every enemy of his purpose for Israel. If the rider of Revelation wears a robe dipped in blood as he rides out to join battle, that is because John chooses to portray him in the language of Isaiah. But, then, to be already heavily blood-stained *before* battle is distinctly curious. Is John teasing us, challenging us to look more closely at his message? For, if the Lion is the Lamb, if the victim is the victor, if to conquer is "to love not one's life even unto death," if there is the intriguing suggestion of universal salvation—then, might not John, in a startling rebirth of images, be challenging his hearer/readers to reinterpret the imagery to which he and they are heirs? John has reversed the image of Isaiah. "The blood is his own, the Messiah's blood, the blood of him whom his opponents have 'pierced' (1:7), the blood that either redeems (1:5-6; 9:9-10) or condemns" (Krodel, 323).

"While gentle silence enveloped all things, and night in its swift course was now half gone, thy all-powerful word leaped down from heaven, from the royal throne, into the midst of the land that was doomed, a stern warrior carrying the sharp sword of thy authentic command, and stood and filled all things with death, and touched heaven while standing on the earth" (Wis 18:14-16). This is Wisdom's typically flamboyant description of the tenth plague of Egypt (Exod 12:23, 29-30). Since John has explicitly had the plagues of Egypt in mind (trumpets and bowls) his meaning here would appear to be self-evident: the rider is going to be that inflexible "stern warrior." But, could John's Lamb ever be such? John has reversed the image of an avenger splattered with the blood of his enemies; the Lamb is the one who has been pierced (1:7). The title Word of God means that this rider is the one in whom God himself works and acts. The Lamb is the one who defines God. And our God is a saving God.

Here, again, one must keep in mind John's creative use of his sources. If he does write an apocalypse, following an established tradition, his is a *Christian* apocalypse. If his God is Yahweh, his God is spoken, now, by the Lamb who was slain. We should respect the paradoxical strain—expressed among other ways in the firmly expressed "universal salvation" view—that runs through the work. In respect of our passage we may endorse the position of Boring: "This view that the eschatological Divine Warrior is red with his own blood rather than that of his enemies, while championed by the Church Fathers, has been challenged by some modern scholars and pronounced 'absurd' by one [U. B. Müller, *Die Offenbarung des Johannes* (Gütersloh, 1984) 327)]. Yet it is not absurd for one who can define 'conquering' as 'dying' and 'Lion' as 'Lamb' (5:1-7). It is analogous to the idea that Christians wash their garments and make them white in the blood of the Lamb (7:14). John's theology as a whole calls for this interpretation. He uses the ancient *form* of portraying the ultimate victory of God as winning a great battle in which those who have resisted God are slaughtered. But he fills this with new content. This is simply what has happened in the Christian confession as such, that the Christ, the triumphant military king, is Jesus, the crucified man of Nazareth, who was crucified not as preliminary to his victory but as his victory" (196–97).

The rider leads out the armies of heaven. These are the "called and chosen and faithful" of 17:14, the companions of the conquering Lamb. The "army" is that of the 144,000 who "follow the Lamb wherever he goes" (14:4). These soldiers are clad in white linen, like the bride of the Lamb (19:8), because they "have washed their robes and made them white in the blood of the Lamb" (7:14; see 6:11); and, like their leader, they ride on white horses, symbols of victory. The only weapon the Rider wields is the sword of his mouth (19:21), the proclamation of the gospel. And, if he is to rule the nations with a rod of iron—perhaps even "smash them with an iron bar" (see 2:27; 12:5)—we will discover in 21:24–22:3 how gracious is that "rule."

He, too, is the one who treads the winepress. From the winepress trodden by the Messiah flows the wine of divine wrath which his enemies are to be made to drink. The suggestion that the wine is, in fact, their own blood, finds the excellent supporting text of Isa 49:26, "I will make your oppressors eat their own flesh, and they shall be drunk with their own blood as with wine." The rider wears his royal title prominently displayed, a title which cannot be overlooked or ignored. Now the "kings of the earth" will know with chilling certainty that he, and not the emperor, is King of kings and Lord of lords. The portrait of the divine warrior appearing in sovereign power is designed to encourage John's readers, to assure them that their Lord *has* overcome the world (John 16:33; 1 Cor 8:6). The warrant for the title is the initial victory of the Cross.

Ezekiel's text (Ezek 39:17-20) is concerned with the destruction of the forces of Gog of the land of Magog, a slaughter which is characterized as a sacrifice: God immolates his enemies. Here, too, is a sacrificial meal; but John goes beyond Ezekiel in offering to the birds of prey the bodies of all the slain, not only the bodies of the great. Victory is taken for granted: the solemn invitation to the birds is issued before the battle is joined. In view of this gruesome scenario, a text like Matt 24:28 might well give us pause: "Wherever the body is, there the vultures will be gathered together"—Jesus is referring to the public and certain nature of the parousia. The "kings of the earth" are those of Rev 17:12-14 who blindly follow the beast. When, at his instigation (but, in the last resort, as God's instruments), they have destroyed Rome (17:12, 16-17), he leads them against the Lamb (17:14). This is the assembly of Armageddon (16:16): it is the decisive encounter between Christ and the forces of Antichrist; it is the climax of the conspiracy of "the kings of the earth . . . against the Lord and his anointed" (Ps 2:2).

Victory is not only total; it is immediate (see 17:14)—there is no battle. The "armies of heaven" are spectators. The rider alone "slays" the forces of the beast. He slays by the sword of his mouth, by the "word" (the Word) and the Word of God is life-giving. The captured leaders of the assault—beast and false prophet—were cast into the "lake of fire," the place of final punishment, symbol of their annihilation. On the other hand, the "kings of the earth" (v. 19), obviously among the "slain" of v. 21, will bring their glory into the heavenly Jerusalem (21:24); the "nations" as a whole survive this "final" battle. What is John really telling us?

The Lamb goes out, conquering and to conquer. He wears a cloak dipped in blood; his weapon is the word of his mouth. Here is the summit of John's rebirth of images. In this "war" there is no battle; the two beasts are captured without a blow being struck. The armies of heaven are passive spectators: they take no part in the action. Any "slaying" is done by the rider alone, wielding that sword "which came out of his

mouth." As Michael's victory over the dragon was really the victory of
the Lamb (12:11), so, here, victory over the beasts is his victory alone.
It is, throughout, John's position that the only battle, the decisive battle,
fought by the Lamb was on the cross. There is the Christian victory. Christian victors conquer by the blood of the Lamb and in no other way.

All the violence in Revelation wrought on the side of good is wrought
by God and the Lamb. Indeed, it is all traced back to the Lamb. The breaking of the first seal (6:1) launched not only the first series of plagues, but
the other two as well; they are interconnected. As rider on the white horse,
the Lamb launches the final, decisive battle. In all of this Christians
endure—they do not take violent action against the worshipers of the
beast. The message of Revelation is, in its apocalyptic dress, the message of Jesus. There must be a response to injustice, to oppression. That
courageous response, which may and can demand the ultimate sacrifice,
is always non-violent. That word speaks, paradoxically, through the violent imagery of Revelation. The only weapon of the oppressed is *hypomonē*.
It is the weapon that, in the end, disarms evil. It seems that we have
hardly begun to learn the lesson of Jesus. Have we, Christians, *really*
learned any lesson of Jesus? Our record is not spectacular, perhaps least
of all in our flaccid condoning of the evil of war—not to mention our com-
plicity in "religious" wars.

### For Reference and Further Study

Considine, J. S. "The Rider on the White Horse." *CBQ* 6 (1944) 406–22.
Rissi, M. *The Future of the World: An Exegetical Study of Revelation 19:11–22:5.* Lon-
    don: SCM, 1972.
_____. "Die Erscheinung Christi nach Offenbarung, 19:11-16." *TZ* 21 (1965)
    81–95.

## 47. *The End of Satan (20:1-10)*

[Satan Bound]

1. Then I saw an angel coming down from heaven with the key of the
abyss, and a great chain, in his hand. 2. He seized the dragon, that ancient serpent, who is Devil and the Satan, and bound him for a thousand years; 3. he threw him into the abyss, shutting and sealing it over
him, so that he should not deceive the nations again until the thousand
years were ended. After that he must be let loose for a little while.

[Reign with Christ]

4. I saw thrones, and seated on them were those to whom judgment was committed. And I saw the souls of those who had been beheaded for the testimony of Jesus and for the word of God, those who had not worshiped the beast and its image and had not received its mark on forehead or hand. They came to life and reigned with Christ for a thousand years, 5. while the rest of the dead did not come to life until the thousand years were ended. This is the first resurrection. 6. Blessed and holy is the one who shares in the first resurrection. Over such the second death has no power; but they will be priests of God and of Christ, and they will reign with him for a thousand years.

[End of the Dragon]

7. When the thousand years are ended, Satan will be let loose from his prison, 8. and he will come out to deceive the nations at the four corners of the earth, Gog and Magog, to muster them for battle—their number as the sands of the sea. 9. They marched over the breadth of the land and surrounded the camp of God's people and the beloved city. But fire came down from heaven and consumed them. 10. And the Devil who deceived them was flung into the lake of fire and brimstone, where the beast and the false prophet were, to be tormented day and night for ever and ever.

## NOTES

*Satan Bound*

1. *then I saw:* Not "After this, I saw," see 18:1; 19:1, a phrase which introduces a new vision. In contrast, "then I saw" links, loosely, a number of visions: (19:11, 17, 19; 20:4, 11, 12; 21:1).

   *coming down from heaven:* As in 18:1 an angel comes down from heaven, charged with a special mission.

   *the key of the abyss:* See 9:1. The abyss is the prison of demonic spirits before their final relegation to the "lake of fire."

   *a great chain:* Satan will not only be firmly imprisoned but heavily shackled.

2. *the dragon, that ancient serpent:* Identified as in 12:9.

   *bound him for a thousand years:* The number is symbolic, related to the thousand years of vv. 4-6.

3. *he threw into the abyss:* See 9:1-2. "The threefold verbs 'threw,' 'shut,' and 'sealed' have the same ring of finality as our 'signed, sealed, and delivered' " (Boring, 200).

   *so that he should not deceive the nations again:* Because of the parallelism, the expression echoes that of 12:9, "the deceiver of the whole world." See v. 8.

   *he must be let loose for a little while:* "There is a necessity for it (*dei*), founded on some mystery of the Divine Will" (Swete, 261). See 12:12, "his time is short."

*Reign with Christ*

4. *I saw thrones . . . .:* See Dan 7:9, 21-22, 26. Literally, v. 4 reads: "And I saw thrones, and they sat on them, and judgment was given to them, and the souls. . . ." Obviously, it is difficult to determine what John really means; at least we may say that we should not be going contrary to the trend of the book if we assume that the occupants of the thrones are "those who have been beheaded." Note the promise of 3:21: "The victor I will grant a seat beside me on my throne" (see 2:26-27). Despite appearances, here as in 7:1-17 and 11:4-13 we have to do with one group.

*those to whom judgment was committed:* They were given authority to be judges (Dan 7:22), as they will be priests and kings in v. 6. They achieve their true status as victors.

*for the testimony of Jesus and for the word of God:* See 1:9; 6:9; 12:17; 19:10.

*who had not worshiped the beast:* See 13:15; 14:9; 16:2; 19:20.

*they came to life:* Like the Lamb (1:18; 2:8) and the two witnesses (11:11).

*Christ:* ho Christos occurs in Revelation only in 11:15; 12:10; 20:4, 6 and is probably in each instance a reminiscence of Ps 2:2: the Lord's anointed against whom the kings of the earth conspired has triumphed, and his victory assures that of his faithful.

5. *the rest of the dead:* Who await the general resurrection, 20:12-13.

*the first resurrection:* The standard Jewish view was that of a general resurrection of the dead at the end. John is alone in his idea of two resurrections. His "first resurrection" means that "those who have been beheaded" already reign with Christ, he "who was dead and came to life" (2:8). "In short, the millennium is nothing other than the *special* resurrection of Christians that *precedes* the general resurrection of the dead" (Krodel, 336). See 1 Thess 4:16.

6. The fifth of the seven beatitudes of Revelation (see 1:3; 14:13; 16:15; 19:9; 22:7, 14); here the one who receives the blessing is not only happy but holy as well.

*the second death:* See 2:11. Jer 51:39, 57 warns that the inhabitants of Babylon, objects of divine chastisement, "shall sleep a perpetual sleep and not wake." In each case the *Targum of Jeremiah* renders the phrase: "they shall die the second death and shall not live in the world to come" (which means exclusion from the resurrection—they will remain in the grave). The "second death," identified with the "lake of fire" in 20:14; 21:8 is also named in 2:11. In all cases it means annihilation, or, at very least, may justifiably be interpreted in that sense.

*priests . . . and they will reign:* See 1:6; 5:9-10; the first fruits of the redeemed (14:4), they partake, in a privileged manner, in the royal priesthood of Christians (see 1 Pet 2:9).

*End of the Dragon*

7. *Satan will be let loose:* The "loosing" of Satan is in view of his instigation of, and defeat in, the battle of vv. 8-10, which is the same battle as that of 19:11-

21. John has four references to this same eschatological battle: 16:12-16; 17:14; 19:11-21; 20:7-10. Compare his several references to the destruction of Rome (14:8; 16:19; 17:16-17; 18:21) and his two descriptions of the judgment (14:14-20; 20:11-15).

8. *at the four corners of the earth:* Satan gathers his forces from the most remote regions of the world (see 16:12-16). In 7:1 the harmful winds which will hurt the earth blow from the four angles or corners of the earth; perhaps John sees the destructive hosts proceeding from the same sources. See Ezek 7:2, "An end! The end has come upon the corners of the land."

*Gog and Magog:* See Ezek 38–39. With his "Gog and Magog" in place of Ezekiel's "Gog, of the land of Magog," John followed current tradition. See *Sib. Or.* 3. 319, 512.

*to muster them for battle:* See 16:14.

*their number as the sands of the sea:* See Jos 11:4; "They came out, with all their troops, a great host, in number like the sand that is upon the seashore." See Gen 22:17; Judg 7:12; 1 Sam 13:5; 2 Sam 17:11; Jdt 2:20; 1 Macc 11:1.

9. *they marched over the breadth of the earth:* See Ezek 38:18, 21-22; Hab 1:6; 2 Kgs 1:12. See 1 Enoch 56:6-7: "And they will go up and trample upon the land of my elect ones. . . . But the city of my righteous ones will become an obstacle to their horses."

*camp . . . beloved city:* The two terms, "camp of the saints" (Palestine) and "beloved city" (Jerusalem), stand together for the people of God. "Camp" is the word used in Exodus for Israel's wilderness home; "God's people" is still a Church in pilgrimage. The "beloved city" stands in contrast to "the great city" (11:8); it is the new Jerusalem.

*fire came down from heaven:* See 2 Kgs 1:10, "The fire came down from heaven and consumed him and his fifty"—the captains and troops sent to arrest Elijah. The destruction of Gog by fire from heaven, with the resurrection following immediately (20:9, 11-15) is paralleled in the *Targum of Pseudo-Jonathan* on Num 11:26: "And they [Gog and his forces] wage war in the land of Israel against the sons of the captivity. The Lord, however, is near them [the Israelites] in the hour of affliction and kills all of them by a burning breath, by a flame of fire, that goes out from beneath the throne of glory."

10. *the lake of fire and brimstone:* The place of final punishment (see 20:10, 14); it is, effectively, a symbol of annihilation. The deceiver of the whole world (12:9) is not slain with his forces but is cast into the "lake of fire."

*tormented day and night for ever and ever:* The language is liturgical—and surely ironical.

### INTERPRETATION

Looking at the whole passage 20:1-10, we find that two events are juxtaposed: on the one hand, the overthrow of Satan in two phases; on the other hand, the reign of a thousand years. Chapter 7 of Daniel, with its two phases, Dan 7:2-14 and 7:23-27, furnishes the background of John's vision. The first condemnation of the dragon coincides with the Danielic moment of judgment when dominion is given to the "one like a son of man" (Dan 7:9-14); henceforth, in Revelation, the dragon's power has passed to Christ and God's people. In Revelation, while Christ and his faithful reign, Satan will remain powerless in their regard, imprisoned in the abyss, his "place." The binding of Satan for a thousand years also coincides with his downfall described in the parallel passage Rev 12:7-12: Satan, the "accuser of our brethren," is cast out of heaven by the victory of Christ; he can no longer accuse or harm the victors.

## Satan Bound

In a fresh vision John sees the dragon, identified again as "the ancient serpent" (12:9), made a prisoner "for a thousand years": the number is symbolic. The key to the expression is to be found in the thousand years' *reign* of 20:4-6; the thousand years' imprisonment of Satan is dictated by this. Making assurance double sure, the angel, sent from heaven for the purpose, cast the shackled Satan into the abyss and sealed the shaft of the abyss (see 9:1-2). This temporary imprisonment of the dragon, preceding his definitive fate (20:10), coincides with his banishment from heaven described in 12:7-12. The declaration "that he should not deceive the nations again" echoes his characterization in 12:9 as "the deceiver of the whole world." It has the same significance as "the accuser of our brothers and sisters" (12:10). All depends on the meaning of the "thousand years." In our view it has no chronological value but serves to symbolize the blessedness of the victors and the helplessness of Satan in their regard. The statement, "After that he must be let loose for a little while," has the same meaning as "his time is short" (12:12). The difficulty in our passage is due to the fact that the "thousand years," though it is a symbol without time value, is linguistically cast in time mode; it invites, indeed demands, chronological phraseology. Hence the phrases: "until [when] the thousand years were ended" (12:3, 5, 7), "after that" (20:3).

## Reign with Christ

From v. 7 it is clear that the vision situation of vv. 4-6 is coterminous with Satan's captivity. Those who had been "beheaded for the testimony of Jesus" are now seated on thrones. They are there as representatives of the whole Church pictured as, distinctively, a Church of martyrs. "They came to life and reigned with Christ for a thousand years" (v. 4). The origin of the notion of millennium is to be found in Jewish speculation on the messianic reign. In the Old Testament this reign is presented as final and permanent (see Dan 2:44; 7:14, 27). Later, extrabiblical speculation, from about 100 B.C.E. to 100 C.E., looked for a temporary triumph of righteousness before the consummation of all things. To this golden age various periods were assigned: one hundred, six hundred, one thousand, seven thousand years. Since it was commonly held that the age of the world would correspond to the time taken for its creation, and each day of creation was said to be a thousand years (see Ps 90:4; 2 Pet 3:8), the seventh day, equivalent to the sabbath rest, would be the reign of the Messiah. Thus, a thousand years is a particularly satisfactory length for the duration of the Messiah's reign on earth.

Since John has used the image of resurrection to describe the bliss of the victors (v. 4), he is careful to distinguish it from the general resurrection (see vv. 12-13); he calls it the "first resurrection." This is a classic instance of John's creativity. He surely had acknowledged the standard Jewish view of a general resurrection of the dead at the End. He is alone in his notion of two resurrections. It is yet another way of emphasizing the destiny of the victors. For a faithful Christian death *is* resurrection. Surely, Paul believed no less: "I long to be dissolved and be with Christ." John, too, knows that the death of the faithful is the "first resurrection"; one is, then and there, with the Lord. But, protagonist that he is of "universal salvation," he cannot, realistically, put "the rest" on the same level as the followers of the Lamb. He has to find some way of underlining the Christian privilege. Seen in this light, his concept of a "first resurrection" makes sense.

### End of the Dragon

If we take the "thousand years" as a symbol, without chronological value, then the phrase, "when the thousand years are ended," does not at all mean that the "loosing" of Satan comes after his internment. His "binding" is strictly in relation to those who reign with Christ. The situation is much like that of 12:10-11 where, cast out of heaven, he is powerless to exercise his role of "accuser of the brethren" in regard to the victors. The "loosing" of Satan is required by the literary construction of the passage: the author, who has already described the eschatological battle (19:11-22), with the defeat and capture of the beast and false prophet and the destruction of their forces, now describes the same battle over again. This time, however, he concentrates on the dragon, who is the real villain of the piece. With his defeat we have really come to the end, and the judgment can follow (20:11-15).

In 19:17-19 John had been inspired by Ezekiel 39; now he looks to Ezekiel 38. There the prophet (Ezek 38:2, 14-16) warns of the emergence of Gog, of the land of Magog, the foe whose invasion from the north had been heralded by Jeremiah (Jer 4:6) and by Zephaniah (Zeph 1:7). Gog figures as the type of victorious barbarian who, in an unspecified distant future, will launch the final attack on Israel, only to be utterly destroyed by Yahweh. Whereas in Ezekiel Gog is king of (the region of) Magog, in Revelation "Magog" has become a personage side by side with Gog. Together they symbolize all the "inhabitants of the earth" leagued against God's people. Here John follows (as much as ever he chooses to follow a source!) current tradition. In apocalyptic and rabbinical writings, Gog and Magog, as nations, represent Israel's enemies.

The assault is on "the beloved city." Standing in contrast to "the great city," it is the new Jerusalem. As in 17:14; 19:20-21, the hosts of evil are immediately and utterly destroyed; there is no battle. The "deceiver of the whole world" is not slain with his forces but is cast into the lake of fire. It is instructive to keep in mind that this "lake of fire" accommodates not only the dragon but also the two beasts, patent personifications of political and religious systems; the three ringleaders are involved in the same hopeless ruin. These symbolical figures are the "destroyers of the earth" for whose destruction the wrath of God was unleashed (11:18). Their total destruction in the "lake of fire" signals the absolute end, the annihilation, of evil.

John is preparing his people for the great tribulation. He is sure that their *hypomonē*, their patient endurance, will mean the death of many of them. In his eyes they are the "rest of the offspring" of the woman, object of the vindictive spite of the dragon. They need encouragement. He hits upon a way of assuring them that though their martyr death might seem to be victory for the dragon, it will, in fact, mean their transfer to heaven, wholly and for ever beyond his reach. While they "reign" he is "bound." Victory is theirs, not his.

John finds another way of stressing not only the blessedness but the privilege of the martyrs. He shared the common view of a final resurrection of humankind. Yet, it is not enough that his faithful martyrs, followers *par excellence* of the Lamb, should be grouped with "the rest of the dead." He comes up with his singular image of a "first resurrection." Since the martyrs are "first fruits" they are representative of Christians. It is they, the "blessed and holy," who share in the first resurrection. John has neatly achieved a twofold purpose.

The forces ranged against God's people, the cynical exploiters of the rest of humankind, are the dragon and the beasts. They are personifications of evil—in fact, the sum total of evil. In the "new heaven and new earth" (21:1) evil has no place. The "lake of fire" signifies its total annihilation. A lurking evil, though powerless to hurt, would take from the absolute triumph of Good. The disappearance of evil is inevitable when it is understood that evil is nothing other than the absence of good (*malum est privatio boni*).

## For Reference and Further Study

Bailey, J. W. "The Temporary Messianic Reign." *JBL* 53 (1934) 170–87.
Bietenhard, H. "The Millennial Hope in the Early Church." *SJT* 6 (1953) 12–30.
Fiorenza, E. Schüssler, "Die tausendjährige Herrschaft der Auferstandenen (Apk 20:4-6)." *BibLeb* 13 (1972) 107–27.
Gourgues, M. "The Thousand-Year Reign (Rev 20:1-6): Terrestrial or Celestial?" *CBQ* 47 (1985) 676–81.
Hughes, P. E. "Revelation 20:4-6 and the Question of the Millennium." *WTJ* 35 (1973) 281–302.
_____. "The First Resurrection: Another Interpretation." *WTJ* 39 (1977) 315–18.
Michaels, J. R. "The First Resurrection: A Response." *WJT* 39 (1976) 100–109.
Page, S. H. T. "Revelation 20 and Pauline Eschatology." *JETS* 23 (1980) 31–43.
Prigent, P. "Le Millennium dans L'Apocalypse johannique." In F. Raphael, ed., *L'Apocalyptique* (Paris: Geuthner, 1977) 139–56.
Rochais, G. "Le règne des mille ans et la seconde mort: origine et sens: Ap 19:11–20:6." *NRT* 103 (1981) 831–56.
Shea, W. H. "The Parallel Literary Structure of Revelation 12 and 20." *AUSS* 23 (1985) 37–54.
Vivian, A. "Gog e Magog nella tradizione biblica, ebraica e cristiana." *RivB* 25 (1977) 389–421.
White, R. F. "Reexamining the Evidence for Recapitulation in Rev 20:1-10." *WTJ* 51 (1989) 319–44.
Wikenhauser, A. "Weltliche und 1000-jährige Reich." *TQ* 127 (1947) 390–417.

## 48. The Last Judgment (20:11-15)

11. Then I saw a great white throne and the One who sat upon it; from his presence earth and heaven fled away, and no place was found for them. 12. I saw the dead, great and small, standing before the throne; and books were opened. Then another book was opened, the book of life; and the dead were judged according to their works as written in the books. 13. The sea gave up the dead that were in it, and Death and Hades gave up the dead in them; and all of them were judged according to their works. 14. Then Death and Hades were thrown into the lake of fire. This is the second death, the lake of fire. 15. And if anyone's name was not found written in the book of life, that one was thrown into the lake of fire.

NOTES

11. *a great white throne:* See 4:2. Strikingly, there is an echo of 19:11, obvious in literal translation: "I saw a great white throne and him who sat upon it"; "behold: a white horse and he who sat upon it."

*the One who sat upon it:* The Almighty Father (see 4:2-3, 9; 5:1, 7, 13; 6:16; 7:10, 15; 19:4; 21:5), the supreme judge at the last judgment (see Matt 18:35; Rom 14:10).

*earth and heaven fled away:* See 6:14; 16:20. Earth and sky flee from the presence of the judge; material creation itself has been contaminated by the sin of humankind (see Gen 3:17; Rom 8:19-22). The old order must make way for a new creation (21:24-26). "The boundaries of the old order disappear: there is nothing between men and God" (Sweet, 294).

*no place was found for them:* May equally well be rendered, "leaving not a trace to be found." See Dan 2:35, ". . . so that not a trace of them could be found"; Rev 12:8. The vanished sky and earth will be replaced by a new heaven and a new earth (21:1). Elsewhere, the New Testament speaks of a renewal or rebirth of creation (Matt 19:28), or the setting free of creation (Rom 8:21). One way or another, the old creation must be transformed in the new age. See Mark 13:31, "Heaven and earth will pass away." For the vanishing of earth and sky immediately before the judgment, see 2 Enoch 65:6, "When the whole of creation, which the Lord has created, shall come to an end, and when each person will go to the Lord's great judgment."

12. *the dead:* The "rest of the dead" (v. 5); the faithful have already been vindicated (vv. 4-6).

*books were opened:* See Dan 7:10, the books that contain a record of the deeds of every human being now come for judgment. See 4 Ezra 6:20, "When the seal is placed upon the age which is to pass away, then I will show these signs: the books shall be opened before the firmament, and all shall see it together"; 1 Enoch 90:20, "he took all the sealed books and opened those very books in the presence of the Lord of the sheep"; 2 Baruch 24:1, "For behold, the days are coming, and the books will be opened in which are written the sins of all those who have sinned."

*the book of life:* See 3:5; 13:8; 17:8; 20:15; 21:27; Dan 12:1; Exod 32:32-33; Ps 69:29; Mal 3:16; Luke 10:20; Phil 4:3; Heb 12:23. See 1 Enoch 47:3, "I saw him, the Antecedent of Time, while he was sitting upon the throne of his glory, and the books of the living ones were open before him." The book of life is the register of the citizens of the heavenly Jerusalem; it is "the book of life of the Lamb, slain since the foundation of the world" (13:8). Verses 13-15 will develop the data of v. 12.

13. *the sea gave up . . . :* The resurrection of the dead, implied in v. 12, is here described. It was widely believed that those lost at sea had no access to Sheol (Hades); in specifically naming the sea John emphasizes that he is describing the *general* resurrection. Death and Hades (see 1:18; 6:8) are personified. "Here they appear as two voracious and insatiable monsters who have swallowed

all past generations, but are now forced to disgorge their prey'' (Swete, 270).
*all of them were judged,* lit. ''they were judged each of them according to their
works'': Personal responsibility is underlined.

14. *Death and Hades:* ''The immersion of this symbolical pair in the lake of fire
is parallel to that of the Beast and the False Prophet (19:20); it can only mean
the annihilation of the forces indicated'' (Swete, 270). See 1 Cor 15:26, ''The
last enemy to be destroyed is death''—the death of death.

*the second death:* See 2:11; 20:6. Identified here and again at 21:8 with the ''lake
of fire.'' See *Targum Isaiah* 65:5-6, ''Their punishment shall be in Gehenna
where the fire burns all the day. Behold, it is written before me: '. . . I will
deliver their body to the second death.' '' Evidently, ''Gehenna'' and ''the
second death'' are one and the same.

15. *if any one's name was not found:* Here and at 21:8 only is the ''lake of fire'' associated with the fate of human beings. See 1 Enoch 90:26, ''I saw how another abyss, full of fire, was opened wide in the middle of the ground; and
they brought those blinded sheep, all of which were judged, found guilty,
and cast into the fiery abyss, and they were burned.''

### INTERPRETATION

In the earliest of his heavenly visions, the first thing that John saw
was a throne (4:2); now, again, he sees ''a great white throne,'' white
like the raiment of the Ancient of Days (Dan 7:9). The One seated on the
throne has dominated Revelation. He is invisibly, but vibrantly, present
in the Lamb. Now is the moment for his final word. The old earth and
heaven fade away for ever. Now is the time for the ''new heavens and
a new earth in which righteousness dwells'' (2 Pet 3:13). In the new world
of God righteousness reigns not only supreme but wholly. There is no
place for any shadow of evil.

The dead, ''great and small'' (*all* the dead), stand before the throne
of judgment. ''Books were opened,'' the books that contain a record of
the deeds of human beings now come for judgment. But there is ''another book'': this book of life is the register of the citizens of the heavenly
Jerusalem; it is the book of life of the Lamb. ''Books were opened . . .
the book of life'': we are faced with the mystery of salvation—people are
judged by their deeds, and yet salvation is free gift (v. 15). God's choice
is not arbitrary and John had warned that a name might be canceled from
the book (3:5). ''In these two books are pictured the paradox of works
and grace. We are ultimately responsible for what we do, for it has eternal consequences—we are judged by works. God is ultimately responsible for our salvation, it is his deed that saves, not ours—we are saved
by grace. Propositional language will always sound paradoxical on such

ultimate issues; John's pictorial language makes both statements in one picture'' (Boring, 212).

Our God has created us as free beings. He respects our freedom totally; that is why his grace is, so often, thoroughly disguised. We come, later, to discern his graciousness in our most painful episodes. Freedom is costly; it exacts the price of responsibility. We are responsible for our deeds and for our omissions. Yet, all the while, our salvation is wholly grace. "Whoever does not receive the kingdom of God like a child shall not enter it" (Mark 10:15). "Justified by his grace as a gift, through the redemption which is in Christ Jesus" (Rom 3:24). John, like the Bible in general, does not attempt to resolve the tension. Later Christian theologians courageously, stubbornly—and vainly—strove to find a way past the dilemma. The theologians of the Bible, in their wisdom, were content to leave the matter in the hands of God.

The "lake of fire" is the place of final punishment of dragon and beasts (19:10). Here, more startlingly, it is the last home of Death and Hades. These have served their purpose; they no longer have any *raison d'être*. The "second death," identified with the "lake of fire" here and in 21:8, is also named in 2:11 and 20:6. In each case it is most reasonably taken to signify annihilation. The evidence of the Targums appears to stand in support. So, for instance, Jer 51:39, 57 warns that the inhabitants of Babylon, objects of divine chastisement, "shall sleep a perpetual sleep and not wake." Both times the Targum renders the phrase: "they shall die the second death and shall not live in the world to come." This means exclusion from the resurrection; they will remain in the grave.

If, in Rev 20:15 (as in 21:8), to be cast into the lake of fire is the fate of one whose name is not written in the book of life, surely, the negation of eternal life is eternal death. Here and at 21:8 only is the "lake of fire" associated with the fate of human beings. Yet this is enough to show that for John the lake of fire/second death awaits not only the symbolic figures but unfaithful humans as will. However he understands "universal salvation," he views it against the awfulness of sin and evil and in a context of human responsibility. But his lake of fire has little in common with the "hell" of tragic Christian tradition. It is reasonable to understand lake of fire/second death in Revelation as annihilation—the absolute end of anything, or anyone, not fit to be present in the New Jerusalem.

It seems to me that the observation of Edward Schillebeeckx is irrefutable: "It is an unimaginable scenario for me as a Christian, familiar with the gospel, that while there is said to be joy among the heavenly ones, right next to heaven people are supposed to be lying for ever, gasping for breath and suffering the pains of hell for ever (however you imagine this—spiritually or physically). On the other hand, the idea of the second or definitive death respects God's holiness and his wrath at the evil that is done, to the detriment of the poor and the oppressed'' (*Church*, 137). If living communion with God is the foundation of eternal life, the absence of such communion is the basis of non-eternal life. There is no longer any ground of eternal life. ''That seems to me to be the 'second death' of the fundamental, definitive sinner (if there is such a person). That is 'hell': not sharing in eternal life; it does not mean someone who is tortured eternally; rather, it means no longer existing at death. That is the biblical 'second death' (Rev 20:6)'' (Schillebeeckx, *Church*, 137).

FOR REFERENCE AND FURTHER STUDY

Glasson, T. F. ''The Last Judgment in Rev 20 and Related Writings.'' *NTS* 28 (1982) 528–39.
Harrington, W. ''No Negative Eschaton: Revelation and Universal Salvation.'' *PIBA* 15 (1992) 42–59.

## XIII. THE NEW JERUSALEM

### 49. *The New Heaven and Earth* (21:1-8)

1. Then I saw a new heaven and a new earth, for the first heaven and the first earth had passed away, and the sea was no more. 2. I saw the holy city, new Jerusalem, coming down out of heaven from God, made ready like a bride adorned for her husband. 3. I heard a loud voice from the throne say: Behold, God's dwelling is with humankind! He will dwell among them, and they will be his peoples, and God himself will be with them [as their God], 4. and he will wipe away every tear from their eyes; and death will be no more; mourning and crying and pain will be no more—for the old order has passed away.
5. The One who sat on the throne said: Behold, I am making all things new! and he said: ''Write this down, for these things are trustworthy and true.'' 6. Then he said to me: It is done! I am the Alpha and the Omega, the beginning and the end. To the thirsty I will give, as a gift, water from the spring of the water of life. 7. The victors will have this heritage; and I will be their God and they will be my children. 8. As for the cowardly, the faithless, the polluted, the murderers, fornicators, sorcerers, idolators, and liars of every kind—their lot will be the lake that burns with fire and brimstone, which is the second death.

## NOTES

1. *a new heaven and a new earth:* See Isa 65:17, see "For, behold, I create new heavens and new earth"; see 66:2. See 1 Enoch 91:16, "The first heaven shall depart and pass away; a new heaven shall appear." The text of 2 Pet 3:10-13 offers a close parallel; this author, like John, is sure that the end of this world of ours will mark the emergence of the "new heavens and a new earth in which righteousness dwells" (3:13). But it will still be heaven and earth—a dwelling for humankind. The "new" will be a transformation of the "old." It "is not another world (that would mean contempt for and rejection of the original good creation), but our earthly world redeemed from being out of joint—though I do not know how to imagine this" (Schillebeeckx, *Church,* 133).

   *and the sea was no more:* The sea is the primeval ocean, symbol of chaos; its disappearance is assurance of God's total victory. Caird (262) observes that the formula "was no more" dismisses seven elements of the old order: sea, death, mourning, crying, pain, every accursed thing, and night (21:1, 4; 22:3, 5).

2. *the holy city, new Jerusalem:* Structurally, 21:1-2 is modeled on Isa 65:17-19: the appearance of a new world, the disappearance of the former things, and the manifestation of a new Jerusalem. See Isa 52:1, "Awake, awake, put on your strength, O Zion; put on your beautiful garment, O Jerusalem, the holy city." See Isa 61:10.

   *coming down out of heaven from God:* A permanent attribute of the new Jerusalem; see 3:12. It is a city of heavenly origin—originating in *God's* true heaven—a city "whose builder and maker is God" (Heb 11:10; see 12:22; 13:14). See Gal 4:26, "the Jerusalem above is free, and she is our mother"; Phil 3:20.

   *like a bride adorned for her husband:* See 19:7; 21:8-14; Isa 49:18, "You [Zion] shall put them on as an ornament, you shall bind them on as a bride does"; Isa 61:10, "He has clothed me with the garments of salvation . . . and as a bride adorns herself with her jewels." The double image of "city" and of "bride" is traditional. The image of "city" comes from an apocalyptic strand going back to Ezekiel 40; the metaphor of "bride" is common in Old Testament and New Testament (see Hos 2:16, 19; Isa 54:6; Ezek 16; Tob 13:16; 2 Cor 11:2; Eph 5:25). John combines the images; already, in ch. 17, the harlot is also the city Rome. In 4 Ezra 9:38–10:54 Ezra has a vision of a mourning woman and, suddenly, "the woman was no longer visible to me, but there was an established city. . . . This therefore is the meaning of the vision. . . . This woman whom you saw, whom you now behold as an established city, is Zion" (10:27, 40, 44).

3. *a loud voice:* As in 19:5 the voice is not identified. It explains the significance of the vision.

   *God's dwelling:* See Ezek 37:27, "My dwelling place shall be with them; and I will be their God, and they shall be my people"; see Zech 8:8. "Dwelling," *skēnē* (see Rev 13:6; 15:5) may recall the *shekinah:* the presence of God among his people.

*his peoples:* Plural, *laoi* (Sinaiticus, A); the singular *laos* is well attested. The plural is the more difficult reading; the singular would represent copyists' assimilation to familiar LXX texts, notably, Ezek 37:27: "My dwelling place shall be with them; and I will be their God, and they shall be my people." "One important and doubtless deliberate change has been made in terms of these prophecies [Lev 26:11-12; Jer 38:33; Ezek 37:27; Zech 8:8]; our writer has substituted "peoples" for "people"—the many peoples of redeemed humanity for the single elect nation, the world for Israel" (Swete, 278).

*[as their God]:* Read in A.

4. *he will wipe away every tear:* See Isa 25:8; Rev 7:17.

*death will be no more:* Renews the assurance of 20:14. If in Babylon the sounds of joy have ceased for ever (18:22), in the new Jerusalem sorrow and pain will have no place. The whole passage is reminiscent of the Beatitudes (Matt 5:3-12).

*the old order,* lit. "the former things": The things belonging to the first heaven and the first earth (v. 1). See 4 Ezra 8:53, "And Death is hidden, Hades fled away; corruption forgotten, sorrows passed away; and in the end the treasures of immortality are made manifest"; 2 Enoch 65:10, "For everything corruptible will pass away, and the incorruptible will come into being, and will be the shelter of the eternal residences."

5. *The One who sat on the throne said:* God speaks, as at 1:8. The vision of 21:1-4 has become reality.

*I am making all things new:* See Isa 43:19, "Behold, I am doing a new thing; now it springs forth, do you perceive it?"; 2 Cor 5:17, "If anyone is in Christ, he is a new creation; the old has passed away, behold, the new has come." Note that God does not declare that he is making new things, but that he is making all things new—renovation rather than new creation.

*and he said:* This *kai legei,* coming between *kai eipen* in v. 5 and v. 6, might indicate a change of speaker; it is simpler, and raises no difficulty, to suppose that God is speaker throughout.

*write this down:* A command to write has been given before: by an angel (1:10-11), by Christ (1:19), by "a voice from heaven" (14:13), and by another angel (19:9).

*these words are trustworthy and true:* Repeated in 22:6; see 3:14; 19:9, 11.

6. *it is done:* See 16:17. The solemn *gegonan* ("it is done") is final. L. L. Thompson notes that the verb (perfect tense) can be translated, "All has been transformed" (85).

*the Alpha and the Omega:* See 1:8; 22:13; 1 Cor 15:28, "when all things are subject to him, then the Son himself will also be made subject to God who made all things subject to him, and thus God will be all in all."

*to the thirsty:* See Isa 55:1, "Every one who thirsts, come to the waters; and he who has no money, come, buy and eat! Come, buy wine and milk without money and without price." See 7:16-17; 22:17. Water is a symbol of life and, as such, is to be a feature of the messianic age (See Isa 12:3; 41:17-18; 44:3-4; Ezek 47; Zech 13:1; 14:8).

*as a gift,* lit. "freely" (*dōrean*): The gift is utterly free. See Rom 3:24, "They are justified by his grace as a gift (*dōrean*)"; the same idea of the gratuitousness of God's gifts underlies Paul's doctrine of justification by faith.

7. *the victors,* lit. "victor": Here translated as plural to accommodate inclusive language. It carries the reader back to the messages of chs. 2–3 with their seven promises.

*heritage:* See Matt 25:34, "Come, O blessed of my Father, inherit the kingdom prepared for you from the foundation of the world"; Rom 8:17, "if children, then heirs, heirs of God and fellow heirs with Christ, provided we suffer with him in order that we may also be glorified with him." Such, indeed, is the lot of the victors.

*I will be their God:* See 2 Sam 7:14, "I will be his father and he shall be my son." The author of Hebrews maintains that Nathan's prophecy is perfectly realized in Christ (Heb 1:5; 5:5); John expands its range to embrace all the elect of God who have borne faithful testimony to Christ. See Rom 8:23, "We ourselves, who have the first fruits of the Spirit, groan inwardly as we wait for adoption as children (of God), the redemption of our bodies."

*my children:* Lit. "my son."

8. *as for the cowardly . . . :* Some have thought this verse out of place—not so. John seeks to underline the truth that, in the city of God, there is no room for sin. Its citizens will be those whose sins have been washed away (see 1:5). "His beginning with cowards and ending with 'liars' is no general statement against cowardice and falsehood but has in view the failures of Christians under the pressure of persecution and the threat of it" (Boring, 217).

*liars of every kind:* See "all who love and practice deceit" (22:15)—all who display an affinity with the dragon.

## INTERPRETATION

The final part of Revelation opens with the vision of a new heaven and a new earth, the setting of a new Jerusalem. The apocalyptic drama nears its close. The former creation has passed away (20:11) and all evil has been destroyed. In other words, creation has been renewed. In John's accustomed manner, the new Jerusalem is briefly introduced here; it will be described more fully in 21:9-27. Jerusalem was an accepted figure of the people of Israel, of the people of God; it is a tangible sign of the covenant, the focus of Jewish faith and hope. To present a new Jerusalem was, in the language of imagery, to proclaim the election of a new people and the sealing of a new covenant. In this chapter John combines the traditional images of "city" and "bride," slipping abruptly from one to the other. More significantly, he utters the promise that God will dwell

among his *peoples.* He who was never the God of Israel only is not prepared to be the God of Christians only.

Now, for the second time (see 1:8) unmistakably, God speaks: he
speaks the creative word that calls the new world into being. Could that
creative word involve the repudiation of the product of his first creative
word? The divine word is, unquestionably, "trustworthy and true." God
himself bears witness to the reality of this solemn promise; the hope of
John's readers is firmly grounded on the divine assurance. "It is done":
not only are the visions true, but all has already come to pass, in the timeless reality of heaven. John has seen the new heaven and the new earth,
he has looked upon the new Jerusalem (21:1-4); in 21:9–22:5 the details
of his visions are outlined. God is the beginning and the end. He is at
the origin of all and at the end of all; all things have tended towards God,
and now all things are found in him.

John's use of "a new heaven and a new earth" is not arbitrary. Not
only is the concept thoroughly biblical, but also his "new world" also
opens up the perspective of an eschatological future in which the cosmos
is redeemed and perfected. This is not a restoration of our broken world
to its imagined original state, but a transformation beyond imagining,
a transformation so radical as to be a "new creation." In all of this, the
human aspect is always firmly in mind. So, in this new heaven and new
earth, "death will be no more; mourning and crying and pain will be
no more" (Rev 21:4). Paul had already spoken of the redemption of the
cosmos in the context of human redemption: the whole of nature shares
in the birthpangs which lead to the freedom of the children of God (Rom
8:18-23). The biblical view of the world maintains an intimate link between
the cosmos and humankind (Gen 1–2). This is a matter of primary importance. It underlines the truth that the biblical idea of redemption is
radically anti-dualistic. Furthermore, it means that the promise of a new
world implies a radical questioning of our present relationship with the
world. The promise of a new world is a reminder and a challenge. It is
a reminder that we human beings have sinned grievously against God's
world, which was committed to our responsible care (Gen 1:26-30). It
challenges us to question our present relationship with this world as it
was originally envisaged by God. We are summoned to *metanoia,* called
to work towards the new world held in prospect. True, it is God who
declares, "I make all things new." But God has freely, from the start,
involved humankind in his creation. In his plan a new world for humankind can only come about with human involvement.

Reference to "the victors" carries the reader back to the messages of
chs. 2–3. "The victors will have this heritage" is an eighth promise that
embraces and rounds off the seven promises there. One should keep in
mind the pastoral concern of John. While this is most evident in the pro-

phetic messages of chapters 2–3, it is kept in sight throughout and becomes more pronounced in the final chapters. This explains why here (v. 8) he takes care to list practices that have no place, nor ever could have place, in the holy city. They characterize the "old man" which those who would enter the city must "put off" (Col 3:5-10). His concern is faithful witness in the present. Since the warning is addressed to Christians, John chooses to deck sin in lurid colors; see 9:20-21. The "liars of every kind" are all who are opposed to Christ, the faithful and true (3:14; 19:11), and have been seduced by the dragon, "the deceiver of the whole world" (12:9). Such as they do not share the heritage of the saints. They will not drink the water of life (v. 6) for their lot is in the lake of fire (20:15)—both images are symbolic.

What is eternal life with God? We, in our earthly existence, creatures of time and space, must perforce picture heavenly reality in terms of time and space. Here, John has two central images. There will be a new heaven and a new earth. The dragon once had his place in the old heaven; he had ravaged the old earth. A creation that is, at last, utterly free of evil can only be *new*. Humankind was the summit of God's creation, his pride and joy (Gen 1:26-31). His destined home for humankind was the garden of delights (2:15). There will be a new home for humankind in the new creation: a city, the city of God, the new Jerusalem. It is a heavenly city, yet a habitat of men and women. There the victors find their promised rest.

In v. 8 John's pastoral concern comes to the fore. If he effectively stresses the absence of sin in the new Jerusalem, he also issues a warning to his hearer/readers. They must strive to prepare, on earth, for life in the City. That demands a turning from sin here and now.

### FOR REFERENCE AND FURTHER STUDY

Burggraeve, R. ''Responsibility for a 'New Heaven and a New Earth.' '' *Concilium* 1991/4, 107–117.

Comblin, J. ''La Liturgie de la Nouvelle Jérusalem (Apoc 21:1–22:5).'' *ETL* 29 (1953) 5–40.

Deutsch, C. ''Trnsformation of Symbols: The New Jerusalem in Rev 21:1–22:5.'' *ZNW* 78 (1987) 106–26.

Gaechter, P. ''The Original Sequence of Apocalypse 20–22.'' *Theological Studies* 10 (1949) 485–521.

Karner, K. ''Gegenwart und Endgeschichte in der Offenbarung des Johannes.'' *TLZ* 93 (1968) 39–59.

Prigent, P. ''Le temps et la Royaume dans l'Apocalypse.'' In J. Lambrecht, ed., *L'Apocalyptique Johannique*, (Gembloux: Duculot, 1980) 231–45.

_____. ''Une Trace de Liturgie Judéochrétienne dans le Chapitre XXI de l'Apocalypse de Jean.'' *RSR* 60 (1972) 163–72.

## 50. *The New Jerusalem* (21:9–22:5)

9. Then came one of the seven angels who held the seven bowls full of the seven last plagues and spoke to me, saying, "Come. I will show you the bride, the wife of the Lamb." 10. So he carried me away in a trance to a great and lofty mountain, and showed me the holy city Jerusalem coming down out of heaven from God, 11. possessing the glory of God. It had the radiance of a precious jewel, like a jasper, clear as crystal. 12. It had a great, high wall with twelve gates, and at the gates twelve angels; on the gates were inscribed the names of the twelve tribes of Israel. 13. There were three gates to the east, three to the north, three to the south, and three to the west. 14. The city wall had twelve foundation-stones, and on them were the twelve names of the twelve apostles of the Lamb.

15. And he who spoke with me had a gold measuring rod to measure the city, its gates, and its wall. 16. The city stands foursquare, its length the same as its breadth; and he measured the city with his rod, twelve thousand stadia: its length and breadth and heigth were equal. 17. And he measured its wall: 144 cubits, according to human measure, that is, an angel's. 18. The fabric of the wall was jasper, while the city was of pure gold, clear as glass. 19. The foundations of the city wall were adorned with every kind of precious stone: the first foundation-stone was jasper, the second lapis lazuli, the third chalcedony, the fourth emerald, 20. the fifth sardonyx, the sixth carnelian, the seventh chrysolite, the eighth beryl, the ninth topaz, the tenth chrysoprase, the eleventh jacinth, the twelfth amethyst. 21. The twelve gates were twelve pearls, each gate made from a single pearl. The main street of the city was of pure gold, like translucent glass.

22. I saw no temple in the city, for its temple was the Lord God Almighty and the Lamb. 23. The city had no need of sun or moon to shine on it; for the glory of God gave it light, and its lamp was the Lamb. 24. The nations will walk by its light, and the kings of the earth will bring their glory into it. 25. Its gates will never be shut by day—for there will be no night there. 26. They will bring into it the splendor and wealth of the nations. 27. But nothing unclean will enter it, nor any who practice abomination or falsehood, but only those who are written in the Lamb's book of life. 22:1. Then he showed me the river of the water of life, bright as crystal, flowing from the throne of God and of the Lamb, 2. down the middle of the city's street. And on either side of the river stood a tree of life yielding twelve crops of fruit, one for each month of the year; and the leaves of the tree were for the healing of the nations. 3. There will no more be anything accursed. The throne of God and of the Lamb will be there, and his servants will worship him; 4. and they will see his face, and his name will be on their foreheads. 5. There will be no more night; they will have no need of light of lamp or sun, for the Lord God will shine upon them, and they will reign for ever and ever.

## NOTES

9. *one of the seven angels:* One of the angels of the bowls who had shown John the great harlot (17:1).

   *full of the seven last plagues:* "Perhaps John believed that the demolition squad had also an interest in the reconstruction for which they had cleared the ground" (Caird, 269).

   *the bride, the wife of the Lamb:* See 19:7; 21:2; Eph 5:25.

10. *in a trance,* lit. "in the spirit": see 17:3.

    *to a great and lofty mountain:* Though it might seem that this mountain, like that of Matt 4:8-10, was John's vantage-point for his view of the city, the Ezekiel background (Ezek 40:2) makes clear that the mountain was the site of the city; see the "holy mountain of God" (Ezek 28:14, 16).

    *the holy city Jerusalem:* See Ezek 40:1–47:12; 48:30-35.

    *coming down out of heaven:* This expression, peculiar to John (3:12; 2:2, 10), describes a permanent characteristic of the city.

11. *possessing the glory of God:* Because of its heavenly origin, it reflects the divine glory. For that matter, it is filled with the presence of God (vv. 22-23). See Isa 60:1-2; Ezek 43:2.

    *like a jasper:* In 4:3 the One seated on the throne appeared "like jasper"; here the heavenly city reflects that divine radiance. "The city's main feature is God's glory, the presence of his very nature" (Krodel, 357).

12. *twelve gates:* See Ezek 48:30-35. "If the gates bear the names of the Twelve Tribes, the names of the Twelve Apostles (v. 14) are engraved on the foundations. Thereby the seer maintains the continuity of the Old Testament and the Christian Church" (Charles, 2:162).

13. *to the east . . . :* See Luke 13:29, "And people will come from east and west, and from north and south, and sit at table in the kingdom of God." In Ezek 48:30-35 the gates are the city exits, whereas all traffic is into John's city (vv. 24, 26, 27).

14. *twelve foundation-stones:* These foundation stones are the precious stones listed in vv. 19-20.

    *the twelve apostles of the Lamb:* See Matt 19:28, "In the new world, when the Son of Man shall sit on his glorious throne, you who have followed me will also sit on twelve thrones, judging the twelve tribes of Israel." Of more immediate relevance is Eph 2:20, "built upon the foundation of the apostles and prophets, Christ Jesus himself being the chief cornerstone" (see Heb 11:10). Texts such as Eph 2:20 and Rev 21:14 offer an important and essential balance to Matt 16:17-19—the "Petrine text." Peter may be the "rock"; the Twelve are the *foundation.*

15. *a gold measuring rod:* See Ezek 40:3, 5; Rev 11:1.

16. *the city stands foursquare:* See Ezek 45:2; 48:16; but John's city is a perfect cube.

In Solomon's temple the holy of holies was a cube (1 Kgs 6:20); the cube is a symbol of perfection.

*twelve thousand stadia:* About fifteen hundred miles (see Rev 14:20). This is a symbolic figure (12 x 1000) indicating twelve tribes and twelve apostles (vv. 12, 14).

17. *144 cubits:* The wall (c. 216 feet in height) is ridiculously out of proportion to the gigantic size of the city—if we were dealing with actual figures and measurements! "A hundred and forty-four" (12 x 12) is a fitting symbolic description of a wall that associates the twelve tribes of Israel and the twelve apostles of the Lamb (vv. 12-14). Besides, a wall was a standard feature of ancient cities. See Isa 26:1.

*cubits:* The cubit was originally the distance from elbow to fingertip, later standarized (see "foot"). John seems to suggest that by "cubit" he means, not the standard cubit, but the forearm measure—ultimately the forearm of an angel. "By what calculus then are we to compute 'a hundred and forty-four' measures of 'an angel's' forearm?" (Caird, 274).

18. *jasper:* Jasper is the gem which symbolizes the radiance of the divine splendor, 4:3; see 21:11; the city is shot through with the radiance of the divine presence. See Isa 54:11-12; Zech 2:5, "For I will be to her [Jerusalem] a wall of fire round about, says the Lord, and I will be the glory within her."

*pure gold, clear as glass:* The city itself was built of transparent gold (v. 21).

19. *foundations . . . every kind of precious stone:* In his description John develops Isa 54:11-12: "O afflicted one, storm-tossed and not comforted, behold, I will set your stones in antimony, and lay your foundations with sapphires. I will make your pinnacles of agate, your gates of carbuncles, and all your wall of precious stones"; see Tob 13:16-17: "For Jerusalem will be rebuilt with sapphires and emeralds, her walls with precious stones, and her towers and battlements with pure gold. The streets of Jerusalem will be paved with beryl and ruby and stones of Ophir."

*were adorned:* Though at first sight John seems to be saying that the twelve foundation stones of the wall (v. 14) were decked with precious stones, it appears rather that each stone is one vast gem. For the most part, these jewels correspond to those set on the high priest's breastplate, each one bearing the name of one of the twelve tribes (Exod 28:17-20; 39:10, 13; see Ezek 28:13 [LXX]). But John has linked the stones with the twelve apostles (v. 14), not with the tribes of Israel. John's list does not square with any of the Old Testament lists. There is, besides, the fact that the identification of the stones listed is uncertain: "it was not at all possible at the time of St. John for anybody to establish the identity of the twelve stones in a way that would appear satisfactory in our day" (Jart, *Precious Stones,* 170). John's list may, quite simply, be a measured contrast to the jewels of the harlot, the other city (17:4).

21. *twelve pearls:* See Isa 54:12, ". . . your gates of carbuncles"; for John, the gates are pearls. Pearls are not mentioned in the Old Testament; in the Hellenistic age the pearl was very highly valued: "the *pearl* of great price" (Matt 13:46). Note a Talmudic tradition attributed to Rabbi Jonathan (early

third century C.E.): "One day will the Holy One (blessed be he) bring precious stones and pearls thirty cubits long by thirty cubits broad and excavate openings in them of ten cubits in breadth and twenty cubits in heighth, and they shall stand in the gates of Jerusalem" (*Baba Bathra* 75a).

*the main street: hē plateia* may be generic—"the streets."

*like translucent glass:* Gold that is transparent as glass is typical of John's daring imagery.

22. *I saw no temple in the city:* The city *is* the temple.

23. See Isa 60:1-5, 11, 19-20. John's use of Isaiah 60 is evident.

   *the city had no need of sun or moon to shine on it:* See Isa 60:19, "The sun shall be no more your light by day, nor for brightness shall the moon give light to you by night; but the Lord will be your everlasting light, and your God will be your glory." The glory of the divine presence renders all created light superfluous. "No words could more clearly demonstrate the purely spiritual character of St. John's conception of the new Jerusalem" (Swete, 295).

   *its lamp was the Lamb:* He "reflects the glory of God" (Heb 1:3; see John 1:14). If God replaces the sun, the Lamb gives light by night.

24. *the nations . . . the kings of the earth:* See Isa 60:3, "And the nations shall come to your light, and kings to the brightness of your rising." The divine light of the city is a beacon to the nations. These are the "nations" and "kings" of 16:14; 17:18; 18:9; 19:19; 20:8—those destroyed in 19:21; 20:9!

25. *its gates will never be shut by day:* See Isa 60:11, "Your gates shall be open continually; day and night they shall not be shut."

26. *the wealth of the nations:* See Isa 60:11, "that people may bring to you the wealth of the nations, with their kings led in procession." But where are these nations and kings of the earth to be found? They have been wholly destroyed in the battle of Armageddon!

27. *nothing unclean:* See Isa 52:1; 35:8; Ezek 44:9. This verse is to be read as a pastoral warning to John's hearers. "Unclean" (*koinos*); Mark 7:20-23 tells us what uncleanness or defilement is: "What comes out of a person is what defiles (*koinoō*) a person. For from within, out of the human heart, come evil thoughts, fornication, theft, murder, adultery, coveting, wickedness, deceit, envy, slander, pride, foolishness. All these evil things come from within, and they defile a person." The kingdom of God is not for such.

   *who practices abomination or falsehood:* See 17:2-4; 18:3; 21:8.

   *only those written . . . in the Lamb's book of life:* See 13:8— the "inhabitants of the earth" are those whose names have not been written in the Lamb's book of life. "There is no distinction between sacred and profane in the city. But there is still an 'outside' (as at 22:15): the perspective is that of the letters [messages], in which commerce with the heavenly Jerusalem as with the harlot Babylon is a present possibility" (Sweet, 310).

22:1. *the river of the water of life:* See Gen 2:9-10; Ezek 47:1, 6-7, 12; Joel 3:18; Zech 14:8.

*bright as crystal:* See 4:6, ''a sea of glass, like crystal.''

*flowing from the throne of God and of the Lamb:* The waters which in Ezek 47 flow from the sanctuary here flow from the throne; the heavenly city has no temple. The water of life flowing from the throne of the Lamb has a parallel in John 7:38-39: ''If any one thirst, let that one come to me, and let the one who believes in me drink. As the scripture has said, 'Out of his heart shall flow rivers of living water.' ''

2. *on either side of the river,* lit. ''and on this side of the river and on that'': One must guess at John's meaning here.

   *a tree of life:* May be understood as a generic singular, meaning ''trees,'' as in Ezekiel; a link with the ''tree of life'' of Gen 2:9; 3:22 is more compelling.

   *yielding twelve crops of fruit:* See Ezek 47:12. This is the fruit promised to the victor, the fruit of ''the tree of life that stands in the paradise of God'' (Rev 2:7).

   *for the healing of the nations:* See Ezek 47:12, ''Their fruit will be for food, and their leaves for healing''—John adds ''for the healing *of the nations,*'' the nations of 21:24-26.

3. *there will no more be anything accursed:* See Zech 14:11, ''And it shall be inhabited, for there shall be no more curse; Jerusalem shall dwell in security.'' This is to say, Jerusalem is securely inhabited because the divine curse (the divine ''ban'' or ''anathema''), which sentenced the city to destruction, is no more. John, in his turn, declares that no accursed person, object of God's displeasure, will find a place in the new city (see 21:27).

   *the throne of God and of the Lamb:* See v. 1. ''Throne'' (singular): another facet of the pattern of the assimilation of Lamb of God.

   *his servants will worship him:* The fulfillment of 7:15.

4. *they will see his face:* The Israelites had gone in pilgrimage to the temple to worship and to ''behold the face of God'' (Ps 17:15; 42:2); they had beheld him only in wish because one cannot see God (Exod 33:20, 23). But now, in the new age, that desire is satisfied (see Matt 5:8; 1 Cor 13:12; Heb 12:14; 1 John 3:2, ''Behold, we are God's children now; it does not yet appear what we shall be, but we know that when he appears we shall be like him, for we shall see him as he is.'' Throughout verses 3-4 the pronoun (''shall worship *him* . . . *his* face, *his* . . . name'') refers to God and Lamb in tandem.

   *foreheads (metōpōn):* Occurs in the New Testament only in Revelation, in three different connections: ''the foreheads of those who are sealed for God (7:3; 9:4; 14:1; 22:4), the foreheads of those who bear the mark of the beast (13:16; 14:9; 20:4), and the harlot's forehead which bears 'a mysterious name' (17:5)'' (Ford, *Revelation,* 363).

5. *there will be no more night:* See Zech 14:7, ''And there shall be continuous day . . . not day and not night, for at evening time there shall be light.''

INTERPRETATION

The book closes with a majestic view of the new Jerusalem, the heavenly Church of the future, the veritable kingdom of God. One of the seven angels of the bowls had shown John the great harlot (17:1); one of the seven now steps forward to show him the bride. The contrast between harlot and bride is thus deliberately emphasized, a contrast all the more marked because they are images of rival cities: Babylon and new Jerusalem. The bride-image, however, is not developed but yields to that of the holy city. We find a parallel in 4 Ezra. In the fourth image of that book the seer talks with a woman in mourning for her children; he does not realize that the woman is Zion. But, "while I was talking to her, her face suddenly shone exceedingly, and her countenance flashed like lightning. . . . And I looked, and behold, the woman was no longer visible to me, but there was an established city, and a place of huge foundation showed itself" (10:25-27).

John's model in his presentation of the new Jerusalem is Ezekiel's vision of the new temple (40:1–47:12) and new Jerusalem (48:30-35). Ezekiel was transported, in vision, from Babylon to Israel and was set upon a very high mountain; there he found, opposite him, "a structure like a city": the temple of the future. He was guided throughout this city by an angel carrying a measuring-rod (40:3–43:12). His guide also showed him a spring in the temple and a great stream flowing from it (47:1-12). An epilogue describes the gates of the city (48:30-35).

In antiquity, a wall was an essential feature of a city (see Isa 26:1). In his description of the gates, John follows Ezekiel closely; in v. 13 the repetition, as in Ezekiel, conveys an impression of stability. A significant difference: for Ezekiel the gates are the exit points of the twelve tribes going to their allotted land; for John they are entrances. In vv. 24-26 it is declared that the gates remain always open, inviting the entry of the nations; all traffic is *into* the city (vv. 24, 26, 27). This factor, together with the disposition of the gates according to the four cardinal points, recalls Luke 13:29. Since there are twelve gates, the wall surrounding the city is divided into twelve sections, with each section resting upon a single foundation stone. Like the gates, the foundation stones, too, are inscribed; they bear the names of the twelve apostles. It is precisely as *apostles of the Lamb* that the twelve are foundation stones in the new Jerusalem.

In Rev 11:1 the seer had measured the "temple of God"; but the heavenly temple is measured by a heavenly being (John's angel guide) with a measuring rod of gold. Yet the measurements taken by the angel are those in common human use (v. 17). The measuring here (unlike that of 11:1-2) would seem to serve the purpose of filling out the vision by giving the architectural specifications of the heavenly city: an attempt to convey, in human terms, what outstrips human power to envisage. Like the city of Ezekiel's vision (Ezek 45:2; 48:16) this city "lies foursquare"; but John goes beyond the former prophet in contemplating a city that is a perfect cube. The obviously symbolic figure of twelve thousand stadia (12 x 1000) carries within it a reference to the number of the tribes of Israel and to the twelve apostles (vv. 12, 14). The city wall, made of jasper, is shot through with the radiance of the divine presence at the heart of the city (vv. 22-23). Built of transparent glass, with jewels as foundation stones and pearls for its gates, this city is, indeed, a heavenly city.

We might expect the glowing description of the city to be followed by a particularly striking description of its temple (the Temple was the glory of the earthly Jerusalem). Instead, a brilliant touch, we learn that there is no temple, nor any need of one: God himself dwells there with the Lamb. Now indeed, "God's dwelling is with humankind" (v. 3) and the glory of his presence pervades the whole city (vv. 11, 18) making of the new Jerusalem, city of God, one vast temple. This is reminiscent of 7:15 where God himself is the tent in the heavenly feast of Tabernacles, for the liturgy of that feast appears to be present to the seer throughout the passage 21:22-27. In the light of our verse we may read the assurance of 3:2 ("the victor I will make a pillar in the temple of my God") as a promise of permanent citizenship in the holy city.

While John is manifestly inspired by Isaiah 60, he (unlike Isaiah) is here describing the heavenly Jerusalem. Its inhabitants are not drawn from all nations; they *are* the nations and kings of the earth, thus fulfilling the universalist prophecies of the Old Testament. The divine light of the city ("the glory of God gave it light, and its lamp was the Lamb," v. 23) is a beacon to the nations. These are the "nations" and "kings" that had opposed God's rule and made war on the Lamb and his followers (16:14; 17:18; 18:9; 19:9; 20:8)—the very nations and kings destroyed in the great eschatological battle (19:21; 20:9)! They will bring their glory into the city, "the splendor and wealth of the nations." John does not forget that he is seeking to comfort humans: "splendor and wealth" are symbols of *human* values. A city that is not home for humankind is not a city.

Verse 27 is to be read as a pastoral warning to John's hearers. The new Jerusalem—the kingdom of God—is a reality of a new world wholly free of evil. Christians must, here and now, prepare for citizenship. They must begin to root out of their lives whatever is incompatible with life in this new realm of God. If one keeps in mind the messages to the Churches, one can appreciate why John finds it salutary to include these asides. His word of pastoral comfort is his reference to the "Lamb's book of life." God does look to our commitment; yet, salvation is the achievement of God and the Lamb, not our doing.

In Ezekiel's vision a life-giving torrent of water issued from beneath the threshold of the east gate of the sanctuary. It flowed into the Dead Sea, turning its waters fresh and making them swarm with fish. Along the banks of the river grew trees that bore a crop of fruit each month and whose leaves had curative properties. John has combined Ezekiel's vision with Gen 2:9-10. The seer at last sees the very spring of the waters of life, the waters promised to the thirsty (7:17; 21:6; 22:17). The new Jerusalem has no temple. Consistently, the waters which in Ezek 47 flowed from the sanctuary, here flow from "the throne of God and of the Lamb." John intends, unmistakably, to assimilate the Lamb to God. Hence, "the Lord God Almighty" is present and visible in the Lamb-who-was-slain. The tree (or trees) of life produces the fruit promised to the victor, the fruit of "the tree of life that stands in the paradise of God" (Rev 2:7). Where Ezek 47:12 reads, "their fruit will be for food, and their leaves for healing," healing "*of the nations*" is John's provocative modification. Another word to his readers: John declares that no accursed person, object of God's displeasure, will find a place in the new city (see 21:27).

When the throne of God was first revealed to John, he glimpsed it through an open door in heaven (4:1); now he views it in the heavenly Jerusalem come down to earth; and on it is seated not only the Father but also the Lamb. Throughout vv. 3-4 the pronoun refers to God and Lamb in tandem. The association of God and Lamb, evident elsewhere, is here expressed most forcefully. Night and darkness have no place in the new city. Worshiping him, looking upon his face, basking in the light of his glory, the servants of God "will reign for ever and ever." Christ has made of his own "a royal house of priests to his God and Father" (1:6; see 5:10; 20:6); now at last, in the heavenly Jerusalem, worshiping before the throne of God and Lamb (22:3), these royal priests shall reign without end.

John surpasses himself in his surrealistic painting of the new Jerusalem. After all, how is one to describe a city of God, a city that is the perfect home of wholly redeemed humankind? It is a city without a temple. God and Lamb reign indeed, but not in the formality of a cultic setting. They dwell in the midst of their people. Our God is never an aloof, distant God, though we tend to make him such. Our traditional God is an aloof figure—too often a forbidding figure. Strangely, while he is quite firmly presented as one gravely offended by human sin, he has been made to appear one unaffected by human suffering. Our God deserves better than the insult of ungracious caricature. He deserves the compliment of carefree trust in his graciousness. There is only one answer to the evil that is sin, and to all evil. Violence can never be the answer. Despite the plagues of Revelation, it is not God's answer. Nothing but love, the infinitely patient divine love, can absorb evil and put it out of commission. The Cross shows the earnestness of a gracious God, shows that there is no limit to his desire to win humankind to himself.

Most striking of all is John's picture of the nations streaming into the new Jerusalem. They bring into it splendor and wealth—all that is worthy and lovely in human achievement. Though city of God, it is their city, the true home of humankind. God's saving purpose prevails. John's glowing description is not only encouragement: it is challenge. We are summoned, here and now, to "lay aside every weight, and sin which clings so closely" (Heb 12:1). We are to look, beyond evil, to what is good in our world. We are to turn with confidence to the God who, though the One seated on the throne, is the gracious God who wipes away every tear.

### FOR REFERENCE AND FURTHER STUDY

Delebecque, E. "Où situer l'Arbre de vie dans la Jérusalem céleste? Note sur Apocalypse 22:2." *RevThom* 88 (1988) 124–30.

Gundry, R. H. "The New Jerusalem: People as Place, not Place for People." *NovT* 29 (1987) 106–26.

Jart, U. "The Precious Stones in the Revelation of St John 21:18-21." *ST* 24 (1970) 150–81.

du Rand, J. A. "The imagery of the heavenly Jerusalem (Revelation 21:9–22:5)." *Neot* 22 (1988) 65–86.

Reader, W. W. "The Twelve Jewels of Revelation 21:19-20: Tradition, History and Modern Interpretations." *JBL* 100 (1981) 433–57.

Topham, M. "A Human Being's Measurement, Which is an Angel's." *ExpTim* 100 (1988–89) 217–18.

_____. "The Dimensions of the New Jerusalem." *ExpTim* 100 (1988–89) 417–19.

## XIV. EPILOGUE AND CONCLUSION

### 51. *Epilogue and Conclusion* (22:6-21)

[Epilogue]
6. Then he said to me: "These words are trustworthy and true. The Lord God who inspires the prophets has sent his angel to show his servants what must soon take place."

7. Behold, I am coming soon! Blessed is the one who keeps the words of the prophecy of this book.

8. It was I, John, who heard and saw these things. When I had heard and seen, I fell down to worship at the feet of the angel who had shown them to me. 9. But he said to me: "No, not that! I am a fellow servant with you and your brothers the prophets and with those who keep the words of this book. Worship God!"

10. And he said to me: "Do not seal up the words of the prophecy of this book, for the time is near. 11. Let the evildoer still do evil, and the filthy still be filthy, and the righteous still be righteous, and the holy still be holy."

12. Behold, I am coming soon, bringing my reward with me, to repay everyone according to what one has done. 13. I am the Alpha and the Omega, the first and the last, the beginning and the end. 14. Blessed are those who wash their robes, so as to have the right to the tree of life, and may enter the city by the gates. 15. Outside are the dogs, sorcerers, and fornicators, the murderers and idolators, and all who love and practice deceit.

16. I, Jesus, have sent my angel to give you this testimony for the Churches. I am the root and offspring of David, the bright morning star.

17. The Spirit and the bride say: "Come!" Let the hearer say, "Come!" Let the thirsty come. Let whoever wishes receive the water of life without charge.

18. I warn everyone who hears the words of the prophecy of this book: if anyone adds to them, God will add to that one the plagues that are written in this book; 19. and if anyone should take away from the words of the book of this prophecy, God will take away that one's share in the tree of life and in the holy city, which are described in this book.

20. He who testifies to these things says: Yes, I am coming soon! Amen! Come, Lord Jesus!

[Conclusion]

21. The grace of the Lord Jesus be with all.

## NOTES

*Epilogue*

6. *then he said to me:* The speaker may be the angel guide (21:9, 15; 22:1) or, better, he is Christ's angel of the prologue (1:1).

*these words are trustworthy and true:* See 21:5. "John closes on the same note with which he opened (1:1-2), with the claim that what he communicates is the prophetic word of God mediated through Christ and the revelatory angel" (Boring, 225).

*the Lord God who inspires the prophets:* The God from whom the charism of prophecy proceeds. See Num 27:16, "The Lord, the God of the spirits of all flesh"; 1 Cor 14:32, "and the spirits of prophets are subject to prophets." Verse 6b echoes 1:1, "The revelation of Jesus Christ, which God gave him to show to his servants what must soon take place; and he made it known by sending his angel to his servant John."

*his servants:* See 1:1; 10:7; 11:18; 22:16; here they are the Christian prophets.

7. *I am coming soon:* See 3:11; 16:15; 22:12, 20.

   *Blessed is the one . . . .:* This beatitude (the sixth of the book) is a shorter form of 1:3. Blessings are often appended to an exhortation or to a legal text (see Exod 23:20-33; Lev 26:3-13; Deut 28:1-4); they were designed to encourage the practical implementation of the prophetic message or the observance of the law. The passage 22:6-7 is a conscious echo of 1:1-3—a circle back to the beginning.

8. *I, John:* See 1:1, 9; again, the author names himself; no pseudonymity for John.

   *I fell down to worship:* See 19:10. The "brothers" of 19:10 are here explicitly identified as "the prophets"; and those who "hold the testimony of Jesus" (19:10) are here those who "keep the words of this book."

9. *I am a fellow servant:* "Those who read, hear, and observe John's words in Revelation are one with John the seer and the angels . . . forming an egalitarian *communitas,* one community of worship" (L. L. Thompson, 69f.).

   *worship God:* The positive answer to idolatry.

10. *and he said to me:* Apparently the angel of v. 6, with the same measure of ambiguity. Or, is it the Christ, who speaks in vv. 12-13?

    *do not seal up:* The instruction is the precise reverse of that given to Daniel (Dan 8:26; 12:4, 9; see Rev 10:4). Dan 8:26, "But seal up the vision, for it pertains to many days hence."

    *for the time is near:* See 1:3.

11. *let the evildoer still do evil:* See Dan 12:10, "Many shall purify themselves, and make themselves white, and be refined; but the wicked shall do wickedly; and none of the wicked shall understand; but those who are wise shall understand." Our verse is a warning. See Rev 16:15, "Behold, I come like a thief. Blessed is the one who stays awake." The beatitude of v. 14 shows that it is not too late for conversion. "There is nothing determinist about these words. Rather, they are a plain call to the reader to put his life in order while there is still opportunity for change" (Caird, 284).

12. *bringing my reward with me:* See Isa 40:10, "Behold, the Lord comes with might . . . behold, his reward is with him, and his recompense before him." The time has come "for rewarding your servants the prophets and your people and those who fear your name, both small and great" (Rev 11:18).

    *according to what one has done:* See 2:23, "I will give to each of you what your conduct deserves."

13. *I am the Alpha and the Omega . . . the beginning and the end:* Here predicated of Jesus; elsewhere predicated only of God (1:8; 21:6).

14. *blessed are those:* The seventh and final beatitude of Revelation (see 1:3; 14:13; 16:15; 19:9; 20:6; 22:7).

*who wash their robes:* That is, "in the blood of the Lamb" (7:14). There is surely a suggestion of baptismal washing.

*tree of life:* See 2:7; 22:2. In the liturgical flavor of the epilogue, there is a suggestion of Eucharist.

*the gates:* For the gates of the heavenly city, see 21:12-13, 21, 25, 27.

*so as to have the right . . . by the gates:* Baptism and Eucharist give promise of entry; the victor may stride boldly through the city gates.

15. *outside the dogs . . .:* See 21:8. "Dogs" is a traditional Jewish designation of heathen Gentiles. In Phil 3:2 Paul applied the epithet to some of his compatriots, so turning back on them their own insulting estimation of Gentiles. The catalog is "a reminder of baptismal commitment. The collocation with the beatitude of v. 14 suggests the invitation to the worthy and exclusion of the unworthy at the eucharist" (Sweet, 317).

    *all who love and practice deceit:* Stronger than the "all lies" of 21:8.

16. *this testimony:* The whole of Revelation; see 1:1, 4.

    *the root and offspring of David:* See Isa 11:1; Rev 5:5.

    *the bright morning star:* See Num 24:17, "A star shall come forth out of Jacob, and a scepter shall rise out of Israel." The context is messianic. See Rev 5:5.

17. *the Spirit and the bride:* "The Spirit" is the Spirit of Jesus that inspires the prophets (2:7; 14:13; see 19:10); "the bride" is the Church (21:2, 9).

    *Come!:* Addressed to Christ; it is the *marana tha*, "Our Lord, come!" (see 1 Cor 16:22), of the liturgy. Through liturgical celebration, eschatological expectations are made present to the worshiper.

    *the hearer:* Every hearer of the book; see 1:3.

    *let the thirsty come:* See John 6:35; 7:35-38; Rev 21:6; 22:1.

    *the water of life without charge:* See Isa 55:1, "Every one who thirsts, come to the waters; and he who has no money, come, buy and eat!" See Rev 21:6. On the parallel of U. Vanni's liturgical reconstruction of 1:4-8 (see above), I suggest that 22:17 follows a similar pattern:

    | | |
    |---|---|
    | And the Spirit and the Bride say: | "Come." |
    | And let one who hears say: | "Come." |
    | And let one who thirsts: | Come. |
    | Whoever wills: | Take the water of life, freely. |

18. *I warn everyone:* See Deut 4:2; 12:32. For a similar warning, see *Letter of Aristeas,* 311; 1 Enoch 104:10-11; 2 Enoch 48:74-75.

20. *he who testifies (ho martyrōn):* Jesus is "the faithful witness" (1:5; 3:14).

    *yes, I am coming soon:* "Yes" is *nai* as at 1:7.

    *Amen:* Human response to the divine assurance.

    *Come, Lord Jesus:* "Lord Jesus" (1 Cor 12:3) is found in Revelation only here and in the following verse; it is a favorite title of Christian faith and prayer. "Come, Lord [Jesus]" is a rendering of the Aramaic *marana tha*, which occurs in 1 Cor 16:22. It is found in a Eucharistic context in the *Didache* 10:6—

Let grace [i.e. Jesus] come, and let this world pass away.
Hosanna to the God of David.
Whoever is holy, let him come; whoever is not, let him repent.
*Marana tha. Amen.*

## Conclusion

21. *The grace of the Lord Jesus be with all:* The book, which opens with an epistolary formula (1:4), also closes with a type of final greeting customary in letters. The formula is like those of Pauline letters. There is a variant reading:
"with the saints" (Sinaiticus); the reading, "with all" (Alexandrinus), is
preferable.

*grace:* God's favor, his efficacious desire for human salvation, embodied in
Jesus, is offered to *all.*

### INTERPRETATION

The epilogue is designed to balance the prologue (1:1-8); we are
reminded that John's work is in the shape of a letter. The epilogue fo-
cuses on the hearer/readers of the book. The speaker in 22:6 is, seemingly, an angel; in point of fact, throughout this passage (vv. 6-9) it is
not clear who is speaking. The trustworthy and true words are the teach-
ings of the whole book: Christ, through his angel, authenticates the words
of the prophecy of the book. The God who is the source of the charism
of prophecy has sent his angel to his servants the Christian prophets to
assure them that the End is near. There is a promise: "I am coming soon."
It surely is Christ who speaks, through the voice of his angel. His coming is blessing for the one who has hearkened to the challenging and encouraging prophetic message of John.

As at the beginning of the book (1:1, 9), the author gives his name.
He acknowledges himself to be the seer of all these visions and auditions:
"these things" which he had heard and seen comprise the revelation of
this entire book—the "revelation of Jesus Christ" (1:1-2). There is a curious repetition of the episode of 19:10. Again John falls at the feet of an
angel and again he is restrained. It is reasonable to read this as a warning against a propensity to angel worship in the Churches of Asia. Alternatively, it may be a way of stating that all worshipers of God are equal
in their worship. And worship of the one true God is the effective response to idolatry.

Conventionally (as in Daniel) eschatological prophecies were sealed,
set aside for future disclosure. But for John the moment of fulfillment
is here: the coming of Christ in glory (22:12, 20). John does not seek to
attenuate the anticipation of the nearness of the end which earlier Chris-

tians had felt (see 1:3, 7; 3:11; 22:12, 20). His prologue assures his readers that "the time is near"; his epilogue echoes the assurance.

In 22:11 evil is characterized by the "evildoers" and "filthy" (the immoral) and good by "the righteous" and "the holy." In each case, there is an action ("do evil," "do right") and a state ("be filthy," "be holy")— the twofold attitude of human decision and of submission to a supernatural power, whether diabolical or divine. As at 16:15, v. 12 here is a warning to the reader. In the following verse we will hear of reward; but one must have left oneself open to recompense. The time for reward has come (see 11:18). It is Christ who speaks. He comes, "bringing his reward with him," for he is the reward. He who comes bears divine titles: Alpha and Omega, the first and the last, the beginning and the end. Christ is virtually identified with God. Omega, last, end—"The end, 'the Omega,' is not an event but a person" (Krodel, 370).

The seventh and final beatitude of Revelation is directed at those who wash their robes "in the blood of the Lamb" (7:14). Here not only martyrs but all Christians are envisaged. This verse links up with 1:5; he "has loosed us from our sins with his blood"; in and through Christ alone can they win salvation and gain their reward. The tree of life is within the city, so they must pass through the gates to reach it. The beatitude makes eternal life accessible to all, but only through the Cross of Christ. The list of "those outside" (v. 15) is practically the listing of 21:8, at least as regards the last five terms. They are those whose lot is "the second death," those who worship the beast and bear its mark (14:9-11). The description "all who love and practice deceit" is much more forceful than the "all liars" of 21:8. One who *loves* falsehood is one to whom it has become second nature, one who shows an affinity with Satan, for "he is a liar and the father of lies" (John 8:44).

The whole of Revelation is "the revelation of Jesus Christ," his "testimony" made known, through an angel, to John (1:1); it is a message to "the seven Churches that are in Asia," and for the whole Church (1:4). At the close, Jesus sets the seal of approval on the fidelity of his prophet. Jesus is both root and branch, he combines all the messianic claims of the Davidic family; he is the "beginning and end" (v. 13) of the whole messianic economy. "He is the source of David's line, 'the root,' as well as David's 'offspring,' the promised Messiah, the Lion of the tribe of Judah (cf. 5:5; cf. Mark 12:35-37). This is a daring Christological conception, and it probably represents John's answer to Jewish anti-Christian polemics" (Krodel, 370f.). He is the bright morning star promised to the faithful at Thyatira.

Inspired by the Spirit, the Church ("the bride") prays its *marana tha*, "Our Lord, Come!" The Church (the earthly Church) responds with eager joy to the Lord's announcement of his coming. The prayer is to be caught up by every hearer of the book (see 1:3); the Lord looks for the response of the individual Christian (see 3:20-21). For the Church is no vague personification; it is a living organism, of living men and women. Attention turns to the community: ''the one who is thirsty'' is invited to come to Christ. In Rev 3:20 we observed a Eucharistic flavor in the promise of a meal shared by Christ with the Christians. It would seem that the Eucharistic interest is present here too in this offer of the water of life. The invitation of Spirit and bride blends into an invitation to Eucharistic fellowship.

''I warn everyone . . .'': it was fairly common practice for writers to append a warning of this kind to their books. John can be so firm because he does not regard himself as author of the book; the real author is, ultimately, God (1:1). For the third time in this passage (vv. 7, 12, 20) Christ, who gives his own solemn testimony to the contents of the book, assures his Church that he is coming soon. It is a response to the earnest prayer of the Church: ''Come!'' (v. 17), and a link with the promise at the start of the book: ''Behold, he comes with the clouds'' (1:7). But this time the promise stands in the liturgical context of the Eucharist.

To the divine assurance, ''Yes'' corresponds the human response, ''Amen,'' expressing the absolute faith in his word of the seer and those whom he represents. John closes with the prayer that conveys all the longing of his beleaguered communities: ''Come, Lord Jesus!''

''Behold, I am coming soon!'' It is an assurance that John's hearer-readers longed to hear. Life was not easy for them in the present. John's prospect of imminent tribulation augured much tougher times ahead. His promise to victors was all very well; the reality was that ''conquering'' meant dying! It was comforting to look eagerly to the One who was coming soon, ''bringing his reward with him.'' He was the one who had conquered, by laying down his life. They, if they were faithful, would share his victory and his triumph. They look to his coming.

In the meantime, as they celebrate their Eucharist, they have his presence with them; they have the reminder of his victory and the asssurance of his promise: ''As often as you eat this bread and drink the cup, you proclaim the Lord's death until he comes'' (1 Cor 11:26). They do not have to wait, bereft, for his final coming. Yet, they long. ''My desire is to depart and be with Christ, for that is far better'' (Phil 1:23). It is in their going to him that the Lord will come to them. *Marana tha!*

Perhaps it is in our Eucharistic celebration that Revelation might challenge us. It was on the night on which he was delivered up that the Lord took, gave thanks, and broke bread: ''This is my body which is for you.'' He is the Lamb who was slain. His death is victory for all. The victim is the victor. That is the ''remembrance'' of the Eucharist. That is the message of Revelation. Behind the surreal visions of the plagues is the Lamb.

And with the Lamb is the One on the throne—the Father of our Lord Jesus Christ. "The *grace* of the Lord Jesus be with all." This "revelation of Jesus Christ" is a word of grace. "Blessed is the one who hears," for these words are trustworthy and true.

### FOR REFERENCE AND FURTHER STUDY

Aune, D. E. "The Prophetic Circle of John of Patmos and the Exegesis of Revelation 22:16." *JSNT* 37 (1989) 103–16.

Boyle, W. J. P. "I am Alpha and Omega: Rev 1:8; 21:6; 22:13." *Studia Evangelica* 2 (1964) 526–31.

Collins, T. *Apocalypse 22:6-21 as the Focal Point of Moral Teaching and Exhortation in the Apocalypse.* Rome: Gregorian University Press, 1986.

Hartman, L. "Form and Message: A Preliminary Discussion of 'Partial Texts' in Rev 1–3 and 22:6ff." In J. Lambrecht, ed., *L'Apocalypse Johannique* (Gembloux: Duculot, 1980) 129–49.

Kavanagh, M. A. *Apocalypse 22:6-21 As Concluding Liturgical Dialogue.* Rome: Gregorian University Press, 1984.

Thomas, R. L. "The Spiritual Gift of Prophecy in Rev 22:18." *JETS* 32 (1989) 201–16.

# EXCURSUS

## Positive Eschaton Only:
## Revelation and "Universal Salvation"

### 1. *Imagery of Evil*

Revelation can readily give an impression of implacable divine wrath, with a strong flavor of vindictiveness. A first step towards a proper grasp of this aspect of the book might be a consideration of the Genesis Flood story. There too, at first sight, Yahweh/God is stirred to violent action against sin and sinners. The Flood story is myth, not history: a story of fundamental symbols which are vehicles of ultimate meaning. Myth speaks timeless truth, truth vital to human existence; it brings out the supernatural dimension of events. In the Flood story we see the holy God's radical incompatibility with evil—his grief over human sin. The story assures us that God will have the last word: "never again shall there be a flood to destroy the earth" (Gen 9:13). Revelation, too, is myth. The plagues exist in vision only. The great battle of Armageddon is not an historical but a mythical battle. This is one reason why we find "inconsistencies." All followers of the beast are slain by the rider (19:21). Yet, into the new Jerusalem the nations will come and the kings of the earth will bring their treasures! God has the last word, and his word is ever that of salvation.

There remains Revelation's violent imagery—an unrelenting language of wrath. Nothing of the violence of the plagues is literal action against our world; it is violence in visionary scenes of the future, couched in metaphorical language. Again, just as there was no "real" Flood, there were no "real" plagues of Egypt; and there were not, nor will be, "real" plagues of Revelation. John is convinced of universal human sinfulness (Christians also are sinners, 1:5). The eschatological terrors are an expression of his sense of justice. That is why God and the Lamb are the source of violence—Christians can only be victims, never perpetrators, of violence (13:9-10). After all, it is the Lamb who, by breaking the first seal, unleashes the plagues (for all three cycles are interconnected), the Lamb "who was slain from the foundation of the world." There is NO human violence against evil. What we find in Revelation is a Christological transformation of traditional imagery.


## 2. *Universal Salvation*

If salvation means fellowship with God and blessedness of eternal life with him, universal salvation means that all human beings will finally be redeemed by God's gracious love, a love displayed ultimately in Jesus Christ. On the other hand, a limited salvation view assumes that only those who, in this life, acknowledge the true God—and, in the New Testament setting, confess Christ as Lord—will finally be saved. Both views are found prominently in both Old Testament and New Testament. A stream of texts maintains that ultimate salvation is limited, e.g., Isa 26:20-21; 66:15-16; Matt 25:31-46; John 3:36. Another stream suggests or affirms universal salvation, e.g., Isa 66:18-23; John 3:17; Rom 11:32-36; 1 Tim 2:3-4. In some cases—and this is significant for an assessment of Revelation—both views are juxtaposed, e.g. Isa 66:15-16: "Behold, the Lord will come in fire . . . to render his anger in fury. . . . For by fire will the Lord execute judgment, and by his sword, upon all flesh; and those slain by the Lord will be many." Immediately afterwards, 66:18-23, we read: "I am coming to gather all nations and tongues; and they shall come and shall see my glory, and I will set a sign among them. And from them I will send survivors to the nations . . . to the coastlands afar off, that have not heard my fame or seen my glory; and they shall declare my glory among the nations." Or again, John 3:36: "One who believes in the Son has eternal life; one who does not obey the Son shall not see life, but the wrath of God rests upon that one." This stands in sharp contrast to the statement a few verses earlier (3:17): "For God sent the Son into the world, not to condemn the world, but that the world might be saved through him."

Arguably, the weightiest text of all in favor of universal salvation is found in Paul. One may well find that Romans 9–11 is not the easiest section of Paul's writings. But one cannot fail to be stirred by the passion behind these chapters. Paul simply will not accept that God has rejected his people (11:1). His argument throughout is tortuous, because the problem he addresses is so puzzling: how could God's people have failed to recognize God's last messenger? He wrestles, despairingly, with a humanly incomprehensible situation, but never loosens his grip on his conviction that "the gifts and the call of God are irrevocable" (11:29). At the end, he commits the whole matter to God and declares, in words that have little to do with the forced logic of his argument up to that point: "and so all Israel will be saved" (11:26). A remarkable statement. Then Paul takes a truly gigantic step: "For God has consigned all to disobedience, that he may have mercy upon all" (11:32). His declaration has to be seen in contrast to the unrelieved picture he had painted in chapters 1–3: all humankind stands under sin, cut off from God. But, then, that backdrop was designed to highlight the incredibly gracious gift of God. As Paul Achtemeier puts it: "Hardening in disobedience is temporary and serves the purpose of grace; that is the mystery Paul announces (v. 32)" (*Romans* [Atlanta: John Knox, 1985] 189).

Turning to Revelation, we find here, as elsewhere, texts that imply or assert limited salvation, e.g., 14:9-10; 20:11-15, and texts that imply or assert universal salvation, e.g., 1:7; 5:13; 14:6-7; 21:24-27. While this juxtaposition of seemingly contradictory views is not unique to John (as we have just observed), he has offered a key to his procedure in his judgment scene of 20:11-15 where he contrasts "books" and "the book of life." People are judged by what they have done; yet, what is ultimately decisive is whether one's name is inscribed in the book of life. John maintains this tension throughout. In consciously paradoxical language and imagery he seeks to present, on the one hand, the frightful human responsibility of the decision to reject one's Creator and live in servitude to false gods, and, on the other hand, to portray the finally victorious mercy of a gracious God. M. Eugene Boring maintains that the interpreter's task is not to seek to resolve the tension but rather to sustain it and, indeed, to find the thrust of the book's message in this very tension.

For our purpose, the relevant factor is that a stream, sometimes hidden, yet flowing in steadfast hope, wends through the somber landscape of Revelation. Could it be otherwise for one who had discerned the conquering God in the Lamb who was slain? "John knows that for Christians the question of universal or limited salvation is not an abstract speculative question, addressing the question of 'How many?' It is rather faith's confession of the meaning of the act of God in Christ; the God whose victory does not depend on ours, who loves us when we do not love him or ourselves, who believes in us when we do not believe in him or ourselves, who saves us when we do not believe that we need saving or are worth saving" (Boring, 228).

One may find a goodly number of relevant Revelation passages on the side of universal salvation. Here is the full list:

> 1:2, 5, 7, 18; 5:9-10, 13; 9:20-21; 10:11; 11:13-15; 14:6-7; 15:4; 16:9, 11; 19:16; 21:1, 3, 5, 24-27; 22:2, 21.

Of these, the following are the more significant:

1:7; 5:13; 14:6-7; 15:3-4; 21:3; 21:24-27.

(On the cited texts, see relevant "Notes.")

One should add 20:14, "This is the second death, the lake of fire." While not looking to universal salvation, this verse is germane to the issue and, more particuarly, is pertinent to the subsequent theological assessment. In 19:20 "the lake of fire" is the place of final punishment. It is instructive to keep in mind that, in 20:10, this "lake of fire" accommodates not only the dragon but also the two beasts (potent personifications of political and religious systems) and, even more startlingly (20:14), Death and Hades. These symbolical figures are "the destroyers of the earth" for whose destruction the wrath of God is unleashed (11:18). Their total destruction in "the lake of fire" signals the absolute end, the annihilation, of evil. And if in 20:15 (as in 1:8) to be cast into the lake of fire is the fate of one whose name is not written in the book of life, surely the negation of eternal life is eternal death. All in all, it is reasonable to understand lake of fire/second death, in Revelation, as annihilation—the absolute end of anything, or anyone, not fit to be present in the new Jerusalem. This calls for theological consideration.


3. *No Negative Eschaton*

Having looked not only at the prospect of universal salvation but also, glance-wise, at violent imagery in Revelation, it is helpful, for the sake of perspective, to regard a celebrated Matthean passage. Straightway, a problem arises. Can one, as a Christian, really believe that the suffering victim on the cross who in Luke's passion-story prayed, "Father, forgive them; for they do not know what they do" (Luke 23:34), could, as risen Lord, declare in awful judgment, "Depart from me you cursed, into the eternal fire"? Matthew, it seems (25:41), would have us think so. What matters is that we should view this seemingly irrevocable sentence against what we know of the God of the Old Testament and of the New. He is the God whose heart "recoils within him" at the prospect of losing Ephraim (Hos 11:8); he is the God who desires the salvation of all (1 Tim 2:4); he is the God who did not spare his own Son (John 3:16). Surely, Jesus would have us believe that his God and ours loves us with divine love beyond our human imagining.

Still, what are to make of Matthew's Last Judgment (Matt 25:31-46)? We are to understand it as myth. Though presented in the guise of an historical event (para-historical, to be pedantic), it does not become irrelevant when one recognizes that its value is symbolic. One is challenged to live in such a way that, should it occur, one would not be caught un-awares. The "last judgment" is a warning: it primarily relates to one's conduct in the present. While the King stresses his solidarity with "all," the exhortation is, by Matthew, addressed to Christians. We are being taught how we should prepare for the "coming" of the Lord, how to prepare for our meeting with him. The "last judgment" is taking place in our lives here and now. The "books" are being written. But, have our names "been written in the book of life since the foundation of the world" (Rev 17:8)? There is the true judgment.

Last judgment conjures up visions of heaven and hell. The terms "heaven" and "hell" are human words, and the accompanying images are all too human. Humans, not God, have invented hell. Theologically, what the terms signify is the reality of human decisions for good or evil and consequent human possibilities. God alone knows if a human being can definitively choose evil—and only in such a case is there the possibil-ity of "hell." Still, the prospect of heaven or hell is salutary, pointing up the seriousness of decision in the present.

In a theological reflection on hell (*Church*, 134-39), Edward Schille-beeckx quotes a saying of Thérèse of Lisieux, "Je crois dans l'enfer, mais je crois qu'il est vide" ("I believe in hell but I think there's no one in it"), and characterizes it as anything but unbiblical. He also adverts to the *apokatastasis* doctrine of some Church Fathers—in the end everyone will be saved—and to the similar implication of the doctrine of reincarna-tion in non-Christian religions. His suspicion is that such solutions sug-gest too cheap an estimation of mercy and forgiveness. He proposes his own view with characteristic theological perspicacity and verve. I believe that he offers a satisfying theological answer to the question raised by the optimistic stream in Revelation. And, in so doing, he raises, by im-plication, the further question whether "universal salvation" is an ap-propriate description of what we have been considering under that rubric.

Heaven and hell are symbols, but they are not on the same level; they are asymmetrical affirmations of faith. The basis of "eternal life"—which is what "heaven" means—is living communion with God. God is the source of that bond of life which is already a reality during earthly life, a bond that cannot be snapped at death. Living communion with the liv-ing God abides beyond death; therefore, heaven exists. There can be no hell on the same level. For, if living communion with God is the founda-tion of eternal life, the absence of such communion is the basis of non-eternal life. There is no longer any ground of eternal life. "That seems to me to be the 'second death' of the fundamental, definitive sinner (if there is such a person). That is 'hell': not sharing in eternal life; not being someone who is tortured eternally—but no longer existing at death. That is the biblical 'second death' (Rev 20:6)." The evil have excluded themselves from communion with the living God—excluded themselves from life. They no longer exist. "But there is no shadow kingdom of hell next to the eternally happy kingdom of God. That is inherent in the assymmetry between what we call heaven and hell" (Schillebeeckx, *Church*, 137–39).

A mistake of the past has been to place good and evil on the same level. Evil, as distinct from good, is not something positive; it is the absence of good—*malum est privatio boni* (Thomas Aquinas, *S. Theol.* 1.48.5). Here is the solid Thomistic basis of Schillebeeckx's position. There is nothing in evil that can mark it for eternal life. Through its inherent emptiness the wicked world disappears by its own logic into absolutely nothing. Schillebeeckx claims, and I concur, that, in contrast to the model of the past—the traditional "hell"—he offers a more plausible Christian solution to the problem of evil. And he concludes:

> So there is no future for evil and oppression, while goodness still knows a future beyond the boundary of death, thanks to the outstretched hand of God which receives us. God does not take vengeance; he leaves evil to its own, limited logic! So there is in fact an eternal difference between good and evil, between the pious and the wicked (the deepest intent of the distinction between heaven and hell), but the pious continue to be spared having to rejoice over the torture of eternal doom being inflicted on their fellow human beings. God's unassailable holiness consists, rather, in the fact that he will not compel anyone to enter the kingdom of heaven as the unique kingdom of liberated and free people. The "eschaton" or the ultimate is exclusively positive. There is no negative eschaton. Good, not evil, has the last word. This is the message and the distinctive human praxis of Jesus of Nazareth, whom Christians therefore confess as the Christ. (*Church*, 138f.).

There is no negative eschaton. This, it seems to me, is a better way of describing what we have been studying under the rubric "universal salvation." The trouble with the expression "universal salvation" is that it might be taken in a manner that trivializes the deadly conflict between evil and good in our history and that cheapens our view of God's mercy and forgiveness. I do not suggest that the scholars named here take "universal salvation" in any trivializing sense—most certainly not. Indeed, "universal salvation," properly understood, may be an adequate expression. But, *positve eschaton only* might be a better statement. Salvation is offered to all. But God is God of freedom; he will not compel. Whether any human person, faced with Infinite Love, can choose to embrace evil (and, at some point, the choice must be stark—anything less would be unworthy of our God), we do not know. What we may say is that one who does so choose has lost a grip on life. There is no future for such a one, because evil has no future. Good has an eternal future.

God alone and the Lamb know what names are inscribed in the book of life.

## For Reference and Further Study

Boring, M. E. "The Language of Universal Salvation in Paul," *JBL* 105/2 (1986) 269–92.

_____. *Revelation*. Louisville: John Knox, 1989. Especially: "Universal Salvation and Paradoxical Language," 226–31.

Caird, G. B. *The Revelation of St. John the Divine*. New York: Harper & Row, 1966.

Giblin, C. H. *The Book of Revelation: The Open Book of Prophecy*. Collegeville: The Liturgical Press, 1991.

Harrington, W. "No Negative Eschaton: Revelation and Universal Salvation." *PIBA* 15 (1992) 42–59.

Schillebeeckx, E. *Church: The Human Story of God*. London: SCM, 1990.

Sweet, J. P. M. *Revelation*. Pelican Commentaries. Philadelphia: Westminster, 1979.

# COMPLETE TRANSLATION

In the Introduction, above, I have suggested that one should, to capture something of the charm of this work, read Revelation as a whole. This translation, the basis of my commentary throughout, while keeping close to the lines of the original, aims at readable English. I have not tried to capture the idiosyncrasies of John's Greek. I have been sensitive to the use of inclusive language.

## Prologue and Address

1. The revelation of Jesus Christ, which God gave him to show his servants what must shortly come to pass. He made it known by sending his angel to his servant John, 2. who, in telling all that he saw, bore witness to the word of God and to the testimony of Jesus Christ. 3. Blessed is the one who reads aloud and blessed are they who hear the words of this prophecy and heed what is written there, for the time of crisis is near.

4. John, to the seven Churches of Asia: Grace to you and peace, from him who is, who was, and who is to come, and from the seven spirits before his throne, and from Jesus Christ, the faithful witness, the first-born of the dead, and ruler of the kings of earth. To him who loves us and has loosed us from our sins with his blood, 6. and has made us a royal house of priests to his God and Father—to him be glory and dominion for ever and ever. Amen. 7. Behold, he will come with the clouds, and every eye will see him, even those who pierced him, and all the tribes of the earth will wail because of him. So be it. Amen. 8. ''I am the Alpha and the Omega,'' says the Lord God, who is, who was, and who is to come, the Almighty.

## Vision of One Like a Son of Man

9. I, John, your brother and sharer in the tribulation and sovereignty and endurance which are ours in Jesus, was on the island called Patmos on account of the word of God and the testimony of Jesus. 10. The Spirit came upon me on the Lord's day and I heard behind me a great voice like a trumpet, 11. which said, ''What you see write in a scroll and send it to the seven Churches: to Ephesus, Smyrna, Pergamum, Thyatira, Sardis, Philadelphia, and Laodicea.'' 12. I turned to see whose voice it was that spoke to me, and having turned, I saw seven golden lamps, 13. and among the lamps one in human form dressed in a robe that came to his feet, with a gold girdle around his breast. 14. The hair of his head was white as snow-white wool, and his eyes flamed like fire; 15. his feet were like brilliant metal refined in a furnace, and his voice was like the roar of many waters. 16. In his right hand he had seven stars, and from his mouth came a sharp two-edged sword; and his face was like the sun shining in its strength. 17. When I saw him I fell at his feet as though I were dead. But he laid his right hand on me, and said, ''Do not be afraid. I am the first and the last, 18. the living one who was dead, and I hold the keys of Death and Hades. 19. Write down therefore what you see, what now is, and what is to take place hereafter. 20. As for the secret of the seven stars you saw in my right hand: the seven stars are the angels of the seven Churches, and the seven lamps are the seven Churches.''

## The Messages to the Seven Churches

2:1. To the angel of the Church at Ephesus write: These are the words of the One who holds the seven stars in his right hand, who walks among the seven golden lamps: 2. I know your works—your toil and endurance. I know you cannot bear evil people and have put to the test those who call themselves apostles but are not, and you have found them to be false. 3. Endurance you have; you have borne up for my name's sake and have not grown weary. 4. But I have this against you: you have lost the love you had at first. 5. Be mindful, then, of how far you have fallen; repent, and do as you did before. If not, I will come to you and remove your lamp from its place, unless you repent. 6. You have this to your credit: you hate the works of the Nicolaitans, as I do. 7. You have ears—so listen to what the Spirit is saying to the Churches! To the victor I will grant the right to eat from the tree of life that stands in the paradise of God.

8. To the angel of the Church at Smyrna write: These are the words

of the first and the last, who was dead and came to life again. 9. I know your tribulation and your poverty—yet you are rich—and the slander of those who claim to be Jews but are not: they are a synagogue of Satan. 10. Do not fear what you are about to suffer. For the devil will throw some of you into prison, to be put to the test, and for ten days you will suffer tribulation. Be faithful unto death, and I will give you the crown of life. 11. You have ears—so listen to what the Spirit is saying to the Churches! The victor will not be harmed by the second death.

12. To the angel of the Church at Pergamum write: These are the words of the One who has the sharp two-edged sword. 13. I know where you dwell, where Satan has his throne—yet you hold fast to my cause. You did not deny your faith in me even in the days of Antipas, my faithful witness, who was slain in your city, where Satan dwells. 14. But I have a few things against you: you have there some who hold to the teaching of Balaam, who taught Balak to set a pitfall for the Israelites; he tempted them to eat meat sacrificed to idols and to commit fornication. 15. In like manner you also have some who hold to the teaching of the Nicolaitans. 16. So repent! Otherwise I will come to you quickly and make war on them with the sword of my mouth. 17. You have ears—so listen to what the Spirit is saying to the Churches! To the victor I will give some of the hidden manna; I will also give to such a one a white stone, with a new name written on the stone, known only to the one who receives it.

18. To the angel of the Church at Thyatira write: These are the words of the Son of God whose eyes are like a flame of fire and whose feet are like brilliant metal: 19. I know your works: your love and faithfulness and service and endurance—indeed, your latest works are better than your earlier works. 20. But I have this against you: you tolerate that Jezebel, that woman who claims to be a prophetess, whose teaching lures my servants into fornication and eating meat sacrificed to idols. 21. I have given her time to repent, but she refuses to repent of her fornication. 22. So, I will throw her on a bed of pain, and throw those who commit adultery with her into great tribulation, unless they repent of her works. 23. And her children I will strike with pestilence. So all the Churches will know that I am the searcher of heart and mind, and that I will give to each of you what your conduct deserves. 24. But this I say to the rest of you in Thyatira, all who do not accept this teaching and have no experience of the deep secrets of Satan—as they call it—I do not lay upon you any further burden. 25. Only hold fast to what you have until I come. 26. To the victor, to the one who keeps my works until the end, I will give authority over the nations—as I myself received from my Father. 27. He will smash [rule] them with a rod of iron, as earthenware he will smash them to pieces. 28. And I will give him the morning star. 29. You have ears—so listen to what the Spirit is saying to the Churches!

3:1. To the angel of the Church at Sardis write: These are the words of the One who has the seven spirits of God and the seven stars: I know your works—you have the name of being alive, though you are dead! 2. Wake up and put some backbone into what still survives—if only on the point of death. For I have found no work of yours perfect in the sight of my God. 3. Be mindful, therefore, of what you received and heard: heed it, and repent. If you do not wake up, I will come as a thief, and you will not know the hour of my coming. 4. Yet you have a few persons in Sardis who have not defiled their garments, and they will walk with me in white, for they are worthy. 5. The victor will likewise be robed in white. I will never strike the victor's name from the book of life, but will acknowledge that name before my Father and his angels. 6. You have ears—so listen to what the Spirit is saying to the Churches!

7. To the angel of the Church at Philadelphia write: These are the words of the holy One, the true One, who has the key of David, who opens and none may shut, who shuts and none may open: 8. I know your works. Therefore, I have set before you an open door, which no one can shut. Though you have little power, yet you have kept my word, and have not disowned my name. 9. Therefore, I will make those of the synagogue of Satan who claim to be Jews and are not, but lie; therefore, I will make them come and fall at your feet—they will know that I love you. 10. Because you have kept my word of endurance, I will in turn keep you safe through the hour of testing which is about to fall upon the whole world, to test those who dwell upon the earth. 11. I am coming soon; hold fast to what you have, and let no one rob you of your crown. 12. The victor I will make a pillar in the temple of my God, never to leave it. I will inscribe on the victor the name of my God, and the name of the city of my God, the new Jerusalem which comes down out of heaven from my God, and my own new name. 13. You have ears—so listen to what the Spirit is saying to the Churches!

14. To the angel of the Church at Laodicea write: These are the words of the Amen, the faithful and true witness, the beginning of God's creation: 15. I know your works: you are neither cold nor hot. How I wish you were either cold or hot! 16. But because you are lukewarm, neither hot nor cold, I will spit you out of my mouth. 17. For you say, ''I am rich, I have made my fortune, I have no need of anything,'' not realizing that you are a pitiful wretch, poor, blind, and naked. 18. I advise you to buy from me gold refined in the fire to make you rich, and white garments to put on to cover the shame of your nakedness, and ointment for your eyes that you may see. 19. All whom I love I reprove and chasten; so, be zealous, and repent. 20. Here I stand knocking at the door; if anyone hears my voice and opens the door, I will come in and will dine with such a one and that one with me. 21. To the victor I will grant a

seat beside me on my throne, as I myself was victorious and sat down with my Father on his throne. 22. You have ears—so listen to what the Spirit is saying to the Churches!

## *The Scroll Vision*

4:1. After this I looked: a door stood open in heaven! And the voice that I had first heard speaking to me like a trumpet said: "Come up here, and I will show you what must take place hereafter." 2. At once, I fell into a trance. There in heaven stood a throne with One seated on it. 3. He who sat there was in appearance like jasper or cornelian; and round about the throne was a rainbow, bright as an emerald. 4. Round about the throne were twenty-four other thrones, and on them sat twenty-four elders clothed in white garments, wearing gold crowns. 5. From the throne came flashes of lightning and peals of thunder, and burning before it were seven flaming lamps, the seven spirits of God, 6. and in front of the throne was what appeared to be a sea of glass, like crystal. In the center, round the throne itself, were four living creatures, with eyes all over, front and back. 7. The first creature was like a lion, the second like an ox, the third had a human face, and the fourth was like an eagle in flight. 8. Each of the four living creatures had six wings, and eyes all over and inside them. Day and night unceasingly they sing: Holy, holy, holy is the Lord God Almighty, who was, and is, and is to come! 9. Whenever the living creatures give glory and honor and thanks to the One who sits on the throne, who lives for ever and ever, 10. the twenty-four elders fall down before the one who sits on the throne, and worship him who lives for ever and ever, and cast their crowns before the throne, saying: 11. "Worthy are you, our Lord and God to receive glory and honor and power, for you created all things; by your will they were created and came into being!"

5:1. Then I saw in the right hand of the One seated on the throne a scroll with writing inside and on the back, sealed with seven seals. 2. And I saw a mighty angel proclaiming in a loud voice: "Who is worthy to open the scroll and break its seals?" 3. But there was no one in heaven or on earth or under the earth to open the scroll or to look inside it. 4. And I wept bitterly because no one was found worthy to open the scroll or to look inside it. 5. But one of the elders said to me: "Do not weep; the Lion from the tribe of Judah, the root of David, has won the right to open the scroll and its seven seals." 6. Then I saw between the throne and the four living creatures and among the elders a Lamb standing as though it had been slain; he had seven horns and seven eyes which are the seven spirits of God sent out into all the world. 7. Then he went and took the scroll from the right hand of the One seated on the throne. 8. And as he took the scroll, the four living creatures and the twenty-four elders fell down before the Lamb; each had a harp, and they held golden bowls full of incense, the prayers of God's people. 9. And they sang a new song: "You are worthy to take the scroll and break its seals, for you were slain and by your blood you bought for God those of every tribe, tongue, people, and nation; 10. you have made them a royal house of priests for our God, and they [shall] reign on earth." 11. As I looked, I heard the voice of many angels round about the throne and the living creatures and the elders, myriads of myriads and thousands of thousands, 12. proclaiming with a loud voice: "Worthy is the Lamb who was slain to receive power and wealth, wisdom and might, honor and glory and blessing!" 13. Then I heard all creatures, in heaven and on earth and under the earth and in the sea, crying: "Blessing and honor, glory and might, to the One seated on the throne and to the Lamb for ever and ever." 14. And the four living creatures said, "Amen"; and the elders fell down and worshiped.

## The Seven Seals

6:1. I watched as the Lamb broke the first of the seven seals, and I heard one of the four living creatures say in a voice like thunder, "Come!" 2. And there, as I watched, was a white horse, and its rider held a bow; he was given a crown and he rode out, conquering and to conquer. 3. When he broke the second seal, I heard the second creature say, "Come!" 4. And out came another horse, blood red. Its rider was given power to take away peace from the earth that people might slaughter one another; and he was given a great sword. 5. When he broke the third seal, I heard the third creature say, "Come!" And there, as I watched, was a black horse, and its rider held in his hand a pair of scales. 6. And I heard what sounded like a voice from among the four creatures say, "a quart of wheat for a denarius, and three quarts of barley for a denarius. But do not harm the oil and the wine!" 7. When he broke the fourth seal, I heard the fourth creature say, "Come!" 8. And there, as I watched, was a pale horse, and its rider's name was Death, and Hades followed with him. They were given power over a quarter of the earth, to kill by sword and famine, by pestilence and wild beasts.

9. When he broke the fifth seal, I saw underneath the altar the souls of those who had been slaughtered for the word of God and for the testimony they bore. 10. They cried aloud, saying, "How long, Master, holy and true, must it be before you pronounce judgment and avenge our blood on the inhabitants of the earth?" 11. Then each of them was given a white robe, and they were told to rest for a little while longer until the number of their fellow-servants and brothers and sisters, who were to be killed as they themselves had been, was completed.

12. I watched as he broke the sixth seal. There was a great earthquake; the sun turned black as a hairy sackcloth, and the moon all red as blood; 13. the stars in the sky fell to the earth as a fig tree shedding its unripe figs when shaken by a gale; 14. the sky was torn apart like a scroll being rolled up, and every mountain and island was dislodged from its place. 15. Then the kings of the earth, the nobles and the commanders, the rich and the powerful, and every slave and freeman, hid themselves in caves or under the mountain crags; 16. and they cried to the mountains and to the crags, "Fall on us and hide us from the One who sits on the throne and from the wrath of the Lamb; 17. for the great day of their wrath has come, and who can stand?"

7:1. After this I saw four angels standing at the four corners of the earth, holding back the four winds of the earth so that no wind should blow on land or sea or on any tree. 2. Then I saw another angel ascend from the rising of the sun, holding the seal of the living God, and he cried aloud to the four angels who had been given power to devastate land and sea: 3. "Do not devastate land or sea or trees until we have set the seal of our God on the foreheads of his servants." 4. I heard how many had been marked with the seal—a hundred and forty-four thousand from all the tribes of Israel: 5. twelve thousand from the tribe of Judah, twelve thousand from the tribe of Reuben, twelve thousand from the tribe of Gad, 6. twelve thousand from the tribe of Asher, twelve thousand from the tribe of Naphtali, twelve thousand from the tribe of Manasseh, 7. twelve thousand from the tribe of Simeon, twelve thousand from the tribe of Levi, twelve thousand from the tribe of Issachar, 8. twelve thousand from the tribe of Zabulon, twelve thousand from the tribe of Joseph, twelve thousand from the tribe of Benjamin.

9. After this I looked, and there was a vast throng, which no one could count, from all nations and tribes and people and tongues, standing before the throne and the Lamb, robed in white and with palm branches in their hands. 10. They were shouting aloud, "Victory to our God who sits on the throne, and to the Lamb!" 11. All the angels who stood round the throne and the elders and the four living creatures fell on their faces before the throne and worshiped God, crying: 12. "Amen! Praise, glory and wisdom, thanksgiving and honor, power and might, be to our God

for ever and ever! Amen." 13. Then one of the elders spoke to me and asked: "These people robed in white—who are they and where have they come from?" 14. I answered, "My lord, it is you who know." He said to me, "They are those who have passed through the great tribulation; they have washed their robes and made them white in the blood of the Lamb. 15. That is why they stand before the throne of God and worship him day and night in his temple, and he who sits on the throne will be their tabernacle. 16. They shall not hunger anymore, or thirst anymore; never again shall the sun strike them, nor any scorching heat. 17. For the Lamb who is at the center of the throne will shepherd them, and will guide them to the springs of the water of life; and God will wipe away every tear from their eyes."

8:1. When the Lamb broke the seventh seal, there was silence in heaven for about half an hour. 2. I saw the seven angels who stand before God, and they were given seven trumpets. 3. Then another angel came and stood at the altar, holding a golden censer. He was given much incense to offer with the prayers of all God's people on the golden altar before the throne, 4. and the smoke of the incense went up before God with his people's prayers from the angel's hand. 5. The angel took the censer, filled it with fire from the altar, and threw it down on the earth; and there came peals of thunder, flashes of lightning, and an earthquake.

### The Seven Trumpets

6. Then the seven angels who held the seven trumpets prepared to blow them. 7. The first blew his trumpet; and there came hail and fire mixed with blood cast upon the earth. A third of the earth was burnt up, a third of the trees were burnt up, and all the green grass was burnt up. 8. Then the second angel blew his trumpet; and what looked like a great mountain flaming with fire was cast into the sea. A third of the sea was turned to blood, 9. a third of the living creatures in it died, and a third of the ships were destroyed. 10. Then the third angel blew his trumpet; and a great star fell from the sky, blazing like a torch, and fell on a third of the rivers and springs of water. 11. The name of the star was Wormwood; and a third of the water turned to wormwood, and many died from drinking the water because it had become bitter. 12. Then the fourth angel blew his trumpet; a third of the sun was struck, a third of the moon, and a third of the stars, so that a third part of them turned dark, and a third of the day did not appear, and likewise the night. 13. Then I

looked, and I heard an eagle [vulture] crying aloud as it flew in mid-heaven: "Woe, woe, woe to the inhabitants of the earth because of the remaining trumpet blasts which the three angels are about to blow."

9:1. Then the fifth angel blew his trumpet; and I saw a star fallen from heaven to earth, and he was given a key to the shaft of the abyss. 2. He opened the shaft of the abyss, and smoke came up from the shaft like smoke from a great furnace, and the sun and the air were darkened by the smoke from the shaft. 3. Out of the smoke came locusts over the earth, and they were given the powers of earthly scorpions. 4. They were told to do no harm to the grass of the earth or to any green plant or any tree, but only to those people who did not have God's seal on their foreheads; 5. they were not permitted to kill them, but only to torment them for five months; and their torment was like the torment of a scorpion when it stings. 6. In those days people will seek death but will not find it; they will long to die, but death will elude them. 7. In appearance the locusts were like horses equipped for battle. On their heads were what looked like gold crowns; their faces were like human faces, 8. and they had hair like women's hair and teeth like lions' teeth. 9. They had chests like iron breastplates; the sound of their wings was like the sound of many chariots with many horses charging into battle. 10. They had tails like scorpions, with stings, and in their tails lay their power to harm people for five months. 11. They had as their king the angel of the abyss, whose name in Hebrew is Abaddon and in Greek Apollyon. 12. The first woe has passed; but there are still two woes to come.

13. Then the sixth angel blew his trumpet; and I heard a voice coming from the horns of the golden altar before God. 14. It said to the sixth angel, who held the trumpet: "Release the four angels held bound at the great river Euphrates!" 15. So the four angels were released: they had been held in readiness for this very hour, day, month, and year, to kill a third of humankind. 16. The number of the troops of cavalry was twice ten thousand times ten thousand; I heard their number. 17. This is how I saw the horses and their riders in my vision: they wore breastplates, fiery red, dark blue, and sulphur yellow; and the horses had heads like lions' heads, and from their mouths came fire, smoke, and sulphur. 18. By these three plagues—the fire, the smoke, and the sulphur that came from their mouths—a third of humankind was killed. 19. The power of the horses lay in their mouths and in their tails; for their tails are like serpents—they have heads, and with them they wound. 20. The rest of humankind, who were not killed by these plagues, still did not renounce the gods their hands had made, nor give up worshiping demons, and the idols of gold and silver and bronze and stone and wood, which cannot see or hear or walk; 21. nor did they repent of their murders, their sorceries, their fornication, or their robberies.

10:1. Then I saw another mighty angel coming down from heaven, wrapped in a cloud, with a rainbow over his head; his face was like the sun, and his legs like pillars of fire. 2. He held in his hand a little scroll which was open. He set his right foot on the sea and his left on the land. 3. Then he gave a great shout like the roar of a lion; and when he shouted the seven thunders spoke out. 4. When the seven thunders had spoken, I was about to write, but I heard a voice from heaven saying: "Seal up what the seven thunders have said; do not write it down." 5. Then the angel I saw standing on the sea and land raised his right hand towards heaven 6. and swore by him who lives for ever and ever, who created heaven and everything in it, earth and everything in it, sea and everything in it, that there would be no more delay. 7. When the time comes for the seventh angel to blow his trumpet, the hidden purpose of God will have been accomplished, as he proclaimed to his servants the prophets. 8. Then the voice which I had heard from heaven was speaking to me again and saying, "Go, take the scroll which is open in the hand of the angel who stands on the sea and the land." 9. I went to the angel and asked him to give me the little scroll. He said to me: "Take it, and eat it. It will turn your stomach sour, but in your mouth it will taste sweet as honey." 10. I took the little scroll from the angel's hand and ate it, and it was sweet as honey in my mouth, but when I swallowed it my stomach turned sour. 11. Then I was told: "Once again you must prophesy over many peoples and nations and tongues and kings."

11:1. Then I was given a cane to use as a measuring rod, and was told: "Go and measure the temple of God and the altar and those who worship there. 2. But leave out the outer court of the temple and do not measure it; for it has been given over to the Gentiles, and they will trample over the holy city for forty-two months. 3. And I will commission my two witnesses to prophesy for those one thousand two hundred and sixty days, dressed in sackcloth." 4. These are the two olive-trees and the two lamps that stand before the Lord of the earth. 5. If anyone tries to harm them, fire comes out of their mouths and consumes their enemies; so shall be killed anyone who tries to harm them. 6. They have power to shut up the sky so that no rain may fall during the time of their prophesying; and they have power to turn water into blood and to strike the earth with every kind of plague as often as they wish. 7. But when they have completed their testimony, the beast that comes up from the abyss will wage war on them and will overcome them and kill them. 8. Their corpses will lie in the street of the great city which is figuratively called Sodom and Egypt, where also their Lord was crucified. 9. And people from every nation and tribe and tongue and race will stare at their corpses for three and a half days and will not permit their corpses to be placed in a tomb. 10. The inhabitants of the earth gloat over them; they celebrate and send gifts to one another, for these two prophets were a torment to the inhabitants of the earth. 11. But after the three and a half days, a breath of life from God came into them, and they stood up on their feet, and a great dread fell upon those who beheld them. 12. Then they heard a loud voice from heaven saying to them, "Come up here!" And they ascended to heaven in a cloud, in full view of their enemies. 13. And in that hour there was a great earthquake, and a tenth of the city fell. Seven thousand people were killed in the earthquake; the rest were terrified and gave glory to the God of heaven. 14. The second woe has passed; but the third is coming soon.

15. Then the seventh angel blew his trumpet, and there were loud voices in heaven saying, "The sovereignty of the world has passed to our Lord and to his Christ, and he shall reign for ever and ever." 16. The twenty-four elders, who sit on their thrones before God, fell on their faces and worshiped God, 17 saying, "We give thanks, Lord God Almighty, who are and who was, because you have assumed your full power and entered on your reign. 18. The nations rose in wrath, but your wrath has come. Now is the time for the dead to be judged and for rewarding your servants the prophets, and your people, and those who fear your name, both small and great, and to destroy the destroyers of the earth." 19. Then God's sanctuary in heaven was opened, and the ark of the covenant was seen in his sanctuary; and there came flashes of lightning and peals of thunder and an earthquake and heavy hail.

### The Woman and the Dragon

12:1. A great sign appeared in heaven: a woman robed with the sun, with the moon beneath her feet, and on her head a crown of twelve stars. 2. She was with child, and she cried out in her pangs of birth, in anguish to be delivered. 3. Then a second sign appeared in heaven: a great red dragon with seven heads and ten horns and seven diadems on his heads, 4. and his tail swept down a third of the stars of heaven and hurled them to the earth. The dragon stood before the woman who was about to give birth, so that when her child was born he might devour it. 5. And she gave birth to a son, a male child, who is destined to rule all the nations with a rod of iron; but her child was snatched up to God and to his throne. 6. The woman fled into the desert, where she had a place prepared by God that there she might be sustained for twelve hundred and sixty days.

7. Then war broke out in heaven. Michael and his angels fought against the dragon. The dragon with his angels fought back, 8. and he did not

prevail, nor had they place anymore in heaven. 9. The great dragon was thrown down, that ancient serpent, who is called Devil and the Satan, the deceiver of the whole world; he was thrown down to the earth, and his angels with him. 10. And I heard a loud voice in heaven proclaim: "Now is the salvation and power and sovereignty of our God, and the authority of his Christ; for the accuser of our brothers and sisters is driven out, he who accused them day and night before our God. 11. They have conquered him by the blood of the Lamb and by the testimony they bore, for love of life did not bring them to shrink from death. 12. Rejoice, then, you heavens and you that dwell in them! But woe to you, earth and sea, for the devil has come down to you in great fury, knowing that his time is short!"

13. When the dragon saw that he had been thrown down to the earth, he went in pursuit of the woman who had given birth to the male child. 14. But the woman was given two great eagle's wings so that she could fly to her place in the desert where she was to be sustained for a time, times, and half a time, away from the serpent. 15. Then the serpent spewed a flood of water after the woman, to sweep her away in its flood. 16. But the earth came to the assistance of the woman, and opened its mouth and swallowed the river which the dragon spewed from his mouth. 17. So the dragon was furious with the woman and went off to wage war on the rest of her offspring, those who keep God's commandments and have the testimony of Jesus. 18. And he took his stand on the seashore.

## The Two Beasts

13:1. Then out of the sea I saw a beast rising, with ten horns and seven heads; on its horns were ten diadems, and on each head a blasphemous name. 2. The beast I saw was like a leopard, but its feet were like a bear's and its mouth like a lion's mouth. The dragon conferred on it his own power, his throne, and great authority. 3. One of its heads was wounded, as it seemed, unto death, yet its mortal wound was healed. And the whole world gazed with wonder after the beast; 4. they worshiped the dragon because he had conferred his authority on the beast, and they worshiped the beast, saying, "Who is like the beast? Who can fight against it?" 5. It was allowed to mouth boasts and blasphemy and it was given permission to exercise authority for forty-two months. 6. It opened its mouth in blasphemies against God, blaspheming his name and his dwelling, that is, those who dwell in heaven. 7. It was allowed to wage war on

God's people and conquer them; and it was given authority over every tribe, people, tongue, and nation. 8. All the inhabitants of the earth will worship it, all whose names have not been written in the book of life of the Lamb, slain since the foundation of the world. 9. If you have ears, hear then! 10. "Whoever is for captivity, to captivity he goes; whoever is to be slain by the sword, by the sword must he be slain." This calls for the endurance and faith of God's people.

11. Then I saw another beast rising out of the land; it had two horns like a lamb's, but spoke like a dragon. 12. It wielded all the authority of the first beast in its presence, and made the earth and its inhabitants worship the first beast, whose mortal wound had been healed. 13. It worked great miracles, even making fire come down from heaven to earth in the sight of people. 14. By the miracles it was allowed to perform in the presence of the beast it deceived the inhabitants of the earth, telling the inhabitants of the earth to set up an image to the beast which had received the sword-wound and yet lived. 15. It was allowed to give breath to the image of the beast, so that the image of the beast might even speak, and to cause those who would not worship the image of the beast to be killed. 16. It caused everyone, small and great, rich and poor, free and slave, to have a mark put on the right hand or on the forehead, 17. and no one was allowed to buy or sell unless one had the mark, the name of the beast or the number of its name. 18. This calls for wisdom. Let anyone who has intelligence figure out the number of the beast, for it is the number of a human being; and its number is six hundred and sixty-six.

## Salvation and Judgment

14:1. Then I looked, and there on Mount Zion stood the Lamb, and with him a hundred and forty-four thousand who had his name and the name of his Father written on their foreheads. 2. I heard a sound from heaven like the sound of many waters, like the sound of mighty thunder; the sound I heard was like harpists harping on their harps. 3. They were singing a new song before the throne and the four living creatures and the elders, and no one could learn the song except the hundred and forty-four thousand who were redeemed from the earth. 4. These are they who have not defiled themselves with women, for they are virgins; these follow the Lamb wherever he goes. These have been redeemed from humankind as firstfruits for God and the Lamb. 5. No lie was found on their lips: they are without blemish.

6. Then I saw another angel flying in mid-heaven, with an eternal gospel to proclaim to the inhabitants of the earth, to every nation, tribe, tongue, and people. 7. He cried in a loud voice: "Fear God and give him glory; for the hour of his judgment has come. Worship him who made heaven and earth, the sea and the springs of water." 8. Another angel, a second, followed, saying, "Fallen, fallen is Babylon the great, who has made all nations drink the wine of the wrath of her fornication!" 9. And another angel, a third, followed them, saying in a loud voice, "Whoever worships the beast and its image and receives a mark on his forehead or hand, 10. shall also drink the wine of the wrath of God, poured undiluted into the cup of his anger, and shall be tormented with fire and brimstone before the holy angels and before the Lamb." 11. The smoke of their torment will go up for ever and ever; there will be no respite day or night for those who worship the beast and its image and whoever receives the mark of its name. 12. Hence the endurance of God's people, those who keep the commandments of God and the faith of Jesus. 13. Then I heard a voice from heaven, saying, "Write this: Blessed are the dead who die in the Lord henceforth. Yes—says the Spirit—that they may rest from their labors; for their works go with them."

14. Then I looked, and there appeared a white cloud, and sitting on the cloud one like a son of man, with a gold crown on his head and a sharp sickle in his hand. 15. Another angel came out of the temple and called in a loud voice to him who sat on the cloud: "Put in your sickle, and reap, for the hour to reap has come, for the harvest of the earth is fully ripe." 16. So the one who sat on the cloud swung his sickle over the earth, and the earth was reaped.

17. Then another angel came out of the heavenly temple, and he also had a sharp sickle. 18. And another angel, one who has authority over fire, came out from the altar, and he called to the one who had the sharp sickle, saying, "Put in your sharp sickle and gather the clusters of the vine of the earth, for its grapes are ripe." 19. So the angel swung his sickle over the earth and gathered the vintage of the earth and threw it into the great winepress of God's wrath. 20. The winepress was trodden outside the city, and blood flowed from the winepress up to the horses' bridles for a distance of sixteen hundred stadia.

## The Last Plagues

15:1. Then I saw another portent in heaven, great and astonishing: seven angels with seven plagues, the last, for with them the wrath of

God is spent. 2. And I saw, as it were, a sea of glass mingled with fire and, standing beside the sea of glass, holding harps of God, were those who had been victorious against the beast and its image and the number of its name. 3. They were singing the song of Moses, the servant of God, and the song of the Lamb: "Great and marvelous are your works, Lord God Almighty; just and true are your ways, O King of the nations. 4. Who shall not fear you, Lord, and do homage to your name? For you alone are holy. All nations will come and worship before you, for your righteous deeds have been revealed."

5. After this, as I looked, the sanctuary of the heavenly Tent of Testimony was opened, 6. and out of the sanctuary came the seven angels with the seven plagues. They were robed in fine linen, pure and shining, and had golden girdles round their breasts. 7. Then one of the four living creatures gave the seven angels seven golden bowls full of the wrath of God who lives for ever and ever. 8. And the sanctuary was filled with smoke from the glory of God and from his power, so that no one could enter the sanctuary until the seven plagues of the seven angels were completed. 16:1. Then I heard a loud voice from the sanctuary say to the seven angels: "Go and pour out the seven bowls of God's wrath on the earth."

16:2. So the first went and poured out his bowl on the earth, and foul and grievous sores broke out on the people who had the mark of the beast and worshiped its image. 3. The second poured out his bowl on the sea; and it turned to blood, like blood from a dead body, and every living thing in the sea died. 4. The third poured out his bowl on the rivers and springs of water, and they turned to blood. 5. And I heard the angel of the waters say, "Righteous are you, who are and who was, O Holy One, because you have thus passed judgment; 6. for they shed the blood of your people and your prophets, and you have given them blood to drink. They have their deserts!" 7. And I heard the altar say, "Yes, Lord God Almighty, true and righteous are your judgments." 8. The fourth poured out his bowl on the sun; and it was allowed to scorch people with its flame. 9. They were scorched with a scorching heat, and they blasphemed the name of God who had power to inflict such plagues, but they did not repent and give him glory.

10. The fifth poured out his bowl on the throne of the beast, and its kingdom was plunged in darkness. People gnawed their tongues in pain, 11. and blasphemed the God of heaven for their pains and sores, and did not repent of their works.

12. The sixth poured out his bowl on the great river, the Euphrates, and its water was dried up, to prepare a way for the kings from the sunrise. 13. Then I saw coming from the mouth of the dragon, from the mouth of the beast, and from the mouth of the false prophet, three foul spirits like frogs. 14. For they are demonic spirits, able to work miracles, who

go out to the kings of the whole world, to muster them for battle on the great day of God the Almighty. 15. "Behold, I come like a thief! Blessed is he who stays awake and keeps his garments by him, so that he does not walk naked and his shame be seen." 16. And they mustered them at the place which is called in Hebrew Armageddon.

17. The seventh poured out his bowl on the air; and out of the sanctuary there came from the throne a loud voice saying, "It is done!" 18. And there were flashes of lightning and peals of thunder, and a violent earthquake, so violent that its like had not been since humankind appeared on earth. 19. The great city was split in three, and the cities of the nations fell. And Babylon the great was remembered before God and made to drink the cup of the wine of the fury of his wrath. 20. Every island vanished, and not a mountain was to be found. 21. Huge hailstones, weighing over a hundredweight, fell from the sky on humankind; and they blasphemed God because of the plague of hail, because that plague was exceedingly great.

### The Harlot and the Beast

17:1. And one of the seven angels who held the seven bowls came and spoke to me: "Come," he said, "I will show you the verdict on the great harlot, enthroned on many waters, 2. with whom the kings of the earth have committed fornication, and the inhabitants of the earth have made themselves drunk on the wine of her fornication." 3. He carried me away in spirit into a wilderness, and I saw a woman mounted on a scarlet beast which was covered with blasphemous names and had seven heads and ten horns. 4. The woman was clothed in purple and scarlet and bedecked with gold and precious stones and pearls. In her hand she held a gold cup full of obscenities and the filth of her fornication; 5. and on her forehead was written a mysterious name: "Babylon the great, the mother of harlots and of all obscenities on earth." 6. I saw that the woman was drunk with the blood of God's people and with the blood of the martyrs [witnesses] of Jesus. At the sight of her I wondered greatly. 7. Then the angel said to me: "Why do you wonder? I will tell you the mystery of the woman and of the beast she rides, with the seven heads and the ten horns. 8. The beast you saw was and is not and is to rise from the abyss; and it goes to perdition. The inhabitants of the earth, whose names have not been written in the book of life since the foundation of the world, will be astonished to behold the beast that was and is not and is to come. 9. This calls for a mind with wisdom. The seven heads are seven hills on which the woman sits enthroned. They are also seven kings: 10. five have fallen, one now is, and the other has not yet come, and when he comes he must stay for a short while. 11. And the beast that was and is not is also an eighth, yet he is one of the seven and he goes to perdition. 12. The ten horns you saw are ten kings, who have received no kingdom as yet; but for one hour they are to receive royal authority with the beast. 13. They have a single purpose and will yield their power and authority to the beast. 14. They will wage war on the Lamb, and the Lamb will conquer them, for he is Lord of lords and King of kings, and those who are with him are called, and chosen, and faithful.'' 15. Then he said to me: ''The waters you saw, where the harlot sat enthroned, are peoples and multitudes and nations and tongues. 16. And the ten horns which you saw, and the beast, they will come to hate the harlot and will make her desolate and naked; they will devour her flesh and will burn her with fire. 17. For God has put it into their minds to carry out his purpose by being of one mind, and by yielding their sovereignty to the beast until God's words are fulfilled. 18. The woman you saw is the great city that holds sway over the kings of the earth.''

## The End of Babylon

18:1. After this I saw another angel coming down from heaven; he had great authority and the earth was lighted up by his splendor. 2. With a mighty voice he proclaimed: ''Fallen, fallen is Babylon the great! She has become a dwelling for demons, a haunt for every unclean spirit, a haunt for every unclean and loathsome bird. 3. For all the nations have drunk of the wine of the wrath of her fornication; the kings of the earth have committed fornication with her, and the merchants of the earth have grown rich on the strength of her wanton luxury.'' 4. Then I heard another voice from heaven, saying, ''Come out of her, my people, that you may have no part in her sins, and that you do not suffer her plagues; 5. for her sins are piled high as heaven and God has remembered her crimes. 6. Pay her back in her own coin, repay her twice over for her works! In the cup she mixed, mix her a double draught! 7. To match her pomp and wanton luxury, mete out to her torment and grief!'' She says to herself: ''I sit here as queen! No widow am I, no mourning will I see!'' 8. Therefore in a single day will her plagues come, pestilence, mourning, and famine, and she will be burnt to the ground; for mighty is the God who has condemned her.

9. The kings of the earth who committed fornication with her, and lived wantonly with her, will weep and wail over her, as they watch the

smoke of her burning. 10. Standing far off in terror at her torment, they will say: "Alas, alas, great city, mighty city of Babylon! In one hour your doom has come!" 11. And the merchants of the earth will weep and mourn for her, because no one buys their cargoes any more, 12. cargoes of gold and silver, precious stones and pearls, fine linen and purples, silk and scarlet; all sorts of scented woods and every type of ivory work and all kinds of objects in costly wood, bronze, iron, or marble; 13. cinnamon and spice, incense, myrrh, and frankincense; wine, oil, fine flour and wheat, cattle and sheep, horses, chariots, slaves, and human livestock. 14. The fruit for which your soul longed is gone from you and all your luxuries and splendors are lost to you, never to be found again. 15. The merchants of these wares, who were made rich through her, stand far off in terror at her torment, weeping and mourning, 16. and saying, "Alas, alas, for the great city that was robed in fine linen and purple and scarlet, adorned with gold and precious stones and pearls. 17. In one hour so much wealth laid waste!" Then every sea-captain and seafarer, sailors and those who make a living from the sea, stood far off, 18. and cried out as they watched the smoke of her burning: "Was there ever a city like the great city?" 19. They threw dust on their heads, and cried out, wailing and mourning, saying, "Alas, alas, for the great city, where all who had ships at sea grew rich from her wealth. In one hour she has been laid waste!"

20. "Rejoice over her, heaven, and God's people, and apostles, and prophets, for God has given judgment for you against her." 21. Then a mighty angel lifted up a stone like a great millstone and hurled it into the sea, saying, "Thus will Babylon, the great city, be hurled down with violence, never to be seen again! 22. The sound of harpers and minstrels, flute-players and trumpeters, will be heard in you no more; and any craftsman of any trade will be found in you no more; and the sound of the mill will be heard in you no more; 23. the light of the lamp will be seen in you no more; and the voice of the bridegroom and bride will be heard in you no more. For your merchants were the great ones of the earth and through your sorcery were all nations led astray. 24. And in her was found the blood of prophets and of God's people, and of all who have been slain on earth."

19:1. After this I heard, as it were, the shout of a vast throng in heaven: "Hallelujah! Victory and glory and power belong to our God, 2. for true and just are his judgments. For he has condemned the great harlot who corrupted the earth with her fornication, and has avenged on her the blood of his servants." 3. And again they shouted: "Hallelujah! The smoke from her goes up for ever and ever!" 4. And the twenty-four elders and the four living creatures fell down and worshiped God who sits on the throne, saying, "Amen! Hallelujah!" 5. Then came a voice from the throne, saying: "Praise our God, all you his servants, you who fear him, small and great." 6. And I heard, as it were, the sound of a vast throng, like the sound of many waters and as the sound of mighty thunder peals, saying, "Hallelujah! For the Lord God the Almighty has entered on his reign. 7. Let us rejoice and be glad and give glory to him, for the marriage of the Lamb has come. His bride has made herself ready, 8. and it is granted to her to attire herself in fine linen, shining and clean—for the fine linen is the righteous deeds of God's people." 9. And he said to me, "Write this: blessed are those who are invited to the marriage feast of the Lamb." And he said to me, "These are the very words of God." 10. And I fell at his feet to worship him. But he said to me: "No, not that! I am a fellow servant with you and your brothers and sisters who hold the testimony of Jesus: worship God. For the testimony of Jesus is the spirit of prophecy."

## The End of Evil

19:11. And I saw heaven wide open, and behold, a white horse; its rider's name was Faithful and True and in righteousness he judges and makes war. 12. His eyes flamed like fire, and on his head were many diadems; written on him was a name known to none but himself; 13. he was clothed in a cloak dipped in blood, and he was called the Word of God. 14. The armies of heaven followed him on white horses, clothed in fine linen, white and clean. 15. From his mouth came a sharp sword with which to smite the nations, for it is he who will rule them with a rod of iron, and it is he who treads the winepress of the wine of the fury of the wrath of God the Almighty. 16. On his cloak and on his thigh was written the title: King of kings and Lord of lords. 17. Then I saw an angel standing in the sun, and he cried aloud to all the birds that fly in midheaven: "Come, gather together for the great banquet of God, 18. to eat the flesh of kings and flesh of captains and flesh of warriors, the flesh of horses and their riders, and the flesh of all, the free and the slave, the small and the great." 19. And I saw the beast and the kings of the earth with their armies, mustered to do battle with the rider and his army. 20. The beast was captured, and along with him the false prophet who had worked miracles in its presence, by which he deluded those who had received the mark of the beast and worshiped its image. These two were thrown alive into the lake of fire with its sulphurous flames. 21. And the rest were slain by the sword of the rider on the horse, the sword which came out of his mouth, and all the birds gorged themselves on their flesh.

20:1. Then I saw an angel coming down from heaven with the key of the abyss, and a great chain, in his hand. 2. He seized the dragon, that ancient serpent, who is Devil and the Satan, and bound him for a thousand years; 3. he threw him into the abyss, shutting and sealing it over him, so that he should not deceive the nations again until the thousand years were ended. After that he must be let loose for a little while. 4. I saw thrones, and seated on them were those to whom judgment was committed. And I saw the souls of those who had been beheaded for the testimony of Jesus and for the word of God, those who had not worshiped the beast and its image and had not received its mark on forehead or hand. They came to life again and reigned with Christ for a thousand years, 5. while the rest of the dead did not come to life until the thousand years were ended. This is the first resurrection. 6. Blessed and holy is the one who shares in the first resurrection. Over such the second death has no power; but they will be priests of God and of Christ, and they will reign with him for a thousand years. 7. When the thousand years are ended, Satan will be let loose from his prison, 8. and he will come out to deceive the nations at the four corners of the earth, Gog and Magog, to muster them for battle—their number as the sands of the sea. 9. They marched over the breadth of the land and surrounded the camp of God's people and the beloved city. But fire came down from heaven and consumed them. 10. And the Devil who deceived them was flung into the lake of fire and brimstone, where the beast and the false prophet were, to be tormented day and night for ever and ever.

11. Then I saw a great white throne and the One who sat upon it; from his presence earth and heaven fled away, and no place was found for them. 12. I saw the dead, great and small, standing before the throne; and books were opened. Then another book was opened, the book of life; and the dead were judged according to their works as written in the books. 13. The sea gave up the dead that were in it, and Death and Hades gave up the dead in them; and all of them were judged according to their works. 14. Then Death and Hades were thrown into the lake of fire. This is the second death, the lake of fire. 15. And if anyone's name was not found written in the book of life, that one was thrown into the lake of fire.

## The New Jerusalem

21:1. Then I saw a new heaven and a new earth, for the first heaven and the first earth had passed away, and the sea was no more. 2. I saw the holy city, new Jerusalem, coming down out of heaven from God, made ready like a bride adorned for her husband. 3. I heard a loud voice from the throne say: "Behold, God's dwelling is with humankind! He will dwell among them, and they will be his peoples, and God himself will be with them [as their God], 4. and he will wipe away every tear from their eyes; and death will be no more; mourning and crying and pain will be no more—for the old order has passed away." 5. The One who sat on the throne said: "Behold, I am making all things new!" And he said: "Write this down, for these things are trustworthy and true." 6. Then he said to me: "It is done! I am the Alpha and the Omega, the beginning and the end. To the thirsty I will give, as a gift, water from the spring of the water of life. 7. The victors will have this heritage; and I will be their God and they will be my children. 8. As for the cowardly, the faithless, the polluted, the murderers, fornicators, sorcerers, idolators, and liars of every kind—their lot will be the lake that burns with fire and brimstone, which is the second death."

9. Then came one of the seven angels who held the seven bowls full of the seven last plagues and spoke to me, saying, "Come. I will show you the bride, the wife of the Lamb." 10. So he carried me away in a trance to a great and lofty mountain, and showed me the holy city Jerusalem coming down out of heaven from God, 11. possessing the glory of God. It had the radiance of a precious jewel, like a jasper, clear as crystal. 12. It had a great, high wall with twelve gates, and at the gates twelve angels; on the gates were inscribed the names of the twelve tribes of Israel. 13. There were three gates to the east, three to the north, three to the south, and three to the west. 14. The city wall had twelve foundation-stones, and on them were the twelve names of the twelve apostles of the Lamb. 15. And he who spoke with me had a gold measuring rod to measure the city, its gates, and its wall. 16. The city stands foursquare, its length the same as its breadth; and he measured the city with his rod, twelve thousand stadia: its length and breadth and height were equal. 17. And he measured its wall: a hundred and forty-four cubits, according to human measure, that is, an angel's. 18. The fabric of the wall was jasper, while the city was of pure gold, clear as glass. 19. The foundations of the city wall were adorned with every kind of precious stone: the first foundation-stone was jasper, the second lapis lazuli, the third chalcedony, the fourth emerald, 20. the fifth sardonyx, the sixth cornelian, the seventh chrysolite, the eighth beryl, the ninth topaz, the tenth chrysoprase, the eleventh jacinth, the twelfth amethyst. 21. The twelve gates were twelve pearls, each gate made from a single pearl. The main street of the city was of pure gold, like translucent glass. 22. I saw no temple in the city, for its temple was the Lord God Almighty and the Lamb. 23. The city had no need of sun or moon to shine on it; for the

glory of God gave it light, and its lamp was the Lamb. 24. The nations will walk by its light, and the kings of the earth will bring their glory into it. 25. Its gates will never be shut by day—for there will be no night there. 26. They will bring into it the splendor and wealth of the nations. 27. But nothing unclean will enter it, nor any who practice abomination or falsehood, but only those who are written in the Lamb's book of life. 22:1. Then he showed me the river of the water of life, bright as crystal, flowing from the throne of God and of the Lamb, 2. down the middle of the city's street. And on either side of the river stood a tree of life yielding twelve crops of fruit, one for each month of the year; and the leaves of the tree were for the healing of the nations. 3. There will no more be anything accursed. The throne of God and of the Lamb will be there, and his servants will worship him; 4. and they will see his face, and his name will be on their foreheads. 5. There will be no more night; they will have no need of light of lamp or sun, for the Lord God will shine upon them, and they will reign for ever and ever.

## Epilogue and Conclusion

6. Then he said to me: "These words are trustworthy and true. The Lord God who inspires the prophets has sent his angel to show his servants what must soon take place." 7. "Behold, I am coming soon! Blessed is the one who keeps the words of the prophecy of this book." 8. It was I, John, who heard and saw these things. When I had heard and seen, I fell down to worship at the feet of the angel who had shown them to me. 9. But he said to me: "No, not that! I am a fellow servant with you and your brothers the prophets and with those who keep the words of this book. Worship God!" 10. And he said to me: "Do not seal up the words of the prophecy of this book, for the time is near. 11. Let the evil-doer still do evil, and the filthy still be filthy, and the righteous still be righteous, and the holy still be holy." 12. "Behold, I am coming soon, bringing my reward with me, to repay everyone according to what one has done. 13. I am the Alpha and the Omega, the first and the last, the beginning and the end." 14. Blessed are those who wash their robes, so as to have the right to the tree of life, and may enter the city by the gates. 15. Outside are the dogs, sorcerers, and fornicators, the murderers and idolators, and all who love and practice deceit. 16. I, Jesus, have sent my angel to give you this testimony for the Churches. "I am the root and offspring of David, the bright morning star." 17. The Spirit and the bride

say: "Come!" Let the hearer say, "Come!" Let the thirsty come. Let whoever wishes receive the water of life without charge. 18. I warn everyone who hears the words of the prophecy of this book: if anyone adds to them, God will add to that one the plagues that are written in this book; 19. and if anyone should take away from the words of the book of this prophecy, God will take away that one's share in the tree of life and in the holy city, which are described in this book. 20. He who testifies to these things says: "Yes, I am coming soon!" Amen! Come, Lord Jesus!

21. The grace of the Lord Jesus be with all.

# INDEXES

## 1. *PRINCIPAL ANCIENT PARALLELS*

### Old Testament

*Genesis*

| | |
|---|---|
| 1–2 | 210 |
| 1:7 | 80 |
| 1:21 | 163 |
| 1:26-30 | 210 |
| 1:26-31 | 211 |
| 1:31 | 27 |
| 2 | 58 |
| 2:9 | 216 |
| 2:9-10 | 219 |
| 3:1 | 132 |
| 3:15 | 135 |
| 3:22 | 216 |
| 4:10 | 94 |
| 5:18-24 | 2 |
| 6:1-4 | 130 |
| 6:6 | 169 |
| 8:21 | 24, 111, 118 |
| 9:12-17 | 79 |
| 9:13 | 229 |

*Exodus*

| | |
|---|---|
| 2:23-24 | 26 |
| 3:14 | 46 |
| 4:23 | 108 |
| 7–10 | 107 |
| 7:14-25 | 121 |
| 7:20 | 106 |
| 7:20-21 | 163 |

| | |
|---|---|
| 8:5-6 | 166 |
| 9:8-12 | 163 |
| 9:23-24 | 168 |
| 9:23-24 | 105 |
| 10:14 | 112 |
| 10:21-22 | 165 |
| 12:1-27 | 84 |
| 12:23, 29-30 | 193 |
| 14:19, 24 | 115 |
| 15:1 | 159 |
| 15:11 | 138 |
| 19:6 | 46 |
| 19:16 | 79 |
| 20:11 | 149 |
| 28:17-20 | 79 |
| 29:9 | 160 |
| 29:38-42 | 84 |
| 33:20, 23 | 216 |
| 39:11 | 79 |
| 40:35 | 161 |

*Leviticus*

| | |
|---|---|
| 4:7 | 93 |
| 17:11 | 93 |
| 23:5-6 | 84 |

*Numbers*

| | |
|---|---|
| 11:26 | 198 |
| 24:17 | 223 |
| 27:16 | 221 |

| | |
|---|---|
| 28:3-8 | 84 |
| 31:16 | 61 |

*Deuteronomy*

| | |
|---|---|
| 16:1-7 | 84 |
| 19:15 | 120 |
| 32:11-12 | 136 |

*Joshua*

| | |
|---|---|
| 11:4 | 198 |

*2 Samuel*

| | |
|---|---|
| 7:14 | 209 |
| 24:14 | 162 |

*1 Kings*

| | |
|---|---|
| 8:11 | 161 |
| 17:1 | 121 |
| 19:18 | 123 |

*2 Kings*

| | |
|---|---|
| 1:10 | 198 |
| 2:11 | 122 |
| 9:7 | 186 |
| 9:22 | 64 |

*1 Chronicles*

| | |
|---|---|
| 21:1 | 134 |
| 24:1-19 | 79 |
| 25 | 85 |

**Tobit**

| | |
|---|---|
| 13:16-17 | 214 |

**2 Maccabees**

| | |
|---|---|
| 2:4-8 | 126 |
| 11:8 | 68 |

**Job**

| | |
|---|---|
| 1–3 | 132 |
| 1:6-12 | 134 |
| 2:1-7 | 134 |
| 3:20-21 | 109 |

**Psalms**

| | |
|---|---|
| 2:2 | 166, 194, 197 |
| 2:4 | 146 |
| 2:7 | 130 |
| 2:8 | 65 |
| 2:9 | 65, 129 |
| 17:15 | 216 |
| 29:3 | 115 |
| 33:3 | 85 |
| 40:4 | 85 |
| 42:2 | 216 |
| 45:4 | 190 |
| 74:13-15 | 128 |
| 96:1 | 85 |
| 98:1 | 85 |
| 104:3 | 80 |
| 144:9 | 85 |
| 149:1 | 85 |

**Proverbs**

| | |
|---|---|
| 5:4 | 106 |

**Ecclesiastes**

| | |
|---|---|
| 9:8 | 68 |

**Wisdom**

| | |
|---|---|
| 2:12-20 | 122 |
| 2:24 | 132 |
| 3:2-3 | 8 |
| 11:15 | 164 |
| 11:16 | 163 |
| 11:17-18 | 113 |
| 11:24-26 | 152 |

| | |
|---|---|
| 12:8-9 | 110 |
| 12:20 | 113 |
| 14:22-26 | 112 |
| 17 | 165 |
| 18:4-16 | 192 |
| 18:14-16 | 193 |
| 18:15 | 191 |
| 19:13 | 104 |
| 19:14 | 122 |

**Sirach**

| | |
|---|---|
| 48:1 | 121 |

**Isaiah**

| | |
|---|---|
| 1:10 | 122 |
| 1:21 | 151 |
| 2:19 | 96 |
| 3:9 | 122 |
| 6:3 | 82 |
| 8:7 | 113 |
| 11:2 | 85 |
| 11:4 | 190, 192 |
| 13:20 | 171 |
| 14:12 | 106 |
| 22:22 | 70, 72 |
| 23:15-17 | 171 |
| 23:16-17 | 151 |
| 25:8 | 101, 102 |
| 30:33 | 150 |
| 34:4 | 96 |
| 40:10 | 222 |
| 40:31 | 136 |
| 43:19 | 208 |
| 49:10 | 101, 102 |
| 49:18 | 207 |
| 49:26 | 194 |
| 52:1 | 207 |
| 53:9 | 147 |
| 54:11-12 | 214 |
| 54:12 | 214 |
| 55:1 | 208 |
| 60 | 218 |
| 60:3 | 215 |
| 60:11 | 215 |
| 60:19 | 215 |
| 61:10 | 207 |
| 62:2 | 63 |

| | |
|---|---|
| 63:1-3 | 192 |
| 63:1-6 | 156, 157 |
| 63:3 | 191 |
| 65:17 | 207 |
| 65:17-19 | 207 |

**Jeremiah**

| | |
|---|---|
| 4:6 | 201 |
| 5:14 | 121 |
| 8:3 | 109 |
| 9:15 | 106 |
| 15:2 | 139 |
| 23:15 | 106 |
| 25:10 | 183 |
| 25:30 | 115 |
| 51:6, 45 | 177 |
| 51:7 | 150, 171 |
| 51:9 | 179 |
| 51:13 | 171, 173, 181 |
| 51:25 | 106 |
| 51:39, 57 | 60, 197, 205 |
| 51:49 | 183 |
| 51:63-64 | 183 |

**Lamentations**

| | |
|---|---|
| 3:15, 19 | 106 |

**Ezekiel**

| | |
|---|---|
| 1 | 79, 81 |
| 1:1 | 78 |
| 1:13-14 | 79 |
| 1:28 | 79 |
| 2:1–3:9 | 86 |
| 3:1-3 | 116, 117 |
| 3:4-5 | 86 |
| 3:13 | 116 |
| 3:14 | 116 |
| 7:2 | 198 |
| 9:4-6 | 98 |
| 14:21 | 90 |
| 26–27 | 180 |
| 26:13 | 183 |
| 27–28 | 181 |
| 27:13 | 180 |
| 28:10-13 | 79 |

28:14, 16    213
29:3    136
32:2-3    136
37:10    122
37:27    207, 208
38:2, 14-16    200
39:17-20    191, 194
43:2    98
47    21, 216, 219
47:12    216, 219
48:30-35    213

*Daniel*
2:27-28    144
2:28    43
2:35    203
2:47    51
4:30    150
7–12    3
7:2-8    19, 140
7:2-14    199
7:3    142
7:4-6    138
7:7    128, 138
7:9    51, 68, 204
7:9-14    199
7:10    203
7:11    142
7:13    46, 51, 116, 154
7:22    197
7:24    138
7:25    119
8:10    128, 130
8:17    187
8:26    115, 222
10:8-9    52
10:13, 20, 21    52
11:1    52
12:1    52
12:4-9    117
12:1    102
12:7    115
12:10    222

*Hosea*
1–3    28
8:1    106
10:8    96
11:8    232

*Joel*
2:1-11    110
2:2-11    112
2:11    166
2:30    105, 166
3:12-13    154

*Amos*
3:7    44, 116
5:6-7    106
6:12    106

*Micah*
4:10    129

*Nahum*
1:6    96
3:4    151, 171

*Zephaniah*
1:7    201
1:14-15    96

*Zechariah*
1:8-11    89, 90
1:12    93
2:5    214
2:14    121
3:1-2    134
3:1-5    132
4:2, 10    46
4:6    79
4:10    79, 85
6:1-8    89, 90
6:5    99
12:10    46, 47
13:2    166
14:7    216
14:11    216
14:16-19    100

**New Testament**

*Matthew*
2:1-2    98
4:8-10    213
5:3-12    208
5:8    216
5:12    186
6:33    30
10:32    68, 69
11:15    57
11:28    153
13:9, 43    57, 102
13:41-43    154
13:46    214
16:17-19    213
16:18    131
19:28    203, 213
20:2    90
22:14    173
24:8    92
24:9-14    94
24:12    55
24:28    194
24:29    90
24:30    46
24:43-44    69
25:31-46    184, 232
25:34    209
25:41    232
26:52    139
28:20    53

*Mark*
2:27    145
4:38    119
7:20-23    215
8:34    147, 148
10:15    205
10:42-45    32
10:43    13
13:9-13    94
13:15-16    167
13:20    117
13:22    143
13:24    90
13:26    154

| | | | | | |
|---|---|---|---|---|---|
| 13:26-27 | 155 | 16:20 | 122 | 13:12 | 216 |
| 13:30 | 155 | 16:33 | 27, 77, | 14:32 | 221 |
| 13:31 | 203 | | 119, 194 | 15:20-23 | 147 |
| 13:32 | 154, 155 | 19:37 | 46 | 15:26 | 204 |
| | | 21:19 | 147 | 15:28 | 29, 208 |
| *Luke* | | | | 16:22 | 223 |
| 4:6 | 140 | *Acts* | | | |
| 4:13 | 130 | 1:8 | 123 | *2 Corinthians* | |
| 6:35 | 153 | 1:9 | 122 | 5:17 | 2–8 |
| 9:54-55 | 121 | 2:23 | 139 | 11:2 | 148 |
| 9:57 | 147 | 7:44 | 160 | 12:12 | 57 |
| 10:18 | 133 | 14:15 | 149 | | |
| 10:19 | 110 | 15:28 | 66 | *Galatians* | |
| 10:22 | 190 | 16:14 | 65 | 1:1-5 | 47 |
| 11:50 | 183 | 18:19-21 | 56 | 4:26 | 136, 207 |
| 11:50-51 | 94 | 19–20 | 56 | | |
| 12:8 | 68, 69 | 20:29-30 | 57 | *Ephesians* | |
| 13:29 | 213 | | | 2:20 | 213 |
| 14:33 | 13 | *Romans* | | 5:14 | 69 |
| 17:37 | 106 | 1:1-7 | 47 | 5:25 | 186 |
| 18:1-8 | 104 | 1:20-32 | 112 | 5:26 | 185 |
| 18:7-8 | 94 | 1:24-32 | 173 | 5:26-27 | 186 |
| 21:12-19 | 94 | 2:4-5 | 113 | | |
| 21:25 | 90 | 3:24 | 205, 209 | *Philippians* | |
| 22:28-30 | 75 | 3:24-25 | 46 | 1:23 | 226 |
| 22:31 | 132 | 5:8 | 27, 48 | 3:2 | 223 |
| 22:43 | 72 | 7:24 | 75 | 4:13 | 102 |
| 23:34 | 232 | 8:17 | 209 | | |
| 24:26 | 102, 147 | 8:18-23 | 210 | *Colossians* | |
| | | 8:21 | 203 | 1:7 | 75 |
| *John* | | 8:23 | 209 | 2:18 | 187 |
| 1:29 | 30 | 8:29 | 136 | 3:5-10 | 211 |
| 3:16 | 27, 232 | 9–11 | 230 | 4:12 | 75 |
| 3:16-17 | 57 | 11:32 | 14 | 4:16 | 75 |
| 7:38-39 | 216 | 12:19 | 94 | | |
| 8:36 | 48 | | | *1 Thessalonians* | |
| 8:44 | 225 | *1 Corinthians* | | 1:1 | 47 |
| 10:3-4 | 75 | 1:3 | 47 | 4:16-17 | 16 |
| 12:23 | 133 | 1:23-25 | 25 | | |
| 12:31 | 133, 134, | 2:608 | 122 | *2 Thessalonians* | |
| | 140 | 3:16-17 | 119 | 1:1-2 | 47 |
| 12:31-32 | 149, 152 | 8:1-13 | 66 | 2:4 | 139 |
| 14:9 | 26 | 8:6 | 194 | 2:8 | 191 |
| 14:23 | 75 | 10:20 | 138 | 3:14-15 | 55 |
| 14:28 | 26 | 10:20-30 | 66 | | |
| 14:30 | 125, 130 | 11:26 | 116 | *1 Timothy* | |
| 15:5 | 102 | 12:3 | 223 | 2:2 | 12 |

| | | | | | |
|---|---|---|---|---|---|
| 2:4 | 232 | 1:18-20 | 139 | 6-13 | 109, 130 |
| 3:6 | 134 | 1:19 | 148 | 18:13 | 106 |
| | | 5:8 | 134 | 47:3 | 203 |
| 2 Timothy | | 5:12 | 150 | 56:6-7 | 198 |
| 2:19 | 99 | | | 60:7-10 | 142 |
| 2:24-26 | 55 | 2 Peter | | 66:1-2 | 163 |
| | | 3:8 | 104 | 81:1-3 | 84 |
| Hebrews | | 3:10-13 | 207 | 90:26 | 204 |
| 1:5-14 | 187 | 3:13 | 204 | 91:16 | 207 |
| 1:14 | 29, 188, | 1 John | | 100:1, 3 | 156 |
| | 189 | 2:18-19 | 66 | | |
| 2:5 | 209 | 3:2 | 216 | | |
| 3:5 | 159 | 4:19 | 57 | 2 Enoch | |
| 4:16 | 127 | 5:4 | 67 | 3:3 | 80 |
| 5:5 | 209 | | | 65:6 | 203 |
| 8:5 | 160 | Jude | | 65:10 | 208 |
| 9:14 | 148 | 9 | 134 | 2 Enoch | 79 |
| 10:19 | 127 | | | | |
| 10:31 | 161 | | | 4 Ezra | |
| 12:14 | 216 | **Early Jewish Authors** | | 4:35-36 | 93 |
| 12:24 | 94 | | | 6:20 | 203 |
| | | 2 Baruch | | 6:49-52 | 140 |
| James | | 2 Baruch | 5 | 6:51 | 142 |
| 2:5 | 59 | 24:1 | 203 | 8:53 | 208 |
| | | | | 9:38–10:54 | 207 |
| 1 Peter | | 1 Enoch | | 15:35 | 156 |
| 1:7 | 75 | 1-36 | 79 | | |

**Miscellaneous Sources**

Assumption of Moses 10:4-5   96
Assumption of Moses 10:4   168
baba Bathra 75a   215
Josephus Ant 3.7.2   51
Pss Sol. 17:26-27
Sibylline Oracles 3:350-55; 4:145-48; 8:9-11, 17-18, 33-36, 95-99   183, 184
Targum Isaiah 65:5-6   204
Targum Gen 49:11   156
Targum of Jeremiah   60, 197

## 2. SUBJECTS

Abaddon, 110, 126
Abyss, 109, 196, 199
Affluence, 184
Agapē, 65
Alpha and Omega, 26, 225
Angels, 28, 112, 116, 151, 156, 177, 187, 188, 234
Apocalypse, 1, 13
Apollyon, 110, 126
Ark, 126, 127
Armageddon, 20, 167, 175, 194, 229
Assyria, 113

Babylon, 113, 150, 151, 167, 171, 173, 177, 178
Beasts, 19
Behemoth, 142
Book of Life, 68, 69, 204

Charagma, 143
Church, 130–31, 136, 188, 189
Cross, 30, 87, 89
Cubits, 214

Death, 232
Desert, 173–74
Determinism, 4
Devil, 29
Dispensationalism, 15
Domitian, 9, 10
Dragon, 19, 29, 130, 131, 133, 134, 135, 136

Earthquakes, 95, 168, 169
Elders, 79
Endurance (hypomonē), 141, 201

Ephesus, 56
Euphrates, 167
Evil, 12, 111, 169, 188, 202, 234

Famine, 90, 91
Flood story, 229
Four Horsemen, 25, 90, 91
Futurist interpretation, 15

God, 23–24
Gog and Magog, 21, 191, 198
Great city, 124

Hades, 90, 92, 232
Hallelujah, 185
Harlot, 171, 175
Harvest, 154
Heaven, 233
Hell, 233
Historical interpretation, 15

Idealist interpretation, 14
Imperial cults, 10

Jerusalem, 216
Judgment, 157

Lamb, 25, 26, 27, 32, 84, 85, 86, 91, 96, 119, 134, 139, 140,141, 146, 147, 148, 175, 188, 193
Laodicea, 74, 166, 169
Last judgment, 233
Lex talionis, 164, 178, 179
Lion as Lamb, 87
Literary freedom, 6

Locust, 112
Lord of the Churches, 28

Marana tha, 32, 225, 226
Martyrs, 57, 58 93, 94, 97, 104, 172
Megiddo, 167
Messages, 56, 76
Messianic feast, 188
Metanoia, 113, 114, 151, 210
Michael, archangel, 131, 132, 133, 138, 195
Mount Zion, 147

Nero, 5, 9, 19, 141, 144, 145, 166, 172, 174
New Jerusalem, 21, 101, 157, 217, 218, 219, 229
Nicolaitans, 18, 62, 66, 72, 188

Olive trees, 121
One hundred and forty-four thousand, 98, 99, 100, 101, 146, 147, 148, 193
Open door, 72, 78

Parousia, 155
Parthians, 89, 113, 167
Pastoral Letters, 12
Patmos, 50
Pergamum, 61, 62, 63, 72, 143
Persecution, 11
Philadelphia, 71, 72
Plagues, 20, 107, 108, 113, 169, 173
Poverty, 184
Preterist interpretation, 16
Prophetic dimensions, 7
Prophetic Messages, 17

Rainbow, 79
Reed, 118
Resurrection, 197, 200, 201

Roman emperors, 172, 175
Rome, 12, 151, 153, 165, 173, 183, 184

Sackcloth, 121
Sardis, 68
Satan, 13, 130, 132, 133, 134, 136, 140
Scroll, 83, 84, 87, 91, 115, 116, 117
Scroll Vision, 18
Seals, 18, 91
Serpent, 135
Seven Churches, 50
Six-six-six, 144, 167
Smyrna, 59
Son of man, 154, 155
Sovereignty of God, 24
Statues, 143

Tabernacles, Feast of, 100, 101, 102
Temple, 119
Tent of Testimony, 160
Throne, 79, 81, 82, 138
Thyatira, 18, 65
Tribulation (thlipsis), 23, 32, 64, 141, 152
Trumpets, 18

Universal salvation, 200, 205, 230, 231, 233, 234

Victor, 55, 57, 68, 72, 75, 209, 210
Victory, 30
Visions, 3, 4, 18, 117, 174, 188
Vulture, 106

War, 134
Wealth, 173
Witnesses, 123, 124
Woman, 19, 128, 129, 130, 135, 136, 171, 174, 188
Wormwood, 106
Worship, 30
Wrath, 150, 161

# 3. AUTHORS

Achtemeier, Paul, 231
Allo, E. B., 39
Altink, W., 153
Aquinas, Thomas, 234
Ashcroft, M., 39
Aune, D. E., 34, 35, 40, 53, 54, 77, 88, 227

Bailey, J. W., 202
Barclay, W., 39
Barr, D. L., 34, 36
Barr, J., 33
Barrett, C. K., 63, 88
Bartina, S., 82
Bauckham, R. J., 36, 49, 97, 168, 169
Beale, G. K., 142, 145, 176
Beasley-Murray, G. R., 39
Beckwith, I. T., 39
Bell, A. A., 35
Bergmeier, R., 88, 118
Bieder, W., 45
Bietenhard, H., 202
Blevins, J. L., 34, 36
Bloom, H., 34, 40
Böcher, O., 36, 39
Boismard, M. É., 36, 147, 148
Boring, M. E., xiii, xv, 36, 39, 45, 83, 84, 86, 97, 116, 126, 132, 139, 152, 157, 174, 189, 193, 196, 205, 209, 221, 231, 235
Bornkamm, G., 92
Bousset, W., 39
Bowman, J. B., 36
Boyle, W. J. P., 227
Brewer, R. R., 82
Brown, S, 71, 73

Bruns, J. E., 176
Brutsch, C., 39
Burggraeve, R., 211

Caird, G. B., xv, 39, 47, 65, 74, 87, 93, 96, 106, 111, 113, 117, 122, 133, 139, 141, 151, 154, 160, 172, 175, 178, 188, 190, 207, 213, 214, 222, 235
Cambier, J., 39, 176
Carmignac, J., 33
Casey, J., 108
Cerfaux, L., 39, 136, 153
Charles, R. H., xv, 36, 39, 51, 85, 86, 101, 116, 139, 213
Charlesworth, J. H., 33, 40
Collins, A. Yarbro, 17, 34, 35, 36, 39, 40, 61, 77, 92, 142, 147, 164
Collins, J. J., 1, 4, 9, 33, 34, 36, 40, 129, 144, 171, 183
Collins, T., 227
Comblin, J., 102, 211
Considine, J. S., 125, 195
Corsani, B., 34
Corsini, E., 39
Court, J., 35, 40

Dehandschutter, B., 45
Delebecque, E., 220
Delobel, J., 36
Deutsch, C., 211
Dodd, C. H., 161
Dornseiff, F., 92
Draper, J. A., 103
du Rand, J. A., 220
Dyer, C. H., 176

Ellul, J., 39
Enroth, A. M., 58
Ernst, J., 136
Ezell, D., 34

Farrer, A., 39
Fekkes, J., 189
Feuillet, A., 35, 40, 53, 88, 92, 95, 103, 120, 136
Filippini, R., 49
Fiorenza, E. Schüssler, 7, 33, 34, 36, 39, 40, 49, 54, 88, 148, 202
Ford, J. M., 40, 88, 147, 148, 171, 189, 216

Gaechter, P., 211
Gangemi, A., 58, 60, 63, 67
Geyser, A., 99
Giblin, C. H., 120, 235
Giesen, H., 88
Glasson, T. F., 41, 206
Gollinger, H., 137
Gonzalez Ruiz, J. M., 39
Goulder, M. D., 37
Gourgues, M., 202
Grant, R. M., 35
Gundry, 220
Guthrie, D., 35, 41, 88

Haapa, E., 92
Habicht, C., 35
Hall, R. G., 80, 82
Hanhart, K., 142
Hanson, A. T., 162
Hanson, P. D., 33, 41
Harrington, D. J., 34
Harrington, W. J., 39, 206, 235
Hartman, L., 33, 53, 227
Hayes, Z., 36
Hellholm, D., 33, 41
Hemer, C. J., 41, 55, 65, 69, 70, 71, 77, 90
Hill, D, 35, 41
Hillyer, N., 88
Hubert, M., 77
Hughes, P. E., 39, 202

Jart, U., 214, 220
Jeske, R. L., 49
Johnson, S. E., 35

Kallas, J., 35
Karner, K., 211
Karrer, M., 35
Kavanagh, M. A., 227
Kealy, S. P., 36, 40
Keresztes, P., 35
Kiddle, M., 40
Kirby, J. T., 53
Klassen, W., 179
Koch, K., 33
Kraft, H., 40
Krodel, G. A., xv, 36, 40, 100, 123, 124, 159, 161, 192, 197, 213, 225
Kümmel, W. G., 35

Ladd, G. E., 40
Lambrecht, J., 37, 41
Läpple, A., 88
LaRondelle, H. K., 167
Laws, S., 41
Leconte, R., 77
Lindsay, H., 15
Linton, G., 34
Lohmeyer, E., 40
Lohse, E., 40

Malherbe, A. J., 35
Mazzaferri, F. D., 35
McNamara, M., 53
Michael, J. H., 118
Michaels, J. R., 202
Michl, J., 137
Minear, P. S., 33, 40, 41, 137, 142
Montagnini, F., 137
Morris, L., 33, 40
Mounce, R. H., 40
Mowry, L., 88
Mulholland, M. R., 40
Müller, H. P., 88, 108
Müller, U. B., 40, 193
Muse, R. L., 77
Mussies, G., 37

Nichelsburg, G. W. E., 2, 34

O'Rourke, J., 88
Oberweis, M., 145

Page, S. H. T., 202
Pesch, R., 45
Pleket, H., 35
Porter, S. E., 37
Prete, B., 142
Prigent, P., 37, 40, 137, 145, 202, 211

Ramsay, W. M., 41, 77
Reader, W. W., 220
Reddish, M. G., 125
Reicke, B., 142
Richards, H., 40
Rife, J. M., 77
Rissi, M., 195
Rist, M., 40
Robinson, B. P., 125
Rochais, G., 202
Roller, O., 88
Rollins, W. G., 33
Roloff, J., 40
Rowland, C., 33, 41, 53
Rudwick, M. J. S., 77

Saffrey, H. D., 53, 137
Sanders, E. P., 34
Scherrer, S. J., 35, 145
Schillebeeckx, E., 127, 205, 206, 207, 233, 234, 235
Schmid, J., 35, 36
Schrage, W., 60
Scott, K., 35
Seng, H., 125
Shea, W. H., 77, 137, 202
Silberman, L. H., 77
Skrinjar, A., 148
Smallwood, E. M., 35

Smith, C. R., 53, 99
Spinks, L. C., 37
Staples, P., 164
Stone, M. E., 33
Stott, W., 53
Strand, K. A., 53, 58, 125, 179
Strobel, A., 176
Surridge, R., 88
Sweet, J. P. M., xv, 40, 51, 55, 66, 74, 80, 104, 108, 166, 171, 178, 183, 190, 203, 215, 235
Swete, H. B., xv, 40, 67, 74, 80, 91, 116, 122, 163, 180, 191, 196, 204, 208, 215

Thomas, R. L., 227
Thompson, L. L. xv, 10, 25, 36, 41, 53, 81, 82, 85, 88, 103, 208, 222
Topham, M., 220
Trites, A. A., 46

Ulrichsen, H., 35

van den Eynde, P., 95
van Schaik, A. P., 155
van Unnik, W. C., 51, 53, 88
Vanhoye, A., 88, 182
Vanni, U., 36, 37, 41, 48, 49, 92, 137, 202
Vivian, A., 202
Vorster, W. S., 34

Waldensberger, W., 92
Walker, N., 82
Westermann, C., 27
White, R. F., 202
Wikenhauser, A., 35, 36, 40, 202
Wilken, R. L., 36
Wilson, R. R., 34
Wolff, G., 103

Zahn, T., 40